Technically-Write!

Canadian Seventh Edition

Ron Blicq

RGI International

Lisa Moretto

RGI International

PEARSON

Prentice Hall

Toronto

Library and Archives Canada Cataloguing in Publication

Blicq, Ron S. (Ronald Stanley), 1925-
    Technically-write! / Ron Blicq, Lisa Moretto. — Canadian 7th ed.

Includes index.
ISBN 978-0-13-173723-5

    1. Technical writing—Textbooks.   I. Moretto, Lisa A.   II. Title.

T11.B55 2007   808'.0666   C2007-903096-3

ISBN-13: 978-0-13-173723-5
ISBN-10: 0-13-173723-6

Vice-President, Editorial Director: Gary Bennett
Acquisitions Editor: Chris Helsby
Marketing Manager: Sally Aspinall
Developmental Editor: Joel Gladstone
Production Editor: Katie Hearn
Copy Editor: Tara Tovell
Proofreader: Lenore Latta
Production Coordinator: Avinash Chandra
Composition: Debbie Kumpf
Art Director: Julia Hall
Cover Design: Kerrin Hands
Interior Design: Geoff Agnew
Cover Image: IStock Photo

Weblinks are included throughout each chapter and may occasionally present alternative points of view. Because the World Wide Web is a dynamic medium, website addresses may sometimes change over time.

4 5   11 10

Printed and bound in the United States of America.

Contents

Chapter 4
Short Informal Reports   54

Chapter 5
Longer Informal and Semiformal Reports   84

Chapter 6
Formal Reports   105

Chapter 7
Technical Proposals   163

Chapter 8
Instructions and Procedures   181

Chapter 12
The Technique of Technical Writing   272

About the Authors

Ron Blicq and Lisa Moretto are Senior Consultants with RGI International, a consulting company specializing in oral and written communication. They teach workshops, based on the Pyramid Method of Writing presented in this book, to audiences all over the world. In 2001 they opened a second company—RGI Learning Inc—specifically to deliver their courses on the web. Their website is **http://www.rgilearning.com.**

Ron is Senior Consultant at RGI's Canadian office. He has extensive experience as a technical writer and editor with the Royal Air Force in Britain and CAE Industries Limited in Canada, and taught technical communication at Red River College from 1967 to 1990. Ron has authored six books with Pearson Education Canada and has written and produced six educational video programs, such as *Sharpening Your Business Communication Skills* and *So, You Have to Give a Talk?* He is a Fellow of the Society for Technical Communication and the Association of Teachers of Technical Writing in the US, and of the Institute of Scientific and Technical Communicators in Great Britain, and is a Life Member of the Institute of Electrical and Electronics Engineers Inc. Ron lives in Winnipeg, Manitoba.

Lisa is Senior Consultant at RGI's United States' office. She has experience as an Information Developer for IBM in the US and as a Learning Products Engineer for Hewlett-Packard in Great Britain. Lisa holds a BSc in Technical Communication from Clarkson University in New York, and an MSc in User Interface Design from the London Guildhall University in England. Her specialties include developing online interactive information, designing user interfaces, and writing product documentation. She is a senior member of the Society for Technical Communication and a member of the Institute of Electrical and Electronics Engineers Inc. Lisa lives in Rochester, New York, and teaches Effective Technical Communication to engineering students at the Rochester Institute of Technology.

(Photo: Mary Lou Stein)

Preface

Not long after you graduate with your university degree or college diploma, you will start having to write business-oriented emails, letters, reports, and possibly technical proposals. This book contains numerous examples of informal and semiformal documents, all based on the unique "pyramid" method for structuring information, a technique that has helped countless technical people overcome "writer's block."

In each edition of *Technically-Write!*, we introduced changes that reflect the way technical professionals currently present information in various industries and in engineering consulting firms. This edition is no exception: here are some of the most noticeable revisions:

- The writing style is tighter and more direct, to reflect the style that has recently evolved in business and in the scientific and technical industries.

- Many of the shorter documents are shown as emails rather than as memos or faxes, because memos and faxes are used much less today.

- There are more detailed suggestions for making oral presentations.

- There are fewer project assignments at the end of most chapters. Many of the assignments are now available online.

If you have seen previous editions, you will notice that the shape of the book has also changed because we have reduced the number of pages by about 15%. We have done this by placing some of the assignments and exercises in an instructor's manual and by making them available electronically.

We continue to use two companies—H L Winman and Associates and Macro Engineering Inc—for many of the model letters and reports and for end-of-chapter assignments, to provide a logical environment for the documents and exercises.

Along the way, we have appreciated the advice and helpful suggestions from users of the book, both teachers and students, and the advice of reviewers. In particular, we thank the following reviewers: Sue Ackerman (Nova Scotia Community College), Kim Jones (McMaster University), Betti Sheldrick (Mohawk College), Susan Stott-Hood (Georgian College), and Una Wilson (New Brunswick Community College, Saint John). Their ideas have guided us in preparing this seventh edition. We are also celebrating, for it's 36 years since the first edition of *Technically-Write!* was published!

RB & LM

Supplements

The seventh Canadian edition of *Technically-Write!* is supported by a comprehensive supplements package, which includes the *Instructor's Resource CD-ROM* (978-0-13-204300-7). This includes the following instructor supplements:

- **Instructor's Manual:** This manual includes additional exercises, teaching tips, transparency masters, and other useful material, based on the authors' extensive teaching and workshop experience.

- **Test Item File:** Available in Microsoft Word format, this test bank includes over 300 test questions, including multiple-choice, fill-in-the-blank, and true/false.

- **PowerPoints:** There are 10 separate PowerPoint presentations included on a variety of topics, including "An Introduction to the Pyramid Method of Writing" and "Writing Plan for a Job Application Letter."

- **Additional Projects—Instructor's Notes:** The complete Additional Projects that are available to *Technically-Write!* students on the Text Enrichment Site at http://www.pearsoned.ca/text/blicq are offered here along with Instructor's Notes that provide suggestions and answers.

- **Text Enrichment Site** (ISBN 978-0-13-207328-8): This site contains additional exercises for each chapter, more sample documents, and links to all weblinks cited in the text.

Most of these instructor supplements are also available for download from a password-protected section of Pearson Education Canada's online catalogue (http://vig.pearsoned.ca). Navigate to your book's catalogue page to view a list of those supplements that are available. See your local sales representative for details and access.

People as "Communicators"

We are equipped with a highly sophisticated communication system, yet we consistently fail to use it properly. The system comprises a transmitter and receiver combined into a single package controlled by a built-in computer, the brain. It accepts multiple inputs and transmits in three ways: action, speech, and writing.

We spend many of our waking hours communicating, half the time as a transmitter, half as a receiver. If, as a receiver, we mentally switch off while someone else is transmitting, we contribute to information loss. Similarly, if as a transmitter we permit our message to become disorganized, unconvincing, or uninteresting, we confuse our readers or listeners. They simply tune out, think about lunch, or wonder if they should rent a DVD tonight.

As long as a person transmits clearly, efficiently, and persuasively, people receiving the message keep their receivers "locked on" to the transmitting frequency (this applies to all written, visual, and spoken transmissions). Such conditions expedite the transfer of information, or "communication."

When you are speaking directly to another person, you as a receiver have the opportunity to ask the transmitter to clarify vaguely presented information. But in more formal speech situations, and in all forms of written and most visual communication, you no longer have this advantage. You cannot stop a speaker who mumbles or uses unfamiliar terminology, and ask that parts of the talk be repeated or clarified; neither can you easily ask a writer in another city to explain an incoherent business letter. This scenario also applies to electronic messages (unless you start a string of messages back and forth, which allows you to ask questions but also wastes time).

The results of poor communication soon become apparent. If people fail to make themselves clear, the consequences are likely to be different from those they anticipated, as Cam Collins has discovered.

Cam is an electrical engineer, and his specialty is high-voltage power generation. He has read about an extra-high-voltage (EHV) DC power conference he wants to attend. In an email to Fred Stokes, the company's chief engineer, Cam described the conference in glowing terms that he hopes will convince Fred to approve his request:

> Fred
>
> The EHV conference described in the attached brochure is just the thing we have been looking for. Only last week you and I discussed the shortage of good technical information in this area, and now here is a conference

Cam's request fails to convince

featuring papers on many of the topics we are interested in. The cost is only $365 for registration, which includes a visit to the Freeling Rapids Generating Station. Travel and accommodation will be about $850 extra. I'm informing you of this early so you can make a decision in time for me to arrange flight bookings and accommodation.

Cam

Fred Stokes was equally enthusiastic and wrote back:

Cam

Thanks for informing me of the EHV DC conference. I certainly don't want to miss it. Please make reservations for me as you suggested.

Fred

Cam was the victim of his own carelessness: he failed to communicate clearly that it was *he* who wanted to go to Freeling Rapids!

Elizabeth had a good idea...

Elizabeth Drew, on the other hand, did not realize she had missed a golden opportunity to be first with an innovative computer technique until it was too late to do anything about it. Her story stems from an incident that occurred several years ago, when she was a recently graduated engineer employed by a manufacturer of agricultural machinery. Elizabeth's job was to design modifications to the machinery, and then prepare the change procedure documentation for the production department, service representatives, sales staff, and customers.

For each modification she had to coordinate three different documents:

- A design change notice that was sent out to everyone concerned.
- An "exploded" isometric drawing showing a clear view of every part, with each part cross-referenced to a parts list.
- The parts list itself, with every item labelled fully and accurately.

Elizabeth found that cross-referencing a drawing to its parts list was a tedious, time-consuming task. The isometric drawing of the part was computer generated by the drafting department. The parts list was also keyed into a computer, but by a separate department. However, because the two computer systems were not always compatible, cross-referencing often proved to be a problem.

...it was simple and efficient...

Elizabeth developed a technique for interfacing the two programs. It was so simple, she wondered why no one else had thought of it. So, without telling anyone, she modified a copy of one of the company's software programs and tested her idea with five different modification kits. Her modification not only worked but also reduced the cross-referencing time by 70–80%.

Elizabeth felt her employer should know about her idea: possibly the company could market the software, or even help her copyright it. So the following day she stopped Mr Haddon, the Engineering Manager, as they passed in the hallway, and blurted out her suggestion. This is how the conversation went:

Elizabeth	Mr Haddon
Oh! Mr Haddon! You know how long it takes to do the documentation for a new part…?	Yes..s..s..?
The problem is in trying to interface between the graphics computer and the parts list…	(*Mr Haddon appeared to be listening politely, but internally he was growing impatient.*)
…It has to be done by hand, you see…	Doesn't the drafting department do all that?
Oh, yes! They do. I was just trying to help them…to speed up their work a bit.	You're working for the chief draftsman now?
Oh, no! It was just an idea I had— to modify the software we use…	I don't remember issuing you a work order…
No. You didn't. I was doing it on my own… (*She meant she was doing it on her own time.*)	You mean the I.T. people asked you to do it?
Well — uh — no. Not exactly…	But you have been modifying one of our software programs? Without authority?
(*Reluctantly*) Uh-huh.	I thought I had made it quite clear to all the staff: No projects are to be undertaken without my approval! (*His tone was cold and abrupt.*)
I wanted to try…	That's final! (*He turned and continued down the hall.*)

…but Elizabeth didn't know how to articulate her ideas clearly

Elizabeth's simple suggestion had become lost in a web of misunderstanding. By the time she was through explaining what she had been doing, she had given up trying to offer her idea to the company. And so her idea lay dormant for two years, until a major software company came out with a comparable program. Elizabeth knew then that perhaps there *had* been market potential for her design.

If Cam Collins and Elizabeth Drew had paused to consider the needs of the people who were to receive their information, they would never have omitted essential details. Cam had only to start his memorandum with a request ("May I have your approval to attend an EHV DC conference next month?"), and Elizabeth with a statement of purpose ("I have designed a software program that can save us hundreds of dollars annually. May I have a few moments to describe it to you?"), to grab the attention of their department heads. Both Mr Stokes and Mr Haddon could then have much more effectively evaluated the information.

Such circumstances occur daily. They are frustrating to those who fail to communicate their ideas, and can be costly.

In business and industry we must communicate clearly and understand fully the implications of failing to do so. A poorly worded order that results in the wrong part being supplied to a job site, a weak report that fails to motivate the reader to take the urgent action needed to avoid a costly equipment breakdown, and even an inadequate job application letter and resume that fail to sell an employer on the right person for a prospective job—these all increase the cost of doing business. Such mistakes and misunderstandings waste time and money. Many of them can be prevented by more effective communication—communication that is receiver-oriented rather than transmitter-oriented, and that transmits messages that are clear, concise, and complete.

Chapter 1
Why Technical People Need to Write Well

Over the past four years we have asked numerous technical professionals: "What is the publication date of the earliest book on technical writing that you own?"

Nearly everyone listed books from the 1960s and 1970s. Yet our research shows that the teaching of technical writing in science and engineering courses began more than one hundred years ago, in 1901, when the Society for the Promotion of Engineering Education (SPEE) reported that

> The writing skills of engineering students are deplorable and need to be addressed by engineering colleges.

These words did not go unheeded. Although technical communication was not part of a technical student's curriculum in those days, and was rarely included even in the range of courses taught by the English department, some engineering and English professors, both in North America and Great Britain, quietly began teaching the importance of good writing as part of other technical courses. After doing this for many years, some of them published books based on the notes they had typed up for their students. The following is a brief history of those texts.

The First Fifty Years

In 1908 T A Rickard, an associate of the Royal School of Mines in London, England, published a book titled *A Guide to Technical Writing*.[1] He wrote:

> Conscientious writers try to improve their mode of expression by precision of terms, by careful choice of words, and by the arrangement of them so that they become efficient carriers of thought from one mind to another.

Rickard titled one of his chapters "A Plea for Greater Simplicity in the Language of Science," having noticed that technical people tended to write in a long-winded way that was not easy for anyone outside their discipline to understand.

In 1922 Karl Owen Thompson, who taught English at the Case School of Applied Science in Cleveland, Ohio, published a book titled *Technical Exposition*.[2] In the introduction to his book he commented on the differences between literary and technical writing:

Technical Communication Overview http://saulcarliner.home.att.net/idbusiness/historytc.htm This site includes a brief history of technical communication.

In the early 1900s, technical communication was taught by engineering professors.

1

The study of English at a scientific school has a more directly professional application than it has at an academic college. Instead of courses in literature with their cultural purposes, courses are given that prepare the students for the types of reading and writing that will be required of them after they are graduated from college…. English is more than a tool, it is a part of life itself in its many activities.

At the University of Michigan's College of Engineering, J Raleigh Nelson insisted from 1915 onward that his students write clearly. In 1940 he summed up his thoughts in a book titled *Writing the Technical Report*,[3] in which he wrote:

> In report writing, in particular, there is an increasing demand that the first page or two shall provide a comprehensive idea of the whole report.

This was the first documented reference to what we now refer to as the Executive Summary, which precedes a long report or proposal (see Chapter 6).

Reginald Kapp taught electrical engineering at University College in London. Like Nelson, he insisted his students write well. In 1948 he summed up his thoughts in a pocket-sized reference book titled *The Presentation of Technical Information*,[4] in which he particularly drew attention to the importance of identifying the audience before (in those days) putting pen to paper. He wrote:

> You must consider carefully the extent of the reader's knowledge, his range of interests, and…any peculiarities…that might influence his receptivity for the information you have to impart.

Similarly, forty years earlier, T A Rickard had written:

> If you describe a stamp-mill to an experienced mill-man, a mining student, or a bishop, you will vary the manner of telling. The most effective will be that which has a sympathetic appreciation of the other fellow's receptiveness. Do not plant carnations in a clay soil, or rice in a sand-heap.[5]

(These authors were writing books for technical professionals, who were almost entirely male in the early part of the 20th century. They would write very differently today: for example, T A Rickard would probably change *mill-man* to *mill worker* and *other fellow's* to *other person's*.)

A Change in Style

Tyler G Hicks was a mechanical engineer who taught at Cooper Union School of Engineering. He had written numerous articles and three technical books before turning his attention to engineering writing. In 1959 Hicks wrote *Successful Technical Writing*,[6] a major milepost for books on technical writing because of his refreshing directness and style. Here are three examples:

> Technical writing always pays off. You never lose when you write a good technical piece…. Good writing is a sure road to professional recognition.

> Talk directly to the reader. Bring him into the discussion. Use the personal pronouns "we" and "you," but with discretion.

Rickard and Kapp strongly stressed the need to identify the audience before starting to write

Technical Communication Quarterly
http://www.attw.org/
Technical Communication Quarterly is the journal of the Association of Teachers of Technical Writing.

Hicks's writing still sits well with today's readers

Choose verbs that create active impressions to the reader, and steer clear of the passive voice. You thus give life to your style.

The five writers discussed here were very conscious that they were preparing their students to take up important roles in the engineering and technical professions. What they had to say to their students then is just as relevant today.

Although writing styles may have changed, the message remains constant

REFERENCES

1. T A Rickard, *A Guide to Technical Writing* (San Francisco: Mining and Scientific Press, 1908), p 8.

2. Karl Owen Thompson, *Technical Exposition* (New York: Harper & Brothers Publishers, 1922), p vii.

3. J Raleigh Nelson, *Writing the Technical Report* (New York: McGraw-Hill Book Company, 1940), p 39.

4. Reginald O Kapp, *The Presentation of Technical Information* (London: Constable & Company Ltd, 1948), p 20. (Reprinted, with slight revisions, and published by the Institute for Scientific and Technical Communicators, UK, 1998.)

5. Rickard, p 12.

6. Tyler G Hicks, *Successful Technical Writing* (New York: McGraw-Hill Book Company, Inc, 1959), p 1 and 194.

In 2007, the Kapp book was still in print

Chapter 2
A Technical Person's Approach to Writing

Engineering technologist Dan Skinner has a report to write on an investigation he completed seven weeks ago. He has made several attempts to get started, but never seems to find the right moment: maybe he was interrupted to resolve a problem, or it was too near lunchtime, or a meeting was called. And now he is up against the wire.

Unless Dan is one of those unusual people who can produce only when under pressure, he is in danger of writing an inadequate, hastily prepared report that does not represent his true abilities. But if he were to relax a little, instead of worrying that he has to organize himself and his writing task, he would find the physical process of writing a much more pleasant experience. But first he must change his approach.

Simplifying the Approach

Throughout this book we will be advising you to *tell your readers right away what they most need or want to know*. This means structuring your writing so that the first paragraph (or, in short documents, the first *sentence*) satisfies their curiosity and answers their most urgent question. This reader-oriented style is known as the "pyramid technique." Imagine every letter, memorandum, email, or report you write is shaped like a pyramid: there is a small piece of essential information, the **Summary Statement**, at the top, supported on a base of details, facts, and evidence, the **Supporting Details**.

Figure 2-1 shows the basic pyramid structure. In later chapters we will show you how to break the supporting details section into smaller compartments to create well-organized documents. For example, in the opening paragraph of his letter report in Figure 2-2 (see page 6), Wes Hillman summarizes what Tina Mactiere most wants to know (whether the training course was a success and what results were achieved). In the remainder of the letter he fills in background details, states briefly how the course was run, reports on student participation and reaction, and suggests additional topics that could be covered in future courses.

Every document shown in this textbook has been structured using the pyramid technique, which is the simplest, fastest, most effective way to plan and write any document, regardless of its length. If Dan Skinner had known about the pyramid, he would have found it much easier to get started.

The writer's pyramid helps you focus your letters and reports

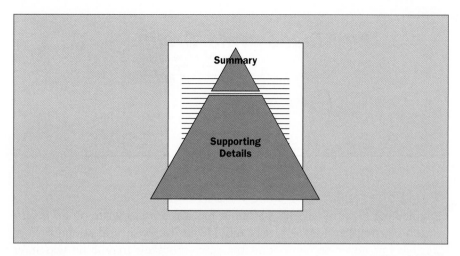

Figure 2-1 The pyramid writing technique.

Society for Technical Communication
http://www.stc.org
With more than 20 000 members worldwide, STC is the largest professional organization serving the technical communication profession. The society's diverse membership includes writers, editors, illustrators, printers, publishers, educators, students, engineers, and scientists employed in a variety of technological fields.

"Disorganize" the writing task!

Planning the Writing Task

The word "planning" seems to imply that report writers must start by thoroughly organizing both themselves and their material. We disagree. Organizing too precisely or too early in the writing process slows rather than speeds writing. The key is to organize your information in a spontaneous, creative manner, allowing your mind to brainstorm in the initial planning stages until you have collected, scrutinized, sorted, grouped, and written the topics into a logical outline that appeals to the reader. These stages are shown in Figure 2-3 (see page 7) and are the steps Dan should have followed.

1. Gather Information

Dan's first step should be to assemble all the documents, results of tests, photographs, samples, computer data, specifications, and other supporting material that he will need to write his report, or that he will insert into it. He must gather everything now, because later he will not want to interrupt his writing to look for additional facts and figures.

2. Define the Reader

Next, Dan must clearly identify his audience. This is probably the most important part of his planning, for if he does not, he may write an unfocused report that misses its mark. He needs to ask himself six questions:

1. *Who, specifically, is my reader?* If it is someone he knows, his task is simplified. If it is someone he is not acquainted with (such as a customer in an out-of-town firm), he must imagine the type of person and the work he or she does.

2. *Is he or she a technical person?* This will help Dan decide whether he can use technical terms.

The Meadowvale Group

Communication Consultants
Box 181 – RPO Graydon
Winnipeg MB   R3M 3J2

October 16, 2008

Tina R Mactiere, President
Macro Engineering Inc
600 Deepdale Drive
Toronto ON   M5W 4R9

Dear Ms Mactiere

Results of Pilot Report-Writing Course

The report-writing course we conducted for members of your engineering staff was completed successfully by 14 of the 16 participants. The average mark was 63%.

Summary (main message)

This was a pilot course set up in response to an August 13, 2008, enquiry from Mr F Stokes. At his request, we placed most emphasis on providing your staff with practical experience in writing business letters and technical reports. Attendance was voluntary, the 16 participants having been selected at random from 29 applicants.

Best results were achieved by participants who recognized their writing problems before they started the course, and willingly became actively involved in the practical work. A few said they had expected to attend an "information" type of course, and at first were mildly reluctant to take part in the heavy writing program. We have attached our comments on the work done by individual participants.

Supporting Details
(all the facts)

Course critiques completed by the participants indicate that the course met their needs from a letter- and report-writing viewpoint, but that they felt more emphasis could have been placed on technical proposals and oral reporting. Perhaps such topics could be covered in a short follow-up course.

We enjoyed developing and teaching this pilot course for your staff, and particularly appreciated their enthusiastic participation.

Sincerely

Wesley G Hillman
Course Leader

enc

Figure 2-2   A letter report written using the pyramid technique.

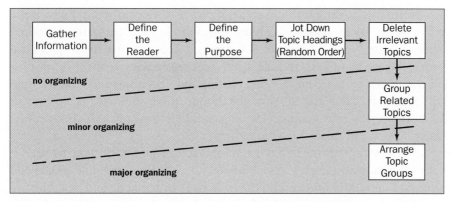

Figure 2-3 The seven planning stages. In practice, these stages can overlap.

3. *How much does the reader know about the subject I will be describing?* This will give Dan a starting point, since he won't need to cover information the reader already knows.

4. *What does the reader want to know or expect to be told?* Dan must anticipate whether the reader will be receptive or hostile to the information he is presenting.

5. *Will more than one person read my report?* If so, Dan must repeat questions 2 through 4 for additional readers.

6. *Who is my **ultimate** reader?* The **ultimate** reader is the person who will make a decision or take action after reading the report. Often this is the person to whom the report is directed called the primary reader. On occasion the ultimate reader may not be the person to whom the report is directed, but may be a secondary reader. For example, a report may be addressed to a department manager, but the person who uses it or does something about it may be an engineer on the manager's staff.

Pay attention to the ultimate reader

Dan's inability to identify his reader was one of the reasons he had difficulty getting started on his report-writing task.

3. Define the Purpose

Now Dan needs to ask himself one or possibly two more questions:

7. *Why am I writing to this person (or these people)?* He needs to decide whether his objective is to pass along information (to **inform** the reader about something), or to convince the reader to act or react (to **persuade** the reader to reply, make a decision, or approve a request).

Decide: Why am I creating this message?

8. If Dan's purpose is to persuade, then he also needs to ask: *What action do I want the reader to take?*

Now Dan is ready to develop a *focused* writing plan.

4. Jot Down Topic Headings

Dan needs to brainstorm ideas and pieces of information to convey to his audience.

Normally, at the outlining stage, a technical person will type or write down a set of familiar or arbitrary headings, such as "Introduction," "Initial Tests," and "Material Resources," and arrange them in logical order. But we want Dan to take a different approach: we want him to list all the topics he plans to discuss, writing only brief headings rather than full sentences. He must do this in random order, making no attempt to force the topics into groups. The topics he knows best will come easily; those he knows less well may take longer.

When he finishes his initial list, he should examine each topic to see if it suggests less obvious topics. As additional topics come to mind he should add them, still in random order, until he finds he is straining to find new ideas.

Dan must not try to decide whether each topic is relevant during this initial brainstorming session. If he does, he may stifle his creativity; he may become too logical and organized. He must let his list develop in random order, regardless of the importance and eventual position of the topics in the final report. At the end of this session Dan's list should look like Figure 2-4.

Building OK – needs strengthening

Elevators – too slow, too small

Talk with YoYo – elev mfr (10% discount)

Waiting time too long – 70 sec.

Shaft too small

How enlarge shaft?

      Remove stairs?

Talk with fire inspector

Correspondence – other elev mfrs

Talk with Merrywell – Budget $950 000

Sent out questionnaire

Tenants' preferences –

    Express elev   No stop – 2nd flr

    Executive elev   Faster service

    Prestige elev   No stop – ground flr

    Freight elev

Freight elev – takes up too much space

Shaft only 10.85×2.5 m (when modified)

Big freight elev – omit basement

Tenants "OK" small freight elev

    (YoYo "C" – 2.45 m)

YoYo – has office in Montrose

Basement level has loading dock

Service reputation – YoYo?

    – Others?

Figure 2-4 Initial list of topic headings, typed in random order.

5. Delete Irrelevant Topics

The fifth step calls for Dan to print a copy to work on, then to examine his list of headings with a critical eye, dividing them into those that bear directly on the subject and those that introduce topics of only marginal interest. His knowledge of the reader—identified in stage 2—will help him decide whether each topic is really necessary, so he can delete irrelevant topics as has been done in Figure 2-5.

Start grouping your topics into compartments

6. Group Related Topics

Now Dan needs to group the headings that remain into "topic areas" that he will discuss together. He can do this by simply coding related topics with the same symbol or letter. In Figure 2-5, letter (A) identifies one group of related topics, letter (B) another group, and so on.

Start pulling the pieces together

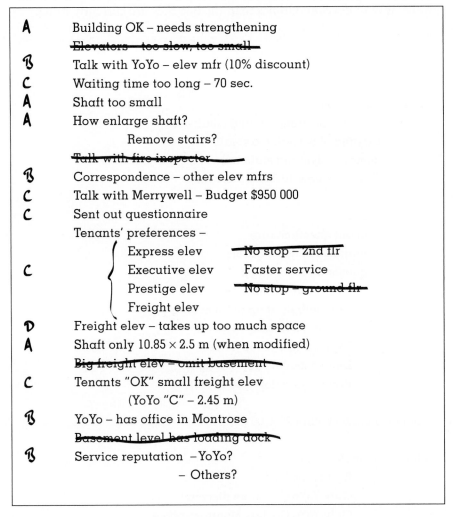

Figure 2-5 The same list of topic headings, but with irrelevant topics deleted and remaining topics coded into subject groups (A–structural implications; B–elevator manufacturers; C–tenants' preferences; D–freight elevator).

7. Arrange the Topic Groups

At this stage Dan takes his first major organizational step: he arranges the groups of information into the most suitable order, considering which order of presentation will be

- most interesting,
- most logical, and
- simplest to understand.

The result becomes the writing plan for his report: his outline, as shown in Figure 2-6.

A final comment about outlining: if you have already developed an outlining method that works well for you, or you are using outlining software successfully, then we suggest you continue as you have been doing. The outlining method suggested here is for people who are seeking a simpler, more creative way to develop outlines than the one they are currently using.

Let the final outline evolve from the subject matter...

Building condition:
       OK – needs strengthening (shaft area)
       Existing elev shaft too small
       Remove adjoining staircase
       Shaft size now 10.85×2.5 metres

Tenants' needs:
       Sent out questionnaire
       Identified 5 major requests
       Requests we must meet:
              Cut waiting time: 32 sec (max)
              Handle freight up to 2.3 m long
       Requests we should try to meet:
               Express elev to top 4 floors
              Deluxe models (for prestige)
              Private elev (for executives)

Budget: must be within $950 000

Elevator manufacturers:
       Researched 3
       Only YoYo Co. offers discount
       Only YoYo Co. has Montrose office

...rather than force the subject matter into a prescribed pattern

Figure 2-6 Topic headings arranged into a writing outline.

Writing the First Draft

Continuity is the key to getting your writing done. This means writing at fairly long sittings during which you know you will not be disturbed. You need to be out of reach of the telephone, friends, and even family, so you can write continuously.

Write where you won't be disturbed: no telephone, no pager, no cellphone, no email

The problem of finding a quiet place to write can be hard to resolve for technical students, who frequently have to work on a tiny writing space in a crowded classroom, or in a dorm room full of distractions. Outlining in the classroom, followed by writing at home or in the seclusion of a library cubicle, is a possible alternative.

Dan Skinner is ready to start writing, but now he encounters another difficulty: he does not know where to begin. Or he may tackle the task enthusiastically, determined to write a really effective introduction, only to find that nothing he writes really says what he wants to say.

We frequently advise technical people who encounter this block that the best place for them to start writing is at paragraph two, or even somewhere in the middle. For example, if Dan finds that a particular part of his project interests him more than other parts, he should write about that part first. His interest and familiarity with the subject will help him write those few first words, and keep him going once he has started. The most important thing is to *start* writing, to put any words down, even if they are not exactly the right words, and to let them lead naturally into the next group of ideas.

Tips for combatting "writer's block"

This is where continuity becomes essential: don't interrupt the writing process to correct a minor point, write perfect grammar, find exactly the right word, fiddle with page layout, or construct sentences and paragraphs of just the right length. That can be done later, during revision. The important thing is to keep building on the rough draft.

Write without stopping to revise; that comes later

Writing and revising are two entirely separate functions, and they call for different approaches. Writing calls for creativity and total immersion in the subject so the words tumble out in a constant flow. Revision calls for lucidity and logic, which force a writer to reason and query the suitability of the words. The first requires excluding every thought but the subject; the second demands an objectivity that challenges the material from the reader's point of view. Writers who try to correct their work as they write soon become frustrated, because creativity and objectivity are constantly fighting for control.

Taking a Break

When Dan has written the final paragraph of his report, he has to resist the temptation to start revising it immediately. Certainly he can pass the draft through a spell-checker, make a back-up copy, and print a copy. But then he needs to set them aside while he tackles a completely unrelated task.

Let time "distance" you from your writing

Reading without a suitable waiting period encourages writers to look at their work through rose-tinted glasses. Sentences they would normally recognize as weak or too wordy appear to be fine. Gross inaccuracies that under other circumstances would stand out go unnoticed. Paragraphs that might not be understood by a reader new to the subject seem clear. Writers' familiarity with their work blinds them to its weaknesses. The remedy is to wait.

Reading with a Plan

Read all the way through without a pen in your hand

Dan Skinner's first reading should take him straight through the draft without stopping to make corrections, so he can gain an overall impression of his report. Subsequent readings should be slower and more critical, with Dan writing changes in as he goes along. As he reads he should check for clarity, tone and style, and technical and grammatical accuracy.

Checking for Clarity

To check for clarity, search for passages that are vague or ambiguous. If the following paragraph remained uncorrected, it would confuse and annoy a reader:

Confusing!

Muddled Paragraph

When the owners were contacted on April 15, the assistant manager, Mr Pierson, informed the engineer that they were thinking of advertising Lot 36 for sale. He has however reiterated his inability to make a definite decision by requesting his company to confirm their intentions with regard to buying the land within two months, when his boss, Mr Davidson, general manager of the company, will have come back from a business tour in Europe. This will be June 8.

The only facts you can be sure about are that the owners of the land were contacted on April 15 and the general manager will be returning on June 8. The important information about the possible sale of Lot 36 is confusing. The writer was probably trying to say something like this:

Clear!

Revised Paragraph

The engineer spoke to the owners on April 15 to enquire if Lot 36 was for sale. He was informed by Mr Pierson, the assistant manager, that the company was thinking of selling the lot, but that no decision would be made until after June 8, when the general manager returns from a business tour in Europe. Mr Pierson suggested that the engineer submit a formal request to purchase the land by that date.

The more complex the topic, the more important it is to write clear paragraphs. Although the paragraph below is quite technical, it would be generally understood even by nontechnical readers:

Technical, but still clear

Clear Paragraph

A sound survey confirmed that the high noise level was caused mainly by the radar equipment blower motors, with a lesser contribution from the air-conditioning equipment. Tests showed that with the radar equipment shut down the ambient noise level at the microphone positions dropped by 10 dB, whereas with the air-conditioning equipment shut down the noise level dropped by 2.5 dB. General clatter and impact noise caused by the movement of furniture and personnel also contributed to the noisy working conditions, but could not be measured other than as sudden sporadic peaks of 2 to 5 dB.

This writer has made sure that

- the topic is clearly stated in the first sentence (the topic sentence),
- the topic is developed adequately by the remaining sentences, and
- no sentence contains information that does not substantiate the topic.

If any paragraph meets these basic requirements, its writer can feel reasonably sure the message has been conveyed clearly.

Checking for Correct Tone and Style

How do you know when your writing has the right tone? One of the most difficult aspects of technical writing is establishing a tone that is correct for the reader, suitable for the subject, and comfortable for you, the writer. If you know your subject well and have thoroughly researched your audience, you will most likely write confidently and will often automatically establish the correct tone. But if you try to set a tone that does not feel natural, or if you are a little uncertain about the subject and the reader, your reader will sense unsureness in your writing.

Finding the Best Writing Level

If Dan Skinner is writing on a specific aspect of a very technical topic, and knows that his reader is an engineer with a thorough understanding of the subject, he can use technical terms and abbreviations. On the other hand, if he is writing on the same topic for a nontechnical reader who has little or no knowledge of the subject, rather than state specific details, Dan may have to write a simplified narrative, explain technical terms, and generally write more informatively.

Keep coming back to your readers: plant yourself in their shoes

For example, when engineer Rita Corrigan wrote the following in a modification report, she knew her readers would be electronics technicians at radar-equipped airfields:

> We modified the MTI by installing a K-59 double-decade circuit. This brightened moving targets by 12% and reduced ground clutter by 23%.

But when Rita reported on the same subject to the airport manager, she included more description and eliminated some technical details that might not be meaningful:

Adjust the level of writing to suit the reader

> We modified the radar set's Moving Target Indicator by installing a special circuit known as the K-59. This increased the brightness of responses from aircraft and decreased returns from fixed objects on the ground.

Suppose Rita also had to write to the local Chamber of Commerce to describe improvements to the airport's air traffic control system. This time her readers would be entirely nontechnical, so she would have to avoid using *any* technical terms:

> We have modified the airfield radar system to improve its performance, which has helped us to differentiate more clearly between low-flying aircraft and high objects on the ground.

Keeping to the Subject

Dan Skinner must now check that he has kept to the subject. He must look at each paragraph and ask: Is this truly relevant? Is it direct? And is it to the point?

Technical writers should convey just enough information for their readers to understand the subject thoroughly. This is apparent in the following descriptions of the same equipment.

Technical writing is *functional* writing

Literary Description	The new cabinet has a rough-textured dove grey finish that reflects the sun's rays in varying hues. Contrary to most instruments of this type, its controls are grouped artistically in one corner, where the deep black of the knobs provides an interesting contrast with the soft grey and white background. A cover plate, hardly noticeable to the layperson's inexperienced eye, conceals a cluster of unsightly adjustment screws that would otherwise mar the overall appearance of the cabinet and would nullify the esthetic appeal of its surprisingly effective design.
Technical Description	The grey cabinet is functional, with the operator's controls grouped at the top right-hand corner where they can be grasped easily with one hand. Subsidiary controls and adjustment screws used by the maintenance crews are grouped at the bottom left-hand corner, beneath a hinged cover plate.

A technical description concentrates on details that are important to the reader (it tells *where* the controls are and *why* they have been so placed), and so maintains an efficient, businesslike tone.

Using Simple Words

Don't use a 90-cent word when an equally suitable 25-cent word exists

A writer who uses unnecessary big words sets an unnaturally pompous tone. The engineer who writes that a design "contains ultrasophisticated circuitry" seems to be justifying the importance and complexity of the work instead of saying that the design has a very complex circuit. Unnecessary use of big words, when smaller, more generally recognized and equally effective synonyms are available, clouds technical writing and destroys the smooth flow.

In technical fields, there are so many required technical words and abbreviations that it is better to surround them with small words. This allows your reader to focus on the technical details.

Removing "Fat"

During the editing stage Dan should be critical of sentences and paragraphs that seem to contain too many words. He should check that he has not inserted words of low information content; that is, phrases and expressions that add little or no information. Their removal, or replacement by simpler, more descriptive words, can tighten up a sentence and add to its clarity. Low-information-content words and phrases are often hard to identify because we see these expressions used in other people's writing. Consider this sentence:

> For your information, we have tested your spectrum analyser and are of the opinion that it needs calibration.

The expressions "for your information" and "are of the opinion that" are words of low information content. The first can be deleted, and the second replaced by "consider," so that the sentence now reads:

Weed out unnecessary expressions

> We have tested your spectrum analyser and consider that it needs calibration.

For a list of low-information-content words and wordy expressions, see Tables 12-1 and 12-2 on pages 295 and 296.

Repeating information can also contribute to excessive length:

> We tested the modem to check its compatibility with the server. After completing the modem tests we transmitted messages at low, medium, and high baud rates. The results of the transmission tests showed...

Deleting the repeated words in sentence 2 ("After completing the modem tests") and sentence 3 ("...of the transmission tests...") makes a much tighter paragraph.

> We tested the modem to check its compatibility with the server, and then transmitted messages at low, medium, and high baud rates. The results showed...

Checking for Accuracy

Nothing annoys readers more than to discover they have been given inaccurate information (particularly if they have been using the information before they discover the error). Readers of Dan's report assume that he knows his facts and has checked that they are correct. If readers discover even a single technical error, they may question his credibility.

Maintain quality control

It's difficult to prevent some errors from occurring when copying quantities and details from one document to another, so carefully check all facts, figures, equations, quantities, and extracts from other documents.

Checking for accuracy also means ensuring that grammar, punctuation, and spelling have not been overlooked. Dan must check spelling with care, because his familiarity with the subject may blind him to obvious errors. How many of us have inadvertently written "their" when we intended to write "there"? And "too" when we meant "two"? A spell-check program will not identify these correctly spelled words used in the wrong context.

Revising Your Own Words

Proofread on a printed copy

We recommend that Dan print out his report and read and revise it on paper rather than on his computer screen. Our experience, and also that of many report writers, is that he will catch many more typographical errors that way.

As he reads, Dan should continually ask himself five questions:

1. **Can my readers understand me?**
   Will the person I am writing for be able to read my report all the way through without getting lost?
   What about other readers who might also see my report? Will they understand it?

2. **Is the focus right?**
   Is my report reader-oriented?
   Are the important points clearly visible?
   Have I summarized the main points in an opening statement that the reader will see right away?

Make yourself a check-list, and then *use* it!

3. **Is my information correct?**
   Is it accurate?
   Is it complete?
   Is all of it necessary?

4. **Is my language good?**
   Is it clear, definite, and unambiguous?
   Are there any grammatical, punctuation, or spelling errors?
   Does every paragraph have a topic sentence (preferably at the start of the paragraph)?
   Have I used any big, "overblown" words where simpler words would do a better job?
   Are there any low-information-content words and phrases?

5. **Have I kept my report as short as possible while still meeting my readers' needs and covering the topic adequately?**

By now Dan's draft should be in good shape and any further reading and revising will be final touches. Dan Skinner will now be able to issue his report with confidence, knowing that he has fashioned a good product. The approach described here will not have made report writing a simple task for him, but it will have helped him through the difficult conceptual stages, and helped him to read and revise more efficiently. When he writes his next report, he will be less likely to put it off until it is so late that he has to do a rush job.

Exercise 2.1
Describe why the pyramid method of writing will help you become a better presenter of information.

Exercise 2.2
Which do you feel is the better way for you to develop an outline for a report: the organized method or the "random" method? Explain why.

Be comfortable with your writing method

Exercise 2.3
(a) What are the seven stages advocated for planning a report?
(b) Which is the most important stage? Explain why.
(c) Must the stages be followed exactly in the sequence listed?

Exercise 2.4
If several people are likely to read a report, how would you identify which one is your primary reader?

Exercise 2.5
Is it better to write a report without stopping to "clean up" the construction along the way, or to write a page at a time and edit that page before going on to the next? Explain why.

Exercise 2.6
What two factors will help you write more easily, and set the right tone?

Exercise 2.7
From the list of five main questions that you, as a writer, should ask yourself during the revision stage (see the boldface questions on page 16), which do you think is the most important? Explain why.

Chapter 3
Letters, Memos, and Emails

How to Write Business Letters That Get Results
http://www.bly.com/
Pages/documents/
File136.doc
Well-known copywriter Robert W Bly provides valuable advice about writing correspondence: "Failure to get to the point, technical jargon, pompous language, misreading the reader—these are the poor stylistic habits that cause others to ignore the letters we send."

Readers want to know *right away* what you most need to tell them

When you write a personal letter to a friend or relative, you probably don't worry whether your letter is too long or contains too much information. You assume your reader will be pleased to hear from you, so you insert comments without concerning yourself very much about organization.

But when you write a business letter you have to be disciplined. Your readers are busy people who want only the details they need to act or make a decision. Extra information annoys and frustrates them. Your letters must be focused, well planned, brief, and clear.

Using the Pyramid

The pyramid technique helps you structure your documents. Figure 3-1 shows the basic pyramid. You can see that only so much information can fit into the top part of the pyramid and is followed by the supporting details and facts. Your readers will know right away why you are writing to them.

Identifying the Main Message

When you write pyramid-style, you will automatically focus the reader's attention on your main message. Before you write, decide *why you are writing* and *what you most want your reader to know*. Then focus on this information by placing it right up front, so it is the first thing your reader reads.

If you begin a letter with background information rather than the main point, your reader will wonder why you are writing. Don McKelvey's letter to Jim Connaught is a typical example of an unfocused message.

Dear Mr Connaught

I refer to our purchase order No. 21438 dated April 26, 2008, for a Vancourt micro-copier model 3000, which was installed on May 14. During tests following its installation your technician discovered that some components had been damaged in transit. He ordered replacements and in a letter dated May 20 informed me that they would be shipped to us on May 27 and that he would return here to install them shortly thereafter.

It is now June 10, and I have neither received the parts nor heard from your technician. I would like to know when the replacement parts will be installed and when we can expect to use the microcopier.

Sincerely

Don McKelvey

Jim had to read more than 70 words before he discovered what Don wanted him to do. If Don had written pyramid-style, starting with a main message, Jim would have known immediately why he was reading the email:

Readers don't want to plough through paragraphs of background information before they encounter your main message

Dear Mr Connaught

We are still unable to use the Vancourt 3000 microcopier we purchased from you on April 26, 2008. Please inform me when I can expect it to be in service.

The microcopier was ordered on P.O. 21438 and installed on May 14. During tests, your technician discovered that some components had been damaged in transit. He ordered replacements, then in a letter dated May 20 informed me that they would be shipped to us on May 27, and that he would return here to install them. To date, I have neither received the parts nor heard from your technician.

I am asking you to phone me directly at (204) 493-5555 to tell me when your technician will come to finish the repairs.

Sincerely

Don McKelvey

Unfortunately, finding exactly the right words to put at the top of the pyramid is often difficult. And that is where many technical people have trouble.

Getting Started

To overcome this block, when you are ready to start, first type these six words:

I want to tell you that...

This proven technique will never fail you!

And then finish the sentence with what you *most* want to tell your reader. For example:

Dear Ms Reynaud

I want to tell you that...the environmental data you submitted to us on October 8 will have to be substantiated if it is to be included with the Labrador study.

Then, when your sentence is complete, delete the *I want to tell you that...* expression. What you have left will be a focused opening statement:

Dear Ms Reynaud

The environmental data you submitted to us on October 8 will have to be substantiated if it is to be included with the Labrador study.

Often you can use an opening statement formed just as it stands when you remove the six "hidden" words. However, if the opening statement seems a bit abrupt, you can soften it by inserting a few additional words. For example, in the letter to Ms Reynaud, you might add "I regret that...":

Dear Ms Reynaud

I regret that the environmental data you submitted to us on October 8 will have to be substantiated if it is to be included with the Labrador study.

Figure 3-1 shows that in business letters the main message is more often referred to as the **Summary Statement**. Good news or bad news, you must place the main message right up front.

Avoiding False Starts

If you do not use the six hidden words to start, you may inadvertently open with an awkward sentence that seems to be going nowhere. For example:

A "dragged out" start

Dear Mr Corvenne

In answer to your enquiry of December 7 concerning erroneous read-outs you are experiencing with your Mark 17 Analyser, and our subsequent telephone conversation of December 18, during which we tried to pinpoint the fault, we have conducted an examination into your problem.

This long, rambling opening is "spinning your wheels," because it does not state the topic early enough. Figure 3-2 contains a list of expressions that can easily cause you to write complicated, unfocused openings. In their

The writer's pyramid helps draw attention to the most important information

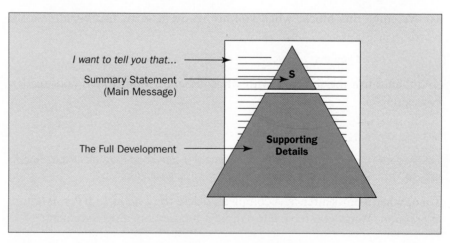

Figure 3-1 Creating a letter's summary statement.

Try inserting *I want to tell you that...* in front of these openings: it doesn't work!

When You Write a Letter...

Never start with a word that ends in "ing":
> *Referring...*
> *Replying...*

Never start with a phrase that ends with the preposition "to":
> *With reference to...*
> *In answer to...*
> *Pursuant to...*
> *Due to...*

Never start with a redundant expression:
> *I am writing...*
> *For your information...*
> *This is to inform you...*
> *The purpose of this letter is...*
> *We have received your letter...*
> *Enclosed please find...*
> *Attached herewith...*
> *My name is...*

IN OTHER WORDS...

Don't Spin Your Wheels!

Figure 3-2 Avoiding awkward starts.

place, start with *I want to tell you that...*, which will help you focus your reader's attention on the main message. If the letter referring to the Mark 17 Analyser had started this way, it would have been much more direct:

Dear Mr Corvenne

(I want to tell you that...) The problem with your Mark 17 Analyser seems to be in the extrapolator circuit. Following your enquiry of December 7 and your subsequent description of erroneous read-outs, we examined... (etc).

A direct start

Planning the Letter

Once you have identified and written the main message, your next step is to select, sort, and arrange the remaining information in a logical order.

This information should relate to what you have said in the Summary Statement and provide evidence of its validity. For example, when Paul Shumeier wrote the following Summary Statement, he realized he would be presenting his reader with costly news:

Dear Mr Larsen

Tests of the environmental monitoring station at Wickens Peak show that 60% of the instruments need to be repaired and recalibrated at a cost of $7265.

He also realized that Mr Larsen would expect the remainder of the letter to tell him why the repairs were necessary, exactly what needed to be done, and how Paul had derived the total cost. To provide this information, Paul had to identify which questions would be in Mr Larsen's mind after he had read the Summary Statement. This meant asking himself six questions, all based on *Who?*, *Where?*, *When?*, *Why?*, *What?*, and *How?*:

Who (was involved)?
Where (did this happen)?
When (did this happen)?
Why (are the repairs necessary)?
What (repairs are needed)?
How (were the costs calculated)?

Six questions: six answers. The answers provide the facts, forming the body of a letter

The answers to these questions become the **Full Development** (or *supporting details*) of the writer's pyramid shown in Figure 3-1. Paul must also determine which facts the reader needs to know to understand the situation. Any "Nice to Know" details can be left out of the message.

Opening Up the Pyramid

To help Paul—and you—organize a letter, the lower part of the pyramid is divided into three compartments: the **Background**, **Facts**, and **Outcome** (see Figure 3-3).

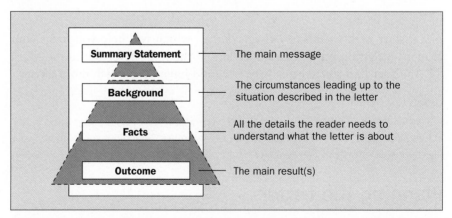

Figure 3-3 Basic writing plan for an informative business letter, interoffice memo, or email.

The **Background** covers *what* has happened previously, *who* was involved, and, sometimes, *for whom* the work was done and *where* and *when* the event occurred or the facts were gathered. Paul wrote:

Our electronics technicians examined the Wickens Peak Monitoring station on May 16 and 17, in response to your May 10 request to Patrick Friesen.

The **Facts** expand on the main message. They provide specific details the reader needs to fully understand the situation or to be convinced of the need to take further action. Here, Paul wrote:

Most of the damage was caused by a tree northwest of the site that fell onto the station during a storm on April 23 and damaged parts of the roof and north and west walls. Instruments along these walls were impact-damaged and then soaked by rain. Other instruments in the station were affected by moisture.

Major repairs and recalibration are required for the 16 instruments listed in Attachment 1, which describes the damage and estimated repair cost for each instrument. This work will be done at our Shepperton repair depot for a total cost of $4485. Minor repairs, which can be performed on site, are necessary for the 27 instruments listed in Attachment 2. These on-site repairs will cost $2780.

These two paragraphs clearly answer the *Why?*, *What?*, and *How?* questions. Note that, rather than clutter the middle of his letter with a long list, Paul placed the details in two attachments and summarized only the main points in the body of his letter. (The attachments are not shown here.)

The **Outcome** describes the result or any effect the facts have had or will have. Because the reader is not expected to take any action, the **Outcome** simply sums up the main result:

I have obtained Ms Korton's approval to perform the repairs and a crew was sent in on May 23. They will complete their work by May 31.

Sincerely

Paul Shumeier

But if the reader is expected to take some action, or approve somebody else taking action, then the **Outcome** becomes a *request for action*. Because Paul wanted an answer, he wrote:

If these repair costs are acceptable, please telephone, fax, or email your approval to me so I can send in our repair crew.

Sincerely

Paul Shumeier

These three parts will help you arrange the full development of any letter, memo, or email into a logical, coherent structure. Before starting, however, you have to decide whether you are writing to inform or persuade.

Writing to Inform

Normally, letters, memos, and emails that purely inform, with no response or action required from the reader, are organized around the basic Summary-Background-Facts-Outcome writing plan shown in Figure 3-3. Kevin Toshak's email to Tina Mactiere, in Figure 3-4, falls into this category.

Another example is a confirmation letter, in which the writer confirms previously made arrangements:

	Christine
Summary	I am confirming that you will represent both Macro Engineering Inc and H L Winman and Associates at the Materials Handling conference in Montreal on May 15 and 16, 2008, as agreed at
Background	the Planning Meeting on March 23. At the conference you will
Facts	• take part in a panel discussion on packaging electronic equipment from 10:00 to 11:15 a.m. on May 15, and
	• host a wine-and-cheese reception for delegates from 5:00 to 7:00 p.m. on May 16.
	Janet Kominsky is making your travel and hotel reservations, and the catering arrangements for the reception. Anna King will provide brochures from Calgary, and my secretary will make up packages for you to distribute.
Outcome	I'll brief you on other details before you leave.
	Wayne

An informative letter *tells* the reader what has been done or what has to be done...

...it doesn't expect the reader to respond

Although the basic writing plan has four compartments (see Figure 3-3), you do not have to write exactly four paragraphs. As both Wayne's and Kevin's examples show, you may combine two compartments into a single paragraph, or let one compartment be represented by several paragraphs.

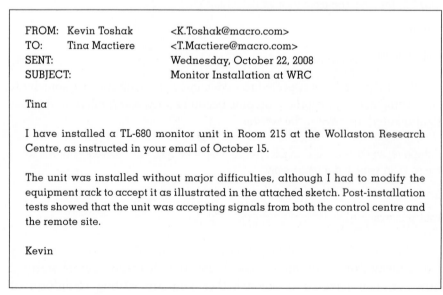

Figure 3-4   An informative email.

When you first use the pyramid technique you'll find yourself writing separate paragraphs for each compartment, but as you become more comfortable with this method you'll understand that keeping the compartments in the correct order is the most important idea and you will blend the compartments into the same paragraph.

Writing to Persuade

In a persuasive letter you expect your reader to respond to you or to take action. Consequently, the writing plan's **Outcome** compartment is renamed **Action,** as shown in Figure 3-5. A request and a complaint are typical examples of persuasive letters or emails, and so is the informal proposal described in Chapter 7.

A persuasive letter *sells* the reader to take some form of action

Making a Request

Many technical people claim that placing the message at the start of a letter is not a problem until they have to ask for something or give the reader bad news. They then tend to lead gently up to the request or negative information.

Bill Kostash is no exception. He has to write to customers to ask if they will accept a change in the preventive maintenance contracts they have with his company:

Many writers hesitate to open with a request

Strategies for Writing Persuasive Letters http://www.washburn. edu/services/zzcwwctr/ persuasive_menu.html **This step-by-step guide covers the purpose of the persuasive letter, prewriting questions for the writer, writing strategies, and revision tips.**

June 18, 2008

Dear Ms Nguyen

I am writing with reference to our contract with you for the preventive maintenance services we provide on your RotoMat extruders and shapers. Under the terms of the current contract (No. RE208) dated January 2, 2008, we are required to perform monthly inspection and maintenance "…on the 15th day of each month or, if the 15th falls on a weekend or holiday, on the first working day thereafter."

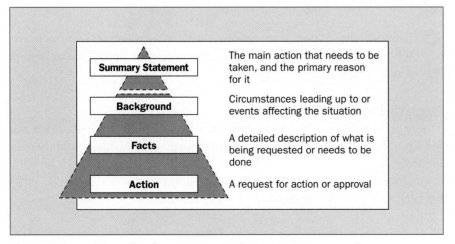

Except for the last compartment, tell and sell writing plans are similar

Figure 3-5 Writing plan for a persuasive letter, memo, or email.

Bill is off to a bad start. Instead of opening with a summary statement he has inserted all the background details first, so Bea Nguyen does not yet know why he has written to her. He has also opened with one of the expressions listed as an awkward start in Figure 3-2. He continues:

Our problem is that almost all of our clients ask that we perform their maintenance service between the 5th and 25th of each month, to avoid their end-of-month peak accounting periods. This in turn creates difficulties for us, in that our service techni-cians experience a peak workload for 20 days and then have virtually no work for 10 days.

(Bea Nguyen still does not know why he is writing.)

Consequently, to even out our workload, I am requesting your approval to shift our inspection date from the 15th to the 29th of each month. If you agree to my request, I will send our technician in to service your machine on June 29—a second time this month—rather than create a six-week period between the June and July inspections. Could you let me know by June 25 if this change of date is acceptable?

Sincerely

William J Kostash

Now Bea knows why Bill has written to her—but she had to read a long way to find out. And she probably had to reread his letter to fully under-stand the details.

If Bill had used the writing plan in Figure 3-5 to shape his letter, his request would have been much more effective. The revised letter is shown in Figure 3-6 with the following numbered comments:

1 contains his **Summary Statement** (he states his request and what the effect will be),

2 contains the **Background** (the contract details),

3 contains the **Facts** (it describes the problem), and

4 contains the **Action** statement, in which he mentions *two* actions: what he wants Bea to do (to call him) and what he will do (schedule a second visit).

Registering a Complaint

The approach is the same if you have to write a letter of complaint or ask for an adjustment, but the third compartment is relabelled as shown in Figure 3-7.

Figure 3-8 on page 29 shows a typical complaint letter using the writ-ing plan in Figure 3-7 with the following comments:

June 18, 2008

Ms Bea Nguyen
Contracts Administrator
Multiple Industries Limited—Manufacturing Division
18 Commodore Bay
Cambridge ON N1R 5S2

Dear Ms Nguyen

(1) I am requesting your approval to change the date of our monthly preventive maintenance visits to service your RotoMat extruders and shapers to the 29th of each month. This will help spread my technicians' workload more evenly and provide you with better service.

A focused, definite, direct request

(2) Our contract with you is No. RE208 dated January 2, 2008, and it requires that we perform a monthly inspection and maintenance on the 15th day of each month. Unfortunately, almost all of our clients ask that we perform their **(3)** maintenance service between the 5th and the 25th. This creates a problem for us in that our service technicians experience a peak workload for 20 days and then have very little work for 10 days.

(4) Could you let me know by June 25 if you can accept the change? Then I will send a technician to your plant on June 29 for a second visit this month, rather than create a six-week space between the June and July inspections.

Sincerely

William J Kostash
Service Manager

Figure 3-6 A request letter written pyramid-style.

(1) In the **Summary**, it is often better to generalize what action is needed and then later, in the Action compartment, state exactly what has to be done.

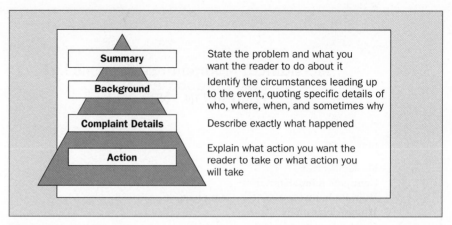

Figure 3-7 Writing plan for a complaint.

2 If there are only a few **Background** facts, you may combine them with either the Summary Statement or the Complaint Details rather than place them in a paragraph by themselves.

3 In the **Complaint Details**, describe in chronological order what happened so the reader will understand the reason for your complaint or request for adjustment.

4 The **Action Statement** must be strong and confident and specifically identify what action you want the reader to take or, in some cases, what action you will take.

Responding to a Complaint

You may need to answer a complaint someone has written. It is easier when you agree with the complaint and can perform the requested action. This will be a shorter response than if you don't agree with the complaint, because you don't have to go into as much detail about why you are agreeing. However, if you disagree with the complaint, your response is more difficult to write and you have to be sure to provide a detailed description of why you cannot act as requested. Figure 3-9 shows the pyramid for responding both positively and negatively to complaints.

Creating a Confident Image

Your writing will create an image of you, your confidence, and your competence. You have only one chance, in writing, to convey a positive image through the quality of your writing and the physical appearance of the information. Everything you write must be clear, concise, and complete. We call these the "Three Cs of Effective Communication."

RGI Video Productions
316 St. Mary's Road
Winnipeg MB   R2H 1J8

November 12, 2008

Mr Bruyere
Sales Manager
Professional Image Business Equipment
Suite 100
1675 Mattingly Drive
Winnipeg MB   R3J M2C

Dear Mr Bruyere

(1) The Nabuchi 700 portable computer you recently sold me had a defective lithium-ion battery that had to be replaced while I was outside Canada. Consequently I am requesting reimbursement of the expenses I incurred to replace the battery.

(2) I bought the computer and a Nabuchi 701PC international power converter from your Willows Mall store on September 4, 2008. (See attached sales invoice No. 14206A.)

The computer worked satisfactorily for the first six weeks, but during that time I had no occasion to use it solely on battery power.

(3) On October 25 I left for Europe, first giving the batteries an 18-hour charge as recommended in the operating instructions. While using the computer in flight, after only 35 minutes the low-battery lamp lit up and the screen warned of imminent failure. I recharged the batteries the following day, in Rheims, France, but achieved less than 25 minutes of operating time before the batteries again became fully discharged.

As the Nabuchi line is neither sold nor serviced in France, I had to buy and install a replacement lithium-ion battery (a Mercurio Z7S), which has since worked fine. I have enclosed the defective battery, plus a copy of the sales receipt for the replacement battery I purchased from Lestrange Limitée, Rheims.

(4) Please send me a cheque for $244.30, which at the current rate of exchange is the Canadian equivalent of the EUR 123.67 shown on the sales receipt.

Sincerely

Suzanne Dumont

Suzanne Dumont, P.Eng
enc 3

Set the scene

...offer the details...

...and end with a firm Action Statement

Figure 3-8   A complaint letter written pyramid-style.

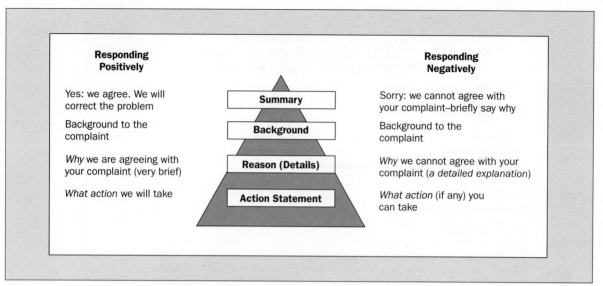

Figure 3-9 Writing plan for responding to a complaint.

Be Clear

A clear letter conveys information simply and effectively, so that the reader easily understands its message. Writing clearly demands creativity and attention to detail. As a writer you must consider not only how you write your letters, but also how you present them.

Create a Good Visual Impression

Clarity depends on appearance as well as clarity of expression

The appearance of a letter creates an impression of the writer and the company he or she represents. If a letter is sloppy or contains typos or spelling errors, then its readers imagine a careless person working in a disorganized office. But if readers are presented with a neat letter, placed in the middle of the page and printed by a quality printer, then they imagine a well-organized person working for a quality company noted for its service.

Develop the Subject Carefully

The key to effective subject development is to present the material logically, progressing gradually from a clear, understood point to one that is more complex. This means developing and consolidating each idea so the reader can fully understand it before presenting the next idea. The sections on paragraph unity and coherence in Chapter 12 (see pages 280 and 281) provide examples of coherent paragraphs. Using the pyramid technique will also help you structure your information in a logical sequence.

Be Concise

For technical business correspondence, concise means writing short letters, short paragraphs, short sentences, and short words.

Short Letters

In business, no one ever complains about reading short letters, but they do moan, whine, and resist diving into long, drawn-out letters, memos, and emails. Just by looking at the length of your information, your reader will begin to judge the content and you. A short letter introduces its topic quickly, discusses it in sufficient depth, and then closes with a concluding statement, its length dictated solely by the amount of information that needs to be conveyed.

The key word here is "short"

Too often business letters will run on for several pages. This creates a problem not only with the length but also with the point of view and the tone. It starts out as a message addressed to an individual but by the time it gets to page 3, it has lost the personal voice. Then, at the end, a signature appears which is too distant from the original greeting. To avoid this, we suggest borrowing a technique from report writing. Instead of placing all the information in the letter, change the letter into a semiformal report and then summarize the highlights—particularly the purpose and the outcome—into a one-page letter placed at the front of the report (so that the report becomes *an attachment* to the letter, as shown in Figure 3-10).

If you use this format, refer to the attachment in the letter *and* insert a main conclusion drawn from it:

> During the second week we measured sound levels at various locations in the production area of the plant, at night, during the day, and on weekends. These readings (see attachment) show that a maximum of 55 dB was recorded on weekdays, and 49 dB on weekends. In both cases these peaks were recorded between 5 and 6 p.m.

A short cover letter is like an executive summary (see page 125)

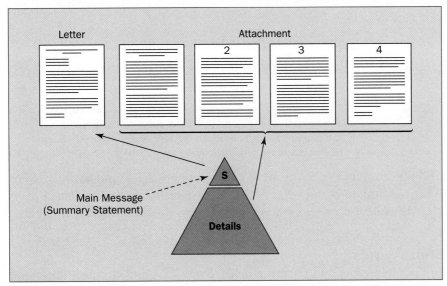

Figure 3-10 A short letter with an attachment is an adaptation of the pyramid method of writing. An example can be seen in Figure 5-4 (page 92).

Short Paragraphs

Think of a paragraph as a miniature pyramid

In business and industry, readers want short paragraphs containing easy-to-digest information. To do this let the first sentence of each paragraph introduce one idea, then make sure that all remaining sentences in that paragraph develop the idea adequately and do not introduce any other ideas. This is known as a "topic sentence," which is shown here in italics:

We have tested your 15 Vancourt 801 DVD drives and find that 11 require repair and recalibration. Only minor repairs will be necessary for 6 of these drives, which will be returned to you next week. Of the 5 remaining drives, 3 require major repairs which will take approximately 20 days, and 2 are so badly damaged they will have to be replaced.

If an idea you are developing results in an overly long paragraph, try dividing the information into a short introductory paragraph and a series of subparagraphs:

My inspection of the monitoring station at Freedom Lake Narrows revealed three areas requiring attention, two immediately and one within three months:

Paragraphs that are longer than eight or nine printed lines are too long

1. The water stage manometer is recording erratic read-outs of water levels. A replacement monitor needs to be flown in immediately so that the existing unit can be returned for service.
2. The tubing to the bubble orifice is worn in several places and must be replaced (30.5 metres of 8 mm tubing will be required). This work should be done concurrently with the monitor replacement.
3. The shack's asphalt roof is wearing and will need resurfacing before winter.

There is more information about writing paragraphs in Chapter 12.

Short Sentences

If you write short, uncomplicated sentences, you help your readers quickly grasp and understand each thought. Compare these two examples of the same information:

Convoluted sentences create the impression that their writer is confused

Complicated	There has been intermittent trouble with the vacuum pumps, although the flow valves and meters seem to be recording normal output, and the 18 cm pipe to the storage tanks has twice become clogged, causing backup in the system.
Clear	There has been intermittent trouble with the vacuum pumps, and twice the 18 cm pipe to the storage tank has become clogged and caused backup in the system. The flow valves and meters, however, seem to be recording normal output.

The first example is confusing because it jumps back and forth between what the trouble is and what is working normally. The second example is clear because it uses two sentences to express the two different thoughts.

Short Words

Short words are especially important for readers whose first language is not English.

In the engineering and scientific fields, many long and complex terms and acronyms have to be used. To make your information more readable, surround technical terms with simple words. Be aware, too, that in today's global society, many of your readers may read and write English as a foreign language. Long words that are not in the average person's vocabulary may cause confusion and misunderstanding. Chapter 12 has more information about writing for an international audience.

Be Complete

As a writer, you must evaluate your information and determine what is "Need-to-Know" and what is "Nice-to-Know" information. Don't just dump all the details you have into your letter, memo, or email and expect your reader to sift through it. On the other hand, don't be thin with your details and leave too many unanswered questions with your reader. To find the right balance, ask yourself: "What details does the reader *need* to fully understand the situation to make a decision, to respond intelligently, or to react accordingly?" The answer to this question will guide you to the level of detail you need to include. Any added remarks or side comments can be left out.

Be Definite

People who think with their fingers on a keyboard or a pen in their hand sometimes produce indecisive letters that are irritating to read. These writers seem to examine and discard points without really grappling with the problem. By the time they have finished a letter, they have decided what they want to say, but it has been at the reader's expense. We call this a "brain dump."

Using the writer's pyramid will help you avoid this trap:

1. Decide exactly what you want to say (i.e. develop your main message).

2. Place the main message right up front (use *I want to tell you that…* to get started).

3. Ask yourself what questions the reader might have after reading the main message, and then answer those questions in the remaining compartments.

If you write primarily in the active voice, you will sound even more definite. Active verbs are strong; passive verbs are weak. For example:

These passive expressions	Should be replaced with
it was our considered opinion	we considered
it is recommended that	I recommend
an investigation was made	we investigated
the outage was caused by a defective transmitter	a defective transmitter caused the outage

For more information on how to use the active voice, see Chapter 12 (page 288).

Know clearly what you want to say before *you start writing*

Write directly from person to person, and name the "doer"

Adopting a Pleasant Tone

To achieve the right tone, your correspondence should be simple and dignified, but still friendly. Approach your readers on a person-to-person basis.

Whether you are writing a letter, memo, or email, you have to develop a tone and style that allow your "voice" to be heard. The more experience you have with business and technical writing, the more developed your style will become. You never want to "sound" like a large, bureaucratic organization. To avoid this, you should write the way you speak, in a comfortable, conversational tone, without slang, regional idioms, or humour.

Be careful, though, not to make your correspondence *too* chatty or informal. In business and technical writing you should consistently sound professional. You can never tell when your letter or email may be forwarded to someone else! We offer the following suggestions to help you develop a professional tone.

Know Your Reader

Reminder: Know who you are writing to!

If you have not identified your reader properly, you may have difficulty setting the correct tone. You need to know your reader's level of technical knowledge and whether he or she is familiar with the topic you are describing. Without this focus you may seem condescending to a knowledgeable reader or overwhelming to a reader who has only limited technical knowledge.

Often you will know exactly whom you are writing to, in which case it is relatively easy to identify an appropriate tone and level of detail. However, there will be other times when you will not personally know your reader, and then you have to identify the *type* of person—or people— who will be reading your words. Be aware that you may have multiple readers at multiple knowledge levels. If you identify a secondary reader, also identify that person's knowledge level and choose your tone and language appropriately. Your main message will always be directed to the primary reader or decision maker.

Be Sincere

Care about both your topic and your reader

Sincerity is the gift of making your readers feel that you are personally interested in them and their problems. You convey this by the words you use and the way you use them. A reader would be unlikely to believe you if you came straight out and said, "I am genuinely interested in your project." The secret is to be so involved and interested in the subject that you automatically convey the ring of enthusiasm that would appear in your voice if you were talking about it. One way to do this is to vary the sentence length. A crisp, short sentence placed between two longer sentences can provide additional emphasis.

Be Human

Too many letters lack humanity. They are written from one company to another, without any indication that there is a human being at the sending end and another at the receiving end. The letters might just as well be sent from computer to computer.

Do not be afraid to use the personal pronouns, "I," "you," "he," "she," "we," and "they." Let your reader believe you are personally involved by using "I" or "we," and that you know he or she is there by using "you." Contrary to what many of us were told in school, letters may be started in the first person. If you know the reader personally, or you have corresponded with each other before, or if your topic is informal, let a personal touch appear in your letters by using "I" and the reader's first name:

Let your presence be apparent

Dear Ben

I read your report with interest and agree with all but one of your conclusions.

If you do not know your reader personally and are writing formally as a representative of your company, then use the first person plural and the person's last name:

Dear Mr Wyndam

We read your report with interest and agree with all but one of your conclusions.

Avoid Words That Antagonize

In writing, you have only one chance to explain your point. If your reader interprets your words differently from the way you had intended, you don't have the opportunity to rephrase them. You also don't have the benefit of body language, voice inflection, or facial expressions.

Be careful not to use words that imply the reader is wrong, has not tried to understand, or has failed to write clearly to you; otherwise, you may place the reader on the defensive. For example, when field technician Des Tanski omitted sending receipts with his expense account, Andy Rittman (his supervisor) wrote this to him:

You may unknowingly upset or antagonize your reader

You have failed to include receipts with your expense account.

This antagonized Des, because the words *you have failed* seemed to imply that he was a failure! Andy should have written:

Please send receipts to support your expense account.

Other expressions that may annoy readers or put them on the defensive are listed in Table 3-1, with a suggested way to make them more positive.

When your goal is to achieve some sort of action or response from the reader, using words that may antagonize will hinder communication. You can still be clear and direct without using these words, and you will find that you are more likely to get the result you expect.

Table 3-1 Expressions that may prove abrasive.

	Sentences containing abrasive words	Much more positive sentences
1. Words that make a reader feel inadequate or guilty:	When completing your application *you neglected* to include your tax number.	Your tax number needs to be included on your application.
	Clearly, *you have not understood* the implications.	Let me explain the implications in more detail.
	We could not accept your bid because *you failed* to submit a complete price proposal.	We could not accept your bid because it did not include a complete price proposal.
	You ought to know that staff working after 11 p.m. have to be sent home by taxi.	It's company policy that staff working after 11 p.m. be sent home by taxi.
	When rejecting the request *you overlooked* human rights legislation.	Before rejecting the request you needed to consider human rights legislation.
2. Words that provoke and so create resistance in a reader:	*I am sure you will agree* that no further action is required.	I regret that no further action can be taken.
	We must insist that you return the form by November 30.	Please return the form by November 30.
	To ensure prompt payment *we demand* that you file your invoice within three days of job completion.	To ensure prompt payment please file your invoice within three days of job completion.
	You must bring the application to Room 117.	Please bring the application to Room 117.
	In your letter *you claim* that the food processor was incorrectly priced.	In your letter you state that the food processor was incorrectly priced.
3. Words that imply the writer is "talking down" to the reader:	*We have to assume* that you understand the problem.	We assume that you understand the problem.
	Undoubtedly you will be present at the hearings.	We request that you attend the hearings.
	We simply do not understand how you misinterpreted our instructions.	Apparently you misinterpreted our instructions.
	You must understand that we cannot reopen the file.	I regret we cannot reopen the file.
	If you are applying for reassessment, then *I must request* that you attend a preliminary hearing on October 5.	If you are applying for reassessment, then I request that you attend a preliminary hearing on October 5.

Close on a Strong Note

You may feel you should always end a letter with a polite closing remark, such as: *I look forward to hearing from you at your earliest convenience*, or *Thanking you in advance for your kind cooperation*. In contemporary business correspondence—and particularly in technical correspondence—such closing statements are not only outdated but also weaken your impact on the reader. Today, you should close with a strong, definite statement:

Please send your comments to me by Friday January 14.

I will complete the project and deliver my report to you on September 21.

You should resist the temptation to add a polite but uninformative closing remark. Simply sign off with "Regards" or "Sincerely."

Using Business Formats

There are many opinions about what is the "correct" format for business correspondence. Most popular word-processing packages include templates for writing business letters, memos, faxes, and proposals. Some are good and easy to use; others are less practicable. The example shown here is the format most frequently used by contemporary technical organizations.

Letter Style

The letter format most commonly used today is the full block (see Figure 3-11). The comments below refer to the circled numbers beside the figure.

1 The trend today is to eliminate all but essential punctuation from the address, salutation, and signature block (more punctuation is used in the US than in Canada). This also is the standard in European countries. The Post Office now requests one space between the city and the province or state, two spaces between the province and the postal code (or the state and the zip code), and no punctuation. The province or state is always printed as two capital letters (e.g. "ON" for Ontario), and the postal code or zip code is on the same line as the province or state.

Most business letters in North America are written full block style

2 Today's trend toward informality encourages writers to use first names in the salutation: "Dear Jack," especially after the first exchange between two people.

Never address a letter to "Dear Sir or Madam" or "To Whom It May Concern." This indicates that you do not know who the recipient is and that the content can't possibly be personalized. If you don't know a name, address the letter to *the position the person holds:* "Dear Customer Service Manager" or "Dear Human Resources Manager." This shows that you at least know how they spend their time at work *and* it allows a mail clerk to direct your letter to the right department.

If you are replying to a letter or email signed by A J Winters, and you don't know if A J is male or female, then write "Dear A J Winters."

3 The subject line should be informative (not just "Production Plan" or "Spectrum Analyser"); it may be preceded by Subject:, Ref:, or Re:. It should be set in boldface and not underlined.

Never refer to the subject line in the body of the letter, as in "The defect is with the above-mentioned product model." This forces your reader to stop and search for information. Repeat the information so your message is clear and easy to read.

4 In the full block format every line starts at the left margin.

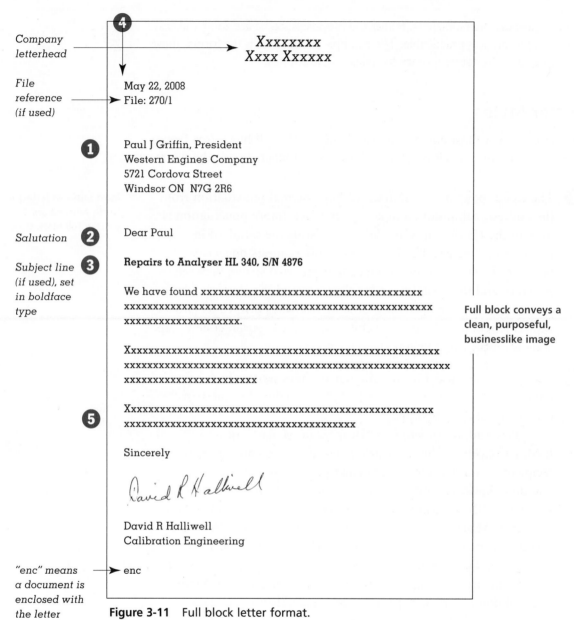

Figure 3-11 Full block letter format.

The labelled callouts in the figure read:

Company letterhead →

Xxxxxxxx
Xxxx Xxxxxx

May 22, 2008
File reference (if used) → File: 270/1

1 Paul J Griffin, President
Western Engines Company
5721 Cordova Street
Windsor ON N7G 2R6

Salutation **2** Dear Paul

Subject line (if used), set in boldface type **3** **Repairs to Analyser HL 340, S/N 4876**

We have found xxxxxxxxxxxxxxxxxxxxxxxxxxxxxxxxxxxxxxxxxx
xxxxxxxxxxxxxxxxxxxxxxxxxxxxxxxxxxxxxxxxxxxxxxxxxxxxxxxxxxxx
xxxxxxxxxxxxxxxxxxxx.

Xxxxxxxxxxxxxxxxxxxxxxxxxxxxxxxxxxxxxxxxxxxxxxxxxxxxxxxxxxx
xxxxxxxxxxxxxxxxxxxxxxxxxxxxxxxxxxxxxxxxxxxxxxxxxxxxxxxxxxxxx
xxxxxxxxxxxxxxxxxxxxxxxx

5 Xxxxxxxxxxxxxxxxxxxxxxxxxxxxxxxxxxxxxxxxxxxxxxxxxxxxxxxxxxx
xxxxxxxxxxxxxxxxxxxxxxxxxxxxxxxxxxxxxxxxxxxxxxxx

Sincerely

David R Halliwell

David R Halliwell
Calibration Engineering

"enc" means a document is enclosed with the letter → enc

Full block conveys a clean, purposeful, businesslike image

5 Close confidently. Most of us were taught in school that we should end a letter with a polite "complimentary close." In business, however, it is better to close with a definite statement that says exactly what action you want the reader to take (for a *persuasive* message), or what action you have taken (for an *informative* message).

These five closing statements are overused, weak, and indefinite:

- Your cooperation in remedying this problem will be greatly appreciated.

- I look forward to hearing from you at your earliest convenience.

- Thanking you in advance for your attention to this matter.

- If we do not hear from you within 21 days we shall consider handing the matter over to another authority.

- Thank you.

These three closing statements create a much stronger impression (of both the writer and what will or has to be done):

- I will call you on May 30 to set up a meeting date.

- Please call me by February 15 and inform me what action you intend to take.

- I need your approval by June 8 if I am to obtain a discount airfare and a reduced conference registration fee.

And then add just one more word: Regards, *or* Sincerely.

Interoffice Memo

The memo is strictly an internal document. Historically, memos were printed on a prepared form, but today email is used instead. In the past, a memorandum would be written to convey information to an internal audience and the tone would be less formal because it was understood that only people inside the organization would receive it. A formal letter would be used if the information was to be sent outside the organization. Email has changed this: we use email for both internal and external messages.

The memo is quickly being replaced by email

Many organizations still use prepared memo formats similar to the one shown in Figure 3-12 keyed to the numbered comments below. You will notice how email formats follow the same basic plan. Often a memo will be written as a separate document and then attached to an email message for distribution.

1 The informality of an interoffice memorandum means titles of individuals (such as Office Manager and Senior Project Engineer) may be omitted.

2 The subject line must be specific; a subject entry such as "Pay Cheques" would be insufficient.

3 No salutation or identification is necessary. The writer can jump straight into the content.

4 Paragraphs and sentences are developed properly. The informality of the memo is not an invitation to omit words.

5 A signature is not required in a memo; however, some people will initial the memo either next to their name in the "From:" field or at the end of the memo. This is omitted if the memo is sent electronically.

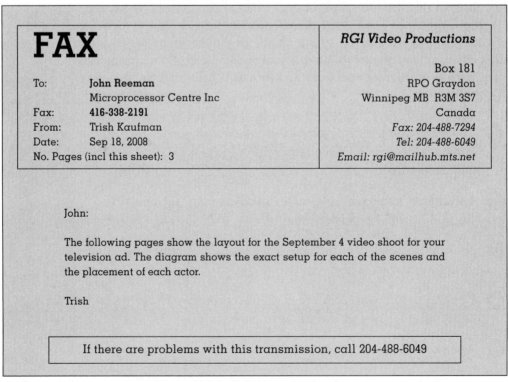

H L WINMAN AND ASSOCIATES

INTEROFFICE MEMORANDUM

(1)
To: A Rittman
From: R Davis
Date: December 3, 2007
(2) **Subject: Early Mailing of Pay Cheques for Field Personnel**

(3) I need to know who you will have on field assignments during the week
before Christmas so that I can mail their pay cheques early. Please provide
(4) me with a list of names, plus their anticipated mailing addresses, by
December 8.

Cheques will be mailed on Friday, December 14. I suggest you inform your
field staff of the proposed early mailing.   *RD*

(5)

Figure 3-12 Interoffice memorandum.

Fax Cover Sheet

Faxed messages, like the memo, are used less today; however, they are a convenient way to communicate information that is not stored electronically.

FAX

RGI Video Productions

Box 181
RPO Graydon
Winnipeg MB R3M 3S7
Canada
Fax: 204-488-7294
Tel: 204-488-6049
Email: rgi@mailhub.mts.net

To: **John Reeman**
         Microprocessor Centre Inc
Fax: **416-338-2191**
From: Trish Kaufman
Date: Sep 18, 2008
No. Pages (incl this sheet): 3

John:

The following pages show the layout for the September 4 video shoot for your
television ad. The diagram shows the exact setup for each of the scenes and
the placement of each actor.

Trish

If there are problems with this transmission, call 204-488-6049

Figure 3-13   A cover sheet for a facsimile (fax) transmission.

Any document sent by facsimile machine is normally preceded by a single-page fax cover sheet that identifies both addressee and sender, and their contact information (see Figure 3-13). The cover sheet usually has a space for the sender to write a short note. A sender who has only a short message to send may write the message directly onto the fax cover sheet and then transmit just the single page.

A fax cover sheet may carry a message in addition to being a transmittal document

Writing Electronic Mail

The criterion for writing email remains the same as for all other forms of written communication: keep the message brief but clear. You want to avoid having your reader make a telephone call or email you to find out exactly what you were trying to say.

Although it is a fast way to communicate...

When Mike Toller in Vancouver, BC, opened up a shipment of parts from Carlson Distributors, he found the order was incomplete and contained some items he had not ordered. He made a note of the deficiencies, sat at his keyboard, and typed in this message:

To: Carlson Distributors, Montreal

Your inv 216875 Oct 19, our P.O. W1634. Short-shipped
10 toolsets MKV, 4 801 sockets plus 2 doz mod 280A lathe bits unordered.
Advise.

M Toller
Crown Manufacturing, Vancouver

...email needs just as much care and attention as business letters

A Beginner's Guide to Effective Email http://www.webfoot.com/advice/email.top.html This useful guide includes an introduction to email and a discussion about why it differs from ordinary correspondence.

In Montreal, Chantal Goulet puzzled over the message, and then typed this brief reply:

To: M Toller, Crown Manufacturing, Vancouver
From: C Goulet, Carlson Distributors, Montreal

The message you sent regarding our invoice 216875 and your P.O. W1634 was difficult to understand. Please explain your concerns.

Chantal Goulet

Mike was surprised: he thought his message was crystal clear. So he again sat at his keyboard and wrote:

> To: Chantal Goulet, Carlson Distributors, Montreal
> From: Mike Toller, Crown Manufacturing, Vancouver
>
> My message was quite clear: You short-shipped us 10 toolsets type MKV and 4 No. 801 sockets. You also shipped 2 dozen model 280A lathe bits we did not order. Please ship the missing items and advise how you want the bits returned.
>
> Mike Toller

Chantal replied in six words:

> Mike:
>
> Thanks. I will investigate the situation.
>
> Chantal

Keep the message short but keep it clear

If Mike had been more explicit when he wrote his original message, both he and Chantal would have saved time.

Email Etiquette

Email is one of the most used and abused tools we have in business and, if you are not careful, it can cause you problems. In today's global society you will find that you communicate with people by email that you may never meet in person or talk with on the phone. Often the only impression they have of you and your competence is based on the email messages you send. For this reason, we encourage you always to be professional when using email. If you are careless and sloppy, you create an image that you and your organization are careless and sloppy.

Text messaging from electronic devices such as a BlackBerry or a cell-phone is different. You will develop a cryptic language that you know your audience will understand. Try not to fall into the bad habit of using this same shortcut in your email messages. Remember, you are creating an image of yourself through your communication skills and you must always be clear, concise, and complete.

There are no established guidelines for writing email, but we can give you some suggestions that will help you be an efficient email communicator. Remember, email does *not* give you a licence to

- write snippets of disconnected information,
- write incorrectly constructed sentences,
- forget about using proper punctuation,
- ignore misspelled words, or
- be abrupt or impolite.

Writing Effective Email http://jerz.setonhill.edu/ writing/e-text/e-mail.htm This document offers 10 tips to help you write effective professional emails. If you want to be taken seriously by professionals, you should know email etiquette.

And never use your work email as a forum for telling long stories, anecdotes, or jokes.

Adopt the Right Tone

Too often, we hear people say "It's only email. It's supposed to be casual and quick." That's true. With email you can be less formal in tone but you still need to be professional. You still need to address the recipient and you still need to "sign" your name to the message. Even if you have a signature file attached to every message you should still type your name at the end. This helps humanize this very technical mode of communication.

Inside your small work groups you will develop a more casual style for quick messages. But be aware that email is not a conversation, and short, one-line comments are ineffective if one person leaves the desk area and returns to several messages. It takes too long to catch up to the flow of the interactions.

Use a Specific Subject Line

Because people receive so much email, the subject line must grab their attention. Consider it a mini Summary Statement. It is the first indication to the reader of what your message is about.

Mark Hoylston, an engineering technician responsible for installing a new network at a client site, was writing to his supervisor to explain that there was going to be a delay in the project because they had discovered some additional work that needed to be done first. His subject line on the email was simply

Subject: Progress

Because it seemed routine, his supervisor decided to read it later, when she had more time. If Mark had written

Subject: Delay in Project Progress

the word "Delay" would have caught her attention.

Make sure you always use a subject line. Some people forget, or do not realize the importance of using one. In many cases, if your audience does not recognize your name, they will delete your message without reading it. A specific subject line encourages them to open and read the message. Be aware that many spell-checkers don't check the subject line so you have to check it yourself.

If you have been replying to a message several times, make sure the subject line still reflects the content of the message. You may have to initiate a new message or change the subject line in the reply message.

Write "Pyramid-Style"

You can use the pyramid method for writing email messages, just as you do for ordinary letters:

1. Start with what you most want your reader to know and, if appropriate, what action you want the reader to take.

2. Follow with any background information the reader may need to understand your message, and provide details about any point that may need further explanation.

Check that each message contains *only* the information your reader will need to respond or to act—and no more. Separate the essential "Need-to-Know" information from the less important "Nice-to-Know" details. Your email will still have four compartments (Summary, Background, Details, Outcome/Action) but they may be much shorter than they are in a letter format. For example, the Summary and Background may be in the same sentence.

Make sure you have a strong action statement if your email message is a sell message. Too often we hear people complain that their audience is not responding to a message. Usually, it's because they have written it as a tell message and the audience does not understand that a reply is expected.

If you need to include extensive details, use the email message as the summary and then put the details in a file attachment so your message uses the structure shown in Figure 3-10. Your readers will appreciate this since they are not forced to read the entire document; they read the highlights in the email message and turn to the details in the attachment when they need them.

Proofread with Care

Reread what you have typed, even for a one-sentence reply

Proofread email *very* carefully: the informality of the medium and the speed with which you can write messages can invite carelessness. If a message is long or particularly important, we recommend you print a copy of the message and proofread your words on paper. You will catch more of the errors this way than reading them on the screen. It's too easy to read what you wanted to write rather than what you did write. Remember, a sloppy email message, with spelling errors and poor organization, is creating a poor image of you and your content.

Be Cautious

If you are annoyed or irritated by a message you receive, *wait* before replying. Let your irritation cool down. Email is ideal for transmitting facts; it's the wrong medium for sending emotional messages. Too many people sit at their desk and send email messages when the telephone or a personal visit with someone is more appropriate. With email, you can't hear a person's voice and may misinterpret the tone as being aggressive when it wasn't meant to be. A quick phone call can resolve an issue, where a series of emails might escalate it.

Remember that email is not a good medium for conveying confidential information, and it is particularly not a medium for making uncomplimentary remarks about other people. Never put anything in an email that you would feel uncomfortable saying to someone in person. Email messages can too easily be forwarded or copied to other readers, and then you have no control over who else may see what you have written. Be just as professional as you are when writing regular letters and memos.

Similarly, be just as sensitive when deciding to copy a message to another person. Be sure that the original sender would want the message distributed to a wider audience.

Tailor the Content

If you are writing to multiple readers, consider sending *two* messages rather than a single all-embracing message. Write

1. a short summary, which you send to readers who are interested only in the main event and the result, and
2. a detailed message, which you send to readers who need all the details.

It may take more of your time to write two messages, but your varying audiences will be more satisfied and able to use your information.

Avoid Overloading the System

Be selective when replying to a multiple-reader message. Don't simply click the "Reply All" button rather than taking the time to address your reply only to those readers who need it. If everyone uses the "Reply All" command, the system—and everyone else's inbox—will quickly become overloaded.

Limit how many readers receive your message

Help Identify the Originator

Write your name at the foot of every message you create, even though your name appears in the "To-From" list at the top or in a signature file. If a recipient decides to forward the message, your name will be associated with your text. You can insert a signature file at the bottom of the message which contains information on other ways to contact you. Typically you can include your name, company name, title, phone number, fax number, and website.

When replying to a message, particularly if your reply is going to multiple addressees, copy a line or two from the original message to help put your reply in context. Identify the excerpt by placing a ">" sign before each line, like this:

Make sure the originator's name is evident

> Dan Reitsma wrote on May 12:
>
> > The Society's constitution was last updated in
> > 2002 and needs amending.
>
> I agree, but first we need to check how much editing was done by Karen Ellsberg before she retired in 2006.

This reduces the frustration your reader will experience from having to scroll down through all the attached messages (often called the "history" or the "train").

Avoid Complex Formatting

Use only simple formatting if you are sending messages outside your email system. Bold, italic, and colour formatting may not convert correctly in transmission or may not be available in the recipient's system. If the message is printed on a black and white printer or photocopied, the colour will be lost.

Write short paragraphs and separate each paragraph with a blank line. Avoid creating columns and indenting subparagraphs, because what you see on screen may not be what your readers see. For example, your screen may look like this:

Facilities are located as follows:

Facility	Location	Distance
Master Control	Calgary, AB	28.6 km south of transmitter
Remote Site 1	Regina, SK	Downtown
Remote Site 2	Thunder Bay, ON	2.5 km north of university

But your readers may see something like this:

Facilities are located as follows:

Facility Location Distance

Master Control Calgary, AB 28.6 km south of transmitter

Remote Site 1 Regina, SK Downtown

Remote Site 2 Thunder Bay, ON 2.5 km north of university

If you need to format columns, consider sending the information as an attachment to an email message.

Indicate Emphasis with Care

Use upper- and lower-case letters, just as this sentence has been written (not like the one below).

PARAGRAPHS COMPOSED OF ALL CAPITAL LETTERS ARE HARD TO READ. YOU CANNOT EASILY IDENTIFY WHICH ARE THE KEY WORDS.

This may be perceived as if you are shouting or that you are angry. The opposite is also true:

paragraphs composed of all lower-case letters are hard to read. you cannot easily identify which are the key words.

Don't use decorative backgrounds. They can make your information hard to read and can take up large amounts of computer resources.

In your professional emails there is no room for short, cryptic notations such as *<lol>*, *btw*, *thx*, *B4*, and *cuz*. These conventions should only be used between friends in quick text-messaging communications. If your audience does not understand the notation, you risk misinterpretation or lack of communication.

And never use your work email address for sending out jokes or forwarding chain messages. Your employer is paying you to work, not to socialize. Many companies have policies about personal use of email and it may be grounds for firing.

ASSIGNMENTS

Project 3.1:   Write Better Opening Sentences

Each of the examples below is an ineffective opening statement to a letter, memo, or email. Revise each to make it more effective. (Remember that each opening sentence is preceded by *Dear....* Don't be afraid to use the first person, singular or plural, and the active voice. For information about the active voice, see page 288.)

1. Accompanying this memorandum is the revised forecast for the second online documentation phase.
2. The purpose of this letter is to inform you that, on or about March 16, you are scheduled to be transferred to the Waverley Heights office for a period of approximately nine weeks to three months.
3. Enclosed please find three copies of the Lakeland Agreement for your review and to sign and return.
4. Further to my memorandum of January 30, the briefing on interconnection services has currently been rescheduled. It will now take place at 9 a.m. on Friday March 13, in conference room B.
5. For your information, it is our company's policy to provide a diversified workforce that encourages employment of employees with different ethnic backgrounds and without reference to their colour or sexual orientation.
6. I am writing to inform you that shortly there will be a vacancy on the company's workplace safety committee and am encouraging you to apply.
7. In answer to your inquiry of October 13, it is possible that approval for your Class C operator's licence, if it is to be granted, will occur before the end of the current financial year.
8. With reference to your January 27 letter, we have conducted an extensive examination into your records. The examination shows that, if you will complete the enclosed Form 2710, you will be entitled to a refund.
9. This is to confirm that, in our discussion of April 13, it was mutually agreed that next year you will represent us on the Provincial Environmental Resources Committee.

10. In the matter of changes to product pricing, it is our recommendation that the conditions pertaining to last year's pricing should be extended to the end of the current year.

Project 3.2: Improve an Email Message

Read this email message and then answer the questions that follow it.

To: Annette.Lesk@winman.ca

From: Mark.Hoylan@winman.ca

Date: Friday, 11 April, 2008

Subject: Progress

Annette:

As you are well aware Ken Poitras and I have been at Morriss Machine Works for two and a half weeks now where we are shoring up the floor and building the racks for the Nortel 2720 Switching Unit and accessories to be installed this week and have had to build a 3.8 metre extension along the width of the north wall.

All this work is now complete and we should've been heading back to the office by now accept theres a problem with the Nortel unit which arrived today and instead of being installed its sitting outside under a tarp. Why? Because no one seems to of calculated you can't grease a 1.06 metre wide piece of equippment (which is it's narrowest dimension) through a 0.92 metre door!!! So... Mr Grindelbauer, who's the MMW works manager (actually I think he's the owner too), has asked Ken and yours truly to stay behind and tear out part of the wall to make the door wider (which we're doing now) so the machine can be put in tommorrow and then to rebuild the wall and reinstal the door which I reckon will take two extra day's. I tried to explain to Mr G there would be an extra charge for doing all this as its not in the contract but he didn't seem to understand, maybe you'd better call him.

Mark

P.S. I reckon the additional time will be 32 hrs and there will be two more nights accomodation and meals, plus some extra lumber and wallboard at a cost that'll probably come in about $135.

PPS We'll be back in the office on the 23rd, ok?

Part 1: List faults that you have noticed in Mark Hoylan's email.
Part 2: Rewrite the email to make it more effective.

Project 3.3:   Resolve a Billing Error

Today you receive a credit card statement covering last month's purchases. There are five entries for expenses you incurred during a business trip between the 10th and 14th of last month:

Item	Date	Vendor/Location	Control No.	$
1	10th	St James Motel, Burntwood Lake	0134652	73.90
2	11th	Burntwood Auto Service	0148167	49.44
3	12th	Wapiti Autos Ltd	0203916	624.80
4	14th	Wapiti Inn	0205771	256.50
5	14th	Burntwood Auto Service	0211606	53.63

Items 2, 3, and 5 are for purchasing gasoline for the panel van. But item 3 puzzles you because the van simply would not hold that amount of gas! You do not have your credit card receipts (you sent them to the Accounting Department at head office, with your expense account), but you do have a travel log in which you recorded your gasoline purchases:

11th — 51.02 L @ $0.969/L
12th — 63.17 L @ $0.989/L
14th — 52.63 L @ $1.019/L

You consider that a data entry error must have occurred on the 12th, which put the decimal point in the wrong place in the transaction.

Write to the manager of customer accounts at WindsorCard (Suite 2160 – 24 Hudson Avenue, Toronto, Ontario, M4J 2B5). Explain the situation and ask for credit.

Project 3.4:   Correct Inaccurate Software Delivery

Three weeks ago you ordered Release 5.6 of *CalcuWrite for Windows XP Professional*, an integrated database and word-processing package. Today the software arrived, accompanied by invoice No. 10402. Details of the purchase are:

- You are buying the software for your company, Harbison Design Group, on company purchase order No. HD 2786.
- The software was ordered from Metroware Limited, 300 Medway Road, Toronto, Ontario.
- You specified on the order that the software was to be supplied on a CD-ROM disk.

But when you open the carton you discover that Metroware has sent you the newer version, for Windows Vista, which you cannot use. You also notice that the handbook has several folded corners, and the user registration card has been filled out by someone:

Klugman, Peter F. 26C Oxnard Road, Halifax, Nova Scotia

You suspect the software was sold previously to Mr Klugman, who subsequently returned it, and you are not happy about that! So you pack up the software, ready to ship back to Metroware Limited, and insert a letter inside the carton in which you describe what has happened and ask for a replacement. From the literature in the box you identify that Metroware's customer service manager is Connie Vetterland.

Write the letter.

Project 3.5:   Explain a Delivery Problem

Rewrite the following email to make it less aggressive and more easily understood.

To: admin@medallionmetals.ca

From: j.hartley@willesden.com

Date: 13 February 2008

Subject: Bad order

Can't you guys fill a simple order correctly? On Oct 5 I ordered eight spigots, Medallion Part No. 34116-3B, and 6 shut-off valves, Medallion Part No. 21360-2A with reverse thread, against my purchase order 2128 and you know what you sent me? 6 spigots and eight valves! Please fill my order properly (it's your shop order 39273) and tell me what you want me to do with the 2 extra valves.

Jim Hartley

Project 3.6:   Acknowledge a College Award

Assume that you are in the last year of the course you are enrolled in, and that three weeks ago the head of the department told you that you have been chosen as this year's winner of the Inter-Provincial Engineering Association (IPEA) award for "proficiency in technical studies."

Yesterday you attended an awards luncheon with other award winners and representatives of the firms and organizations donating the awards. You sat next to Calvin Reiman, vice-president of the local chapter of the IPEA, who presented the award to you.

Today, write to the president of the local chapter of the IPEA to thank the association for the award. Use these details:

- The president is Marjorie Wiens.
- IPEA's address is 710 Durham Avenue of your city.
- The award is $500 plus a wall plaque inscribed with your name.

Project 3.7:   Describe Unexplained Absence Procedure

Rewrite the following memorandum so that it makes its point clearer without being wordy or "talking down" to the reader.

MEDALLION METALS

To: B Darragh, Production Department

From: A K Willesden, Manager, Human Resources

Date: June 12, 2008

Ref: Absences

It has come to our attention that on five occasions at not very widely separated intervals during the month of May, you chose to absent yourself from work on the production line without what we feel is a valid explanation such as a doctor's certificate. At no time on any of the above occasions has this office been provided with supporting evidence that you were suffering from a health condition of sufficient severity to prevent you from travelling to your place of work and functioning at your assigned task.

It is the policy of this department that you be informed of the effect that such unexplained actions can have: that each of these five days will be documented as an "absence without pay," which will be reflected as a deduction from your pay cheque on June 28. It also is necessary for me to draw your attention to paragraph 18.2 of the company's booklet *Terms of Employment with Medallion Metals*, a copy of which was issued to you on your first joining the company, that states that more than three undocumented and unexplained absences can mean that your term of employment may be terminated with only one week's notice. At this point in time, no further disciplinary action is being taken, but consider this as a warning before allowing any further unexplained absences to occur.

If you have any questions or concerns about this information, please feel free to contact me.

A K W

Project 3.8:   Complain About an Entertainment Centre

Assume that you have recently returned from a holiday in Waverley, some 1200 km from your home, where you visited friends Martin and Joan Lamont. You were impressed with the features of Martin's Nabuchi 98 Portable Entertainment Centre, which looked just like a laptop computer. Joan had given it to Martin at Christmas and bought it from Craven's Discount Centre at 1837 Kelly Street in Waverley. You decided to buy one for yourself.

But you were disappointed to discover that Craven's had sold out, no more were on order, and they were the sole distributor in Waverley. However, Harry Craven, the shop owner, said he still had the demonstrator, which he could sell you for 5% off the regular discount price. You suggested a 15% discount would be more appropriate, but Mr Craven insisted on 5%. He added that he would have his technician give it a good checkover, if you would leave it with him for 48 hours. Two days later you picked it up, paid $759.95, and received Craven's invoice stamped "Paid in Full." The following day you flew home without opening the carton.

When you plugged in the Nabuchi 98, you found the CD player worked okay but the DVD player would not work. You also discovered there is no local service centre for Nabuchi products, so you took the unit to Modern TV and Radio at 28A Waltham Avenue. When you picked it up three days later, shop manager Jim Williams said it's working fine now and handed you a tiny circuit board.

"There's your problem," he said. "Craven's in Waverley must have replaced the original board, because the name Craven is stamped on this one." He said that whoever inserted the board did not align it properly and bent the pins by forcing it into its socket.

You paid $103.50 for the repair job on Modern's invoice No. 1796. Now write to Harry Craven, tell him what happened, and ask for a refund of $... (you decide how much).

Project 3.9:   Request Free Parts

Assume that today is March 23 and that you are an engineering technologist engaged in a lake-level measurement project in northern Quebec, working under Government Environmental Studies contract WM-23357. You are employed by Manfred Industries Ltd.

Yesterday, at a critical moment in the program, your Hektik Model 370 Water Stage Manometer broke down. You took it apart and identified that it needed a replacement spring and drive assembly. So you emailed a purchase order to the supplier: Hektik Canada Inc, 21 Avenue St Pierre, Montreal, requesting a replacement be shipped to you by air express. You quoted purchase order No. 26019. (The Model 370 is manufactured by Hektik Industries GmbH in Dusseldorf, Germany.)

But you are concerned: this is the third time that the fault has occurred in the past eight months, and each time the thread on the drive shaft has been stripped. You previously ordered replacement spring and drive assemblies on July 16 and October 6 of last year, at a cost of $238.50 apiece. So today you decide to write to Hektik Canada to complain about the repeated failures (you may attribute the cause to any condition you wish, if you feel you need to point out the cause), and to request that the current replacement part be supplied free of charge.

Write the letter.

Project 3.10:   Request Approval to Attend a Course

Assume that this is the second Monday of the current month, and that for the past four weeks you have been on a field assignment in Quebec City, where you have been conducting an extensive hardware and software installation program for Inter-Provincial Telephones (IPT). You have been assisted by two technicians (Ted McCourt and Carolyn

Freedman), and you are now three days ahead of schedule. The task is to be completed by the 12th of next month.

Today you receive an email with a link to a website from McGill University in Montreal advertising a one-week course. Details are:

Course title:	Managing in a Technological Environment
Course dates:	Monday 5th to Friday 9th of next month
Type of course:	Maximum immersion: 9 a.m. to 5 p.m. daily, plus 7 to 10 p.m. Wednesday evening; approximately 20 hours of home assignments
Cost:	$695; includes materials, books, and lunches, plus a guest speaker from industry at each lunch
Registration:	No later than noon on the 23rd of this month; telephone registrations accepted
No. of participants:	16

You are impressed by the technical standard of the course described on the website and want to attend. (Because of previous assignments, you missed a similar extension department evening course offered by your local university last winter. Your company sponsored four engineers to attend that course, for which the fee was $365 each.)

Write an email to your department head, Dennis Copthorne, in which you

- describe the course (convince him it is a good one),
- ask if you can attend,
- ask if the company will pay the tuition fee plus travel and lodging,
- ask to be spared from the IPT task for one week (be convincing), and
- ask for a quick reply (because time is short).

Assume that Dennis can give you technical and financial approval to attend. Also assume that you have a rental car for the IPT project, which you can use to drive to Montreal, but that $34.95 per day will have to be added to your expenses to reimburse IPT for using the car. The hotel cost in Montreal will be $129 per night.

Chapter 4
Short Informal Reports

The word *report* may make you think of a formal document, yet most reports are written as letters, memos, and email. This chapter describes the short informal reports you are likely to write as an engineer, engineering technologist, or technician.

Although there are many types of informal reports, all are based on the writing plan outlined in Figure 4-1. Each report contains

1. a brief statement describing what the reader most needs to know,
2. a short introduction to the problem or situation,
3. a detailed description of the data, situation, or problem, and what has been done or could be done about it, and
4. a conclusion that sums up the results and possibly recommends what should be done next.

Keep in mind that these pyramids are just templates. You can use them as is or you can adapt them to your unique situations.

Short Informal Reports
http://jerz.setonhill.edu/writing/technical/reports/index.html
This document introduces two basic principles of technical communication—meeting the reader's needs and using the inverted pyramid.

The writing plan for basic reports is similar to the plan for business letters

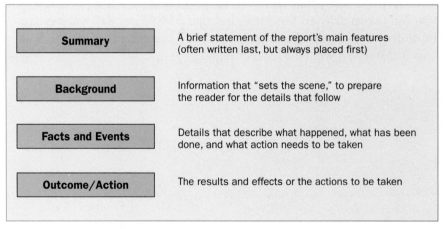

Figure 4-1 Basic writing plan for short reports. The plan is modified slightly to suit each situation.

Writing Style

The reports described in this chapter are written in a direct, informative style that is to the point. The writers are usually describing events that have already occurred, so they write mostly in the past tense, which helps them to be consistent. They switch to the present or future tense only when they have to describe something that is presently occurring, outline what will happen in the future, or suggest what needs to be done. All three tenses occur in the report shown in Figure 4-2.

To: Don Gibbon <dgibbon.ho@winman.ab.ca>
From: Dan Skinner <dskinner.fld@winman.ab.ca>
Date: January 24, 2008
Subject: Carpet problem at KMON-TV

Don

	The indoor/outdoor carpet we installed in KMON-TV has corrected the noise problem but is "pilling" badly. I will examine the carpet with the manufacturer's representative to find the cause.	*Summary*
Past tense	The carpet was installed in the satellite studio control room during the night of January 8–9, to reduce the ambient noise level by 3.6 dB.	*Background*
Mainly past tense	At the station manager's request, I returned to the control room today and checked the carpet's condition. After only two weeks it has tight little balls of carpet material adhering to its surface. I called the manufacturer's rep, who said that the condition is not unusual and does not mean that the carpet is wearing quickly. He suggested that it may be caused by improper cleaning techniques and probably can be easily corrected. However, our client is not pleased with the carpet's appearance.	*Facts*
Present tense		
Future tense	The manufacturer's rep and I will return to the control room between midnight and 2 a.m. on January 31 to study the carpet-cleaning techniques used by maintenance staff. I will email our findings to you later in the day.	*Outcome*

Dan

Figure 4-2   A short report transmitted by electronic mail.

Dan Skinner has written the Background and most of the Facts paragraph mainly in the past tense because those sections deal with what has already been done. At the end of the Facts he has shifted into the present tense to report how the station manager feels now. For the Outcome he has written in the future tense to outline what he plans to do. This past-present-future arrangement is natural and logical. Even Dan's Summary follows the same pattern.

Incident Report

Anytime you are involved in or witness an accident, whether equipment is damaged or people are injured, you need to write a report describing what you saw. An incident report informs management and others of what happened and is often kept in a permanent file.

Anna King is working late in the H L Winman office in Calgary when the telephone rings. The caller is Bob Walton, a member of the electrical engineering staff, who is on a field trip to Dryden, Ontario. He tells Anna he has been involved in a traffic accident near Brandon, Manitoba, his co-traveller has been injured, and some of his equipment has been damaged. He wants Jim Perchanski, his department head, to send out replacement equipment by air express.

Anna jots down notes while Bob talks. Because she will be out of the office the following day, she writes a report of the conversation and emails it to Jim Perchanski (see Figure 4-3), knowing he will access his email immediately after he arrives in the morning.

Anna's message is an incident report, written pyramid-style (see Figure 4-1). Because she will not be available to answer questions, Anna takes care to describe the situation clearly:

1 A subject line must be informative; it must tell what the message is about and stress its importance to the reader. If Anna had simply written "Transcript of Telephone Call from R Walton," she would not have captured Jim Perchanski's attention.

2 This brief **Summary Statement** gets right to the point by immediately telling Jim in general terms what he most needs to know:

Why the message was written.
What happened.
What action has been taken.
What action he has to take.

3 In this **Background** paragraph Anna tells what she knows about the accident and its effects. That serves as background to the important facts that follow.

4 Anna knows that Jim must act quickly to ship the replacement equipment, so in this **Facts** section she uses a list as an attention-

To: Jim Perchanski <perchanski.ho@winman.ab.ca>
From: Anna King <aking.ho@winman.ab.ca>
Date: September 18, 2007
Subject: Accident report and request for spare parts **1**

Jim

Bob Walton and Pete Crandell have been involved in a high-way accident, which will delay their inspection of the Sledgers Control project at Dryden, Ontario. They need replacement parts shipped to them tomorrow (Wednesday, September 19). **2**

Bob telephoned from Brandon, Manitoba, at 19:35 to report the accident, which occurred at 17:15 some five kilometres west of Brandon. Pete has been hospitalized with a fractured left knee and a suspected concussion. Bob was unhurt. The van and some of their equipment were damaged. **3**

Bob wants you to ship the following items by air express on an Air Canada Wednesday evening flight to Winnipeg, and to mark the shipment "HOLD FOR PICK UP BY R WALTON SEP 20":

- 1 Spectrum analyser, HK7741
- 1 Calibrator, Vancourt model 23R
- 24 Glass vials, 300 mm long; 50 mm dia **4**

He will rent a van and drive to Winnipeg to pick up the items Thursday morning. He will then drive on to Dryden and expects to arrive there about 16:00 hr. He has informed the duty engineer at site RJ-17 at Dryden of the delay. **5**

Bob is preparing an accident report for you. He is staying at Hunter's Motel in Brandon (Tel: 204-453-6671). **6**

Anna

Address your recipient and "sign" your name in an email

Figure 4-3   A third-person incident report with an added request.

getter: if Anna had described the items in a paragraph, they would not have been nearly as noticeable.

5 Instructions must be explicit, otherwise Bob Walton may not connect with the equipment in Winnipeg. Anna has identified specific days, and the date, to make sure that no misunderstandings occur. To state "tomorrow" or "the day after tomorrow" might cause Jim Perchanski to assume a wrong date, since he will be reading the report one day later than it was written.

Accuracy of information is essential in report writing

6 In this brief **Action** paragraph Anna indicates what further action is being taken and where Jim can contact Bob Walton if he needs more information.

When Jim reads his email in the morning, he will know immediately what has happened and what action he has to take.

Bob Walton also used the report writer's pyramid when he subsequently wrote to Jim from Hunter's Motel in Brandon, Manitoba, to describe the accident and its effects. His report is in Figure 4-5. Its focus and emphasis differ from those in Anna's earlier report, but it is still an incident report with the following parts:

Where Anna King's report (Figure 4-3) expects reader action, Bob Walton's report (Figure 4-5) does not

A This is his **Summary**: it takes a main piece of information from each compartment that follows.

B This is the **Background**: by clearly describing the situation (*who? where? why? when?*) Bob helps Jim more easily understand what happened:

A well-developed background results in a clear description of the event

- Bob establishes where they were, how they happened to be there, in what direction they were travelling, and who else was involved.
- He itemizes vehicles, licence numbers, and drivers' names in an easy-to-read list.
- He mentions that he is enclosing a sketch (Figure 4-4).

A sketch helps a reader visualize the situation

Figure 4-4 Attachment to Bob Walton's report (Figure 4-5).

H L WINMAN AND ASSOCIATES

INTEROFFICE MEMORANDUM

To: Jim Perchanski   From: Bob Walton
Date: September 19, 2007   Subject: Report of Traffic Accident
                                    at Brandon, Manitoba

Pete Crandell and I were involved in a multiple-vehicle accident on September 18, which resulted in injuries to Pete, damage to our panel van and some equipment, and a two-day delay in our inspection of the Sledgers Control project.

(A)

The accident occurred at 17:15 on Highway 1, about 5 km west of Brandon, Manitoba. We were travelling east in company panel van TLA 711, on our way to site RJ-17 at Dryden, Ontario. Pete was driving and we were approaching the intersection with Highway 459.

(B) Details of other people involved, and their vehicles, belong in the Background, not the Event

Other vehicles involved in the accident were

- Toyota Tercel, license 881 FLM, driven by D Varlick
- Ford truck, license TRB 851, driven by F Zabetts
- Pontiac Grand Am, licence 372 HEK, driven by K Schmitt.

Positions of the vehicles and our panel van immediately before the accident are shown on the attached sketch.

As the Toyota attempted a right turn into Highway 459 it skidded into the Ford truck, which was standing at the intersection waiting to enter Highway 1. The impact caused the Toyota's rear end to swing into our lane, where Pete could not prevent our van from colliding with it. This in turn caused the van to slide broadside into the westbound lane, where the Pontiac approaching from the opposite direction collided with its left side.

(C)

Pete was taken to Brandon General Hospital with a broken left knee and a suspected concussion; he will be there for several days. The panel van was extensively damaged and was towed to Art's Autobody, 1330 Kirby Street, Brandon. As some of our equipment was also damaged or shaken out of calibration, I telephoned Anna King on Tuesday evening and requested replacements (she has prepared a list for you).

(D)

I have rented a replacement van from Budget, and have informed the duty engineer at site RJ-17 that my inspection of the Sledgers Control project will start on Friday, September 21, two days later than planned.

Bob

Figure 4-5 A first-person incident report written in a word-processed document and attached to an email.

C Because his background information is complete, Bob's **Facts** can be concise. He simply provides a chronological description of what happened from the time the Toyota started to slide until all vehicles stopped moving.

D In the **Outcome** Bob describes the results of the accident (injuries, damage) and what he has done since (rented a van, requested replacement equipment). He closes on a strong note: he describes what is being done about the project, which was his reason for passing through Brandon.

Bob knows his role is to be an informative but objective (unbiased) reporter. No doubt he has an opinion of who is at fault, but to state it would have injected subjectivity into his report.

A test for an effective report: Does the reader have to ask questions? (No questions = a good report)

Trip Report

When you work offsite, you need to report your activities

Whenever you are involved in an activity or perform work outside your normal working conditions (visiting a client, attending a conference, working remotely) you will be expected to keep your supervisor, manager, or co-workers informed of your activities by writing a short Trip Report.

You may have been absent only a few hours, inspecting cracks in a local water reservoir; you may have spent several days installing and testing a prototype pump at a power station in a nearby community; or you may have been away for two months, overhauling communications equipment at a remote client site.

You'll find that a trip report will have components of the other types of reports. For example, if you are sent to a remote site to conduct an inspection, your report will be a trip report/inspection report. Or if you have been involved in an accident while onsite, your report will be a trip report/incident report.

The simplest way to write a trip report is to answer the questions shown in Figure 4-6, which, like all examples in this chapter, is a modification of the basic writing plan in Figure 4-1.

Short Trip Reports

Short trip reports do not need headings. A brief narrative following the Summary-Background-Facts-Outcome pattern carries the story:

Summary	A prototype automatic alarm has been installed at the power generation station for a one-month evaluation by the Roper Corporation.
Background	Dave Makepiece and I visited the site from January 15 to 17.
Facts	We completed the installation without difficulty, following installation instruction W27 throughout, and encountered no major problems. However, we omitted step 33, which called for

connections to the remote control panel, because the panel has been permanently disconnected.

Outcome   The alarm will be removed by M Tutanne on February 26, when he visits the site to discuss summer survey plans

Summary	Very briefly: What did you set out to do, and what did you achieve?
Background	Who went where, why, and when?
Trip Details 1. Work done 2. Problems	In more detail: • What did you do? What problems affected your work? • What did you do about them?
Outcome/Action	Is the job complete? What still needs to be done?

Figure 4-6   Writing plan for a trip report.

In practice, the very short Background can probably be combined with either the Summary or the Facts to form a single paragraph.

Long Trip Reports

Long trip reports require headings to help readers identify each compartment. Typical headings might be:

- **Summary**
- **Assignment Details** (Background)
- **Work Accomplished** (Facts)
- **Problems Encountered** (Facts)
- **Suggested Follow-up** or **Follow-up Action Required** (Outcome/Action)

You also need to include any problems you experienced

Anna King's instructions to H L Winman and Associates' engineers (see Figure 4-7 on pages 62–63) tell them how to organize their longer trip reports, describe the information that would normally follow each heading, and include excerpts and sample paragraphs.

Except for the Outcome section, trip reports should be written entirely in the past tense.

Progress or Status Reports

Progress or status reports keep managers aware of how well their project groups are doing. Even for a short-term project, management wants to hear how the project is progressing, especially if problems are affecting its

H L WINMAN AND ASSOCIATES

475 Lethbridge Trail, Calgary AB T3M 5G1

Guidelines for Writing Long Trip Reports

Use a standard format for long trip reports. These instructions suggest how you can organize your information under five main headings: *Summary; Assignment Details; Work Accomplished; Problems Encountered;* and *Follow-up Action.* You may omit the headings from very short reports.

Summary

Make your summary a short opening statement that says what was and was not accomplished. Highlight any significant outcomes.

Assignment Details

State the purpose of the trip and include any other information the reader may want to know. If the information is lengthy, use subheadings such as

- Purpose of Trip
- Background
- Project No./Authority
- Personnel Involved
- Person(s) Contacted
- Date(s) of Field Trip

Work Accomplished

Describe the work you did. Present it in chronological order unless more than one project is involved, in which case describe each project separately. Keep it short: don't describe at great length routine work that ran smoothly. Whenever possible, refer to your work instruction or specification, and attach a copy to your report:

> The manual control was disconnected as described in steps 6 to 13 of modification instruction MI1403, enclosed as Attachment 1.

Go into more detail only if you encountered difficulty, or if work was necessary beyond that anticipated by the job specification:

> At the request of the site maintenance staff, we installed a manual control in the power house as a temporary replacement for a defective GG20 control. I left the parts removed from the panel with Frank Mason, the senior power house engineer, together with instructions for returning the panel to its original configuration.

If parts of the assignment could not be completed, identify them and explain why the work was not done:

1

Figure 4-7   Anna King's instructions for writing long trip reports also show the appearance of a trip report.

We had to omit Test No. 46 because the RamSort equipment had been removed.

Problems Encountered

Describe problems in detail. Knowledge of problems you encountered and how you overcame them can be invaluable to the engineering or operating departments, which may be able to prevent similar problems elsewhere.

Avoid statements that do not tell the reader what the problem was or how it was overcome. For example:

> Considerable time was spent in trying to mount the miniature control panel. Only by fabricating extra parts were we able to complete step 17.

If this information is to be used by the engineering or operating department, it must be more specific:

> We spent three hours trying to mount the miniature control panel according to the instructions in step 17. Because the main frame had additional equipment mounted on it, which prevented us from using most of the parts supplied, we had to fabricate a small sheetmetal extension to the main frame and mount it with the miniature panel, as shown in Attachment 2.

Follow-up Action

Tie up any loose ends here. If any work has not been completed, draw attention to it even though you may already have mentioned it under "Work Accomplished." Identify what needs to be done, if possible indicate how and when it should be done, and say whose responsibility it now becomes:

> The manual control mounted as a temporary replacement in the power house is to be removed when a new GG20 control panel is received onsite. This will be done by Frank Mason, with whom I left instructions for doing the work.

The Outcome looks forward, says "who will do what"

In some cases you may direct follow-up action to someone else in your own or another department:

> The manual control is to be removed from the power house by R Walton, who will visit the site on May 12.

If your report is very long, insert subheadings and use a paragraph numbering system to increase its readability.

Anna King
January 20, 2008

2

Progress Reports
http://www.io.com/
~hcexres/textbook/
progrep.html
This document deals
with the purpose,
timing, format,
and organization of
progress reports.

schedule. Because delays can have a marked effect on costs, management needs to know about them early.

There are three major types of progress or status reports:

1. The **occasional progress report** is written to keep management informed about a project's progress. You decide when it is necessary to write one.

2. The **periodic progress report** is written as a regular update on project status, possibly weekly or monthly.

3. The **personal progress report** is usually written once a month and is used to keep management informed about your personal activities.

Occasional Progress Report

Jack Binscarth, one of Macro Engineering Inc's technicians in Toronto, has been assigned to Cantor Petroleums north of Edmonton to analyse oil samples. The job is expected to take five weeks, but problems have developed that have prevented Jack from completing the work on time. To let his manager know what is happening, he writes the brief progress report in Figure 4-8, adapting the standard Summary-Background-Facts-Outcome arrangement into the five compartments shown in Figure 4-9. (see page 66) This type of progress report is similar to a field trip report.

Periodic Progress Report

If a project continues for several months, normally management will specify that progress reports be submitted at regular intervals.

A periodic progress report may be a one-paragraph statement describing the progress of a simple design task, or it may be a multipage document covering many facets of a large construction project. Regardless of its size, the report should answer the four main questions the reader is likely to ask:

Anticipate your reader's curiosity

1. Will your project be completed on schedule?

2. What progress have you made?

3. Have you had any problems?

4. What are your plans/expectations?

To answer these questions, a periodic progress report can use the standard Summary-Background-Facts-Outcome arrangement:

Summary	A brief overview of the project schedule, progress made, and plans
Background	The situation at the start of the report period
Facts	Progress made and problems encountered
Outcome	Plans/expectations for the next period and impact on the schedule

MACRO
ENGINEERING INC.

600 Deepdale Drive, Toronto ON M5W 4R9

TO: Fred Stokes, Chief Engineer
           Head Office
FROM: Jack Binscarth
           (at Cantor Petroleums)
DATE: October 16, 2007
SUBJECT: Delay in Analysis of Oil Samples

My analysis of oil samples for Cantor Petroleums has been delayed by problems at the refinery. I now expect to complete the project on October 28, twelve days later than planned.

The first problem occurred on September 24, when a strike of refinery personnel set the project back four working days. I had hoped to recover all of this lost time by working a partial overtime schedule, but failure of the refinery's spectrophotometer on October 12 again stopped my work. To date, I have analysed 111 samples and have 21 more to do.

The spectrophotometer is being repaired by the manufacturer, who has promised to return it to the refinery on October 19. Today I informed the refinery manager of the delay, and he has agreed to an increase in the project price to offset the additional time. He will call you about this.

Provided there are no further delays I will analyse the remaining samples between October 24 and 27, and then submit my report to the client the following morning. This means I should be back in the office on October 29.

Jack

Summary Statement

Progress

Progress reports follow a past-present-future arrangement

Situation Now

Future Plans

Figure 4-8 An occasional progress report. (Because the report is short, the Background compartment has been omitted.)

Figure 4-9   Writing plan for an occasional progress report.

Figure 4-10 shows how survey crew chief Pat Fraser used these compartments to write an effective progress report (the numbers below are keyed to parts of the report):

1 The **Summary** tells civil engineering coordinator Karen Woodford how closely the survey project is adhering to schedule, and predicts future progress. This is the information she wants to read first.

2 The **Background** section reminds Karen of the situation at the end of the previous reporting period and predicts what Pat expected to accomplish during this period. Background should always be stated briefly.

3 The **Facts** (or Discussion) section is broken into two parts:

- Work done during the period (3a)
- Problems affecting the project (3b)

Pat Fraser opens each paragraph of this compartment with a topic sentence (a summary statement) that states the main point of the paragraph in general terms:

- Dry, clear weather…enabled us to progress faster than anticipated.
- The electrical fault in the EDM equipment…recurred on May 23.
- I have had difficulty hiring reliable people to clear brush along the route.

H L WINMAN AND ASSOCIATES

INTEROFFICE MEMORANDUM

To: Karen Woodford, Coordinator Civil Engineering
From: Pat Fraser, Survey Crew Chief
Date: May 31, 2007
Subject: Progress Report No. 4—,
             Allardyce Survey Report

The Allardyce Route survey has progressed well during the May 16 to 31 period. The survey crew has regained two days, and now is only four days behind schedule. We expect to be back on schedule by June 30.

The Summary sums up key features from the report's body

Project plan AR-51 shows we should have surveyed positions 30 to 34 during this period. But, as stated in my May 15 report, we were six days behind schedule at the end of the previous period, having surveyed only as far as position 28. Consequently, we expected to survey only to position 32 by May 31.

Dry, clear weather from May 18 to 23 enabled us to progress faster than anticipated. We reached position 31 on May 23, carried out a terrain analysis for the Catherine Lake diversion scheme on May 24 and 25, resumed surveying on May 26, and reached position 32 at 09:00 on May 29, two days earlier than expected. At end of work on May 31, we were just 300 metres short of position 33. Survey results are attached.

Two problems affected the project during this period:

1. The electrical fault in the EDM equipment, which delayed us several times early in the project, recurred on May 23. I had the unit repaired at Fort Wilson on May 24 and 25, while we conducted the terrain analysis, and it has since worked satisfactorily.

Describe any problems that affect the work

2. I have had difficulty hiring reliable local people to clear brush along the route. Most remain with us for only a few days and then quit, and I then have had to hire replacements. This problem will continue until mid-June, when the college students we interviewed in March will join the crew.

We plan to advance to position 37 by June 15, which should place us only two days behind schedule. If we can maintain the same pace, I plan to make up the remaining two days during the June 16 to 30 period.

Pat Fraser

Figure 4-10   A periodic progress report written as a document and attached to an email message.

Pat then describes in more detail what happened, using *facts* (exact dates and position numbers, for example) to support each topic sentence. To prevent the report from becoming too long, Pat attaches the survey results and simply refers to them in the narrative. (Because of their length, they have not been printed with Figure 4-10.)

4 In the **Outcome** paragraph Pat tells Karen what the crew expects to accomplish during the forthcoming period, and even suggests when they might eventually get back on schedule. This final statement clearly supports the opening paragraph, and brings the report to a logical close.

5 Pat types his name at the end of the document to indicate this is the end of the report. This is especially important in a multipage report.

Here are other factors to consider when writing periodic progress reports:

Heading titles parallel the pyramid's parts but are more specific

- If a progress report is long, use headings such as these to help readers *see* your organization:

    Adherence to Schedule (This is your summary.)
    Progress During Period (These are your facts; state the background information at the front of the Progress section.)

    Problems Encountered

    Projection for Next Period (This is the outcome.)

- For lengthy progress or problems sections, start with a summarizing statement describing general progress, then write several subparagraphs, each giving details of a particular aspect of the project.

    For example:

    4. Interior construction work has progressed rapidly but exterior work has been hampered by heavy rain.

        4.1 In the east wing, we constructed all partitions, laid 80% of the floor tiles, and installed 20% of the light fixtures.

        4.2 In the west wing, we laid all remaining floor tiles, installed all light fixtures, bolted down 16 of the 24 benches and connected them to the water supply and drains.

        4.3 Outside, we started landscaping on September 16, but had to abandon the work from September 18 to 23 when heavy rains turned the soil into mud. By the end of the month we had completed only the outer areas of the parking lot.

- Be as brief as possible when describing routine work. Quote specifics rather than generalizations, and place lengthy details in an attachment. If, for example, you are reporting an extensive analysis, in your progress section you might write:

We analysed 142 samples, 88 (62%) of which met specifications. Results of our analyses are shown in Attachment 1.

Attachment 1 would contain several pages of data (numbers, quantities, measurements), which, if included as part of the report narrative, would slow the reader down.

- Describe problems, difficulties, and unusual circumstances in depth. State clearly what the problem was, how it affected your project, what measures you took to overcome it, and whether the remedial measures were successful. For example:

Topic sentence	Juvenile vandalism has proved to be a petty but time-consuming problem. On September 3, youths scaled the fence around the materials compound and stole about $300 worth of
Facts	building supplies. On September 16 they started up a front end loader, drove it into the excavation, then got it stuck in the mud and burned out the clutch. To prevent a recurrence, from
Outcome	September 18 I have doubled the night watch and have had the site policed by a patrol dog. There have been no further attempts at vandalism.

Each problem description is shaped like a miniature pyramid

- Forewarn management of any situation that, although it may not yet affect your project, may become a future problem:

7.1 Unless the strike at Vulcan Steel Works ends shortly, it will soon disrupt our construction program. Our present supply of reinforcing barmats will last until mid-October, after which we must find an alternative source of supply. I have researched other suppliers, but have been warned by union representatives that any attempt to obtain steel elsewhere may result in a walk-out at other plants.

Predict potential developments...

Include any warnings at the end of the Facts (problems) section, immediately before the Outcome.

- If your report is lengthy, number your paragraphs and subparagraphs (see the previous examples). The paragraph numbers can help you refer to a specific part of a previous report:

The possibility of a shortage of steel mentioned in para 7.1 of my September report was averted when the strike at Vulcan Steel Works ended on October 6.

...and then in a subsequent report describe the outcome

- Maintain continuity between reports. If you introduce a problem that has not been resolved in one report, you should refer to it again in your next report, even though no change may have occurred or it was solved only a day later (see the example in the previous paragraph). You must never simply drop a problem because it no longer applies.

- If management expects you to include project cost information in your progress report, insert it in three places:

In the **Summary** comment briefly on how closely you are adhering to projected costs.

In the **Progress** section give more details of costs, and particularly cost implications of problems.

In the **Outcome** section indicate future cost trends.

Costs are usually closely linked with your adherence to schedule: the more you drop behind schedule, the more likely you'll have to report a cost overrun.

Personal Progress Report

A personal progress report serves two purposes:

1. It keeps management informed of your monthly activities.
2. It can be used to document your progress and help you manage your time.

Most organizations use performance evaluations as a tool to help employees grow in their careers and to help focus employee professional development. Managers or supervisors are asked to review each of their employees' performance and recognize their strengths and areas for improvement. As an employee, it is important that you are involved in this process. It is usually done once a year.

To help your manager understand what activities you have been involved in and what you have achieved, we recommend you write monthly personal progress reports. These reports will also help you with your time-management skills because you will have to plan your future activities. Set aside thirty minutes on the last day of each month and write a short report, following the writing plan in Figure 4-11. Eventually you will need to focus only on your future work compartment since the Future Work becomes the Present Work.

There is enough detail in Susan's report (Figure 4-12) for her manager to understand the situation but not too much detail to slow down the reading.

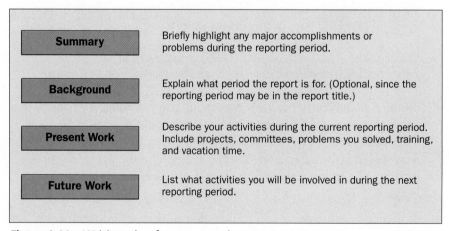

Summary	Briefly highlight any major accomplishments or problems during the reporting period.
Background	Explain what period the report is for. (Optional, since the reporting period may be in the report title.)
Present Work	Describe your activities during the current reporting period. Include projects, committees, problems you solved, training, and vacation time.
Future Work	List what activities you will be involved in during the next reporting period.

Figure 4-11 Writing plan for a personal progress report.

MACRO
ENGINEERING INC.

600 Deepdale Drive, Toronto ON M5W 4R9

Monthly Progress Report for Susan Jenkins
November 1–30, 2008

Summary

Most of my efforts this month were spent diagnosing problems with the CI software. The problems we discovered will need further investigation next month. Although I spent time helping the new intern set up his workstation, it will pay off next month when he is able to help the JCL team begin focus groups for the MarTel project. I was also heavily involved in professional society activities.

Present Work

Centurion Insurance

I completed testing the CI conversion program on two browsers: Netscape and Internet Explorer. This took longer than I originally estimated because I discovered a problem with the program and had to determine if it was on our end or on the CI platform. Both browsers continue to freeze-up immediately after initializing the program. I consulted with the lead technical specialist at CI and we agreed that the code must have not been passing the appropriate parameters. The project is still running two weeks behind schedule.

MarTel Corporation

I worked with the local MarTel account representative to determine who should be involved in the focus group. We determined the demographics and number of participants, the location, and the topics we need to explore.

Intern Orientation

I met several times with Dave Jankowski, the intern from City College. He joined the group this month and will be here for six months. I installed the required software, helped him access the server, and established his passwords. I went over our email guidelines with him so he understands how our team uses it.

Committee Work

I attended the E-learning Administrative Committee meeting in Banff on November 13–14, representing the eastern provinces. We need to stay involved as a firm in what is happening at the national and international level so our computer engineering groups remain competitive.

As the Safety Council representative for our group, I attended a CPR refresher course and met with the other council members to revise our fire evacuation plans.

Future Work

Next month I plan to
- conduct a line item code review of the CI conversion program with the technical specialist to determine any bugs that may be causing the freeze problems,
- monitor the progress of the MarTel focus group,
- supervise the intern's activities,
- prepare a proposal to present a paper at the IEEE Computer Society annual conference,
- investigate adding client testimonials to our website, and
- update all engineer resumes on the company server.

Figure 4-12 A personal progress report.

If the manager needs more detail, he will ask Susan. However, it must have enough detail so both Susan and her manager can understand the points a year later if they need to refer to it for her performance evaluation. She decided to use paragraphs rather than a list so there is more continuity when reading. Notice how each topic is a mini-pyramid with a topic sentence as the summary.

If you are writing regular project status reports you don't need to repeat specifics from earlier reports. Remember, this is about what *you* did, not about the project. Susan decided to break her report into topic areas so the manager understands her activities in each area. You can decide how you want to organize your report but be consistent from month to month.

Project Completion Report

It's mostly the facts compartment that gets expanded and relabelled

A project completion report may be the only report evolving from a short project, or the last in a series of progress reports concerning a lengthy project. Thus the Summary-Background-Facts-Outcome arrangement shown in Figure 4-1 can be adhered to fairly closely, with the facts compartment being separated into two compartments labelled **Project Highlights** and **Exceptions** (see Figure 4-13). The Exceptions section draws attention to deviations from the original project plan.

The project completion report written by Jack Binscarth at the end of his analysis of oil samples for Cantor Petroleums identifies the five writing compartments. (See Figure 4-14; Jack's progress report for this project is in Figure 4-8.) In a short report like this it's acceptable to combine two, or sometimes more, writing compartments into a single paragraph. In Jack's project completion report, paragraph 1 contains both the **Summary** and the **Background,** and paragraph 2 contains both the **Project Highlights** and the **Exceptions.**

Summary	A brief statement that the project or job is complete, plus a short description of the result(s)
Background	The circumstances affecting the job, such as purpose, terms of reference, schedule, budget, and people involved
Project Highlights	Major achievements, such as work accomplished, problems encountered (plus how they were resolved, and how they affected the project), targets met, and results obtained
Exceptions	Variances from the project plan (if there are any), which may be work that could not be completed or that deviated from the plan; includes the reason for each exception, and its effect
Outcome/Action	A closing statement that either comments on the outcome or identifies any follow-up action that must be taken, such as remedying an exception

Figure 4-13   Writing plan for a project completion report.

MACRO
ENGINEERING INC.

600 Deepdale Drive, Toronto ON M5W 4R9

TO: Fred Stokes
FROM: Jack Binscarth
DATE: October 29, 2007
SUBJECT: Finalizing Cantor Petroleums' Project

I completed the analysis of oil samples for Cantor Petroleums on October 26, nine days later than planned. The work was done at the refinery, as requested in Cantor Petroleums' purchase order No. 376188 dated September 4, 2007, and was scheduled to start on September 11 and end on October 16. I was assigned to the project under work order No. 2716.

The work plan called for me to analyse 132 oil samples within the five-week period, but three problems caused me to overrun the schedule and complete four fewer analyses than specified. The delay was caused by a strike of refinery personnel and a faulty spectrophotometer that had to be sent out for repair and recalibration. The incomplete analyses were caused by four contaminated samples that could not be replaced in less than six weeks.

Russ Dienstadt, the refinery manager, agreed to a cost overrun and has corresponded with you separately on this subject. He also agreed that it would be uneconomical for me to return to analyse replacements for the four contaminated samples. When I delivered the 128 analyses to him on October 26, he accepted the project as being complete.

Summary
Statement

Background

Project
Highlights

Exceptions

Outcome

Figure 4-14   A project completion report.

Inspection Report

An inspection report is an extended trip report

An inspection can range from a quick check of a small building to assess its suitability as a temporary storage centre, to a full-scale examination of an airline's aircraft, avionics equipment, repair facilities, and maintenance methods. In both cases the inspectors report their findings in an inspection report. The building inspector's report will be brief: it will state that the building either is or is not suitable, and give reasons why. The airline inspector's report will be lengthy: it will describe in detail the condition of every aspect of the airline's operations and list every deficiency (condition that must be corrected). In both cases the reports can follow the Summary-Background-Facts-Outcome arrangement, as shown in Figure 4-15.

Kevin Doherty's building inspection report in Figure 4-16 on page 75 shows how these compartments helped shape a logical, easy-to-follow document:

1 His **Summary** tells the Production Manager the one thing he most wants to know: can they use the building?

2 The **Background** describes who went where, why, and when.

3 Kevin has opened the **Conditions** section with a summarizing general statement, and then supported it with facts (3a). Because they are not in any particular order, he used bullets for the itemized list.

He has presented the **Deficiencies** (3b) as a briefly stated list, which makes it easy to identify what has to be done, and has used active verbs to demonstrate that the actions *must* be performed. Because he may need to refer to these items later, he used numbers for this list.

4 The recommendation in his **Outcome** supports his summary.

For a short inspection report like this, Kevin presented all the Conditions first and then listed all the Deficiencies. But such an arrangement

It's better to describe conditions and deficiencies in two separate sections

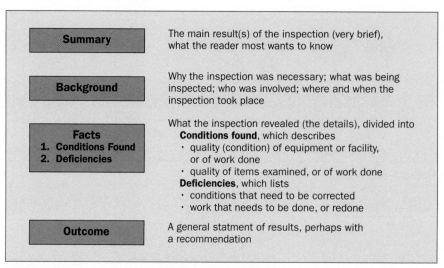

Figure 4-15 Writing plan for an inspection report.

MACRO
ENGINEERING INC.

600 Deepdale Drive, Toronto ON M5W 4R9

TO: Hugh Smithson Production Manager
FROM: Kevin Doherty
DATE: January 8, 2008
SUBJECT: Inspection of Carter Building

① The Carter Building at the corner of River Avenue and 39th Street will make a suitable storage and assembly centre for the Dennison contract.

② Christine Lamont and I inspected the Carter Building on January 6 to assess its suitability both for storage and as a work area for 20 assemblers for 15 months. We were accompanied by Ken Wiens of Wilshire Properties.

③ We found the interior of the building to be spacious and to have good facilities, but to be unsightly. Our inspection showed the following:

③a
- There are 460 m^2 of usable floor space (see attached building plan, supplied by Mr Wiens); we need 350 m^2 for the project.
- There are two offices, each 16 m^2, and a large unimpeded space ideal for partitioning into a storage area and four work stations.
- The building is structurally sound and dry, but it is very dirty and smells strongly (the previous tenant was a fertilizer distributor).
- There are numerous power outlets, newly installed with heavy-duty circuits, and the building has excellent overhead lighting.
- Several walls are damaged and many contain obnoxious graffiti.
- There is a new loading ramp on the north side of the building, suitable for semitrailers.
- Washroom facilities are adequate for up to 30 people, but one toilet and two washbasins are broken.

Before we rent the building, the rental agency will have to

③b
1. clean it thoroughly,
2. repair damaged walls, partitions, and toilet facilities, and
3. redecorate the interior.

Ken Wiens said his firm will do this.

④ I recommend we rent the Carter Building from Wilshire Properties, with the provision that the deficiencies listed above be corrected before we move in.

K D

Figure 4-16   A short informal inspection report.

could become cumbersome for a long report that covers many items. For example, for an inspection at Remick Airlines, the organization of the Facts section would look like this:

A plan for a short inspection report

A. **Conditions Found:**
 1. Electrical Shop
 2. Avionics Calibration Centre
 3. Flammable Materials Storage
  (etc...)
B. **Deficiencies:**
 1. Electrical Shop
 2. Avionics Calibration Centre
 3. Flammable Materials Storage
  (etc...)

The more departments inspected, the longer the report becomes and the further apart each department's Conditions and Deficiencies sections grow.

To overcome this difficulty, treat each department as a *separate* inspection and reorganize the report so that for each department the Deficiencies section immediately follows the Conditions section. The organization of the whole report then becomes:

A plan for a longer, more detailed inspection report

Summary
Background
Facts:
 1. Electrical Shop
  A. Conditions Found
  B. Deficiencies
 2. Avionics Calibration Centre
  A. Conditions Found
  B. Deficiencies
 3. Flammable Materials Storage
  A. Conditions Found
  B. Deficiencies
 (etc...)
Outcome:
 Conclusions
 Recommendations

Laboratory Report

Lab reports are written frequently in colleges, less often in industry

There are two kinds of laboratory reports: those written in industry to document laboratory research or tests on materials or equipment, and those written in academic institutions to record laboratory tests performed by students. The former are generally known as "Test Reports" or "Laboratory Reports"; those written by students are simply called "Lab Reports."

Industrial laboratory reports can describe a wide range of topics, from testing a piece of metal to determine its tensile strength, through analysing a sample of soil (a drill core) to identify its composition, to checking a microwave oven to assess whether it emits radiation. Academic lab reports can also describe many topics, but their purpose is different since they describe tests that are intended to help students learn something or prove a theory rather than produce a result for a client.

Laboratory reports generally conform to a standard pattern, although emphasis differs depending on the purpose of the report and how its results will be used. Readers of industrial laboratory or test reports are usually more interested in results than in how a test was carried out. Readers of academic lab reports are usually professors and instructors, who are more likely to be interested in thoroughly documented details, from which they can assess the student's understanding of the subject and what the test proved.

A laboratory report has identifiable compartments, each usually preceded by a heading.

Compartment	Heading	Contents	
Summary	**Summary**	A very brief statement of the purpose of the tests, the main findings, and what can be interpreted from them. (In short laboratory reports, the Summary can be combined with the next compartment.)	**A generic writing plan for a lab report**
Background	**Objective**	A more detailed description of why the tests were performed, on whose authority they were conducted, and what they were expected to achieve or prove.	
Facts	**Equipment Setup**	*There are four parts here:* A description of the test setup, plus a list of equipment and materials used. A drawing of the test hook-up may be inserted here. (If a series of tests is being performed, with a different equipment setup for each test, then a separate equipment description, materials list, and illustration should be inserted immediately before each test description.)	

Compartment	Heading	Contents
	Test Method	A detailed, step-by-step explanation of the tests. In industrial laboratory reports the depth of explanation depends on the reader's needs: if a reader is nontechnical and likely to be interested only in results, then the test description can be condensed. For lab reports written at a college or university, however, students are expected to provide a thorough description of their method.
	Test Results	Usually a brief statement of the test results or the findings evolving from the tests.
	Analysis (or Interpretation)	A detailed discussion of the results or findings, their implications, and what can be interpreted from them. (The analysis section is particularly important in academic lab reports.)
Outcome	Conclusions	A brief summing-up, which shows how the test results, findings, and analysis meet the objective(s) established at the start of the report.
Backup	Attachments	These are pages of supporting data such as test measurements derived during the tests, or documentation, such as specifications, procedures, instructions, and drawings, which will interrupt reading continuity if placed in the report narrative.

In practice, the writing plan is adapted to suit the industry and the circumstances

The compartments described here are those most likely to be used for an industrial laboratory report, although emphasis and labelling will differ depending on the requirements of the organization and the authority for whom the report is being written.

In a college or university you will often see a slightly different arrangement, with the report being divided into three parts in which the report writer answers the questions listed in Figure 4-17.

Because test laboratories are audited regularly, *every* report they produce must clearly account for every step that is taken in each test. The tests and reports must also comply with professional industry standards such as ISO, GLP (General Lab Practices), and GMP (General Manufacturing Practices). Even at the college level your objective should be to consistently achieve a similar standard.

Plan for a Laboratory Report

Introduction

1. What was your **Objective**? Describe what you were trying to achieve.
2. What **Safety Considerations** did you have to take into account when performing the tests?
3. What **Method** did you use? Either describe the test method or refer to the description in a standard operating procedure (SOP).

Test Description

4. What **Materials** did you use? Be very exact: quote *exact* machine(s) and source(s) of materials, so that a reader can replicate exactly what you did.
5. What **Calculations** did you make?
6. What **Information** did you capture? Describe *exactly* what you saw happen, but without offering opinions. You are an objective observer of the work.
7. What **Results** did you obtain? Present factual data, such as graphs, tables, calculations evolving from the test, and comparisons with previous data (again, avoid offering opinions).

Discussion

8. What did the results mean to you? This is your **Analysis**: interpret the results in light of the objectives you established in Step 1, and discuss their significance (*now* your opinions can be heard!).

Figure 4-17   Sample plan for a college laboratory report.

ASSIGNMENTS

Project 4.1:   Damage in the Test Lab

This happened so quickly, you had no time to think or move!

It's 11:25 a.m. and you are talking to Dave, an electrician, who is standing on a stepladder beside the bench on which you are running tests on Torstar Batch 81. Batch 81 is contained in a vat and you are using a Vancourt 2120 calibrator to measure the results.

Dave is replacing a burnt-out fluorescent lamp from over the bench. As he loosens the lamp, he shouts: "Oops! Watch out below!!"

The lamp slips from his hands, falls on the bench and calibrator, smashes, and bits of glass drop into the vat. Dave climbs down from the ladder, apologizes, examines the meter dial on the calibrator, and shows you that its glass has been smashed.

You stop the test, realizing you'll have to rerun it *and* get a replacement calibrator. You phone Majestic Electronics, the supplier, who says: "We'll have one for you the day after tomorrow."

To avoid letting the schedule get even further behind, you search for someone who can work at night to rerun the test. Phil Maybank volunteers to do so. The overtime labour will cost $320.

Write an email to Pat Wyvern, the project manager, to report the incident and the effect on the project schedule. Pat's email address is pwyvern@multind.com.

Project 4.2: Checking an Insurance Claim

When you arrive at work this morning, branch manager Vern Rogers calls you into his office.

"We've had a call from Hugh Smithson in our Sudbury branch," he says. "Twelve cartons of special instruments they shipped yesterday were in a truck that rolled 8 km east of North Bay. The insurance company wants someone to look over the damage with one of their adjusters, to confirm how much can be repaired or salvaged."

At North Bay you meet Noella Redovich of Milltown Insurance Company. She takes you to a warehouse where you examine the crates, which are a jumble of broken glass, tangled wire, and chipped and splintered instrument cases. As you check each container, Noella notes the numbers in her book: 10, 4, 12, 11, 6, 3, 1, 9, 8, and 2 are totally beyond repair and obviously have no salvage value. Crate number 5 surprisingly is hardly marked: somehow it must have been cushioned, because its contents are not damaged.

Noella adds up the totals: "Not very good for us," she says. "Ten out of eleven means a heavy claim."

"Twelve," you say. "There were twelve crates."

Noella checks her figures: "One is missing," she says. "Number 7." She suggests it might have been stolen before the accident occurred. "The police were on the scene immediately. There would not have been time after the accident."

When you return to your office, Vern Rogers asks you to write a report and email it to Hugh Smithson. Here is additional information you may need for your report:

- The shipping company was Merryhew Van Lines of Hamilton, Ontario.
- The waybill number was C2719.
- The 12 crates were being shipped to Melwood Test Labs, Ottawa.
- The crates are being held at C and J Storage Limited, 63 Crane Street, North Bay.
- You reported the missing crate to the police in North Bay, at 2:25 p.m., immediately after completing your inspection.

Hugh Smithson's email address is h.smithson@winman.ca. Assume the inspection occurred today.

Project 4.3: Reporting Progress

You have a summer job conducting traffic studies for the Department of Highways. The work started June 1 and will end August 31. Your task is to monitor traffic counts at six locations within a 50 km radius of Lake Katrine. You are required to send in a progress report at the end of each month. As it's now June 30, you are about to write your first report. Here are the notes you made during the month:

- First task: put cables down (across highway) at locations A through F (exact locations on six different highways are listed in Work Order 203). Done June 1, 2, and 3. The cables are black rubber and as a vehicle crosses a cable it records twice on a counter in a control box beside road (it records once for each set of wheels).
- Problem at Site D: No power outlet beside Highway 216, as shown on map. Found one 325 metres north, so laid cable there. (Not a problem: won't affect count—there's no traffic intersection between the original and new site.)
- Set counters to start recording June 3. Started 6:00 p.m., ended 9:00 p.m. (it takes 3 hours to drive to all 6 sites).
- Took first readings June 4: all counters working. Took readings daily, emailed them daily to Department of Highways office.
- Reset counters. (The instructions say to do this every seven days.) Done June 11.
- Site F: Highway 2166, gravel road, cable torn and ragged. Road had been graded overnight; grader must have torn cable away. Phoned in for new cable and counter and box (because box was torn from its mounting); all delivered June 13. Installed same day. Set counter to start at 8:35 p.m.
- June 18: read and reset counters.
- No readings June 19 & 20: involved in traffic accident June 18, evening. I wasn't injured, but car needed repair. Got it back June 21, 10 a.m.
- Emailed results June 21, but with a caution: the count was for 3 days, not one.
- June 25: Reset counters except site B. Counter box burnt and damaged (I think it was struck by lightning). Phoned in for new box, delivered June 26, installed same day and set it to start recording at 7:45 p.m.
- No problems June 26 to 30.

Your supervisor at the Department of Highways is Karen Cottrell. (kcottrell@doh7.gov.ca). All your reports go to her. Write your report as an email.

Project 4.4: Theft at Whiteshell Lake

You are the team leader of a four-person inspection crew enroute to a remote site 920 km from your office, where construction of a new power generating station is in progress. You are travelling in a company-owned van and after 615 km you and the crew stop for the night at the Towpath Inn, a small motel beside the road that skirts around Whiteshell Lake.

Early the following morning you discover the van has been broken into: the window on the front passenger door has been smashed and the radio and about $8 in loose change (for parking meters) has gone. You check further and find a video camera and videotapes also have gone (from a locked storage box in the back of the van—the lock has been broken off).

You try telephoning your office, but it is too early. The motel has a wi-fi connection so you write an email to your manager, M B Corrigan (mbcorrigan@multind.com), in which you describe what has happened and ask that a replacement video camera be sent to you. Here is some additional information you draw on to write your report:

- You are driving a company panel van, licence number HLW 279; it is a Chevy.
- Your trip was authorized by company Travel Order N-704, dated one week ago.
- The power generating station is being constructed beside the Mooswa River, 27 km north of the small town of Freehampton.
- The video camera is a Nabuchi TX350 "Portacam." You rented it from Meadows Electronics at 212 Grassmere Road. Its serial number is 21784B.
- The purpose of the video camera is to record construction progress visually. The videotape will be edited and then shown at the Power Authority Directors' Meeting scheduled for the 22nd of next month.
- You telephone the police at Clearwater Village, to report the break-in and theft. They ask you to report in person, which you will do when you leave Whiteshell Lake.
- Ask your manager to ship you the replacement video camera by bus the day after tomorrow. You will meet the bus when it stops in Freehampton.
- Use today's date as the date of your report.

Project 4.5: Accident Above the North Saskatchewan River

You are supervising construction of a temporary bridge over the North Saskatchewan River near Gillam, Manitoba. The bridge is being built to connect two construction sites, one on each side of the river. A vertical pier has been built on each side of the river and cables are being strung from the top of each pier to mooring posts along the length of the bridge.

Yesterday, you accompanied Frances Willis, a surveyor with No. 13 Architectural Group in Winnipeg, who was taking theodolite sitings from a platform halfway up the south pier. You were working out construction details with crew chief Dan Kerfauver when, at 2:15 p.m., you heard a shout and Dan shoved hard against your right side so that you fell to the floor of the platform. Simultaneously you heard a "coiled zinging" sound and felt a thud as Frances fell violently to the platform floor beside you.

Dan got to his feet first and immediately examined Frances, who was in extreme pain but conscious. Dan explained that the far end of a tautly strung cable had let go from its mooring on the bridge deck and had coiled back to the top of the pier. As it went, the loose end had swung past the platform, whipped the theodolite and tripod away, and struck Frances a glancing blow. Dan suspected that the blow had fractured her left arm and possibly dislocated her shoulder. You radioed for medical assistance and Frances was taken to the medical centre at Gillam. You tried to find the theodolite, but with no success; you suspected it was swept into the river. You noticed that your right shoulder was becoming increasingly painful and you found that a 1 cm-wide by about 5 cm-long wood splinter had pierced your jacket and was embedded in your shoulder. You visited the medical centre, where the splinter was rather painfully removed and the wound was treated and bound.

Now it is the next morning (today) and you have seen Frances in the medical centre. She is suffering from a broken left arm (broken both above and below the elbow), is sedated, and has a mild concussion. (Your injury is very painful too, but you don't mention it to Frances because you sense her condition is much worse than yours.) The doctor tells you she will be released within 48 hours and will be able to travel back to Winnipeg.

You now have two email reports to write:

Report 1: Write a brief note to Charles Severin, your department head in Winnipeg. Report what has happened and say there will be a construction delay for two reasons: a new theodolite is required from No. 13 Architectural Group (it should be here in two days), and a new cable has to be strung (it will take three days). Charles's address is cseverin@constructionhouse.ca.

Report 2: Write an email incident report to Ken Forster, chief architect at No. 13 Architectural Group, to inform him of the incident and of Frances's condition. Ask him to send a replacement surveyor and to airship a replacement theodolite and tripod. His email address is k.forster@13Group.com.

Chapter 5
Longer Informal and Semiformal Reports

Longer Informal and Semiformal Reports
http://www.csee.umbc. edu/~sherman/Courses/ documents/TR_how_ to.html
This website gives some excellent advice on writing a technical report, covering how to write the thesis, the components of the technical report, organization, as well as common mistakes to avoid.

The previous chapter discussed short reports that deal primarily with facts, in which the writer identifies the relevant details and presents them briefly and directly. This chapter describes longer reports that often deal with less tangible evidence, in which the writer analyses a situation in depth before drawing a conclusion and, sometimes, making a recommendation.

Longer reports may describe an investigation of a problem or unsatisfactory condition, an evaluation of alternatives to improve a situation, a study to determine the feasibility of taking certain action, or a proposal for making a change in methods or procedures. All are written in a fluid narrative style that is both persuasive and convincing; their writers have concepts or new ideas to present and they want their readers to understand their line of reasoning.

Investigation Report

The term *investigation report* covers any report in which you describe how you performed tests, examined data, or conducted an investigation using tangible evidence. You start with known data and then analyse and examine it so that the reader can see how you conducted the investigation and reached the final results. You may write the report as a letter, as a memo, or as a semiformal document.

A well-written investigation report contains standard parts that help guide the reader to a full understanding of its topic. They are shown in Figure 5-1, which is an expanded version of the basic writing plan described at the start of Chapter 4 (Figure 4-1). The parts are identified by circled numbers in the three-page investigation report in Figure 5-2.

1 The **Background** is only one sentence, which refers to the memo that initiated the investigation. It is short because the reader already knows the circumstances.

2 The **Investigation Details** start here, with a very brief reference to the **Approach**.

3 These are the **Findings**. It also is the start of a comparative analysis (see page 88).

4 This is the first of three **Ideas** for resolving the problem.

Comparing each plan, idea, method, or product *only* against the criteria helps a writer be objective

5 These are the **Criteria**: the requirements against which each idea will be measured.

6 The **Analysis** starts here. The table provides a convenient, easy-to-access summary of what each idea will achieve and cost.

7 In the Analysis, each idea is compared to the Criteria. (Note that the ideas are *not* compared one against another.)

8 The **Outcome** starts by drawing **Conclusions**, and continues with a **Recommendation**.

9 The **Attachments** contain drawings, specifications, and detailed cost estimates for each idea.

This expanded writing plan is still based on the pyramid seen in earlier chapters

Summary	A brief statement of the situation or problem and what should be done about it	
Background	A description of the situation or problem and its history	
Investigation Details	The **Facts**, comprising:	
	Approach	How the investigation was tackled
	Findings	What the investigation revealed
	Ideas	Different ways the situation can be improved or the problem resolved
	Criteria	Factors that influence the analysis
	Analysis	Evaluation of each idea
Conclusions	The **Outcome**, or result of the investigation; a summing-up	
Recommendation	A positive statement advocating action*	
Attachments	Evidence: detailed facts, figures, and statistics that support the Investigation Details*	

Included only when appropriate.

Figure 5-1   Writing plan for an investigation report.

MEMORANDUM   KCMO-TV

TO: Dennis Carlisle, Operations Manager
FROM: Phyllis van der Wyck, Engineering Department
DATE: October 21, 2007
SUBJECT: Investigation of High Ambient Sound Level,
           Satellite Studio Control Room

I have investigated the high ambient sound level reported in the control room of our satellite studio at 21 Union Road, and have traced it to the building's air-conditioning equipment. The sound level can be reduced to an acceptable level by replacing the blower motor and soundproofing the air-conditioning ducts and blowers. The cost will be $9800.

Summary

1 My investigation was authorized by your memo of August 28, 2007, in which you described the audio difficulties your production crews are experiencing when programming from the satellite studio.

Background

2 Tests conducted with a sound level meter at various locations in the control room established that the average ambient sound level is 36.8 dB, with peaks of 38.7 dB near the west wall. This is approximately 7 to 9 dB higher than the sound levels measured in the control room for Studio 1 on Westover Road, where the average ambient sound level is 29.5 dB with peaks of 30.2 dB near the south wall.

Approach

This two-and-one-half page memo report would benefit from having headings inserted at appropriate places

The unusually high sound level is caused by the air-conditioning equipment, which is in an annex adjacent to the west wall of the control room. Air-conditioner rumble and blower fan noise are carried easily into the control room because the short air ducts permit little noise dissipation between the equipment and the work area. The flat hardboard surface of the west wall also acts as a sounding board and bounces the noise back into the room.

Findings

3

Ideas are numbered consecutively for ease of reference

I have considered three methods we could use to reduce the ambient sound level:

Ideas

4

1. Move the air-conditioning equipment to a storage room at the other end of the building, for an estimated 10–12 dB reduction in sound level. This would, however, require major structural alterations that will cost between $22 000 and $26 000.

Figure 5-2   A memo investigation report with primarily objective development.

2. Replace the existing blower fan assembly with a model TL-1 blower manufactured by the Quietaire Corporation of Hamilton, Ontario, and line the ducts with Agrafoam, a new soundproofing product developed by the automobile industry in Germany. Together, these methods would reduce the ambient sound level by about 6.5–7.5 dB. The cost will be $9800.

3. Cover the vinyl floor tiles with Monroe 200 indoor/outdoor carpet, a practice that has proved successful in air traffic control centres, and mount carpet on the control room's west wall, for a sound level reduction of about 4.0–4.5 dB. The cost will be $2400.

The remedy we select must

5 • reduce the ambient sound level by at least 7.3 dB, to provide conditions similar to those at the Westover Road control room,

• be implemented quickly (ideally by November 15, when the Christmas Pageant programs will be recorded), and

• cost no more than $10 000, if the modifications are to be completed within the 2007–2008 budget year.

Criteria

6 As the table shows, none of the three methods meets all of the above criteria, although Method 2 comes close to doing so.

Analysis

	Required	Method 1 Relocation	Method 2 Blower/Ducts	Method 3 Carpet
Projected sound level reduction (min)	7.3 dB	10–12 dB	6.5–7.5 dB	4.0–4.5 dB
Time to implement (max)	3 weeks	12 weeks	3 weeks	1.5 weeks
Approximate cost (max)	$10 000	$22–26 000	$9800	$2400

A table simplifies a comparison, making it easier to analyse

7 • Method 1—relocating the air-conditioning equipment—would reduce the sound level more than the required minimum but cannot be implemented quickly or within budget.

• Method 2—replacing the blower motor and lining the ducts—probably would reduce the sound level to an acceptable level, but only just. It could be implemented quickly and within budget.

- Method 3—covering the floor and one wall with carpet—would reduce the sound level by only one-third of the desired reduction. It could be implemented quickly and within budget.

8 The only method that comes close to meeting our immediate requirements is Method 2. If we were to combine it with Method 3, we could achieve a probable total sound reduction of 8.3–9.8 dB, which would meet the required reduction but would exceed the budget by $2200. (Note that, when combining methods, the total reduction will be *less* than the summation of the two individual sound level reductions.)

Conclusions

Because Method 2 comes close to the required minimum reduction in sound level, I recommend we replace the blower motor and line the ducts with Agrafoam for a total cost of $9800. However, because actual sound level reductions can differ from those projected, I suggest we retest the sound levels following installation. If a further reduction in sound level proves necessary, then I recommend we install Monroe 200 carpet on the floor and west wall in March 2008 at a total cost of $2400, using $200 from the 2007–2008 budget year and $2200 from the 2008–2009 budget year.

Recommendation

These modifications will provide the quieter working environment needed by your production crews.

P. van der Wyck

9 Att: Specifications and cost estimates

Attachments

A major recommendation and a minor recommendation

Conducting a Comparative Analysis

A comparative analysis is also a justification

Phyllis van der Wyck's evaluation of three sound level methods (Figure 5-2) is known as a *comparative analysis*. In a comparative analysis you compare different products, plans, ideas, or methods to identify which is the most suitable for a particular situation. It can be written either objectively or subjectively:

- In an *objective* comparative analysis you do not allow your opinions to intrude until the very end of the report, when you make your recommendation (as Phyllis van der Wyck did).

- In a *subjective* comparative analysis you allow your voice to be heard—your opinions to be apparent—much earlier in the report, usually when you analyse the alternatives.

The objective and subjective methods are shown side-by-side in Figure 5-3.

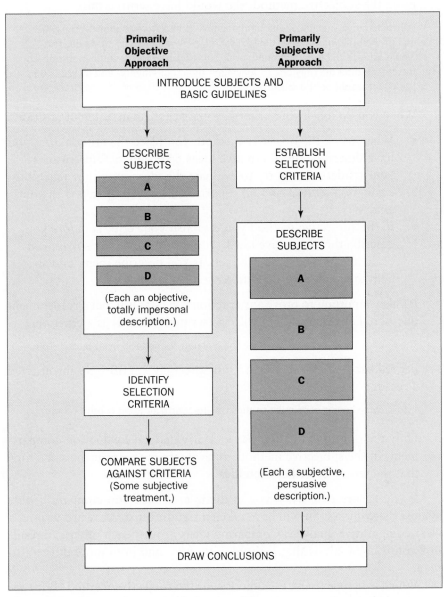

Both objective and subjective development methods provide opportunities to arrange your information for maximum effect

Figure 5-3 Alternative methods for describing a comparative analysis.

There are three primary differences between the two methods:

1. In the objective method (on the left in Figure 5-3) you describe each idea or product you are evaluating as a series of facts, without commenting on the product's quality or value. For example, when describing idea 1, Phyllis writes:

Present only facts to maintain objectivity

> Move the air-conditioning equipment to a storage room at the other end of the building, for an estimated 10–12 dB reduction in sound level. This would, however, require major structural alterations that will cost between $22 000 and $26 000.

But in the subjective method (on the right in Figure 5-3) you can insert comments and opinions about the idea or product. If Phyllis had been using the subjective method, she would have written this:

When you offer an opinion, you are immediately subjective

> We could move the air-conditioning equipment to a storage room at the other end of the building for an estimated sound level reduction of 10–12 dB. This would achieve the greatest sound level reduction among the three methods—in fact it would be the only one to fully meet the requirements—but at $22 000 to $26 000 it would be the most costly.

2. When you establish your criteria, you place them in different positions:

   - When using the objective method, you place the criteria *after* you have described the alternative ideas or products. This ensures your readers do not try to evaluate the ideas until they reach the evaluation section of your report, and so keep in step with your analysis.
   - In the subjective method you establish your criteria *before* you describe the alternative ideas. You do this precisely so you *can* evaluate the ideas and products as you describe them, and so help the reader see the difference.

It's also important to prove any criterion you establish that a reader might question. For example, if Phyllis had written only this as a criterion,

> The remedy we select must...reduce the ambient sound level by at least 7.3 dB.

Anticipate your readers' questions

her readers might have asked: "Why precisely 7.3 dB?" So she inserted a reason:

> ...to provide conditions similar to those at the Westover Road control room.

3. Only the objective method has a clearly defined Evaluation compartment. In the subjective method, an evaluation occurs at the same time that the writer describes each idea.

If you ensure that when you evaluate each idea you compare it *only* against the criteria, you will have taken a significant step toward writing a clear comparative analysis. Comparing ideas against each other can result in a confusing analysis that is difficult to write and even more difficult to read.

Which is better: to use the objective or the subjective method? Both are equally valid; however, for a beginning report writer, we recommend using the objective method. Using the subjective method demands more skill, because there is a danger that your comments will make you appear too opinionated and so offend the reader.

Evaluation Report/Feasibility Study

Evaluation reports are similar to investigation reports—both names are frequently used interchangeably. Evaluation reports often start with an idea or concept their authors want to develop, prove, or disprove. Their authors first establish guidelines to keep their report within prescribed bounds, and then research data, conduct tests, and analyse the results to determine the concept's viability. At the end of the evaluation they draw a conclusion that the concept either is or is not feasible, or perhaps is feasible in a modified form.

Two titles, but a similar function

The writing plan shown in Figure 5-1 can also be applied to an evaluation report. Morley Wozniak's evaluation of landfill sites in Figures 5-4 and 5-5 follows this plan.

Morley's report is significant in that it is preceded by a one-page cover letter that *describes and comments on* key implications within the report. Its addressee (Quillicom's town engineer) has the option of distributing it to the town councillors with the report or detaching it and replacing it with a cover letter of his own.

A cover letter can introduce a sensitive issue or confidential information

The parts of the writing plan shown in Figure 5-1 are identified in Morley's report by circled numbers beside the narrative; they are keyed to the additional comments provided here.

Recommendation and Feasibility Reports http://www.io.com/ ~hcexres/tcm1603/ acchtml/feas.html This document is one chapter from the online textbook used in Austin Community College's online course, Online Technical Writing (http://www.io.com/ ~hcexres/tcm1603/ acchtml/acctoc. html). It describes feasibility reports in detail and includes several samples.

❶ Although several factors affect site selection, in his **Summary** Morley focuses primarily on environmental impact because he believes it is of overriding importance.

❷ The **Introduction** provides Background details leading up to the study assigned to H L Winman and Associates, and then to Morley.

❸ The **Evaluation Details** start here, with a single paragraph in which Morley outlines his **Approach** (i.e. how he tackled the study). Note that he mentions the three components *in the same sequence* that he will describe them further on in the report.

❹ These are Morley's **Findings**—the results of his research. He describes the findings in detail because his readers must fully understand the geology of the area if they are to accept the conclusions he will draw later in his report. He is totally objective here, reporting only facts without letting his opinions intrude.

H L WINMAN AND ASSOCIATES

May 23, 2007

City, province, and postal code, correctly placed all on one line

Robert D Delorme, P.Eng
Town Engineer
Municipal Offices
Quillicom ON P8R 2A2

Dear Mr Delorme

Our assessment of the three sites selected as potential landfills for the Town of Quillicom shows that each has a disadvantage or limitation. The most serious exists at Lot 18, Subdivision 5N, which is the site preferred by the Town Council. A distinct possibility exists that a landfill located here could contaminate the town's water supply.

The disadvantages of the two other sites affect only cost and convenience:
- Lot 47, Subdivision 6E, will be considerably more expensive to operate.
- Lot 23, Subdivision 3S, will have a much lower capacity.

If the Town Council still prefers to use Lot 18, a drilling program must first be conducted to identify the soil and bedrock structure between the lot and Quillicom. Providing the boreholes show no evidence that contamination will occur, then the site would be a sound choice.

The enclosed report describes our study in detail. I will be glad to discuss it and its implications with you.

Regards

Morley Woyzuck

for Vincent Hrabi
Branch Manager
H L Winman and Associates
Thunder Bay, Ontario
enc

A cover letter accompanying an in-depth report or proposal may be signed by the author for the department manager

Figure 5-4   The cover letter preceding an evaluation report. This letter is also an executive summary.

5 Morley presents the three possible landfill sites as his **Ideas** (even though they were originally presented to him by the client, the Town of Quillicom). In effect he is saying to his readers: "Now that I have described the geology of the land to you, here are three locations within the area for you to choose from." He is still totally objective.

6 Morley now identifies three general **Criteria** he will use to evaluate the sites. He does not identify specific criteria because they have not been defined.

7 In his **Analysis,** Morley must clearly establish the factors on which he will base his conclusions. Now he allows some subjectivity to appear in his writing (we can hear his voice behind his words). He is moving down the right side of the plan for a comparative analysis, as shown in Figure 5-3.

8 Morley's **Conclusions** identify the main features affecting each site. Note that he simply offers the alternatives without saying or even implying which is preferable. This part of the report, together with the Recommendations, is the Outcome (sometimes referred to as the *terminal summary*).

9 In the **Recommendations** Morley states specifically what he believes the Town Council must do. He must sound definite and convincing, so he starts with "We recommend…" rather than the passive "It is recommended that…"

10 The **Attachment** brings together all the site details in an easy-to-read form, and simultaneously provides readers with evidence to support what Morley says about the landfill sites in the report narrative.

Morley's rationale for organizing and writing his report

Proposals
http://www.io.com/ ~hcexres/textbook/ props.html
Also from Online Technical Writing, this document describes types of proposals, their organization and format, and the common sections in a proposal. Included are several sample proposals and a revision checklist.

H L WINMAN AND ASSOCIATES

Evaluation of the Proposed Landfill Sites for the Town of Quillicom, Ontario

Summary

Two of the three locations selected as potential landfill sites for the Town of Quillicom, both southeast of the town, are environmentally safe. There is insufficient data to determine whether the third site, to the north of Quillicom, poses an environmental risk. All three sites are financially viable although one, because of its greater distance from Quillicom, would be more costly to operate.

1

Introduction

The Town of Quillicom in Northwestern Ontario currently operates a landfill 3.7 km southeast of the town. The landfill was constructed in 1958, and since 1974 has also served the mining community of Melody Lake, 2.8 km to the southwest of the landfill. In a report dated February 27, 2007, Quillicom town engineer Robert Delorme identified that the existing landfill was nearing capacity and that a new landfill must be found and operational by April 30, 2008.

The Background traces the history leading up to the present study

2

Previously, in 2004, the town had identified two sites as potential replacement land-fills: Lot 18, Subdivision 5N, 3.4 km north of Quillicom; and Lot 47, Subdivision 6E, 14.6 km to the southeast. The costs to set up and operate both sites were determined, and Lot 18 proved to be more economical ($2000 more to purchase and develop, but $17 000 a year less to operate). It was favoured by the Town Council. However, in a letter to the Council dated November 15, 2005, Mr Delorme expressed his concern that leachate from the site could possibly contaminate the town's source of potable ground water, and recommended that the town first carry out an environmental study.

The town subsequently engaged H L Winman and Associates to examine the sites and determine both their financial viability and their environmental safety. In a letter dated March 15, 2007, Mr Delorme commissioned us to carry out the study, and to include a third potential landfill site at Lot 23, Subdivision 3S, immediately adjacent to the existing landfill, in our assessment.

Figure 5-5 The evaluation report (6 pages).

Study Plan

(3) We divided our study into three components: (1) an examination of the area geology and its ability to constrain leachate movement; (2) an examination of the physical properties of the proposed landfill sites; and (3) an evaluation of the financial and environmental suitability of the sites.

Area Geology and Hydrogeology

(4) Bedrock at Quillicom and in the area of all three proposed landfill sites is chiefly granite and gneiss lying 15 to 30 metres below the surface. A layer of till varying in thickness from 10 to 20 metres covers the bedrock, and is itself covered by 1 to 15 metres of lacustrine silts and clays.

The whole area has experienced repeated glaciation, with the most recent occurring about 20 000 years ago with the advance of the Late Wisconsonian Ice Field. The advancing ice severely scarred this granite and gneiss. When the ice began to retreat 10 000 years later, till was deposited over the region. In addition, meltwater streams below the ice field deposited vast quantities of alluvial material, which today exist as eskers.

The melting ice also created Lake Agassiz and caused silts and clays to be deposited to a depth of up to 30 metres over the entire lake bed. (In the Quillicom area these lacustrine deposits range from 5 to 15 metres deep.) Then, as the lake drained and water levels receded, streams cut into the lacustrine and till deposits. These streams eventually dried up and their channels were filled with windblown silts and sands. Today the channels are known as buried stringers and, if they are water bearing, as stringer aquifers in the weathered bedrock and eskers.

The Town of Quillicom obtains its potable water from a stringer aquifer on the surface of the weathered bedrock. Other stringer aquifers are known to exist in the area to the east and south of Quillicom, and likely also exist to the west and north.

The Ontario Water Resources Branch provided us with logs obtained during drillings for ground water wells in the mid 1980's, all to the south and east of Quillicom. We have plotted the locations and types of materials on a topographic map, which shows that

- the bedrock in the area slopes downward, toward the south, from the Town of Quillicom, and
- a major 350-metre wide glacial esker starts 1 km southeast of Quillicom and continues for several kilometres southeast under Highway A806, to beyond the proposed landfill at Lot 47, Subdivision 6E.

As there are very few borehole records for the area north of Quillicom, we could not plot a similar map for that area.

Presenting technical details so they will be understood by all readers takes skill!

2

The Proposed Landfill Sites

The attributes of the three proposed landfill sites are discussed briefly below and itemized in detail in the attachment. The anticipated life of each site is based on the 2006 population of Quillicom. Similarly, projected operating costs are based on 2006 prices.

Lot 23, Subdivision 3S

This narrow, 7.81-hectare strip of land is immediately east of and adjacent to the existing landfill, 3.7 km southeast of Quillicom on Highway A806. As it is the smallest site, it will cost only $9000 to purchase and develop. Its annual operating cost will be $47 000, the same as at the present landfill, and it will have an operational life of 12 to 14 years.

Lot 47, Subdivision 6E

Judicious use of white space makes technical details more readable...

The largest of the three proposed sites at 35.91 hectares, but also the most distant, Lot 47 is a rectangular parcel of land 14.6 km southeast of Quillicom on Highway A806. Its combined purchase and development price will be $20 000, and its annual operating cost will be $64 000. (The high operating cost is caused primarily by the much greater distance the garbage collection vehicles will have to travel.) It will have a lifespan of almost 60 years.

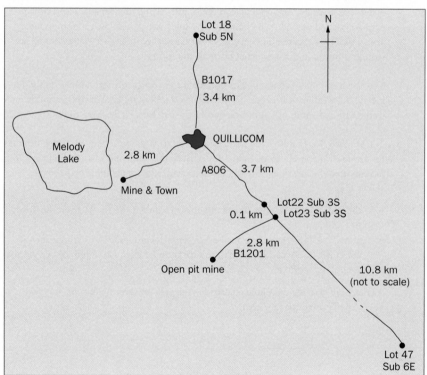

3

Lot 18, Subdivision 5N

A roughly square, 22.75-hectare parcel of land, this lot is 3.4 km directly north of Quillicom on Highway B1017. It will cost $22 000 to purchase and develop, and $47 000 a year to operate (the same as at present). At the current fill rate, it will last for 36 to 40 years.

Site Comparisons

We considered three factors when comparing the three proposed landfill sites: cost, environmental impact, and convenience (see attachment).

Cost. We examined cost from two points of view: the immediate expense to purchase and develop the site, and the annual cost to operate it.

- Lot 23, adjacent to the existing landfill, offers the lowest purchase and development cost at $9000, compared with $20 000 and $22 000 for the two alternative sites.
- Lot 23 and Lot 18 (the site north of Quillicom) offer comparable operating costs at $47 000 per year, whereas Lot 47 (14 km southeast of Quillicom) would have the highest annual operating cost of $64 000.

However, if the purchase and development costs are spread over 10 years and added to the operating costs, Lots 18 and 23 show a more comparable cost structure:

Site:	Lot 18	Lot 23	Lot 47
Annual Cost:	$49 200	$47 900	$66 000

Environmental Risk. The primary environmental risk is the effect that leachate from the landfill could have on Quillicom's source of potable water. If a landfill lies on a glacial esker, leachate from the landfill will probably contaminate ground water aquifers in the esker. If these aquifers are connected hydraulically to stringer aquifers, the stringer aquifers also probably will become contaminated.

- Lots 23 and 47 (and the existing landfill) lie on a major esker south of Quillicom but offer no environmental risk because the slope of the bedrock in the area is to the south, away from the town. Consequently, even if leachate from the landfill contaminates the ground water, it will flow away from Quillicom and will not contaminate the town's water supply.
- Lot 18, however, is in the uncharted area north of Quillicom, where neither the presence of eskers nor the slope of the bedrock has been determined. Consequently it offers a potential risk that leachate from a landfill located here could contaminate the town's water supply. This will be particularly true if the slope of the bedrock north of Quillicom is the same as south of the town, since then the leachate will flow south, toward Quillicom.

Convenience. To establish convenience we considered the size of each landfill site (measured as the number of years it can be used before another site must be found) and its proximity to Quillicom.

4

...as does the author's choice not to justify the right margin

This analysis sets the scene for the conclusions the report author will draw

- Lot 47 is the largest site, offering close to 60 years of use, but is four times farther from Quillicom than either of the two other sites.
- Lot 18, to the north, is next largest and can provide between 36 and 40 years of use. It is a comfortable 3.4 km from Quillicom.
- Lot 23, adjacent to the current landfill, is the smallest site and so will have a life span of only 12 to 14 years. It also is 3.4 km from Quillicom.

Conclusions

The possibility of leachate contamination of the Town of Quillicom's water supply makes Lot 18, Subdivision 5N, a doubtful choice until sufficient drilling has been done to create a profile of the strata between the lot and Quillicom.

8

The remaining two sites are environmentally sound but have different advantages:

- Lot 47, Subdivision 6E, provides the greatest space but will be costly to operate.
- Lot 23, Subdivision 3S, offers the lowest cost but will have only a limited life span.

Recommendations

We recommend that the Town of Quillicom purchase Lot 23, Subdivision 3S, and operate it as a temporary landfill from 2008–2018. We also recommend that the town concurrently conduct a drilling program to the north of Quillicom to determine whether Lot 18, Subdivision 5N, will be an environmentally sound site to use after the year 2018.

9

Morley Wozniak

Morley Wozniak, P.Eng

Remember: conclusions and recommendations must never introduce new information

5

Attachment

(10)

Comparison of Proposed Landfill Sites
for the Town of Quillicom

Comparison Factor	Lot 18 Sub 5N	Lot 23 Sub 3S	Lot 47 Sub 6E
Distance from Quillicom (driving dist in km)	3.4 N	3.7 SE	14.6 SE
Size (hectares)	22.75	7.81	35.91
Life (years)	36–40	12–14	58–60
Environmental risk (the site's potential for contaminating the Quillicom water supply)	Unknown	None	None
Development costs:			
Purchase price ($)	10 000	2 000	5 000
Construction cost ($)	12 000	7 000	15 000
Ten-year cost ($/yr)	2 200	900	2 000
Operating costs ($/yr)	47 000	47 000	64 000
Combined development and operating costs:			
Year 1, w/o amortization ($)	69 000	56 000	84 000
Per year, w amortization ($)	49 200	47 900	66 000

An "open" table (no lines drawn around it) is cleaner for a simple presentation

6

We encourage using the
first person in letter and
report writing

Compare how Phyllis van der Wyck and Morley Wozniak each use the first person (see Phyllis's investigation report in Figure 5-2, pages 86 to 88). Phyllis uses the informal "I" because she is writing a memo report to another member of the television station where she works. Morley uses the slightly more formal "we" because he knows his semiformal report will be distributed to the Quillicom town councillors. (Note, however, that he uses "I" in the personal cover letter to Robert Delorme that accompanies the report.)

Like an evaluation report, a feasibility study starts by introducing an idea or concept, and then develops and analyses the idea to assess whether it is technically or economically feasible. The chief difference lies in the name and application of each document. An evaluation report is generally based on an idea that is originated and evaluated within the same company; hence, it is nearly always informal. A feasibility study is normally prepared at a slightly higher level: the management of company *A* asks company *B* to conduct a feasibility study for it, because company *A*'s staff is not experienced in a specific technical field. For example, if a national wholesaler engaged solely in the distribution of dry goods were to consider purchasing an executive jet, it would seek advice from a firm of management consultants. The consultants would examine the advantages and disadvantages, and publish their results in a feasibility study that they would issue as either a letter or a formal report. Often the differences between a feasibility study and an evaluation report are so slight that only personal preference dictates which label is used for a particular document.

ASSIGNMENTS

Project 5.1: Resolving a Landfill Problem

You are the assistant engineer for the Town of Quillicom in Northern Ontario. Your boss is Robert D Delorme, P.Eng, who is the town engineer.

Start by researching and
reading about what has
gone before

Mr Delorme has assigned a landfill project to you: the existing landfill site—at Lot 22, Subdivision 3S—is nearly full and a new site must be found quickly. He hands you a report by H L Winman and Associates and instructs you to read it. (Turn to Figure 5-5, on pages 94 to 99 to read the report.)

Mr Delorme tells you that before the town councillors can make a decision on which site to develop, they will need to know how much it will cost to drill a dozen boreholes north of Quillicom and analyse the results. He asks you to get some price quotations for the work. He also says, privately, that you need to be aware that the councillors have indicated their preference for Lot 18, Subdivision 5N, rather than any other location. Here are some other details:

- Morley Wozniak, at H L Winman and Associates in Thunder Bay, will plot the results of the borehole drilling.
- The positions for the boreholes are to be shown on a map (see Figure 5-5, page 96).

- A list titled "Borehole Specifications for the Area North of Quillicom" contains the exact positions where the drilling must be carried out.
- You are to get at least two (and preferably three) price quotations for the drilling.

From two drilling companies you know of in the area, you obtain the following quotations:

Northwest Drillers, Ltd Quillicom, Ontario	$78 520 (GST incl)
M J Peabody and Company Dryden, Ontario	$75 900 (GST extra)

You could not find a third company to give a quotation, but you did talk to Bert Knowles, the assistant superintendent at Melody Lake Mines. He had a suggestion: their open-pit mine is nearly worked out and shortly will close. When it does so, the Department of the Environment will insist that Melody Lake Mines cover it with earth and seed it with grass.

Mr Knowles suggested that Melody Lake Mines will lease the open pit mine to the Town of Quillicom as a landfill site, for a nominal one dollar a year. There is, however, a condition: the town must spread soil over the compacted garbage—and do it progressively as the site is filled, so there will be no obnoxious smell for the people who live near the mine to contend with—and seed it and plant trees.

You agree: it's something the Town would do anyway, before closing a landfill site.

Mr Knowles drives you to the site and you stand on the lip of a shallow, roughly oval excavation varying from about 3 to 18 metres deep. Then you talk to Inga Paullsen, the mine geologist, who calculates the size of the excavation as 24.86 hectares.

You describe the difficulty the Town Council is having in finding a landfill site, mention the three other sites, say the one north of the town could create an environmental problem, and explain you won't know until drilling has been completed there.

Inga tells you that drilling has already been done there. When she was a junior at college she worked one summer with an exploration crew that drilled quite a few boreholes north of Quillicom. They were looking for an alternate place to sink a mine shaft, but found no ore deposits north of either Melody Lake or Quillicom. She says the mine does not have the records, only a report from the drilling company.

The drilling company Inga worked for was Mayquill Explorations, but she says it does not exist anymore. It was owned by Ernie Mays, and when he retired he simply closed down the company. Inga suggests he may still have the records.

Ernie Mays lives at 211 Westerhill Crescent in Quillicom. When you visit him, he tells you that he remembers drilling for Melody Lake Mines and that they sank about 20 boreholes, all north of Quillicom. He could not, however, remember if the bedrock slopes, but he does remember there was evidence of a large sand esker running roughly south-southwest toward Quillicom.

You ask Ernie if he still has the drilling records, but he says he doesn't. He explains that about three years ago Mr Caldicott came to see him and asked for the records. Mr Caldicott now has them.

A second piece of information introduces still another aspect!

Suddenly, everything falls into place. Frank Caldicott is not only general manager of Melody Lake Mines, but also a very influential Quillicom town councillor. And his youngest sister, Julie, is married to the town engineer—Robert Delorme, your boss.

Because you have so much new information to include, you decide to write a semiformal report of your findings. (You will have to decide whether you will include the information you now have about the previous drilling north of Quillicom, and the location of the records.)

Here is some additional data you may need to write your report:

- You are concerned about groundwater contamination problems if the open-pit mine is used as a landfill, so you call Morley Wozniak at H L Winman and Associates in Thunder Bay, who tells you that it will not be a problem because both the lake and the mining community are north of the pit, and the bedrock slopes to the south.
- You calculate that costs to develop the open-pit mine as a landfill will be only $3000, because you can use the buildings and approach roads that are already there.
- The open-pit mine is 4.1 kilometres directly south of Quillicom, but 6.6 kilometres by road (3.8 kilometres southeast along highway A806, then 2.8 kilometres southwest along highway B1201).
- The annual operating cost for using the open-pit mine as a landfill will be $49 500, which is $2500 more than the cost for operating the current landfill.
- You obtain a third drilling estimate from Quattro Drilling and Exploration Company in Kenora, which quotes $83 200, GST included.

A question of ethics: do you mention the "family" connection?

On a hunch you visit the Land Titles Office in Thunder Bay and look up the surveys for the area north of Quillicom. Against Lot 18, Subdivision 5N, you find the owner listed as *Julie Sarah Caldicott, 207 Northern Drive, Quillicom, Ontario.*

Your assignment: Write the report.

Project 5.2: Identifying a Power Plant Problem

You are an independent consultant and operate a business known as Pro-Active Consultants Limited from your home. Four days ago you received a telephone call from Paullette Machon, who is vice-president, operations, of Baldur Agricultural Chemicals (BAC), a company with manufacturing plants across Canada. She assigned you a task: to drive to the BAC plant at Gordontown, where you are to look into a technical problem in the power house. Ms Machon is concerned because power house costs have been rising at Gordontown just at the moment when world fertilizer prices have been decreasing. This is causing BAC to be uncompetitive in both national and international markets.

Ms Machon explained that BAC requires a lot of hot water and steam in its manufacturing operations. However, over the past two years fuel consumption at Gordontown has risen by 18%, numerous breakdowns have occurred that have interfered with production, and there has been a sharp rise in production costs. She has visited the power house repeatedly, but has never found anything that could be attributed to poor operation. In fact, the power house has always been immaculate.

Now Ms Machon wants an independent consultant to take a look, talk to the people in the power house, and try to identify any production problems.

She also hinted that the problem may not only be technical. She explained that the present chief engineer at the BAC power house is Curt Hänness; he is to retire in three months, and she has to decide whether to promote Harry Markham, the existing senior shift engineer, or to bring in a new chief engineer from outside the company. On paper, Markham is ideal for the job. He has worked in the power house for 15 years (he is now 36) and always under Hänness, so his knowledge of the plant and its operations cannot be challenged. Yet the rising costs indicate that all is not as it should be in the plant, and Ms Machon wants to be sure that the new chief engineer does not perpetuate the present conditions.

A technical problem affected by the personalities involved

She said she would inform Hänness and Markham that she has engaged you to study the hot water and power generating system in their power house, and that they are to expect you.

You visit the BAC power plant in Gordtontown today. During your talks to plant staff and tours of the plant you make the following notes:

1. Housekeeping excellent—whole place shines (but is this only surface polish for impression of visitors?)
2. Maintenance logs are inadequately kept—need to be done more often. Need more detail. Equipment files not up-to-date and not properly filed.
3. Boiler cleaning badly neglected. Firm instructions re boiler cleaning need to be issued by head office.
4. Flow meters are of doubtful accuracy. May be overreading. Not serviced for three years. Manufacturer's service department should be contacted (these are Weston meters). Manufacturer needs to be called in to do a complete check and then recalibrate meters.
5. Overreading of meters could give false flow figures—make plant seem to produce more steam than is actually produced.
6. Good housekeeping obviously achieved by neglecting maintenance. Incorrectly placed emphasis probably caused by frequent visits from company president,

These are the "technical" details...

who likes to bring in important visitors and impress them. Hänness likes reflected glory (so does Markham).

7. Shift engineers are responsible for maintenance of pumps and vacuum equipment. Not enough time given over to this. They seem to prefer straight replacement of whole units on failure rather than preventive maintenance. Costly method! Obviously more breakdowns: they wait for a failure before taking action. A preventive maintenance plan is needed.

8. Markham seems O.K. Genial type; obviously knows his power house. Proud of it! But seems to resist change. Definitely resents suggestions. Does he lack all-round knowledge? Is he limited only to what goes on in his plant? Is he afraid of new ideas because he doesn't understand them? Young staff hinted at this: too loyal to say it outright, but they seem to be restive, hampered by his insistence that they use old techniques that are known to work but are slow. Nothing concrete was said—it is just an impression.

...and these are the "personal" details

9. Hänness has done a good job training Markham. Made him a carbon copy. Hänness doesn't do much now. Markham runs the show, and has for over a year. He expects to get the job when Hänness retires. It'll be a real blow to him if he doesn't! BAC might even lose a good company man.

10. Discussed microprocessor-controlled CORLAND 200 power panel with staff. Young engineers had read about it in *Plant Maintenance*—eager to have one installed similar to the one at Pinewood Paper Mill. But Hänness and Markham knew nothing about it—didn't seem to be interested. Are they not keeping up-to-date with technical magazines?

Your assignment: Write two evaluation reports for Ms Machon:

1. The first is to address the technical problems in the power house at Gordontown.

2. The second is to address the personnel difficulties.
   In each case you are to make a recommendation. Here is some additional information you may need:
   - Gordontown is 124 km from your city/town. It has a population of 15 700 and its primary employer is the BAC plant.
   - The BAC office in your city/town is at 1450 Disraeli Crescent.

Chapter 6
Formal
Reports

Formal reports require more careful preparation than the informal and semiformal reports described in previous chapters. Because they will be distributed outside the originating company, their writers must consider the impression their report will convey of the entire company. A well-written, good-looking report can do much to convince prospective clients that you should handle their business, whereas a poorly written, badly presented report can cause clients to question your capability.

The presentation aspect must convey the originating company's "image," suit the purpose of the report, and fit the subject it describes. For instance, a report by a chemical engineer evaluating the effects of diesel fumes on the interior paint of bus garages would most likely be printed on standard bond paper, and its cover, if it had one, would be simple and functional. At the other end of the scale, a report by a firm of consulting engineers selecting a college site for a major city might be printed professionally and bound in an artistically designed book-type folder.

Formal reports are made up of several standard parts, not all of which appear in every report. Each writer uses the parts that best suit the particular subject and the intended method of presentation. There are six major and several subsidiary parts on which to draw, as shown in Table 6-1.

Table 6-1 Traditional arrangement of formal report parts.

Cover or Jacket

Title Page

Summary

Table of Contents

Introduction

Discussion

Conclusions

Recommendations

References or Bibliography

Appendices

Notes:
1. **Major Parts** are in boldface type.
2. A Cover Letter or Executive Summary normally accompanies a formal report.

Technical Reports
http://www.io.com/
~hcexres/textbook/
techreps.html
This document is one chapter from the online textbook used in Austin Community College's online course, Online Technical Writing (www.io.com/~hcexres/textbook/acctoc.html). It describes types of technical reports and their general characteristics and audience, and provides a checklist that can be used for writing technical reports.

The acronym SIDCRA is formed from the first letter of each major report part

Major Parts

Six major parts form the central structure of every formal report. In the traditional arrangement they are known by the acronym SIDCRA.

Summary

The summary is considered by many to be the most important part of a report and the most difficult to write. It has to be informative, yet brief. It has to attract the reader's attention, but must be written in simple, nontechnical terms. It has to be directed to the executive reader, yet be readily understood by almost any reader.

Normally the summary appears immediately after the title page, where it can be found easily. A summary must be *informative*. In as few words as possible it has to state why the project was carried out and the report was written (the purpose), highlight the most important features of the report, state the main conclusion, and possibly make a recommendation:

The criteria for a summary are difficult to meet

Informative Summary

We have tested a specimen of steel to determine whether a job lot owned by Northern Railways could be used as structural members for a short-span bridge to be built at Peele Bay in the Yukon. The sample proved to be G40.12 structural steel, which is a good steel for general construction but subject to brittle failure at very low temperatures.

Although the steel could be used for the bridge, we consider there is too narrow a safety margin between the –51C temperature at which failure can occur, and the –47C minimum temperature occasionally recorded at Peele Bay. A safer choice would be G40.8C structural steel, which has a minimum failure temperature of –62C.

An informative summary answers readers' questions...

Other informative summaries preface the two formal reports presented in this chapter and the semiformal evaluation report in Figure 5-5 (page 94).

You need to avoid writing a *topical* summary. As its name implies, a topical summary simply describes the topics covered in the report without attempting to draw inferences or capture the reader's interest:

Topical Summary

Construction of the Minnowin Point Generating Station was initiated in 2004, and first power from the 1340 MW plant is scheduled for 2010. A general description of the structures and problems peculiar to the construction of this large development in an arctic climate is presented. The river diversion program, permafrost foundation conditions, and major equipment are described. The latter include the 16 propeller turbines, among the largest yet installed, each rated at 160 000 horsepower.

...whereas a topical summary only suggests what can be found within a report

Because they are less results-oriented, topical summaries are *not* recommended for most formal reports.

You write the summary last, after you have written the remainder of your report. Only then will you be fully aware of the report's highlights, main conclusions, and recommendations, so you can draw on them to form your words. It should have a page to itself, be centred on the page, and be prefaced by the word "Summary." If it is very short, it may be indented equally on both sides to form a roughly square block of information. For examples, see pages 133 and 149.

Introduction

The introduction begins the major narrative of the report by preparing readers for the discussion that follows. It orients them to the purpose and scope of the report and provides sufficient background information to place them mentally in the picture before they tangle with technical data. A well-written introduction contains exactly the correct amount of detail to lead readers quickly into the major narrative.

The length of an introduction and its depth of detail depend mostly on the readers' knowledge of the topic. If you know that the ultimate reader is technically knowledgeable, but at the same time you have to cater to the executive reader who is probably only partly technical, write the introduction (and conclusions and recommendations) in semitechnical language. This permits semitechnical executives to gain a reasonably comprehensive understanding of the report without devoting time and attention to the technical details contained in the discussion.

Knowing your reader influences the depth of detail required

Most introductions contain three parts: **purpose, scope,** and **background information.** Frequently the parts overlap, and occasionally one of them may be omitted because there is no reason to include it. The introduction always starts on a new page (normally identified as page 1 of the report) and is preceded by the report's full title. The title is followed by the single word "Introduction," which can be either a centre heading or a side heading, as shown in Figure 6-1.

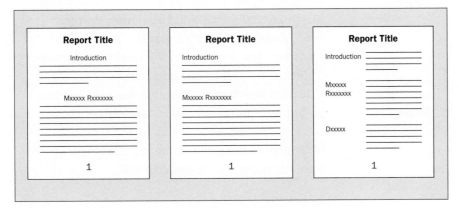

Figure 6-1 Different ways to integrate headings and text.

The **purpose** explains why the project was carried out and the report is being written. It may indicate that the project has been authorized to investigate a problem and recommend a solution, or it may describe a new concept that the report writer believes should be brought to the reader's attention.

The **scope** defines the parameters of the report. It describes the ground covered by the report and outlines the method of investigation used in the project. If there are limiting factors, it identifies them. For example, if 18 methods for improving packaging are investigated in a project but only 4 are discussed in the report, the scope indicates which factors (such as cost, delivery time, and availability of space) limited the selection. Sometimes the scope may include a short glossary of terms that need to be defined before the reader starts to read the discussion.

Background information comprises facts readers must know if they are to fully understand the discussion that follows. It may describe conditions or events that caused the project to be authorized, and details of previous investigations or reports on the same or a closely related subject. In a highly technical report, or when a significant time lapse has occurred between it and previous reports, background information may also provide a theory review and references to other documents. If the theory review is lengthy and there is a long list of documents, they are often placed in appendices, with only a brief summary of the theory and a quick reference to the list appearing in the introduction.

The introductions shown here, plus those forming part of the two sample reports later in this chapter, represent the many ways a writer can introduce a topic.

Place a short glossary in the introduction, a longer glossary in an appendix

A good introduction "sets the scene"

Technical Report Writing
http://www.sti.nasa.gov
Scientists at NASA's Lewis Research Center must write reports that are both technically correct and easy to read. This NASA guide was written to make writing reports easier. Separate chapters deal with the stages of report preparation, report style, the introduction, experiment and analysis descriptions, results and discussions, concluding and supporting sections, reviewing reports, and references. An author's checklist and reporting aids provide quick guidelines for technical report writers.

Introduction 1

Background

Purpose

Scope

Northern Railways plans to build a short-span bridge 1 km north of Peele Bay in the Yukon and has a job lot of steel the company wants to use for constructing the bridge. In letter NR-70/LM dated March 20, 2006, Mr David L Harkness, Northern Area Manager, requested that H L Winman and Associates test a sample of this steel to determine its properties and to assess its suitability for use as structural members for a bridge in a very low temperature environment. Two Charpy impact tests were performed, one parallel to and the other transverse to the grain of the test specimen, at 10° increments from +22C down to –50C.

Introduction 2

Purpose

H L Winman and Associates was commissioned by Ms Rita M Durand, president and general manager of Auto Drive-Inns Inc of Toronto, to select a Windsor, Ontario, site for the first of a proposed chain of computerized, automatic drive-in grocery outlets to be built in Canada. Windsor was chosen as the test site because it represents an average community in which to assess customer acceptance of such a service.

Say why you are writing…

Background

Aside from exterior façade and foundation details, Auto Drive-Inns are built to a standard 8.5 by 5.3 metre pattern with an order window at one end of the longer wall and a delivery window at the other end. Auto Drive-Inns carry only a limited selection of groceries, milk and fruit, but boast 60-second service from the time an order is placed to its delivery at the other end of the building. For this reason, Auto Drive-Inns attract people hurrying home from work, the impulse buyer, and the late-night traveller, rather than the selective buyer. The Drive-Inns depend more on the volume of customers than on the volume of goods sold to each individual.

…describe what has gone before, and…

Scope

The chief consideration in selecting a site must be a location on the homeward-bound side of a main trunk road serving a large residential area. The site must have quick and easy entry onto and exit from this road, even during peak rush-hour traffic. The residential area should be occupied mainly by single persons and younger families in which both parents work. And there should be little competition from walk-in grocery stores.

…explain factors affecting both the study and the report

Discussion

The discussion, which normally is the longest part of a report, presents all the evidence (facts, arguments, details, data, and results of tests) that readers need to understand the subject. The writer must organize this evidence logically to avoid confusing readers, and present it imaginatively to hold their interest.

There are three ways you can build the discussion section of a report:

By **chronological development**—in which you present information in the sequence that the events occurred.

By **subject development**—in which you arrange information by subjects, grouped in a predetermined order.

By **concept development**—in which you organize information by concept, presenting it as a series of ideas that imaginatively and coherently reveal how you reasoned your way to a logical conclusion.

Chronological Development

The chronological method of development is simple to organize and write: you simply arrange the major topics in the order they occurred and eliminate irrelevant topics as you go along. You can use it for very short reports, for laboratory reports showing changes in a specimen, for progress reports showing cumulative effects or describing advances made by a project group, and for reports of investigations that cover a long time and require visits to many locations to collect evidence.

But the simplicity of the chronological method is offset by a major disadvantage: because it describes events sequentially, it can result in a dull read. If you are to hold your readers' attention, you have to emphasize the most interesting items and de-emphasize the less important details.

Chronological development is essentially factual

The chronological method works best when time is a factor, such as when reporting tests carried out over a five-year period on the effects of salt on concrete pavement. Your report would record the extent of erosion at specific intervals and how the erosion increased annually in direct relation to the amount of salt used to melt snow each year.

Subject Development

If the previous investigation had been broadened to include tests on different types of concrete pavements, or if both pure salt and various mixtures of salt and sand had been used, then the emphasis would have shifted to an analysis of erosion on different surfaces or caused by various salt/sand mixtures, rather than a direct description of the cumulative effects of pure salt. For this type of report you would arrange the topics in *subject* order.

Subject development sorts information into groups

The subject order could be based on the extent of erosion with different concentrations of salt and sand, starting with a 100% concentration of salt, then continuing with salt/sand ratios of 90/10, 80/20, 70/30, and so on. Alternatively, you could select the different types of pavement as the subjects, arranging them in a specific order and describing the effects of different salt/sand concentrations on each surface.

The subject method of development permits you either to conceal your personal preference until almost the end of the report, or to let your opinions show your preference all the way through. These alternative approaches are illustrated in Figure 5-3 on page 89.

Concept Development

By far the most interesting reports are those using the concept method of development. They need to be organized more carefully than reports using either of the previous methods, but they give the writer a tremendous opportunity to devise an imaginative arrangement of the topic.

They can also be very persuasive. Because the report is organized in the order in which you reasoned your way through the investigation, your readers will much more readily appreciate the difficulties you encountered and frequently will draw the correct conclusion even before they read it. This helps readers feel they are personally involved in the project.

You can apply the concept approach to your reports by thinking of each project as a logical but forceful procession of ideas. If you are presenting a concept (an idea, plan, method, or proposal) that readers are likely to accept, then use a straightforward four-step approach:

1. Describe your concept in a brief overview statement.

2. Discuss how and why your concept is valid; offer strong arguments in its favour, starting with the most important and working down to the least important.

3. Introduce negative aspects, and discuss how and why each can be overcome or is of limited importance.

4. Close with a restatement of your concept, its validity, and its usefulness.

But if you are presenting a controversial concept, or need to overcome reader bias, then you have to modify your approach by carefully establishing a strong case for your concept *before* you discuss it in detail. This means constantly anticipating your readers' likely reaction to your information.

Ella Watson used this approach in a report she prepared for her friend Paul Dobrin, owner/manager of an Edmonton company making extruded plastic and metal parts. Manufacturing costs had risen steeply over the past two years and Paul's prices had become uncompetitive. Paul thought he should replace some of his older, less efficient equipment, so he asked Ella to evaluate his needs.

Ella quickly realized that if Paul was to avoid going out of business he would have to replace much of his equipment with microprocessor-controlled machines, and do it soon. Because the cost would be high, he would have to lease, rather than buy, the new equipment. Here, Ella had a problem. Paul was old-fashioned and throughout his life he had steadfastly refused to purchase anything that he could not buy outright. He was unlikely to change now.

In her report, Ella used a carefully reasoned argument to prove to Paul that he needed a lot of new equipment and that the only feasible way he could acquire it would be to lease it. Throughout, Ella wrote objectively but sincerely about her findings, hoping that the logic of her argument would swing Paul around to accepting her recommendation. Here is the step-by-step approach Ella used:

Concept development has the greatest potential for effectively organizing information

The concept method leads the reader to the right answer...

- She opened with a summary that told Paul that to avoid bankruptcy he would have to invest in a lot of expensive equipment and make extensive changes in his operating methods.
- She produced financial projections to prove her opening statement, and then described the productivity and profitability necessary for Paul to remain in business.
- Ella showed why Paul's equipment and methods were inefficient, introduced the changes Paul would have to make, established why each change was necessary, and demonstrated how each would improve productivity.
- Then she introduced two sets of cost figures: one for making the minimum changes necessary for Paul's business to survive, and the second for more comprehensive changes that would ensure a sound operating basis for the future. She also commented that both would require capital purchases likely to be beyond Paul's financial resources.
- Ella outlined alternative financing methods available to Paul, the implications and limitations of each, and the financial effect each would have on Paul's business. (She included leasing but made no attempt to persuade Paul that he would have to lease; she let the figures speak for themselves.)
- Ella concluded by summarizing the main points she had made: that new equipment *must* be acquired; that to buy even the minimum equipment was beyond Paul's financial resources; and that, of the financing methods available, leasing was the most feasible.
- In her recommendation, Ella suggested that Paul make comprehensive changes and lease the new equipment. (By then, she had become so involved with Paul's predicament that she wrote strongly and sincerely.)

...carefully tracing a logical, persuasive, and sometimes intricate path

Even though the concept method challenges a writer to fashion interesting reports, it is not always the best reporting medium. When a topic and the outcome are clear-cut, there is no need to lead the reader through a lengthy "this is how I thought it out" discussion. Reserve the concept method for topics that are controversial, difficult to understand, or likely to meet reader resistance.

Avoid Clutter

Keep the narrative simple and uncluttered

Whichever method you use, avoid cluttering the discussion with detailed supporting information. Unless tables, graphs, illustrations, photographs, statistics, and test results are essential for reader understanding while the report is being read, banish them to an appendix. But always refer to them in the discussion, like this:

> The test results attached as Appendix C show that aircraft on a bearing of 265°T experienced considerably weaker reception than aircraft on any other bearing. This was attributed to...

Readers *interested only in results* will consider that this statement tells them enough and continue reading the report. Readers interested in *knowing how the results were obtained*—who want to see the overall picture—will turn to Appendix C.

If an illustration or table is essential, try to extract the key points from an appendix and use them to create a miniature illustration or table that you can insert beside or embed into the narrative.

Unless the discussion is very short, divide it into a series of sections that are each preceded by an informative heading. After each heading, start the section with an overview statement to describe what the section is about and suggest what conclusion will be drawn from it. (Overview statements are miniature summaries that direct a reader's attention to the point you want to make.) And then, at the end of each major section, insert a concluding statement that summarizes the result of the discussion within that section. From these section conclusions you can later draw your main conclusions.

Conclusions

Conclusions briefly state the major inferences that can be drawn from the discussion. You must base them entirely on previously stated information. *Never* surprise readers by introducing new material or evidence to support your argument. If there is more than one conclusion, state the main conclusion first and follow it with the remaining conclusions in decreasing order of importance. This is shown in the two examples below, which present the same conclusions in both narrative and tabular form.

There should be no surprises here

Narrative Conclusion

If we upgrade to version 4.1 of the *Mosaic* software, we will also have to upgrade our operating system. The one-time cost will be $7600, but we will increase our multimedia production capability by 65%.

Tabular Conclusion

If we upgrade to version 4.1 of the *Mosaic* software, we will

- experience a 65% increase in our multimedia production capability,
- have to upgrade our operating system, and
- incur a one-time cost of $7600.

Because conclusions are *opinions* (based on the evidence presented in the discussion), they must never tell the reader what to do. This task must always be left to the recommendations.

Recommendations

Recommendations appear in a report when the discussion and conclusions indicate that further work needs to be done, or when you have described several ways to resolve a problem or improve a situation and want to

Now you can let your voice be heard

identify which is best. Write recommendations in strong, definite terms to convince readers that the course of action you advocate is valid. Use the first person and active verbs, as has been done here:

Strong I recommend that we build a five-station prototype of the Microvar system and test it operationally.

Compare this with the same recommendation written in the third person, using passive verbs:

Weak It is recommended that a five-station prototype of the Microvar system be built and tested under operational conditions.

If you feel you cannot use the personal "I," try using the plural "we," to indicate that the recommendations represent the company's viewpoint. For example:

Strong We recommend building a five-station prototype of the Microvar system. We also recommend that you
1. install the prototype in Railton High School,
2. commission a physics teacher experienced in writing programmed instruction manuals to write the first programs, and
3. test the system operationally for three months.

And no surprises here, either!

Because recommendations must be based solidly on the evidence presented in the discussion and conclusions, they must *never* introduce new evidence or new ideas.

Appendices

Place related data not necessary to an immediate understanding of the discussion further back in the report, in the appendices. The data can vary from a complicated table of electrical test results to a simple photograph of a blown transistor. The appendices are a suitable place for manufacturers' specifications, graphs, analytical data, drawings, sketches, excerpts from other reports or books, cost analyses, and correspondence. There is no limit to what can be placed in the appendices, provided that the information is relevant and reference is made to every appendix in the discussion.

The appendix is *not* a storage place for information that only *might* be useful

The importance of an appendix has no bearing on its position in the report. Whichever set of data is mentioned first in the discussion becomes Appendix A, the next set becomes Appendix B, and so on. Each appendix is considered a separate document complete in itself and is paginated separately, with its front page labelled 1. An example of an appendix appears at the end of Report 1, on page 145.

Subsidiary Parts

In addition to the six major parts of a formal report, there are several additional parts that perform more routine functions. Although referred to here as "subsidiary," they nevertheless contribute much to a report's effectiveness.

Cover

Almost every major formal report has a cover. It may be made of glossy cardboard printed in multiple colours and bound with a dressy plastic binding, or it may be only a light cover of coloured fibre material stapled on the left side. The cover not only informs readers of the report's main topic but also conveys an image of the company that originated it. This "matching" of subject matter and company image plays an important part in setting the correct tone.

The cover should reflect the company's image

The cover should contain the report title, the name of the originating company and, perhaps, the name of its author. The title should be set in bold letters centred horizontally on the page and separated from any other information.

The choice of title is particularly important. It should be short yet informative, implying that the report has a worthwhile story to tell. Compare the vague title below with the more informative version beneath it.

Original vague title

Radome Leakage

Revised informative title

Porosity of Fibreglass Causes Radome Leakage

Technical officers at remote radar sites would glance at the first title with only a muttered, "Looks like somebody else has the same problem we've got." But the second title would encourage them to stop and read the report. They would recognize that someone may have found the cause of (and, perhaps, a remedy for) a trouble spot that has bothered them for some time.

Note how the following titles each *tell* something about the reports they precede:

Reducing Ambient Noise in Air Traffic Control Centres

Effects of Diesel Exhaust on Latex Paints

Salt Erosion of Concrete Pavements

The report title should capture readers' interest

These titles may not attract every potential reader who comes across them, but they will certainly gain the attention of anyone interested in the topics they describe.

Title Page

The title page normally carries four main pieces of information: the report title (the same title that appears on the cover); the name of the person, company, or organization for whom the report has been prepared; the name of the company originating the report (sometimes with the author's name); and the date the report was completed. It may also contain the contract number, a report number, a security classification such as CONFIDENTIAL or SECRET, and a copy number (important reports given only limited distribution are sometimes assigned copy numbers to control and document their issue). All this information must be tastefully arranged on the page, as has been done in the full report in Figure 6-6 (page 132).

Table of Contents

If the T of C seems sparse or disjointed, check that the report narrative has sufficient *descriptive* headings

All but very short reports contain a table of contents (T of C). The T of C not only lists the report's contents, but also tells readers how the report has been arranged.

The pleasing arrangement for a T of C on page 134 uses the single word **Contents** rather than "Table of Contents"; we recommend the shorter title. The contents page also contains a list of appendices, with each identified by its full title. In long reports you may also insert a list of illustrations and their page numbers between the T of C and the list of appendices.

The introductory pages to a report (i.e. the summary and contents pages) are numbered using lower case Roman numerals. All other parts of the report are numbered with Arabic numerals, starting with the **introduction**, which becomes page 1.

References (Endnotes), Bibliography, and Footnotes

Accurate documentation of information sources is essential

A report writer who refers to another document, such as a textbook, journal article, report, or correspondence, or to other persons' data or even a conversation, must identify the source of this information in the report. To avoid cluttering the report narrative with extensive cross-references, the reference details normally are placed in a storage area at the end of the report. This storage area is known as a list of references or a bibliography. Specifically:

A **List of References** is the most convenient and popular way to list source documents. The references are typed as a sequentially numbered list at the end of the narrative sections of the report (usually immediately ahead of the appendices). Such numbered references are sometimes referred to as *endnotes*. For a short example, see page 144. (Footnotes, which are printed at the foot of the page on which the particular reference appears, are seldom used in contemporary reports.)

A **Bibliography** is an alphabetical listing of the documents used to research and conduct a project. The documents are listed in alphabetical order of authors' surnames, and the list is placed at the end of the report narrative. A bibliography may list many more documents than are referred to in the report. An example appears on page 123.

Source references can be written many ways. The most common are the styles recommended by the Modern Language Association (MLA) and the American Psychological Association (APA), although there are many others. The style we show here most closely parallels the MLA approach, but with some differences that have become entrenched in the technical documentation field. If you are writing in industry, the suggested approach will work well for you. If you are writing in an academic situation or for a technical journal, you should enquire which style the professors or the journal editor prefer.

Until the mid-90s, most source referencing was to printed documents. Today, however, you will often be gaining information from an electronic resource, which may be by email or searching on the web. Because internet sources may only be transitory, you will need to quote more source information whenever possible. How to do this will be shown on the following pages.

Preparing a List of References

References should contain specific information, arranged in this sequence:

(a) Author's name or authors' names (in natural order: first name and/or initials, and then surname)
(b) Title of document (article, book, paper, report)
(c) Identification details, such as:

For a book: city and province, state, or country of publication, publisher's name, and year of publication.

For a magazine or journal article: name of magazine or journal; volume and issue number; date of issue.

For a report: report number; name and location of issuing organization; date of issue.

For email: name and email address of sender; name and address of recipient; the date sent.

For correspondence: name and location of issuing organization; name and location of receiving organization; the letter's date.

For a conversation or speech: name and location of speaker's organization; name, identification, and location of listener; the date.

For an excerpt from a web page: the name of the author/designer (if known); the title of the page or source; the name of the organization that owns the site; the latest update; the date the information was accessed; and the URL.

(d) The page number (if applicable) on which the referenced item appears or starts.

Referencing a Book

If you are referring to information in a book authored by only one person, the entry in your list of references should contain:

(a) Author(s)'s name
(b) Title of book (set in italic type)

Bibliography Styles Handbook
http://www.english.uiuc.edu/cws/wworkshop/bibliography.html
The Bibliography Styles Handbook, one section of the University of Illinois's Writers' Workshop, provides information about the bibliographic styles of the American Psychological Association (APA) and the Modern Language Association (MLA), and about the old MLA style.

Each reference source must be recorded exactly as it appears on the original document

(c) City of publication, publisher's name, and year of publication (all within one set of brackets)

(d) Page number (the first page of the referenced pages)

If it is your first reference, and you are referring to an item on page 174 of the book, your entry would look like this:

Each reference entry is given a sequential number

1. Laurinda K Wicherly, *Fibreoptic Modes of Communication* (Toronto, Ontario: The Moderate Press Inc, 2006), p 174.

If a book has two authors, both are named:

2. David B Shaver and John D Williams, *Management Techniques for a Research Environment* (Edmonton, Alberta: Witney Publications, 2007), p 215.

But if there are three or more authors, only the first-named author is listed and the remaining names are replaced by "and others":

3. Donald R Kavanagh and others,... *(etc)*.

If a book is a second or subsequent edition (as this book is), the edition number is entered immediately after the book title:

4. Ron Blicq and Lisa Moretto, *Technically-Write!* Canadian 7th ed (Toronto, Ontario: Pearson Education Canada, 2008).

Some books contain sections written by several authors, each of whom is named within the book, with the whole book edited by another person. If your reference is to the whole book, identify it by the editor's name:

5. Donna R Linwood, ed, *Seven Ways to Make Better Technical Presentations* (Vancouver, BC: Bonus Books Ltd, 2007).

But if your reference is to a particular section of the book, identify it by the specific author, enclose the section title in quotation marks, set the book title in italics, then name the editor:

External document titles are listed in italic type; internal section titles are listed within quotation marks

6. Kevin G Wilson, "Preparation: The Key to a Good Talk," *Seven Ways to Make Better Technical Presentations*, ed Donna R Linwood (Vancouver, BC: Bonus Books Ltd, 2007), p 71.

(In examples 5 and 6, "ed" means "editor" or "edited by.")

Referencing a Magazine or Journal Article

Similarly, if you are referring to an article in a magazine or journal, list these details:

(a) Author(s)'s name(s)

(b) Title of article (always in quotation marks)

(c) Title of journal or magazine (set in italics)

(d) Volume and issue numbers (shown as two numbers separated by a colon)

(e) Journal or magazine issue date

(f) Page on which article or excerpt starts (optional entry)

If an article is your seventh reference, it would look like this:

7. Lilita Rodman, "You-attitude: A Linguistic Perspective," in *Technostyle*, 17:2, Winter 2002, p 55.

If a magazine article does not show an author's name, then the entry starts with the title of the article:

8. "Selling to the EEC: Challenge of the New Millennium," in *Technical Marketing*, 11:5, May 2006, p 113.

Referencing a Report

To refer to a report written by yourself or another person, list this information:

(a) Author(s)'s name(s) if the author is identified on the report
(b) Title of report, in italics
(c) Report number, or other identification (if any)
(d) Name and location (city, plus province or state) of organization issuing report
(e) Report date
(f) Page number (if a specific part of the report is being referenced)

Reports, memos, and email messages can be listed as reference sources...

Here is an example:

9. Derek A Lloyd, *Effective Communication and Its Importance in Management Consulting*. Report No. 61, Smyrna Development Corporation, Montreal, Quebec, February 18, 2007.

Referencing an Email Message, Letter, or Memo

For an email message, the entry should look like this:

10. Christine Lamont (c.lamont@macroeng.com), "Replacing Vancourt Meters." Email to Wayne Kominsky (kominsky@7designgrp.net), 31 October 2006.

For a letter or memo, the email references are replaced by company name and location, the title often is omitted, and the word "email" is replaced by "letter" or "memo"):

11. Christine Lamont, Macro Engineering Inc, Toronto, Ontario. Letter to Wayne Kominsky, No. 7 Design Group, Winnipeg, Manitoba, 31 October 2006.

Referencing a Conversation or Speech

For a conversation or speech follow these examples:

12. David R Phillips, Lakeside Power and Light Company, Thunder Bay, Ontario, in conversation with Anna King, H L Winman and Associates, Calgary, Alberta, January 7, 2008.

...as can talks and telephone or face-to-face conversations

13. Francis R Cairns, Elwood Martens and Associates, Fredericton, New Brunswick, speaking to the 8th Potash Producers' Conference, Regina, Saskatchewan, September 16, 2007.

Referencing an Excerpt from a Web Page

If information is available only on a web page, and is *not* printed elsewhere, list:

(a) Author(s)'s name(s) (if an author is identified).
(b) Title of the specific piece of information (enclosed within quotation marks).
(c) The title of the page or source (in italics).
(d) The name of the institute or organization that owns the web page.
(e) The date the information was entered, or the latest update, using day (numeral), month (first three letters, spelled out), year (numeral).
(f) The date the information was accessed.
(g) The web identification (the URL, within angle brackets).

For example:

> 14. Göran Nordlund, "Documentation for Medical Equipment – a Real Cross-Cultural Challenge," in *Forum 2003 Preliminary Programme*, 19 Nov 2002, retrieved 2 Mar 2003 <http://www.intecom.org/Forum 2003 Preliminary Programme>

However, if the information has also been published in print form, the entry should refer to the original document *and* the website. List:

(a) The full printed identification (for a book, article, technical paper, etc).
(b) The date the information was entered on the website (day, month, year).
(c) The URL identification (within angle brackets).

Here is an example:

> 15. "Keeping Track of Your Performance," in *RGI News*, No. 13, Winter 2001–2002, 18 Mar 2002, retrieved 16 Jul 2003 <http://www.rgilearning.com/newsletters>

Referencing an Excerpt from an Online Book

The entry should contain this information:

(a) Author(s)'s names
(b) Title of chapter (in quotation marks)
(c) Title of book (in italics)
(d) Book identification (city of publication, publisher, copyright date), if available
(e) Date of electronic publication, or latest update
(f) Name of the organization responsible for the website
(g) Date the information was accessed
(h) URL identification

Here is an example:

> 16. Marvin LeTouche, "Maintaining Quality Levels," *Quality Control in the Mining Industry*. Chicago: Bronzeline Publishers, 2006. 15 Oct 2006; Mainstream Mining Inc; retrieved 8 Jan 2007 <http://www.mainstream.ca/qc>

Referencing an Excerpt from an Online Magazine Article

The following information should be recorded:

(a) Author(s)'s names (if author is identified)

(b) Title of article (in quotation marks)

(c) Title of magazine or journal (in italics)

(d) Issue number plus year of publication (in brackets)

(e) Page number

(f) Date accessed

(g) URL identification

For example:

> 17. Margery Leduc, "Are Handheld Computers Taking Over from Laptops?"
> *Computers Unlimited*, 8.3 (2006), retrieved 23 Oct 2006
> <http://www.bearskincollege/lib/online.html>

Referencing Information in an Online Database

The information to be recorded is as follows:

(a) Author(s)'s names (if identified)

(b) Title of information (in quotation marks)

(c) Name of database (in italics)

(d) Name of organization owning site (if available)

(e) Date accessed

(f) URL identification

Here is a typical example:

> 18. "Radiant Heat in Tomorrow's Homes," *Heating Industry Standards Institute*.
> Heating Industry Institute, retrieved 10 May 2003 <**http://www.heating.**
> **standards.com/market/2455/616.html**>

Additional Factors to Consider

Remember that when a magazine article, technical paper, or report is published as one of several documents bound into a volume, then it is listed within quotation marks (only the title of the volume is set in italics). But if the article, technical paper, or report is published as a *separate* document, the quotation marks are omitted and the title of the article, paper, or report is set in italic type, as in entry No. 9.

Every entry in a list of references must have a corresponding reference to it in the body of your report. At an appropriate place in the narrative you should insert a superscript (raised) number to identify the particular reference. It should look like this:

> Earlier tests[3] showed that speeds higher than 2680 rpm were
> impractical.
> *(Alternatively, the raised 3 could go here.)*

Numbering each entry simplifies cross-referencing between the text and the list of references

If you refer to the same document several times, your list of references needs to show full details for that document only the first time you refer to it. Subsequent references can be shown in a shortened form containing only the author's name (or authors' names) and the page number. For example, if the first reference you make is to an item on page 48 of the particular book described below, the entry in the list of references would be

1. Wayne D Barrett, *Management in a Technical Domain* (Halifax, Nova Scotia: Martin-Baisley Books, 2007), p 48.

Now suppose that your second and third sources are other documents, but for your fourth source you again refer to *Management in a Technical Domain*, this time quoting from page 159. Now you need list only the author's surname and the new page number.

4. Barrett, p 159.

Do the same for each future reference to the same document, simply changing the page number each time. (Note that the Latin terms *ibid.* and *op. cit.* are no longer used.) You can even make repeated references to several different documents by the same author by simply inserting the year of publication for the particular document between the author's name and the page number:

9. Barrett, 2007, p 159.

Preparing a Bibliography

A bibliography lists not only the documents to which you make direct reference, but also many other documents that deal with the topic. The major differences between a list of references and a bibliography are:

- Bibliography entries are *not* numbered 1, 2, 3, etc.
- The name of the *first-named* author for each entry is reversed, so that the author's surname becomes the first word in the entry. (If there is a second-named author, that name is *not* reversed.)
- The *first* line of each bibliography entry is extended about 12 mm to the left of all other lines (see Figure 6-2).
- The entries are arranged in alphabetical sequence of first-named authors.
- Punctuation of individual entries is significantly different, with each entry being divided into three compartments separated by periods: (1) author identification (name, etc); (2) title of book or specific article; and (3) publishing details. (Positions of periods are shown in Figure 6-2.)
- Page numbers are usually omitted, since generally the bibliography refers to the whole document. (Reference to a specific page is made within the narrative of the report.)

Figure 6-2 shows how to list bibliography entries from various sources. The entries for this bibliography have been created from some of the "reference" entries listed earlier. The number to the right of each entry is cross-referenced to the explanatory list below:

1 Book by one author

2 Book by two authors, seventh edition

In a bibliography, authors' surnames are used for easy cross-referencing

Most bibliography entries contain three distinct groups of information

3 Conference speech

4 Web source

5 Email

6 Report

7 Conversation

Bibliography

1 Barrett, Wayne D. *Management in a Technical Domain*. Halifax, Nova Scotia: Martin-Baisley Books, 2007.

2 Blicq, Ron, and Lisa Moretto. *Technically-Write!*, Canadian 7th ed. Toronto, Ontario: Pearson Education Canada, 2008.

3 Cairns, Frances R, Elwood Martens and Associates, Fredericton, New Brunswick. Speaker at the 8th Potash Producers' Conference, Regina, Saskatchewan, September 16, 2007.

4 "Keeping Track of Your Performance." *RGI News*, No. 13, Winter 2001–2002. 23 June 2002. Retrieved 30 November 2003 <http://www.rgilearning.com/newsletters>

5 Lamont, Christine, Macro Engineering Inc, Toronto, Ontario. Email to Wayne Kominsky, No. 7 Design Group, Winnipeg, Manitoba, October 31, 2006.

6 Lloyd, Derek A. *Effective Communication and Its Importance in Management Consulting*. Report No. 61, Smyrna Development Corporation, Montreal, Quebec, February 18, 2007.

7 Phillips, David R, Lakeside Power and Light Company, Thunder Bay, Ontario. Conversation with Anna King, H L Winman and Associates, Calgary, Alberta, January 7, 2008.

8 Rodman, Lilita. "You-attitude: A Linguistic Perspective." *Technostyle*, 17:2, Winter 2002.

9 "Selling to the EEC: Challenge of the New Millennium." *Technical Marketing*, 11:5, May 2002.

10 Shaver, David B, and John D Williams. *Management Techniques for a Research Environment*. Edmonton, Alberta: Witney Publications, 2007.

11 Wilson, Kevin G. "Preparation: The Key to a Good Talk." *Seven Ways to Make Better Technical Presentations*, ed Donna R Linwood. Vancouver, BC: Bonus Books Ltd, 2007.

Extending the first line of each entry to the left helps readers find specific source references

Figure 6-2 A typical bibliography.

⑧ Journal/magazine article

⑨ Magazine article, with no author identification

⑩ Book by two authors

⑪ Section of book with section written by one author and whole book edited by another

Because a bibliography is not numbered, you cannot cross-refer directly to it simply by inserting a superscript number in the report narrative, as can be done with a list of references. The most common method is to insert a parenthetical reference in the narrative that includes the author's name (or authors' names) and the page number:

> Although the tests conducted in the Northwest Territories (Faversham, p 261) showed only moderate decomposition...

The full descriptive listing for Faversham's book or report would be carried in the bibliography.

If several publications by the same author are listed in the bibliography, then the date of the particular publication is included as a parenthetical reference to identify which document is being mentioned:

> The most significant tests were those conducted 22 km south of Old Crow, in the Yukon (Crosby, 2006, p 17), which showed that...

Cover Letter

A cover letter is a brief letter that identifies the report and states why it is being forwarded to the addressee. The following letter accompanied the second report in this chapter (see pages 149 to 153).

Dear Mr Merrywell

We enclose our report No. 8-23, "Selecting New Elevators for the Merrywell Building," which has been prepared in response to your letter LDR/71/007 dated April 27, 2007.

If you would like us to submit a design for the enlarged elevator shaft, or to manage the installation project on your behalf, we shall be glad to be of service.

Sincerely

Barry V Kingsley

H L Winman and Associates

Some cover letters include comments that draw attention to key factors described in the report or that evolve from it, and sometimes summarize or interpret the report's main findings. This is done in the cover letter preceding the first report in this chapter (see Figure 6-5 on page 131).

Executive Summary

An executive summary is an analytical summary of the purpose of the report, its main findings and conclusions, and the author's recommendations. Unlike the normal report summary prepared for all readers, the executive summary can present detailed information on aspects of particular concern to senior executives, and often may discuss financial implications. An executive summary can be presented in two ways: externally, as a letter pinned to the front of the report, or internally, as an integral part of the report.

If the executive summary is attached to the report like a cover letter, the recipient may remove it before circulating the report to other readers. Hence, an external executive summary is written like a letter and is addressed to a specific reader, which permits its author to make comments that are intended only for that reader's eyes, or to deal with sensitive issues that for political reasons should not be discussed in the body of the report. The executive summary preceding Report 1 serves this purpose (see Figure 6-5 on page 131).

If, however, the executive summary is bound within the report so that it will be read by everyone, its purpose becomes more general and its author simply summarizes and perhaps comments on the report's major findings. Rather than being written like a letter, the words **Executive Summary** are centred at the top of the page and the summary is presented like a semiformal report. Such an executive summary may be positioned immediately inside the report cover, after the title page (in which case it replaces the normal short summary), or after the table of contents.

When an executive summary is bound inside the report, a brief cover letter may also be prepared as a transmittal document and attached to the front of the report.

An executive summary may often precede a major technical proposal, in which a company describes how it can successfully tackle a task at an economical price for the government or another company (see Chapter 7).

The Complete Formal Report
The Main Parts

Two formal reports are included in this chapter, each typical of the quality of writing and presentation that the technical business industry expects of engineering, science, and computer graduates. The first report is presented in the traditional arrangement (see Table 6-2), and the second in an alternative, pyramidal arrangement. In each case the parts of the report remain the same, but their sequence changes. The reports are typed single-spaced with a clear space between paragraphs, which is the style preferred by industry. In comparison, academic institutions tend to prefer double spacing throughout.

...whereas an executive summary usually has two or more paragraphs

An integral executive summary rarely contains sensitive or confidential information

The same information, but two ways to arrange it

Table 6-2 The main parts of the formal report organized in the traditional arrangement.

Cover:	Jacket of report; contains title of report and name of originating company; its quality and use of colour reflect company image.
Title Page:	First page of report; contains title of report, name of addressee or recipient, author's name and company, date, and sometimes a report number.
Summary:	An abridged version of whole report, written in nontechnical terms; *very* short and informative; normally describes salient features of report, draws a main conclusion, and makes a recommendation; always written last, after remainder of report has been written.
Table of Contents:	Shows contents and arrangement of report; includes a list of appendices and, sometimes, a list of illustrations.
Introduction:	Prepares reader for discussion to come, indicates purpose and scope of report, and provides background information so reader can read discussion intelligently.
Discussion:	A narrative that provides all the details, evidence, and data needed by the reader to understand what the author was trying to do, what the author actually did and found out, and what the author thinks should be done next.
Conclusions:	A summary of the major conclusions or milestones reached in the discussion; conclusions are only opinions, so can never advocate action.
Recommendations:	If the discussion and conclusions suggest that specific action needs to be taken, the recommendations state categorically what must be done.
References:	A list of reference documents that were used to conduct the project and that the author considers will be useful to the reader; contains sufficient information for the reader to correctly identify and order the documents.
Appendices:	A storage area at the back of the report that contains supporting data (such as charts, tables, photographs, specifications, and test results) that rightly belong in the discussion but, if included with it, would disrupt and clutter the major narrative.

The traditional arrangement provides a continuous narrative

Sometimes the appendices are bulkier than the rest of the report

Traditional Arrangement of Report Parts
(Conclusions and Recommendations *after* the Discussion)

In the traditional arrangement there is a logical flow of information: the **introduction** leads into the **discussion**, from which the writer draws **conclusions** and makes **recommendations** (the two latter parts are sometimes referred to jointly as the **terminal summary**), as illustrated in the bird's-eye view of a report in Figure 6-3. This arrangement is used for most technical and business reports.

Formal Report 1: Installing a Radiant Energy Heating System for Hartwell Enterprises Ltd

The author of this report (Figures 6-5 on page 131 and 6-6 on page 132) is Karen Woodhouse, an engineer working for H L Winman and Associates. She chose to break with tradition and automatically justify the right margin (make it vertically straight).

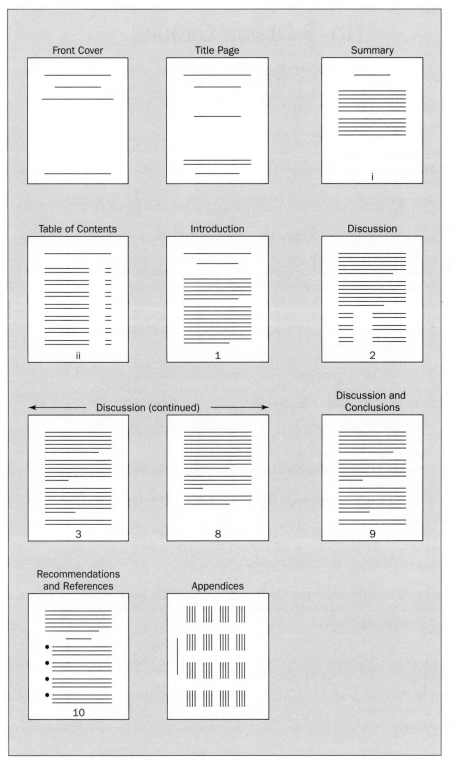

A bird's-eye view shows report parts (compare to Figure 6-8 on page 147)

Figure 6-3 Formal report—traditional arrangement. (These are the individual pages of Formal Report 1; to conserve space, some of the discussion pages have been omitted.)

NO. 5 DESIGN GROUP

240 Victoria Drive – Suite 300
Burlington, Ontario L7R 1R5
Tel: 905 234 1786; Fax: 234 1807
email: 5design@aol.com

November 27, 2007

Vern Rogers, Manager
H L Winman and Associates
970 Birchmount Road
Scarborough ON M1P 3J6

Dear Mr Rogers

As we discussed by telephone earlier today, we are commissioning
H L Winman and Associates to prepare a report on the practicability of
installing a radiant heating system in the new office and assembly plant we
are designing for Hartwell Enterprises Ltd of Peterborough, Ontario. The
plant is to be built at the northwest corner of the intersection of Seymour
Drive and Graveley Street, with construction starting on April 1, 2008 (see
attached preliminary design).

Our client has indicated interest in radiant heating but needs substantive
information before deciding on installing such a system. Consequently, in
your report will you please describe

- how radiant heat works and how it differs from traditional heating
  methods,
- the advantages of installing and using radiant heat,
- the cost to install radiant heat, compared to traditional heating systems, and
- the savings to be accrued by Hartwell Enterprises over, say, a five-
  year period.

Your contact at Hartwell Enterprises will be operations manager Vincent
Correlli. He is aware that you are preparing a study for us and will be ready
to answer questions about their operation.

I would appreciate receiving your report by January 8, 2008, because we will
be submitting our design to Hartwell Enterprises on January 15. Please call
me if you have any questions.

Sincerely

Mark Hesseltine

Mark Hesseltine
Design Associate
No. 5 Design Group

The four bulleted items became Karen's project criteria

Figure 6-4   Letter authorizing the report in Figure 6-6.

Comments on the Report Writer's Approach

To understand the circumstances leading up to the report, first read Mark Hesseltine's letter of authorization in Figure 6-4. Mark is an architect with No. 5 Design Group who has designed a new building for Hartwell Enterprises Ltd, a specialty manufacturer in Peterborough, Ontario. His client has expressed interest in having radiant energy heating installed in the new building. Because No. 5 Design Group does not have radiant energy expertise in-house, Mark contracts with H L Winman and Associates to evaluate the practicability and cost of installing such a system. The task was assigned to Karen Woodhouse.

Although Mark would *appear* to be Karen's primary reader, in reality it would be the executives at Hartwell Enterprises. Rather than rewrite Karen's report, Mark would prefer to briefly list its main points in his report, and then include Karen's report as an attachment. Consequently, Karen tailored her approach to suit nontechnical readers and included more information than she would have done if she had been writing solely for No. 5 Design Group. **Clearly identifying the reader is an essential first step when writing a comprehensive report.**

Check before you place your hands on the keyboard: the person you are writing to may not be your primary reader

Karen also wrote the report *backwards*, which helped her organize her information more effectively. This was her approach:

1. First, she collected data on the three heating systems she would be evaluating, and researched comparative costs with experts in the radiant energy field: Darryl Berkowski in Winnipeg, Manitoba, and Vincent Harding in London, Ontario.

2. Then Karen created a table showing the relative costs of each system (this table became the report's Appendix, on page 145). From this table she also developed smaller tables identifying specific cost factors (these appear in the report's Discussion, on report page 8).

Writing in reverse order may seem unnatural, yet it results in a better report

3. Next, she created two sets of illustrations depicting installation and operating costs at one, three, and five years: first a series of bar charts and then a series of graphs. From these she chose the graph in figure 3 (on report page 9) as the most descriptive and simplest to read.

4. Karen's fourth step was to write the Introduction, to "set the scene." Here, she drew on information in No. 5 Design Group's letter of authorization to establish the background to the report, and its purpose and scope. She knew her primary readers would not have seen the letter.

5. Next, Karen wrote a preliminary outline, which was really an early version of the Table of Contents on page 134. She used this as a loose guide for structuring the report, making changes to it as she wrote.

6. Because her readers would not be knowledgeable about radiant energy heating, she wrote a comprehensive general description, which became the first four pages of the Discussion (see report pages 1 to 4).

7. Next she wrote the comparisons and analyses, using the charts and tables she had prepared earlier. This helped give her the right direction to take.

8. Now Karen wrote the Conclusions. She went back to the Introduction and identified the three questions she had been particularly asked to address, and provided answers to them.

Sometimes inserting a recommendation is optional

9. She deliberated whether to write a Recommendation. The authorizing letter did not specifically ask for a recommendation yet she felt that, because she had researched the information and as such was the local expert, she should identify what route she felt Hartwell Enterprises should take.

10. And *last*, Karen wrote the Summary, drawing principally on the Conclusions to compose it.

Remember Karen's "backwards" approach when you have to write your next long report. By documenting all the details *first*, you will find you can organize your ideas much more easily and write more fluidly.

Comments on the Report

Karen's report is in Figure 6-6, on pages 132 to 145, and is preceded by the cover letter in Figure 6-5. The comments below refer to specific parts of the report.

- Karen's cover letter is equivalent to an executive summary because she comments on the report's contents. Because she knows the cover letter will be seen only by Mark Hesseltine, she uses a friendly tone and the first person "I."

- A quick glance at the Contents (report page ii) tells Karen's readers that she has organized her information into a logical, coherent flow, and that there are three main components: background information on radiant energy systems; a plan for installing a radiant energy heating system in the client's building; and a cost projection and analysis.

- In the Introduction (report page 1), the Background is in paragraph 1, the Purpose is in paragraph 2, and the Scope is in the three bulleted points.

- For the Discussion (starting at the bottom of report page 1), Karen has adopted an overall "concept" arrangement of information, but internally it breaks into a subject arrangement when describing the proposed installation and some of the costs.

Writing in the first person means making a decision: "I" or "we"?

- She has written the entire report in the first person plural. "When I am presenting the results of a study I have done personally," she said, "and I am writing directly to my client, then normally I would use the first person singular: 'I.' But when I am writing on behalf of the company, and simultaneously writing for my client's client, and don't know the client personally, then I use the first person plural: 'We.'"

- The Conclusions, on report pages 9 and 10, are longer than normal because they have to cover all the points the client requested. They

(Comments are continued on page 146)

H L WINMAN AND ASSOCIATES

970 Birchmount Road, Scarborough, ON M1P 3J6

email: kwoodhouse@winman.on.ca

January 7, 2008

Mark Hesseltine
Design Associate
No. 5 Design Group
240 Victoria Drive, Suite 300
Burlington ON L7R 1R5

Dear Mark

I am enclosing our report, *Installing a Radiant Energy Heating System for Hartwell Enterprises Ltd*, as requested in your letter of November 27, 2007. The report shows that in the long term radiant energy will be the most economical heating system for Hartwell Enterprises' new building.

To some extent I am concerned that Hartwell Enterprises may hesitate when they see the high front-end cost, particularly in comparison to electric heat. Hence, I have taken care to include a graph which shows clearly that radiant energy heating will be particularly efficient from a cost viewpoint after the fourth year. If the graph on page 9 were to be extended for another five years, the considerably lower operating cost of radiant energy heating would be even more noticeable. You may want to address this factor in your proposal.

Please call me if you need further information on any of the points addressed by the report. I'll be glad to supply it.

Sincerely

Karen Woodhouse

Karen Woodhouse, P.Eng
enc

> Inserting this second paragraph converted Karen's cover letter into an executive summary

Figure 6-5 Cover letter/executive summary accompanying the formal report in Figure 6-6.

H L WINMAN AND ASSOCIATES

Installing a Radiant Energy Heating System for Hartwell Enterprises Ltd

Prepared for

No. 5 Design Group
Burlington, Ontario

Prepared by

Karen Woodhouse, P.Eng
H L Winman and Associates
Scarborough, Ontario

January 7, 2008

Figure 6-6   Formal Report 1: traditional arrangement (14 pages;
full report minus cover page).

Summary

We have evaluated three methods for heating the proposed Hartwell Enterprises Ltd plant designed by No. 5 Design Group for construction in Peterborough, Ontario. Electric heat is the least expensive to install but the most expensive to operate. Gas-fired forced hot air is moderately expensive to install and moderately expensive to operate. Radiant energy heating is the most expensive to install and the least expensive to operate. Long term, however, radiant energy offers the most efficient and cost-effective method.

Installing a radiant energy heating system in a new building means the system can be incorporated into the overall design so that it becomes unobtrusive as well as efficient and cost-effective. It also provides more gentle warming than the other two methods, and the temperature in each area of the building can be controlled separately. The operating cost will be 39% less than for electric heating, and 30% less than for gas-fired hot air heating.

The Summary: the full story in a capsule—difficult to write!

i

Contents

The preliminary pages bear Roman page numbers; all other pages bear Arabic numbers

If more than one appendix, the title changes to "Appendices" and each appendix is identified by a letter: "A," "B," "C," etc

Appendix

Comparison of Costs: Heating/Cooling Systems for Hartwell Enterprises Ltd

Installing a Radiant Energy Heating System for Hartwell Enterprises Ltd

Introduction

Hartwell Enterprises Ltd assembles and packages modules and specialty products for public and private organizations such as the Department of Defence, NavCan, Multiple Industries Limited, and Northern Paging and Cellular Systems. The company does no original manufacturing itself, confining its role to assembling components supplied by carefully chosen manufacturers. Hartwell Enterprises Ltd has built a solid reputation as a fast, high-quality producer of specialty systems, and the company's business has increased steadily since its inception in 1988. Today, it needs a larger building, but research for suitable accommodation among Peterborough area properties has failed to find a building that can be adapted to the company's special needs.

In August 2007, Hartwell Enterprises Ltd commissioned No. 5 Design Group of Burlington, Ontario, to design a building that will meet the company's particular requirements, and to find a site on which to place it. No. 5 Design Group has, in turn, asked H L Winman and Associates to evaluate the efficacy and cost to install a radiant heating system in the new building, rather than a more traditional heating method. Specifically, they asked us to describe

- how radiant heat works and how it differs from traditional heating methods,
- the advantages of and the cost to install a radiant heating system, and
- the savings to be accrued by Hartwell Enterprises Ltd over the first five years.

Radiant Heating vs Traditional Heating

A traditional heating system warms air directly, which we feel on our skin as immediate heat, but its impact is transitory. Turn off the source of the heat, and the space being warmed immediately starts to cool. On a winter's day, for example, a residential furnace pumps hot air into the rooms until a preset temperature is reached, then the thermostat switches off the furnace. The

1

The Introduction establishes why the project was undertaken and the report has been written

These requirements were copied almost verbatim from the client's letter of authorization warming effect stops immediately and the air temperature, influenced by cooler windows and walls, begins to drop.

A radiant heating system, rather than warming air directly, radiates heat outwards in all directions until the rays contact another surface. If the surface is cooler than the radiant panel, the surface begins to warm up and the air near to it also warms, but gently, and so our skin feels the warmth as a gentle, comfortable heating. On a cool winter's day, a furnace pumps heat into the radiant panels as hot water or they are heated electrically until a preset room temperature is reached, when the source of the heat is switched off. The warming effect, however, does not stop immediately because the radiant panel continues to radiate residual heat for a considerable time. Consequently, the air in the room cools much more slowly than with hot air heating.

Comparing a complex technical concept to a familiar everyday event helps reader understanding

Compare the difference in heat produced by a gas ring and an electric hotplate. The gas ring provides immediate heat to the surrounding air, but the heat stops immediately when the gas is switched off. The electric hotplate builds up its heat more slowly, but *continues to radiate heat* for 10 to 15 minutes after the electricity is switched off.

A 100% radiant heating system is ideal for locations that are unlikely to be affected by external sources that cause sudden changes in temperature. Yet it still can be effective in areas that are subjected to such changes, such as an aircraft hangar. Lawrence Drake, executive director of the Radiant Panel Association, explains that

> Thermal mass in a heated shop or hangar floor responds rapidly to the change of air temperature when a big overhead door is opened. All the heat that has been "trickled" into the slab over time is released quickly to combat the cold air rolling in over the floor. This happens because of the sudden, dramatic increase in temperature difference between the slab and the new air. Once the door is closed the building returns to its normal comfort setting almost immediately.[1]

He adds, however, that under such conditions a combination of radiant energy and a back-up hot air heating system can be even more effective, because occupants of the space immediately feel the heated air.

2

Darryl Berkowski, who installs radiant heating systems in Manitoba and Northwestern Ontario, points out that electric or hot water baseboard heaters may *appear* to produce radiant heat, but in effect they release only a small amount of radiant energy. Primarily, they heat the air.[2]

A particular advantage of radiant heating is that *it can be controlled locally.* In a traditional heating system, hot air is supplied to vents, or hot water to radiators, from a central furnace, the operation of which is controlled by a single thermostat mounted on a wall of only one of the rooms. Thus, the temperature in the other rooms cannot be controlled separately. If, for example, one of the rooms tends to be cooler than the others because it has large windows on a north wall, the heating system is unable to compensate for the variation. Conversely, in a radiant heating system the heat supplied to the radiant panels can be controlled separately in each room. This is true of radiant panels heated either electrically or by hot water.

Radiant Panel Installations

Radiant heating panels may be installed in the wall, ceiling or floor. Because they heat all objects within their line of sight, floor panels heat the ceiling and walls, wall panels heat the opposite wall, and ceiling panels heat the floor and walls. Similarly, all three heat furniture they can "see" and, of course, the people in the room. The radiant energy is felt as a very gentle, subtle warming, never as a searing blast.

Generally, wall panels tend to be smaller than ceiling panels, and ceiling panels tend to be smaller than floor panels, which often use the whole floor as their radiating surface. Also generally, the smaller the panel the greater the temperature at which it must operate to gain a measurable effect. Consequently, wall panels may be as hot as 65°C, ceiling panels as warm as 40°C, but floor panels rarely exceed 25°C. Lawrence Drake writes that

> A heated floor normally "feels" neutral. Its surface temperature is usually less than our body temperature, although the overall sensation is one of comfort. Only on very cold days when the floor is called on for maximum output will it actually "feel" warm.

> Heat coming from a wall radiator can be felt the closer you get to it because its surface is much warmer than your body. Radiant ceiling

3

A statement made in an email message or during a conversation may be documented as a source reference

Introducing excerpts from an existing document adds credibility to a report panels are also generally warmer than your body so you will feel some warmth on your head and shoulders.[3]

Wall and ceiling panels usually come preassembled and are fixed onto the surface of the wall or ceiling. Floor panels normally are embedded in the floor, as part of the floor construction, and then are covered with a layer of concrete or similar floor material. Consequently the whole floor becomes a single, large radiant panel.

When installed as an integral part of a new installation, either electric elements or water pipes are laid in continuous parallel rows in the floor (see Figure 1). The pipes are made of a strong, durable, light, cross-linked poly-ethylene (PEX). Connectors are made of noncorroding copper, brass, or plastic.

Although it's possible to install a radiant heating system as a retrofit in an existing building, the ideal arrangement is to design a radiant heating system specifically for a new building. It can then be installed as an integral part of the new structure.

A cutaway illustration like this helps readers visualize the technology

Figure 1. Various types of radiant energy panels
(Illustration courtesy of Radiant Panel Association)

4

Suggested Installation Plan for the Proposed Hartwell Enterprises Building

Hartwell Enterprises' operation is unique, in that it works on a just-in-time method of delivery for the components that are assembled into products. The company's contracts with its suppliers stipulate that components are to be delivered in small lots only a few hours before they are to be assembled. This has two major effects:

Research into a client's business practices can help you focus information accurately

1. Because components are moved rapidly from the delivery semitrailer to the assembly line, and then to the shipping area for packing and storing in a second semitrailer ready for shipping, Hartwell Enterprises requires only a small warehouse area.

2. Because the loading bay doors have to be opened frequently, the loading bay demands special attention from a heating viewpoint.

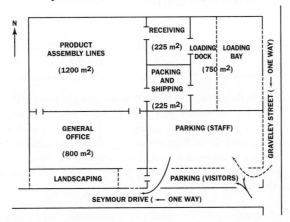

Figure 2. Design of proposed new building for Hartwell Enterprises Ltd

Proposed Heating System

The proposed Hartwell Enterprises building particularly lends itself to heating by radiant energy. The diverse activities in the various parts of the building call for different types and methods of heating. As Figure 2 shows, there will be five main areas of activity, each requiring a different level and form of heating, and each with its own thermostat. The floor in each area will be concrete, but there will be some variations:

The scene has been set: now for the plan!

5

- The general office will have a 0.20 metre thick slab with its upper surface 0.35 metres above grade. It will be covered by Orlando carpet and underlay.

- The product assembly, receiving, and shipping areas will be set on a 0.20 metre thick slab with the floor level at 1.3 metres above grade. There will be basement under these three areas, with a 2.2 metre high ceiling.

- The unloading and loading bays will be at grade level, built on a 0.35 metre reinforced concrete slab.

As the primary source of heat for these areas, we propose installing hot-water pipes embedded in the concrete with a separate circulation system and thermostat for each area. The mechanical room for the hot water boiler and the controls will be set up in the basement. (We are not recommending electrically heated panels, because in southern Ontario it is on average 20% more expensive to heat the radiant panels by electricity than by natural-gas-fired hot water.[4])

The main paragraphs contain the plan...

The product assembly, receiving, and shipping areas will require no supplementary heating. However, the general office and the loading bays will. For these areas we propose the following additional heating arrangements.

- The ceiling in the general office will slope upward, toward the north (the back of the office), which will tend to draw warm air aloft, into the higher part of the ceiling and away from the south side of the area. To maintain an even warmth on the south side, we propose installing two 1.5 × 0.8 metre horizontal radiant panels under the windows along the south wall. These will be heated by hot water and will be controlled by a separate thermostat.

...while the bulleted sub-paragraphs introduce variations and exceptions

- The loading bays will cool rapidly in winter when the doors are opened to admit and exit semitrailers. Here we propose installing two overhead hot-air heaters, one above each door. They also will be hot-water heaters, and the blowers will be triggered to start up when a door opens and to shut down when a predetermined ambient temperature is reached. (In effect, the radiant energy from the floor panels will restore the temperature quite quickly; the hot-air heaters will provide a supplementary, readily noticeable, immediate source of extra heat during extreme cold conditions.)

6

Proposed Cooling System

Although radiant energy panels can provide moderate cooling in the summer, particularly in dry climates, in moist or semimoist conditions they tend to be less efficient.[5] Consequently we propose that all cooling be carried out through a separate system, comprising

- a Hyperion Model 2000 air conditioning unit for cooling the general office, product assembly, and receiving and shipping areas, and
- a Hyperion Model 2720 air conditioning unit for cooling the loading bay.

The two air conditioners will be located in the basement, with the model 2000 at the west end and the model 2720 at the east end. The model 2000 will feed cooled air through ductwork concealed in the ceiling of the office, assembly, and receiving/shipping areas. The model 2720, which will be a fast-response unit designed to recover quickly from rapid changes in temperature, will feed cooled air through ductwork under the roof of the loading bay.

Costs: Radiant vs Traditional Heating

Two cost factors have to be considered when comparing a radiant energy heating system with a traditional heating system: the cost of installation and the cost of operation. The cost of installing and operating air conditioning from May to September also has to be taken into account.

For this study, we have examined the cost of installing and operating three systems:

1. Radiant energy heating, plus a separate air-conditioning system.
2. All-electric heating, plus a separate air-conditioning system.
3. Forced hot-air heating fueled by natural gas, with integral air conditioning.

Installation Costs

The costs to install these three systems in the proposed Hartwell Enterprises building are listed in Table 1, which at first glance shows that electric heating is the least expensive and radiant energy is the most expensive. However, when air conditioning is included, gas-fired hot air becomes the least expensive.

A section opening paragraph should act like a mini-summary, identifying aspects to be discussed

7

The table lists key cost figures, providing a ready comparison

Table 1. Installation Costs

System	Heating System ($)	Air Conditioning ($)	Total ($)
Radiant energy	47 200	21 600	68 800
All-electric plus air conditioning	26 600	21 600	48 200
Gas-fired hot air with integral air conditioning	38 700	(incl)	38 700

The table lists key cost figures, providing a ready comparison

Annual Operating Costs

To calculate potential operating costs, we referred to a 2005 study carried out by Vincent Harding of V Harding Associates, in which he averaged the annual heating costs of 30 industrial buildings in Ontario, Manitoba, and Saskatchewan for the years 1999 to 2004.[6] From these we culled the heating costs for eight light-industry buildings in Southern Ontario, each of a similar size to the proposed 3200 m^2 Hartwell Enterprises Building. Two are heated by electricity, three by gas-fired forced hot air, and three by radiant energy. The results are summarized in Table 2, which shows that radiant energy heating has the lowest annual operating cost and all-electric heating has the highest annual operating cost. A detailed breakdown is shown in the Appendix.

A simple table with key cost figures can be embedded conveniently into the narrative

Table 2. Average Annual Operating Costs

System	Heating Only ($)	With Air Conditioning ($)
Radiant energy	17 300	20 800
All-electric	31 700	35 200
Gas-fired forced hot air	27 600	31 100

8

Projected Costs Over Five Years

In Figure 3, the combined installation and operating costs for both heating and cooling are shown for year one, and then the projected operating costs for heating and cooling are shown cumulatively for years two through five. The graph shows that in the first year the installation and operating cost for electric heating is the least expensive, and radiant energy is the most expensive. However, after 1 year and 5 months the positions are reversed, with the cumulative costs of installing and operating radiant energy heating becoming less expensive than electric heating.

Installing and operating a gas-fired forced hot-air heating and air-conditioning system remains less expensive than radiant energy for the first 3 years and 2 months, after which the cumulative cost of radiant energy heating plus a companion air-conditioning system becomes more economical.

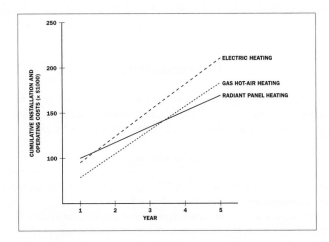

Both this graph and the two previous tables are supported by the detailed cost comparison in the appendix

Figure 3. Comparison of installation and operating costs over five years, for radiant energy, hot air, and electric heating systems

Conclusions

A radiant energy heating system offers several advantages for the proposed Hartwell Enterprises Ltd office and product assembly plant planned for 1650 Seymour Drive in Peterborough, Ontario:

Conclusions sum up key outcomes but never specifically advocate action

- Its operating cost will be 39% less expensive than for electric heating, and 30% less expensive than for gas-fired forced hot-air heating.

- It will provide a softer, less obtrusive, and more stable source of warmth than either electric or hot-air heating.

- It can be controlled separately for each area of the building.

- It can be designed and installed as an integral part of the new structure and thus be less obtrusive.

The chief disadvantage is that its installation cost will be 77% higher than for an electric heating system, and 22% higher than for a gas-fired forced hot-air system.

Conclusions may, however, *imply* the course to be taken

However, in the long term, the combined installation and operating cost of radiant energy heating becomes less than that of electric heating in 17 months, and less than that of forced hot-air heating in 38 months.

Recommendation

Viewing Hartwell Enterprises' move into a new building as a long-term venture, we recommend installing a radiant energy heating system to take advantage of the long-term low operating expenses it will incur.

References

The References section lists all written and spoken information sources

1. Lawrence V Drake, *Radiant Panel Heating and Cooling*. Report: Radiant Panel Association, Hyrum, Utah, 1995, p 3.
2. Darryl Berkowski, D & M Innovators, Winnipeg, Manitoba. Email to Karen Woodhouse, H L Winman and Associates, December 10, 2007.
3. Drake, p 2.
4. Berkowski, p 2.
5. Drake, p 4.
6. Vincent Harding, *Comparison of Costs: Electric, Gas, and Radiant Energy Heating in 30 Industrial Buildings, 1999–2004*. Report: V Harding Associates, London, Ontario, February 23, 2005.

10

Placing a detailed table
like this within the
report narrative would
distract a reader's
attention

Appendix

Comparison of Costs: Three Heating/Cooling Systems
for Hartwell Enterprises Ltd

Heating/Cooling System	Installation Cost ($)	Annual Operating Cost ($)	First Year Costs ($)	Cumulative Three-Year Costs ($)	Cumulative Five-Year Costs ($)
Radiant Energy:					
• Heating	47 200	17 300			
• Air-Conditioning	21 600	3 500			
Combined Systems:	**68 800**	**20 800**	**89 600**	**131 200**	**172 800**
Electric Heat:					
• Heating	26 600	31 700			
• Air-Conditioning	21 600	3 500			
Combined Systems:	**48 200**	**35 200**	**83 400**	**153 800**	**224 200**
Gas-fired Forced Hot Air:					
• Heating	} 38 700	27 600			
• Air-Conditioning		3 500			
Combined Systems:	**38 700**	**31 100**	**68 700**	**130 900**	**193 100**

show the advantages and disadvantages of radiant energy heating but do *not* advocate what action should be taken. Karen has taken care not to introduce new information into her Conclusions.

- The Recommendation advocates action and does so in strong definite terms, using "We recommend…" rather than "It is recommended…."

- The Appendix is a "landscape-view" page, and as such has been turned correctly so that the top of the appendix is on the left side of the page (see page 145).

Pyramidal Arrangement of Report Parts
(Conclusions and Recommendations *before* the Discussion)

A way to address three different levels of reader within a single document

In recent years, more and more report writers have altered the organization of their reports so they more effectively meet their readers' needs. The pyramidal arrangement brings the conclusions and recommendations forward, positioning them immediately after the introduction, so that busy readers do not have to leaf through the report to find the terminal summary (the report's outcome). The advantages of the pyramidal approach are immediately evident: readers have only to read the initial pages to learn the main points contained in the report, and the writer can help them along by gradually increasing the technical content of the report, catering to semitechnical executive readers up to the end of the recommendations, and to fully technical readers in the discussion and appendix. Although the natural flow of information that occurs in the traditional arrangement is disrupted, Figure 6-7 shows there is now a reader-oriented flow, with the three compartments each containing progressively more technical details.

A bird's-eye view showing the pyramidal arrangement of report parts is illustrated in Figure 6-8. Segments of a sample report written using the pyramidal approach are shown in Figure 6-9 on page 149.

Three reports in one, each a complete story in itself

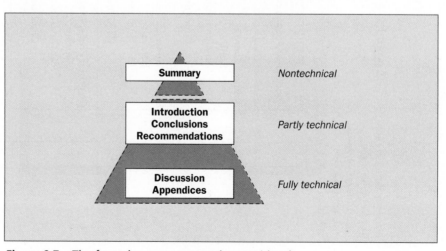

Figure 6-7   The formal report arranged pyramid style.

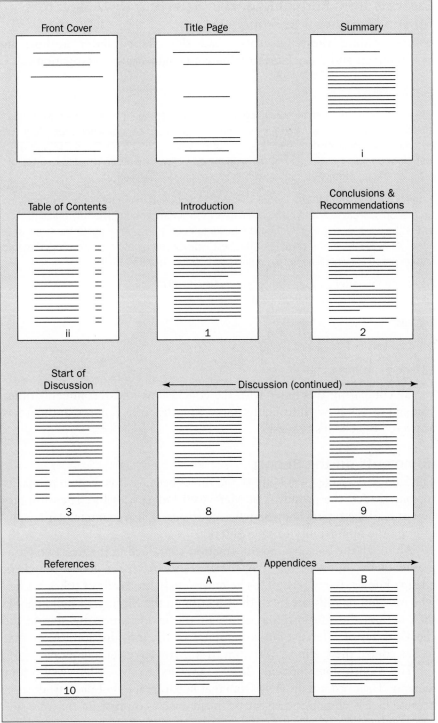

Compare this arrangement with the bird's-eye view in Figure 6-3 on page 127

Figure 6-8   Formal report—pyramidal arrangement (These represent the pages of Formal Report 2; to conserve space, some of the Discussion pages have been omitted.)

Excerpts from Formal Report 2: Selecting New Elevators for the Merrywell Building

Before reading these excerpts, read the client's letter authorizing H L Winman and Associates to initiate an engineering investigation:

Dear Mr Bailey

The elevators in the Merrywell Building are showing their age. Recently we have experienced frequent breakdowns and, even when the elevators are operating properly, it has become increasingly evident that they do not provide adequate service at the start of work, at noon, and at the end of the working day. I have therefore decided to install a complete range of new elevators, with work starting in mid-August.

The report writer used some of these words in the Introduction on page 150

Before I proceed any further, I would like you to conduct an engineering investigation for me. Specifically, I want you to evaluate the structural condition of my building, assess the elevator requirements of the building's occupants, investigate the types of elevators available, and recommend the best type or combination of elevators that can be purchased and installed within a proposed budget of $950 000.

Please use this letter as your authority to proceed with the investigation. I would appreciate receiving your report by the end of June.

Regards

David P Merrywell, President

Merrywell Enterprises Ltd

By comparing this letter with the conclusions and recommendations, you can assess how thoroughly Barry Kingsley (the report's author) has answered the client's requests.

Comments on the Report

The Summary (page 149) is short and direct because it is written primarily for one reader: the president of Merrywell Enterprises Inc. It encourages him to read the report immediately, and to accept its recommendations, by offering the opportunity to save $60 000.

Although the background information contained in the first two paragraphs of the Introduction (page 150) seems to repeat details the client already knows, Barry recognizes he must satisfy the needs of other readers who may not be fully aware of the situation in the Merrywell Building. He then defines the purpose and scope of the investigation by stating the client's terms of reference in paragraph 3 of the introduction. (Note that he has copied them almost verbatim from Mr Merrywell's letter.)

A report may be directed to one reader, but also must consider other readers who may see it

The Conclusions present Barry's answers to Mr Merrywell's four requests. Their order is different from that in paragraph 3 of the Introduction because he has chosen to present the main conclusion first (in this case, the best combination of elevators that can be purchased within the stipulated budget), and to follow it with subsidiary conclusions in descending order of importance. Barry is aware that when using the pyramidal report format he must write conclusions that evolve naturally and logically from the introduction, *because his readers have not yet read the discussion.*

   (Comments are continued on page 154)

H L WINMAN AND ASSOCIATES

Summary

The elevators in the 71-year-old Merrywell Building are to be replaced. The new elevators must not only improve the present unsatisfactory elevator service, but must do so within a purchase and installation budget of $950 000.

Of the many types and combinations of elevators considered, the most satisfactory proved to be four 2.45 × 2.15 metre deluxe passenger elevators manufactured by the YoYo Elevator Company, one of which will double as a freight elevator during off-peak traffic times. This combination will provide the fast, efficient service requested by the building's tenants for a total price of $890 000, which will be 6.3% less than the projected budget.

A simple, straight-forward summary that answers the readers' most immediate question

Figure 6-9 Formal Report 2: pyramidal arrangement (5 pages of excerpts from a 16-page report).

Selecting New Elevators for the Merrywell Building

Introduction

When in 1974 Merrywell Enterprises Ltd purchased the Wescon property in Montrose, Alberta, they renamed it "The Merrywell Building" and renovated the entire exterior and part of the interior. The building's two manually operated passenger elevators and a freight elevator were left intact, although it was recognized that eventually they would have to be replaced.

The Introduction, Conclusions, and Recommendations stand alone as a composite section

Recently the elevators have been showing their age. There have been frequent breakdowns and passengers have become increasingly dissatisfied with the inadequate service provided at peak traffic hours.

In a letter dated April 27, 2007, to H L Winman and Associates, the president of Merrywell Enterprises Ltd stated his company's intention to purchase new elevators. He authorized us to evaluate the structural condition of the building, to assess the elevator requirements of the building's occupants, to investigate the types of elevators that are available, and to recommend the best type or combination of elevators that can be purchased and installed within the proposed budget of $950 000.

Conclusions

The primary conclusion comes first, followed by subsidiary conclusions

The best combination of elevators that can be installed in the Merrywell Building will be four deluxe 2.45 × 2.15 metre passenger models, one of which will serve as a dual-purpose passenger/freight elevator. This selection will provide the fast, efficient service desired by the building's tenants and will be able to contend with any foreseeable increase in traffic. Its price at $890 000 will be 6.3% less than the proposed budget.

Installation of special elevators requested by some tenants, such as a full-size freight elevator and a small but speedy executive elevator, would be feasible but costly. A freight elevator would restrict passenger-carrying capability, while an executive elevator would elevate the total price to at least 20% above the proposed budget.

The quality and basic prices of elevators built by the major manufacturers are similar. The YoYo Elevator Company has the most attractive quantity price structure and provides the best maintenance service.

1

The building is structurally sound, although it will require some minor modifications before the new elevators can be installed.

Recommendations

We recommend that four Model C deluxe 2.45 × 2.15 metre passenger elevators manufactured by the YoYo Elevator Company be installed in the Merrywell Building. We further recommend that one of these elevators be programmed to provide express passenger service to the top four floors during peak traffic hours, and to serve as a freight elevator at other times.

Recommendations should be written in the first person, singular or plural

2

Evaluating Building Condition

The Discussion tells the reader the building is in good shape...

We have evaluated the condition of the Merrywell Building and find it to be structurally sound. The underpinning done in 1985 by the previous owner was completely successful and there still are no cracks or signs of further settling. Some additional shoring will be required at the head of the elevator shaft immediately above the 9th floor, but this will be routine work that the elevator manufacturer would expect to do in an old building.

The existing elevator shaft is only 7.5 metres wide by 2.5 metres deep, which is unlikely to be large enough for the new elevators. We have therefore investigated relocating the elevators to a different part of the building, or enlarging the existing shaft. Relocation, though possible, would entail major structural alterations and would be very expensive. Enlarging the elevator shaft could be done economically by removing a staircase that runs up the centre of the building immediately east of the shaft. This staircase is used very little and its removal would not conflict with fire regulations. Removal of the staircase will widen the elevator shaft by 3.35 metres, which will provide sufficient space for the new elevators.

Establishing Tenants' Needs

To establish the elevator requirements of the building's tenants, we asked a senior executive of each company to answer the questionnaire attached as Appendix A. When we had correlated the answers to all the questionnaires, we identified five significant factors that would have to be considered before selecting the new elevators. (There were also several minor exceptions that we did not include in our analysis, either because they were impractical or because they would have been too costly to incorporate.) The five major factors were:

...and then goes on to assess what needs to be done

- Every tenant stated that the new elevators must eliminate the lengthy waits that now occur. We carried out a survey at peak travel times and established that passengers waited for elevators for as much as 70 seconds. Since passengers start becoming impatient after 32 seconds,[1] we estimated that at least three, and probably four, faster passenger elevators would have to be installed to contend with peak-hour traffic.

- Although all tenants occasionally carry light freight up to their offices, only Rad-Art Graphics and Design Consultants Limited considered that a freight elevator would be essential. However, both agreed that a separate

3

freight elevator would not be necessary if one of the new passenger elevators is large enough to carry their displays. They initially quoted 2.75 metres as the minimum width they would require, but later conceded that with other modifications they could reduce the length of their displays to 2.3 metres. All tenants agreed that if a passenger elevator is to double as a freight elevator, they would restrict freight movements to non-peak travel times.

- The three companies occupying the top four floors of the building requested that one elevator be classified as an express elevator serving only the ground floor and floors 6, 7, 8, and 9. Because these companies represent more than 50% of the building's tenants, we considered their request should be entertained.

- Three companies expressed a preference for deluxe elevators. Rothesay Mutual Insurance Company, Design Consultants Limited, and Rad-Art Graphics all stated that they had to create an impression of business solidarity in the eyes of their clients, and felt that deluxe elevators would help convey this image.

- The managements of Rothesay Mutual Insurance Company and Vulcan Oil and Fuel Corporation requested that a small key-operated executive elevator be included in our selection for the sole use of top executives of the building's major tenants. We asked other companies to express their views but received only marginal interest. The consensus seemed to be that an executive elevator would have only limited use and the privilege would too easily be abused. However, we retained the idea for further evaluation, even though we recognized that an executive elevator would prove costly in relation to passenger usage.[2]

We decided that the first two of these factors are requirements that must be implemented, while the latter three are preferences that should be incorporated if at all feasible. The controlling influence would be the budget allocation of $950 000 stipulated by the landlord, Merrywell Enterprises Ltd. In decreasing order of importance, the requirements are:

1. Passenger waiting time must be no longer than 32 seconds.
2. At least one elevator must be able to accept freight up to 2.3 metres long.
3. An express elevator should serve the top four floors.
4. The elevators should be deluxe models.
5. A small private elevator should be provided for company executives.

Identifying users' needs helps establish clear criteria

4

(The sample stops here; there were 12 more pages in the original report.)

Barry uses the first person plural to open his Recommendations because, although he alone is the report's author, he is representing H L Winman and Associates' views to the client.

We have included the first two pages of the Discussion to show that, early in his report, Barry establishes the criteria that will influence how he selects a combination of elevators that will best meet his client's needs. By carefully identifying the five criteria and describing why each is valid, he shows his readers the direction his report will take. (In later sections of his report—not included in the sample pages—he identifies various combinations of elevators that could be installed, and demonstrates which ones meet the criteria, until he finally reaches an optimum configuration.)

ASSIGNMENTS

Project 6.1: Testing Highway Marking Paints

For the past six years the Department of Highways in your province has used "Centrex CL" for marking highway pavement centrelines and lanes. Recent advances in paint technology, however, have brought several new products onto the market, which their manufacturers claim are better than Centrex CL. To meet this challenge, Centrex Inc has developed a new paint ("TL") and has recommended that the Department of Highways use it in place of CL.

In a letter dated March 18 of this year, senior provincial highways engineer Morris Hordern commissioned you to carry out independent tests of the new paints. (You own a home-based consulting company known as Pro-Active Consultants Limited.) You start your project by obtaining samples of white and yellow highway paint from six manufacturers, transferring the samples into unmarked cans and then coding the cans as shown in Table 6-3A.

You then place the coding list into a sealed envelope, and lock it away in a safety deposit box at a local bank.

You decide to paint sample stripes on two regularly travelled stretches of highway and to assess the samples in four ways:

1. Spraying characteristics
2. Drying time
3. Visibility after three months
4. Visibility after six months

You assess spraying characteristics as excellent, very good, good, fair, and poor. The ratings are:

Very good:	WA,	WB,	WC,	WD,	WF,	YL,	YR
Good:	WE,	WG,	YM,	YN,	YO,	YQ	
Fair:	YP						

Table 6-3A Coding of paint cans.

	Manufacturer	Paint Coding	
		White	Yellow
1.	Centrex Inc, Truro, Nova Scotia Paint type: CL (the "old" paint)	WA	YL
2.	Novell Paint Ltd, Guelph, Ontario Paint type: 909	WB	YM
3.	Hi-Liner Products, Winnipeg, Manitoba Paint type: HILITE	WC	YN
4.	Multiple Industries Corporation, Calgary, Alberta, Paint type: MICC	WD	YO
5.	Wishart Incorporated, Thunder Bay, Ontario, Paint type: ROADMARK 13	WE	YP
6.	Provincial Paint Company, Saskatoon, Saskatchewan, Paint Type: 81-238	WF	YQ
7.	Centrex Inc, Truro, Nova Scotia Paint type: TL (their "new" paint)	WG	YR

New technology creates new products for evaluation

You assess drying time in minutes:

WA:16	WC:18	WE:14	WG:19	YM:26	YO:14	YQ:12
WB:33	WD:11	WF:13	YL:13	YN:18	YP:10	YR:15

Some factors demand personal judgment, others are measurable

After three months you assess visibility by day and by night. You use five drivers (you are one) to rate the stripes independently and to place the stripes' visibility on a scale of 1 to 10. You then average the five assessments (night readings are taken with headlights at high beam) and record them in Table 6-3B.

After another three months the same drivers again assess stripe visibility, with the results shown in Table 6-3C.

You consolidate your results into two tables, one for white paint, one for yellow paint, and then

You will need to create two comparison tables before writing your report

- reject any unacceptable paints (see guidelines below),
- rank acceptable paints in order of suitability,
- identify the best paint(s) to use for highway marking,
- retrieve the paint coding list from the bank deposit box, and
- write your report.

Some factors you use to conduct your study and to write your report are:

- Provincial senior highways engineer Morris Hordern's office address is 416 Inkster Building, 2035 Perimeter Road of your city.
- The paint stripes were painted on two stretches of highway:
  - Highway 26 (concrete surface), 1.7 kilometres north of the intersection with Highway 431.

Table 6-3B Three-month paint check.

Paint	Concrete Pavement		Asphalt Pavement	
Code	Day	Night	Day	Night
WA	8	8	8	9
WB	7	8	7	7
WC	8	9	10	9
WD	9	9	7	8
WE	7	6	7	8
WF	8	9	9	10
WG	7	7	7	8
YL	8	9	9	9
YM	7	7	7	9
YN	7	9	7	8
YO	8	8	7	8
YP	7	8	6	8
YQ	5	6	4	6
YR	9	10	9	9

Table 6-3C Six-month paint check.

Paint	Concrete Pavement		Asphalt Pavement	
Code	Day	Night	Day	Night
WA	6	6	5	7
WB	4	5	5	5
WC	8	8	9	9
WD	6	7	6	8
WE	6	5	6	7
WF	5	7	5	6
WG	6	7	6	7
YL	6	7	7	8
YM	6	7	6	8
YN	6	7	6	7
YO	6	7	6	8
YP	3	4	4	5
YQ	2	3	3	4
YR	8	9	8	9

- Highway 431 (asphalt surface), 1.2 kilometres west of the intersection with Highway 26.
- The paint stripes are applied at night, between midnight and 6 a.m.
- To apply the stripes, you mount a paint stripe applicator on a small garden tractor.
- Paint Manufacturers' Association specification PMA-02-34B states that spraying characteristics for fast-drying highway paint should be at least "Good," and preferably "Very Good." To achieve "Very Good," the paint must flow smoothly and evenly without forming globules or dripping from the nozzle.
- You refer to specification ASTM D-711 to establish the maximum acceptable paint drying time, which is 20 minutes.
- Guidelines you give to the drivers assessing paint visibility are shown in Table 6-3D. You then average the five assessments.
- You establish minimum acceptable visibility levels for the paints to be:

After three months' traffic wear:	7
After six months' traffic wear:	6

These factors help establish acceptability criteria

Note: Calculate real dates for each stage of the study and quote them in your report.

Your assignment: Write the results of your paint evaluation as a formal report addressed to senior provincial highways engineer Morris Hordern. Your report should not only present the results of your tests, but also analyse them, draw conclusions, and make a recommendation.

Table 6-3D Guidelines for evaluating paint visibility.

	Distance Visible	
Rating	**Day**	**Night**
10	500 m	200 m
8	400 m	160 m
6	300 m	120 m
4	200 m	80 m
2	100 m	40 m

Project 6.2: Correcting a Noise Problem

Assume that today is March 3. This morning you receive a letter from Wendy Partridge, the area manager of Mirabel Realty. (You are the owner/manager of Pro-Active Consultants Limited, which you operate from your home.)

Dear (you)

As I mentioned when I telephoned last week, my staff have been complaining for the past three months that the noise level in our office is too high. They claim it is affecting their work and causing fatigue. I have noticed, too, that staff turnover has been higher lately.

Please look into the problem for me to determine whether their complaints are justified. If they are, will you suggest what can be done to remedy the problem, recommend the most suitable method, and include a cost estimate.

Sincerely

Wendy G Partridge

Area Manager, Mirabel Realty

Part 1

At 4:00 p.m. on March 3 you visit Mirabel Realty (the office is in room 210, on the second floor of the Fermore Building at 381 Conway Avenue of your city). You notice a background hum, which you consider to be caused by motors in the computers and printers. You are still there when the office staff quits at 4:30. After they go, you notice you can still hear the hum, but at a lower level.

You walk around the office with Wendy who, you suspect, is hoping for a positive report which she can use to prove to her staff that their complaints are imaginary. You notice that the hum does get significantly louder near the north wall of the office. Then suddenly it stops, or rather, dies away. The time is 4:45 p.m.

From Wendy you determine that

- Superior Giftware, a distributor of cheap imports, occupies the office next door (room 208), immediately north of Mirabel Realty.
- Their manager is Saul Ferguson.
- Wendy has talked to him about the noise, but she says he "was pretty hostile" and refused to admit his machines might be the cause.
- The Superior Giftware office quits work at 4:45 p.m. daily.

You arrange to take sound-level measurements on March 10. You want to identify how much of the noise is generated by equipment in the Mirabel Realty office, and how much by the company next door.

You consider that a visit to Superior Giftware is essential, since you suspect that the machines they use may be the problem. You want to know the sound levels on both sides of the wall between the two companies, to assess the extent of soundproofing you may want to recommend.

Assignment 1: Write to Saul Ferguson and ask for permission to carry out sound-level measurements in his office on March 10.

Part 2

It is now March 10, one week later. You take a Nabuchi Model 1300 sound-level meter with you and return to 381 Conway Avenue. You plan to measure sound levels at various locations in the Mirabel Realty office under four conditions:

- When both businesses are empty.
- When only Superior Giftware is working (4:30–4:45).
- When only Mirabel Realty is working (8:00–8:15).
- When both businesses are working.

You also plan to take readings in Superior Giftware's office.

You suspect the next-door neighbour is being defensive

Because Mr Ferguson has not replied to your letter, you telephoned him on March 9 to ask if you can take measurements in his office on March 10 to which he reluctantly agreed. When you visit Superior Giftware, you notice a packaging and sealing machine only 2.5 metres from the wall separating the two business offices.

You record the measurements you take (see Table 6-4) and compare them to the general ratings for office noise, which you obtain from City of Montrose standard SL2020, dated January 20, 2001. The recommended sound levels for an urban office are:

Quiet office: 30–40 dB
Average office: 40–55 dB
Noisy office: 55–75 dB

You note that the sound level in Mirabel Realty's office increases as you move toward the dividing wall between the two offices (see Figure 6-10).

You also notice there seem to be two components of noise in Mirabel Realty's office, some being transmitted through the air and some being transmitted through the structure (from Superior Giftware's machines, through the floor). When you place a hand on the walls or floor, you can feel the vibration. Floors in both offices are tiled.

You prepare your client for news she does not want to hear

Before leaving, you tell Wendy Partridge that there seems to be a noise problem, which can be corrected, but it may prove to be expensive.

Assignment 2: Summarize your findings in a brief progress report, which you will email to Wendy Partridge.

Part 3

It's now March 14 and you are considering possible ways to reduce the sound levels in Mirabel Realty's office:

You have several options, some of which can be used in tandem

1. You could erect a false wall, insulated internally with Corrugon, from floor to ceiling on Mirabel Realty's side of the wall between the two companies.
2. Black cork panels, 18 mm thick, could be glued on Mirabel Realty's side of the wall.

Table 6-4 Average sound levels, second floor, 381 Conway Avenue.

Location	Both Offices Working (dB)	Only Superior Working (dB)	Only Mirabel Working (dB)	No One* Working (dB)
Mirabel Realty				
A	74	73	48	27
B	71	69	51	27
C	66	65	50	27
D	64	61	52	26
E	63	59	51	28
F	59	53	49	26
G	54	49	44	28
Superior Giftware				
H	86	—	—	25
I	83	—	—	26

*Mostly air-conditioner noise.
Note: Measurements made with Nabuchi Model 1300 Sound-Level Meter set to "A" scale.

3. You could install carpeting throughout Mirabel Realty's office.
4. Superior Giftware's machine could be mounted on Vib-o-Rug (insulating rubber that eliminates transmission of vibration from machine to building structure).

You recognize that remedies 1 and 2 are alternatives (they both deal with sound transmitted through the air). Remedies 3 and 4 are also alternatives (they both dampen vibrations and sound carried through the structure). Remedy 3 also quite effectively dampens internal office noise.

You consider the approximate costs:

Remedy 1: $9600
Remedy 2: $1760
Remedy 3: $16 400
Remedy 4: $1050

You consider possible problems each remedy may present:

Remedy 1. Corrugon is in short supply; delivery time would be a minimum of 3 months.

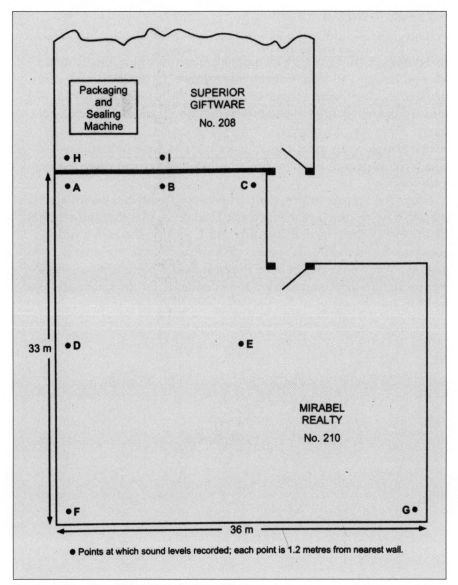

Figure 6-10 Plan of Mirabel Realty's office.

The packaging machine is the problem, but difficult to remedy at source

Remedy 2. Cork has an offensive smell; this can be partly corrected by treating the cork with Odoroff.

Remedy 3. The carpet must be dense and have a good quality rubber underlay (included in the approximate cost).

Remedy 4. Depends on cooperation of Superior Giftware's manager.

You calculate the probable sound-level reductions that could be achieved in Mirabel Realty's office:

Remedy 1: 6–10 dB
Remedy 2: 4–7 dB

Remedy 3: 8–12 dB
Remedy 4: 3–5 dB

Assignment 3: Consider which alternative(s) you will recommend to Mirabel Realty, and then write an investigation report describing your findings and suggesting corrective measures. Remember that Wendy will forward the report to her head office for authorization of the expenditure.

Assignment 4: Also write a brief cover letter to Wendy Partridge in which you very briefly summarize your key findings and corrective measures.

Note: You prepare a *formal* report because Wendy has mentioned that she will have to convince managers at head office that they must authorize the cost of the remedial measures. And, because she knows little about noise and its effects, you decide to include some explanatory information. (You would also be wise to research and document such information at a library, to establish positive evidence for the statements you make in your report.)

Chapter 7
Technical Proposals

Technical proposals can vary broadly. They can be short and informal or long and very formal, and fall into three general categories:

An **informal proposal** offers an idea and discusses why it should be implemented. Most often it is circulated only within an organization and is usually written as an email or a memo. The writer believes there is a better way to do something and proposes that the idea be implemented. Typical informal proposals might be

In an informal proposal you can comfortably use the first person: "I"

- a plan to introduce a new software-driven electronic calibration system throughout the company,
- a proposal to research local resources for replacement equipment components, rather than importing them, or
- a request to attend a conference (a request often is a proposal).

A **semiformal proposal** also offers an idea and suggests that it be implemented, but is sent at management level within an organization or between one organization and another. It can range from a 1-page letter to a 30-page (or longer) document prefaced by a title page and executive summary. It may suggest ways to increase productivity, provide a service, or resolve a problem, or may recommend conducting research. Typical semiformal proposals might

Here, "We" is more prevalent

- propose researching new office space to alleviate crowded conditions in a company,
- offer specialist consulting services to a potential client,
- suggest amalgamating company departments, to provide a more efficient and cost-effective management structure, or
- recommend providing field crews with portable computers that have integral wireless transmission capabilities.

A **formal proposal** normally is a large, often multiple-volume document designed to impress to the government or a major organization that the proposing company has the capability to carry out an important, often multi-million-dollar task or project. Such proposals are substantial because they describe in detail what will be done, how it will be done, who will be responsible for specific aspects of the work, and why the proposing

"We" is also common here, to maintain a confident active voice company has the potential to complete the project on time, within budget, and to the client's satisfaction.

Formal proposals are usually prepared in response to a Request for Proposal (RFP) that defines exactly how they are to be organized and what must be covered in the proposal. They are always accompanied by a cover letter or letter of transmittal, which often acts as an executive summary. A formal proposal might

- suggest to a city that it develop a deep-water holding pond to over-come an overloaded drainage system and flooding following heavy rainfalls,
- propose to a bank that it hire a consultant to research ways that will improve automatic teller services for customers, or
- recommend to the Department of Communications that it refurbish its mobile communications units.

In this chapter we will focus on writing informal and short semiformal proposals, which are the types you are most likely to encounter during your first years in industry.

Overall Writing Plan

All proposals, regardless of their length, contain the following parts:

- A **summary** that describes briefly what is being proposed and identi-fies any significant factors (such as cost).
- **Background** information that outlines the circumstances that have caused the proposal to be prepared.
- Definitive **details** that describe what needs to be done, how it will be done, what the results will be, and why the proposing company is capable of doing the job. This is the body of the proposal.
- An **action statement** that requests approval to go ahead (for an in-house proposal), or make a decision (for a client who will buy the services being offered).
- **Attachments** or **appendices** that contain detailed evidence to support statements made in the body of the proposal (appropriate for most semiformal proposals; not always present in informal proposals).

On the following pages we will demonstrate how to alter these five writ-ing compartments to suit different proposal configurations.

The overall writing plan is similar to that for semiformal reports

Short Informal Proposal

Marina writes with con-fidence, and it shows

The plan in Figure 7-1 was used by Marina Albrecht to organize the pro-posal in Figure 7-2. It is an in-house proposal because Marina is writing only to her manager, Karen LePage. We have inserted the label for each writing compartment beside the proposal to demonstrate how it was con-structed (they were not shown beside the original document).

Summary	A brief statement that describes what you want to do, or what you want done.
Introduction	The circumstances leading up to the situation that caused you to write the proposal (the **Background** and **Reason**).
Proposal Details	A carefully developed description, in two parts: • **Suggestion:** The proposed changes or improvements, why they are necessary, and what they will cost. • **Evaluation:** An assessment of the viability of the proposed changes and the effect they will have, including any problems that will evolve and how they will be overcome.
Action	A firm statement identifying what you want done, when, and by whom.
Attachments	Supporting data, such as drawings, plans, cost estimates, and spreadsheets. *(This compartment is optional.)*

Figure 7-1   Writing plan for a short informal proposal.

Longer Informal or Short Semiformal Proposal

Marina has written what is known as a single-solution proposal, a proposal that offers only one way to do something. However, there are times when you may want to describe alternative solutions, to demonstrate to the reader that you have considered a number of options, one of which you propose should be adopted.

For example, Terence Watkinson is the Chief Executive Officer (CEO) of a successful and rapidly growing business that develops innovative computer software for controlling and routing shipments for the trucking industry. At a recent managers' meeting, it was decided that the company would have to find larger space. Terence instructed Wally Meyers, the company's office manager, to research a suitable building and prepare a proposal to present to the next management meeting.

Wally found three suitable locations in different parts of the city, each with different advantages. Although he could have selected what he considered the best site and proposed just that to management, he chose also to present the alternative sites because he knew some of the managers had fixed opinions on where the building should be, and he particularly needed to persuade them that another site would be better. The writing plan Wally used to organize his proposal is shown in Figure 7-3.

Several factors affect how you write a proposal that offers alternative solutions:

Satisfy your readers' curiosity

Peterborough Environmental Consultants

To: Karen LePage, Office Manager
From: Marina Albrecht, Project Engineer
Date: March 5, 2008
Re: Proposal to Change to Recycled Copy Paper

Summary Statement

When the current supply of regular office copier paper is exhausted, I propose that we change to recycled paper. The cost will be marginally higher, but our company will be seen to be following the advice we give our customers.

Reason/ Background

This is exactly the right moment to make the change. The Canadian public has become increasingly sensitive to the damage being done to the environment by extensive use of paper manufactured from Canada's timber resources. We will not only make a contribution by using recycled paper, but also can use that fact when proposing that other companies do the same. Coincidentally, we will be changing to a Canadian-made product.

Strong, definite statements...

Details: Suggestion

The paper we have used for the past four years is 20 lb Westburn stock, which is imported from Dayton, Ohio, by Manor Industries Inc of Toronto, Ontario. (Our two other offices have similar arrangements with local distributors of imported paper products.) The recycled paper I am proposing is 20 lb Environ stock manufactured by Repap Canada Ltd in Thunder Bay, Ontario.

Details: Evaluation

I bought 1000 sheets of Environ stock and tested them on a trial basis. I found the following:

- The Environ paper fed as well as the Westburn paper and experienced no paper jams.
- The Environ paper appears very slightly coarser than the Westburn paper, and is slightly less white, but the print image is the same quality.
- 1000 sheets of Environ paper are 1.5 mm thicker than the same quantity of Westburn paper, but that does not affect printing or handling.
- The cost of the Environ paper is $66.95 per 5000 sheets, compared with $59.95 for the Westburn paper.

...and the first-person active voice...

I have discussed the possibility of obtaining a discount from Repap Canada in Thunder Bay, and they have agreed that, providing we contract to bulk-purchase all our copy paper from them for one year, for our offices in Winnipeg and Vancouver as well as Peterborough, they will give us a 10% discount. This will result in a purchase price of $60.26 per 5000 sheets, which is only $0.31 more per 5000 than we are currently paying.

Action Statement

I propose that we use Environ recycled copy paper on a 12-month trial basis. May I have your approval by March 25 to place an order with Repap Canada Ltd of Thunder Bay, for deliveries to start May 1, 2008?

...help convince the reader the idea is valid

Figure 7-2 A short informal proposal prepared for an in-house audience.

Summary	A synopsis of the proposal's key points, which identifies the proposal's purpose, main advantages, result, and cost.
Introduction	A description of the situation, condition, or problem that demands attention, and the circumstances leading up to it. This part represents the **Background** and **Reason**.
Proposal Details	The **Details** section is the body of the proposal. It should open with a brief statement that identifies the overall approach. It is then divided into four subcompartments:
Objective	• The **Objective** defines what needs to be achieved to improve the situation or condition, or resolve the problem, and establishes the **Criteria** that must be met.
Proposed Solution	• The **Proposed Solution** offers what the writer considers to be the best way to achieve the objective. It includes a full description of the solution, the expected result or improvement, its advantages, and its cost.
Alternative Solutions	• The **Alternative Solutions** section describes other ways that the objective can be met. Each alternative addresses the same topics as those covered for the proposed solution.
Evaluation	• The **Evaluation** analyses each solution and compares it against the criteria for an optimum solution established in the Objective. The solutions should be compared only against the criteria, never against each other.
Action	The **Action Statement** recommends what action needs to be taken. It is often titled **Recommendation** and must be written in strong, confident terms.
Attachments	The **Evidence** or **Supporting Data** contains drawings, cost analyses, spreadsheets, etc, that establish the validity of statements made in the body of the proposal.

Avoid saying or implying that this is the best solution...

...let the facts speak for themselves

Figure 7-3 Writing plan for a longer informal proposal or short semiformal proposal.

1. When you establish the criteria that will be used to evaluate the different alternatives, you must "prove" any criterion the reader might question. If Wally writes, "We will need a minimum of 'X' square metres of office space immediately, and another 'Y' square metres within two years," he needs to recognize that not every member of the management committee may be aware of the space requirements. He must explain ("prove") why the figures are valid.

2. When you present your proposed and alternative solutions, you must prevent your opinions from intruding. For example, Wally must present only *facts* about each property, and comment neither on its advantages or disadvantages (that will be done in the evaluation section).

Show you have anticipated your readers' questions

Nor must he compare one property against other properties. His readers must feel he is completely objective.

3. When presenting alternative solutions, to avoid confusing your readers you need to present the facts about each alternative *in the same sequence* that you presented that information for the proposed solution. This means Wally must describe the availability, age, condition, accessibility, and cost of each property in exactly the same order.

Maintain your objectivity until you make your recommendation

4. When writing the evaluation, compare the solutions *only* against the criteria.

5. Be positive when writing the action statement: use the active-voice expression "I recommend..." or "We recommend..." rather than the passive-voice expression "It is considered that..." or "It is recommended that...."

When Meridian Engineering Consultants of Thunder Bay decided to provide courses in technical writing for their staff, they inserted a Request for Proposal (RFP) as a display advertisement in *The Globe and Mail* (see Figure 7-4). One of the companies submitting a proposal was Online Writing Trainers Ltd (OWTL) of Winnipeg, Manitoba. The proposal was written by Arlene Tetrault, OWTL's projects manager, and is shown in Figure 7-5.

Arlene started by listing the advantages of each of the three training methods she would present, and then made in-depth calculations of the cost for each. This showed her that, because the costs were so close, they would not be a governing factor in MEC's choice. She was then able to

---

MEC   Call for Proposals

Provision of Training Services:
Writing Technical Letters, Email, Reports and Proposals

MEC is soliciting proposals from innovative training consultants to provide courses in technical writing for our 120-person staff, 80% of whom are engineers and engineering technologists working primarily in Civil and Structural Engineering, Information Technology, and the Environmental Sciences. The training is to cover letter, email, report and proposal writing, and include methods for sharpening individual writing style.

The training is to start January 15, 2008, and be completed by March 31, 2008. Vendors are to provide three copies of their technical and cost proposal by noon on Wednesday, October 31, 2007, marked RFP 3/014. Late proposals will not be accepted.

Meridian Engineering Consultants Ltd
334 Willows Avenue, Thunder Bay, Ontario, P7B 3X6

Figure 7-4 The Request for Proposal (RFP) that prompted Online Writing Trainers Ltd to prepare the proposal in Figure 7-5.

concentrate on the advantages that each method offered from the MEC learners' point of view.

The design of the proposal, with headings in a narrow column on the left and the text in a wider column on the right, is an effective application of information design principles. Readers can readily see how Arlene has structured her ideas, and can find information easily. The headings also parallel the labels in the writing compartments shown in Figure 7-3. Here are some additional comments on the proposal:

Encourage readers so they *want* to read your words

- The paragraph in the centre of page 1 is Arlene's **Summary**, in which she identifies the preferred training method she recommends and lists its cost. Many people hesitate to state the cost in the Summary, fearing that readers may not continue reading if they feel the cost is too high. We believe it should be there, because it is the first question readers are likely to ask, so they will search for it and be irritated if they find it has been buried far down in the proposal.

- The first paragraph of the Introduction provides the **Background**, which sets the scene for the information to follow. Arlene draws much of this information from the RFP in Figure 7-4.

- The paragraph at the foot of page 1 provides a quick statement that identifies OWTL's capacity to handle the project. Arlene keeps it short, placing the detailed information in an attachment.

- By listing the **Objectives** (on page 2), Arlene identifies the factors she will use to evaluate the three methods. In Objective 1, she lists the topics that need to be taught. She divides them into two groups to suit the two different groups of employees, which she identifies in Objective 2. She drew Objectives 3, 4, and 5 from MEC's RFP.

- The **Proposed Solution** starts in the centre of page 2 and continues two-thirds of the way down page 3. Arlene presents only *facts*, without commenting on their value at this stage in the proposal.

Maintain your objectivity, almost to the end

- The two **Alternative Solutions** appear on pages 3 and 4. Each is shorter than the proposed solution, but the information is presented in the same sequence. Again, Arlene presents only facts.

- In the **Evaluation** of the three methods (page 5), Arlene compares each method against the Objectives she established on page 2. She starts by identifying the objectives met by all three methods, and then continues with comments on the advantages and disadvantages of each method. Here, she allows her (i.e. OWTL's) opinions to appear, for the first time in the whole proposal.

- The **Conclusions** present the outcome of the Evaluation, but Arlene only *suggests* which method MEC should select. Although Figure 7-3 labels this as an **Action Statement**, in which the writer normally makes a strong recommendation that the reader approve the proposal, Arlene chose to move her Action Statement into a cover letter to send with the proposal (see page 175).

Online Writing Trainers Ltd
Suite 200 – 450 Bridgeview Road
Winnipeg MB R2J 3M4

Proposal to Provide Training Services:
Writing Technical Letters, Email, Reports, and Proposals

Prepared for
Meridian Engineering Consultants Ltd
Thunder Bay, Ontario

In response to
MEC RFP 3/014
Proposal prepared October 26, 2007

Indent the summary on both sides to catch readers' attention

We have investigated three methods for providing training in letter, email, report and proposal writing for Meridian Engineering Consultants Ltd. The method we propose is a mix of web-based and traditional classroom-style learning. It will meet the needs of MEC staff who prefer electronic delivery and those who prefer more traditional instruction. The total cost at $51 400 is comparable to solely online or solely classroom instruction.

Introduction

Meridian Engineering Consultants Ltd (MEC) plans to upgrade its technical staff's ability to write effective letters, email, reports, and proposals. Training is to be conducted between January 15 and March 31, 2008, and is to include approximately 96 technical professionals and 24 support staff. MEC published a Request for Proposals (MEC RFP 3/014) in *The Globe and Mail* on October 10, 2007, calling for interested training consultants to submit training and cost proposals for providing the appropriate services.

Highlight company experience only very briefly here; focus on what your company can do for the reader

Online Writing Trainers Ltd (OWTL), of Winnipeg, Manitoba, has been providing onsite courses for engineering and other business organizations in Canada and the US since 1972, and in the UK since 1994 (see Attachment 1 for a detailed company description). To meet the growing demand by both North American and European businesses to access training over the internet, in 2001 we converted our onsite courses for electronic delivery. They are now available online from our corporate website.

1

Figure 7-5   A short semiformal proposal offering alternative solutions.

Objectives

We established the following requirements that must be met:

1. The training is to cover eight main subjects:

   Foundation Topics
   - Getting to the point (identifying and placing key information for immediate access)
   - Organizing the details (developing the remainder of the document)
   - Writing effective email
   - Sharpening language skills

   Advanced Topics
   - Writing business letters and memos
   - Writing short reports
   - Planning and writing formal reports
   - Planning and writing business and technical proposals

2. Technical staff are to receive training on both foundation and advanced topics. Support staff are to receive training only on the foundation topics.
3. The cost for the training must be comparable, whether delivered onsite or online, or in a blended format.
4. The training must be completed within a 2.5 month period, between January 15 and March 31, 2008.
5. The training must accommodate the schedules of technical staff who travel frequently.

Draw on the client's requirements to write the Objectives

Proposed Delivery Method
Blended Training

Our proposal offers a combination of onsite and online courses under a "blended" arrangement, with some portions of the training being taught online and other portions being taught onsite. The costs for implementing blended training will be slightly less than for traditional classroom training.

In the following discussion, we have relabelled the eight topics as four Foundation Courses and four Advanced Courses. See Attachment 2 for course descriptions.

The **online training** will be held first and will cover the four Foundation Courses, which will be taken by all staff. Because the program is maintained on OWTL's server, participants will not need to download the courses to their individual computers. They will also be able to access the courses from any computer at any location at any time. The system will record their progress and each time participants log on they will be taken immediately to the point where they stopped. There will be an examination at the end of each course, which will be evaluated electronically and the results reported to the participant.

Cover new technology or methods in detail

The **onsite training** will cover the four Advanced Courses, which will be presented at spaced intervals, after each person has completed the Foundation Courses online. Support staff will not take the Advanced Courses, because they normally do not write technical correspondence, reports and proposals.

2

Schedule

The **online segment**, comprising the four Foundation Courses, will be taken over a six-week period, between January 21 and February 25, 2008. The four courses require a total of 6 to 8 hours of study.

The **onsite segment**, comprising the four Advanced Courses, will be covered in a single 8-hour class, with a maximum of 12 participants in each class. To cover the 96 technical professionals, the classes will be held on eight separate days, four between March 1 and 4, and four between March 22 and 25. The spread of dates will allow for possible travel absences of engineering staff.

Jan		Feb				Mar				
21	28	04	11	18	28	03	10	17	24	30

120		*4*		*4*

| *Foundation courses* | *Advanced courses* |
| *(all online)* | *(8 onsite groups of 12)* |

Cost

The cost for providing courses under the blended approach will be $51 400. The cost covers provision of

Identify total cost and
what it covers in the
proposal; put detailed
costs in an attachment

- 120 individual IDs and passwords for participants to access the four Foundation Courses,
- 8 one-day onsite training sessions, to cover the four Advanced Courses, with 12 staff members attending each session,
- 2 instructors for each onsite course,
- evaluation of 2 assignments written by each onsite course participant, and
- instructors' travel and accommodation expenses.

In the online training mode, all eight courses will be taken electronically. Participants will be able to access the courses from any computer at any location and at a time convenient to themselves. The system will record their progress and each time participants log on they will be taken immediately to the point where they stopped. There will be an examination at the end of each course.

The 96 technical professionals will register for all eight courses, which will require approximately 14–16 hours of study. They will also write four assignments and submit them electronically to an OWTL instructor, who will return them with feedback.

The 24 support staff will register for the four Foundation Courses, which will require approximately 8 hours of study.

All participants will receive a copy of the course textbook, which will become a permanent resource for future reference.

3

OnlineTraining
(continued)

Schedule

The courses will be taken between January 15 and March 31, 2008. OWTL will monitor course progress and submit a report to MEC every two weeks. The reports will list those who have started, how far each person has progressed, and those who have completed their courses.

Cost

The cost for providing training online will be $49 220, which will include
- 120 individual IDs and passwords for participants to access the four Foundation Courses,
- 120 course textbooks,
- evaluation of four assignments submitted by each person completing courses 5 to 8, and
- submission of progress reports at two-week intervals.

Alternative Delivery Method
Onsite Training

Onsite training is traditional classroom training. We will present eight two-day workshops for the 96 technical professionals, and two one-day workshops for the 24 support staff, with 12 participants attending each workshop. Topics to be covered will include the following:

| 2-day workshop: | All 8 topics |
| 1-day workshop: | 4 foundation topics |

All participants will receive a copy of the course textbook and approximately 30 pages of additional notes. The workshops will be held on MEC's premises.

Schedule

The workshops will be presented in four timeframes to accommodate staff absences while on field assignment:

Dates	2-day Workshops	1-day Workshops
January 19–23	2	1
February 2–5	2	-
March 1–5	2	1
March 15–18	2	-

A table summarizes key points and draws readers' attention

Cost

The cost for providing the 10 workshops will be $52 520, which will include
- 2 instructors for each workshop,
- evaluation of four assignments completed by participants attending the two-day workshops,
- 120 course textbooks and course notes,
- instructors' travel and accommodation expenses.

4

All three of the proposed methods will provide the required depth of training established in the Objectives, can be completed within the required time frame, and will accommodate the schedules of technical staff who travel. The costs also are comparable:

Blended training	$51 400
(online and onsite)	
Solely online training	$49 220
Solely onsite training	$52 520

Identify where cost explanations can be found

The primary differences are in the delivery methods and individual participants' reaction to them. For a detailed cost analysis, see Attachment 3.

Blended Training will meet the needs of both types of course participant: those who prefer electronic instruction and those who prefer the interactive classroom environment. The more basic foundation topics will be taught online. The more intense advanced topics will be presented in person, which will provide participants with personal instruction and the opportunity to ask questions.

The Evaluation permits the writer to air her views

Solely **Online Training** will please participants who prefer privacy and the ability to study at their own time, pace and location. It will not, however, provide personalized instruction or the interactive environment that some participants prefer.

Solely **Onsite Training** will please participants who prefer to work face-to-face with an instructor and like the interactive environment in which they may ask questions and hear the questions of others. It will not, however, offer much flexibility because participants must attend at a fixed time.

Conclusions

Although all three methods will meet MEC's requirements, we consider that the blended training option will provide the flexibility MEC needs to train both technical and support staff, and will suit employees who often have to travel and work offsite.

Online Writing Trainers Ltd
26 October 2007

5

(Note: the three attachments are not printed here to conserve space in this edition of *Technically-Write!)*

Arlene's cover letter reads as follows:

Dear Contracts Manager

I am enclosing an Online Writing Trainers' proposal to present courses on writing technical letters, email, reports, and proposals to Meridian Engineering Consultants' staff, in response to MEC RFP 3/014. We recommend that Meridian Engineering Consultants adopt "Blended Instruction" as the preferred training method, which will be a combination of electronic and in-person delivery of the training. The cost will be $51 400, which is slightly less than for regular classroom-style training. Blended Instruction will also meet the needs of staff who prefer electronic delivery and those who prefer personal instruction.

Our corporate website at www.owtl.com provides a detailed description of Blended Instruction. Please call me at 204.488.1827 if you have further questions.

Sincerely

Arlene Tetrault

Contracts Manager
Online Writing Trainers Ltd

Student Project Proposal

Many technical students nearing the end of their education have to undertake a technical term project, sometimes working alone but more often working in teams. Although the instructor may assign a project to each team, there are times when the instructor invites each team to identify a technical problem and then write a proposal identifying how the team will tackle it. You can use the writing plan in Figure 7-6 to help you.

The plan shows that you cannot simply decide, without considerable forethought, that "We'll put two computers at different ends of the building and work out whether there is less information loss between them, using fibreoptic cable compared with RS-232 wire cable." That would make a good project, but before writing it up as a proposal you need to work out the amount of cable you will need, how you will get the computers, what software you will be using, how you will measure information loss at different frequencies, how long all this will take you, and so on. Only when you have "done your homework" and have the facts at your fingertips will you be ready to write the proposal.

This practical approach is particularly suited to college writing

The Language of Proposal Writing

There can be nothing wishy-washy about the language you use in a proposal. If you have organized your proposal using one of the writing plans shown in this chapter, you will provide a smooth flow of information. Now you must let your language convince your readers that you have a strong case to present. Here are four suggestions.

1. Present Only Essential Information

Before writing, divide all your information into two parts: (1) information the reader *must have* to make a decision (we call this the "Need-to-Know"

Summary	A brief outline of what you plan to do, and what doing it will achieve.
Background	Why the project needs to be tackled. Include historical information concerning the topic and identify the team members.
Proposal Plan	Describe how your project team will carry out the project. Provide the following information:
Details	• Your overall approach or plan. • Who (in your team) will be doing what. • Special equipment or parts you require (attach a list)

Project Schedule	• Identify the dates on which you plan to
	  > complete your research,
	  > finish the design,
	  > complete product construction, and
	  > complete testing and troubleshooting the product.

Reporting Schedule	• Identify the dates when you plan to
	  > submit progress reports,
	  > submit a topic outline for your project report,
	  > submit first draft sections for evaluation,
	  > complete the final project report, and
	  > present your oral report.

Action	Request approval to go ahead with the project.
Evidence	Provide supporting information to validate your plan, plus a list of materials or parts you will need.

Figure 7-6   Writing plan for a student project proposal.

This writing plan parallels how project proposals are written in industry

information); and (2) information that is of general interest but the reader *does not need* to make a decision (we call this the "Nice-to-Know" details). Often, because we know a project well, we tend to present everything we know because it interests us. Take a step back and look at your information from the potential readers' point of view.

2. Use the Active Voice

The active voice will make you sound firm and definite. Instead of writing:

> The two computers would be connected by means of a metal wire and a fibre-optic cable, whereas alternating from one cable to the other would be accomplished by a Model 1880 switching unit. *(Passive voice: 33 words)*

Write strongly and positively

Write:

> A wire and a fibreoptic cable will connect the two computers, while a Model 1880 switching unit will alternate between them. *(Active voice: 22 words)*

In addition to having 33% fewer words, the active voice makes the second writer sound much more confident and knowledgeable. (For more information on using the active voice, refer to Chapter 12.)

3. Avoid Wishy-Washy Words

Replace weak words like *would, could,* and *should* with a strong word like *will*. In the first example about the two cables, the word *would* occurs twice and creates only a "soft" impression (the reader may comment: "Well, I guess that might be okay."). In the second example, the word *would* has been replaced with *will,* creating a much more confident impression (the reader will feel like commenting: "Now that makes sense!")

You can make a similarly weak impression if you insert low-information-content expressions into your proposal. Examples are *bring to a conclusion* (use *concludes*), *in the direction of* (use *toward*), and *by means of* (use *by*). For an extensive list of such words, see the section on Low-Information-Content Expressions in Chapter 12.

A third damaging effect occurs if you write vague statements like *an adequate supply, got some help,* or *many tests will be attempted.* Whenever possible, use descriptive words that convey clear images, words such as *a three-week supply, two technicians helped us,* and *we will carry out thirty tests.*

Use words that convey a strong image

4. Avoid Giving Opinions

Experienced proposal writers know just when to insert an opinion or a subjective statement. As a beginning proposal writer, you will be much safer if you withhold your opinions until the end of the proposal, when you make your recommendation.

ASSIGNMENTS

Project 7.1:   Acquiring Handheld Computers

Assume that you are employed by the local branch of H L Winman and Associates, in a department related to the discipline you are studying—e.g. civil, mechanical, electrical, or computer engineering; biophysics; environmental science; etc. In your work, you and your associates have to travel frequently. Most of you use a portable (laptop) computer.

In the coming year's budget, the company has set $30 000 aside to purchase replacement laptops. However, you feel that a handheld computer such as a palm pilot would be more useful. You discuss the idea with your associates and many agree with you. You describe your idea to Tracey Harcourt, your department manager, who likes your idea and suggests you write a proposal she can take to the next Capital Budget meeting. She recommends that, in your proposal, you describe

Overcome readers' resist-
ance by anticipating
their questions

- why handheld computers would be of value to departmental staff,
- what you can do with a handheld computer, compared to a laptop,
- the advantages of a handheld computer, and
- how many should be purchased.

She also suggests you identify several different handheld computers, evaluate them, and propose that the company buy a specific brand.

Project 7.2: Building a Sunroom

You have friends living in a private home at... (provide the address of a
house you know in your community). Assume that you have had a discussion with these friends, during which you suggested that a sunroom
would be a useful addition to their house. They are doubtful, but you are
very persuasive until finally they say: "As you seem to be the expert, why
don't you get some information for us and *show* us why we should
install a sunroom, and what kind of sunroom would be best."

Now you need to take a more detailed look at the house and assess

- where, and off which room, the sunroom should be built,
- what size it should be,
- what zoning requirements apply,
- whether it should be a four-season or three-season sunroom,
- who makes and installs sunrooms, and what they have to offer, and
- what the cost will be.

You decide to write a semiformal proposal for your friends, in which
you describe what can be done and recommend the best approach and
supplier.

Project 7.3: Installing an Alternative Power Supply

You are a technician employed by H L Winman and Associates and currently you are engaged in a three-month project under contract to a
major client: Terrapin Control Systems. The project started seven weeks
ago and will run for another eight weeks. The difficulty is that over the
past four weeks you have twice experienced power outages that have
destroyed the tests for that particular day, which means you are now two
days behind schedule and there is no more time available if you are to
finish the project by the prescribed completion date. (If there is a delay
beyond that date, Terrapin Control Systems will impose a cost penalty of
$1000 per day.)

Each day you test two sets of switches, one of which is exposed to
extreme heat and the other is exposed to extreme cold. At the start of
each test the switches are placed in an oven or a freezer chamber, the
temperature is increased or decreased to an optimum level, and the
switches are made to operate continuously and automatically for four-
teen hours. To avoid the cost of having a technician present at night, you
have installed timers that shut off the chambers at a prescribed time each

night. The interruption by power outages means the switches have experienced nonstandard testing and have had to be discarded.

To prevent another power outage from affecting the tests, you realize you must have a backup power supply. Write a proposal to your manager, John Grayson, in which you recommend that the company either buy or lease a backup power supply. You will need to do some research to determine

- what types of power supply are available,
- what strength of power supply will be sufficient (to do this you may choose your own specifications),
- whether you will require one or two power supplies (one each for the oven and deepfreeze chamber),
- whether it will be more economical to purchase or to lease the power supply, and
- the cost of purchasing versus the cost of leasing.

In your proposal, describe the various power supplies that are available and compare them. Be ready, too, to counter a possible suggestion that it would be less expensive and more efficient to have a technician on site at night rather than buy or lease a backup power supply. Remember that a technician cannot prevent the power outage and so cannot prevent test degradation.

Project 7.4:   A Proposal to the Student Council

Write a proposal to the Student Council (or its equivalent) at your school or college, describing an innovative idea you have that you would like the council to implement. The idea may be one of the following:

1. A plan to set up a two-or-three-day skiing trip to one of the ski resorts nearest to your college, to be held during a mid-term or between-term break. Work out the details and use them to answer questions the Student Council is likely to ask, such as these:

    - When will it happen?
    - How much will it cost?
    - Where is the resort?
    - What lodgings are available, and at what cost?
    - What arrangements will be made to rent a coach, and at what cost?
    - Who will make all the arrangements?
    - How will it be marketed?

    Answer even more questions than are listed here

2. A plan to set up a money-making event that will generate funds for a charity (you choose which one). Identify an event that will be particularly visible and so promote the charity's need for funds. Propose that students taking part in the event obtain sponsors who promise to donate a specified amount if the student they sponsor completes an

activity such as a 50 km bicycle ride, a 20-lap swim, a 10 km hike, and so on. Describe why the charity is worth supporting, how the event will be organized, who will do the organizing, and how the event will be publicized, either through the school's internal media or to the general public.

3. A plan to clean up the neighbourhood around the school or college. From time to time there have been complaints from residents living on neighbouring streets that students drop gum and candy wrappers, looseleaf pages, cigarette packs and butts, and so on, as they walk to and from the local bus stop or their cars. The residents complain that the students' debris lowers the quality of the neighbourhood and reduces house values. Suggest that the Student Council

    -   set up cleanup crews who will regularly (once a week?) search the neighbouring streets for rubbish and collect it in large garbage bags, and
    -   send out a news release to the local media, to demonstrate that the College's/School's students are very conscious of the image they create and that they want to contribute actively to the neighbour-hood's environment.

    Be ready to counter remarks from the Student Council that the local residents contribute much of the garbage they are complaining about.

Develop your own idea for a project!

Alternatively, if you have a different idea you feel the Student Council should address, you may select it as your topic. Whatever topic you select, you must research it in sufficient depth so that you can write a confident proposal.

Chapter 8
Instructions and Procedures

This chapter describes how to write a user's manual and provides detailed guidelines for writing technical instructions and procedures.

User's Manual

Most manufacturers normally issue a user's manual with their products, which contains (1) a brief description of the product, (2) instructions on how to use it, and (3) suggestions for fixing problems that may occur. For qualified repair specialists they may also produce a set of maintenance instructions containing detailed service and repair procedures. Both publications perform the same task for different readers: user manuals assume the reader has only slight technical knowledge, while maintenance instructions assume the reader is a technical expert.

Identifying the Audience

The problem with many user guides is that they are written from an engineer's or a technical person's point of view and are often too complex or incomplete from the user's point of view. To avoid this, you need to identify your audience before you start writing, and understand their level of knowledge and experience with the product.

We often suggest to engineers that they write a brief description of who the user is, so they can refer back to it as they write. This audience analysis often becomes the first section in the user's guide, called "Who Should Read This Document."

The first step in *any* writing situation: know your audience

Writing Plan

The writing plan for most user manuals has four compartments, as shown in Figure 8-1. The two top compartments describe the product, and the two lower compartments tell the reader how to use it.

The following sections demonstrate how these four compartments are used. The product in this instance is electronic mail software.

Summary	What the product is, and what it does
Product Description	What the product consists of
Operating Instructions	How to use the product
Troubleshooting Techniques	How to remedy a problem

Figure 8-1   Writing plan for a user's manual.

Describing the Product

The **Summary** briefly describes the product and its main purpose:

> This electronic mail software allows you to communicate with other email users by sending and receiving messages. It allows you to connect to a remote computer, called a server, and access messages other people have sent to you. The server computer will also send any messages you have written to other people.

The **Product Description** identifies each part and describes its components. For equipment that has several discrete components or parts, the Product Description may be subdivided into two sections: Overview and Detailed Description.

- The Overview section simply lists the main components:

> The electronic mail program contains four components:
> - The In Tray
> - The Out Tray
> - The File Cabinet
> - The Address Book

List the components in the same sequence you will describe them

- The **Detailed Description** provides more specific information about each component *in the same sequence* that they were presented in the Overview section:

> The In Tray is identified by a square icon with an arrow pointing down. This indicates that messages are directed to you. Any messages that are sent to you are automatically placed in this area. You can view your messages in the In Tray by pointing your mouse on the icon and clicking.

> The Out Tray is identified by a square icon with an arrow pointing up. This indicates that messages are from you to someone else. This is the area where messages you have written are stored until you are ready to send them.

> The File Cabinet is identified by an icon that looks like a traditional two- or three-drawer filing cabinet you might find in an office. This is the area where you can store or file messages that are important or that you want to keep. You can create

different folders for different situations and thus create a filing system for your messages.

The Address Book is identified by an icon that looks like a small book. This is the area where you store the electronic addresses of people to whom you frequently send messages. When you write a message you can select the address of the person or persons you are sending it to directly from the Address Book.

Clear, simple language helps *all* readers understand

Using the Product

The **Operating Instructions** provide step-by-step instructions for each task the user can perform with the product. One of the major problems with many user manuals is that they are not written from the user's perspective: instead of describing *how* to do something with the product, the manual describes *what* can be done with it. Too often, writers jump right into writing the steps without determining what the reader will need. If you follow these three steps, your User's Manual will be user-oriented:

1. Perform a task analysis.
2. Group and label the tasks.
3. Write the steps for each task.

This is similar to the writing process described in Chapter 2 (Figure 2-3 on page 7).

Step 1—Perform a Task Analysis

When you have decided who your audience is, you need to list everything *they might want to do* with the product. Make sure you don't list everything *the product can do*. Instead, focus on the tasks the user will perform. For example, a task analysis for a simple electronic mailing package might look like this:

Tasks:

Sending messages	Deleting messages
Receiving messages	Creating messages
Forwarding messages	Connecting to the server
Addressing messages	Checking spelling
Printing messages	Attaching documents
Adding names to an address book	Installing
	Customizing
Storing messages in folders	Calling manufacturer for
Creating folders	support
Downloading messages	Using the Help system

When writing a task analysis, use verbs that end with "...ing" (*sending, receiving*, etc)

This list is developed while brainstorming and is not meant to be in any particular order. Later, you can add items; for now, just list the tasks.

Step 2—Group and Label Tasks

Looking at the above task list, you can see that certain items are related. For example, Receiving messages and Forwarding messages are related, just as Creating messages, Addressing messages and Checking spelling are. We suggest grouping the related topics and giving them a letter to identify each group. For example, in the following revised list, each task has been assigned a letter (A, B, C, etc) to show which group it belongs to.

Identify which tasks seem related

Tasks:	Groups:
Sending messages	F
Receiving messages	A
Forwarding messages	A
Addressing messages	B
Printing messages	C
Adding names to an address book	B
Storing messages in folders	A
Creating folders	A
Downloading messages	A
Deleting messages	A
Creating messages	B
Connecting to the server	F/A
Checking spelling	B
Attaching documents	F
Installing	D
Customizing	D
Calling manufacturer for support	E
Using the Help system	E

This becomes the first step toward organizing the information

Now you perform your first organizational step: to assign a label to each group. Choose a label that *describes what the user is doing* or is trying to accomplish with the tasks. Use "ing" words whenever you can in your labels, because they *indicate an action performed by the user.* Here are labels for the above groups:

A – Handling Incoming Messages
B – Writing Messages
C – Printing Messages
D – Getting Started
E – Getting Additional Help
F – Sending Messages

Now is the time to organize the groups of topics into a logical sequence for the intended audience. User manuals are usually structured in a sequential arrangement listing what needs to be done first, or by introducing easy tasks first. In this example the structure might look like this:

Getting Started *(D)*
    Installing Your Software
    Customizing Your Software

Writing Messages *(B)*
    Creating Messages
    Addressing Messages
    Adding Names to an Address Book

Sending Messages *(F)*
    Sending Messages You Have Written
    Connecting to the Server
    Attaching Documents

Handling Incoming Messages *(A)*
    Connecting to the Server
    Receiving Messages
    Forwarding Messages
    Creating Folders
    Storing Messages in Folders
    Downloading Messages
    Deleting Messages

Printing Messages *(C)*

Getting Additional Help *(E)*
    Using the Help System
    Calling the Manufacturer for Support

An outline emerges naturally, almost painlessly...

We now have a user-focused, task-oriented structure that describes how to use the product.

Step 3—Write the Steps

Each of the identified tasks now becomes an instruction, and you can write the steps it takes to accomplish each task. Here are two examples from the electronic mail tasks:

Installing Your Software

1. Unpack the contents of the box and make sure you have
    - this manual,
    - the CD, and
    - the software license.
2. Turn your computer on and start Windows.
3. Put the CD into your CD drive.
4. When the Install Wizard initiates, follow the directions on the screen.

...from which a logically flowing instruction can be written

Connecting to the Server

1. Click on the File menu.
2. Choose the Connect to Server command.
3. When a dialog box appears, enter your ID and password.

4. Click OK.

5. Wait while the system initiates the protocol sequence defined in the Server Settings dialog box.

6. When the message **You Are Now Connected** appears on screen, you have successfully connected to the remote server.

You can now send and receive your electronic mail messages.

Note that each step is short, has a number, and uses verbs in the imperative mood. (For more information on writing instructional steps, see "Give Your Reader Confidence" on pages 188 to 189 of this chapter.)

Troubleshooting Techniques tell the reader what to do if, having followed the Operating Instructions correctly, the equipment does not work. They also consist of short, numbered steps and use verbs in the imperative mood.

When all else fails, call for help

If the message **Server Connection Failed** appears, follow this procedure:

1. Click on the Settings Menu.

2. Choose Server Settings.

3. Make sure your ID, password, and IP address are correctly identified.

4. Click OK.

5. Try connecting to the server again.

6. If the problem continues, call the manufacturer for technical support.

Technical Instruction

A technical instruction tells somebody to do something. It may be a simple one-sentence statement that defines what has to be done but leaves the time and the method to the reader. Or it may be a step-by-step procedure that describes exactly what has to be done and when and how. The latter type of technical instruction will be described here.

An instruction *must* be written from the reader's point of view

As with all technical writing, the first step is to define your readers and establish their level of technical knowledge and familiarity with your subject. This helps you decide the depth of detail you must provide. If they are familiar with a piece of equipment, you may assume that the simple statement "Open the cover plate" will not pose a problem. But if the equipment is new to them, you may have to broaden the statement to help them first identify and open the cover plate:

Find the hinged cover plate at the bottom rear of the cabinet. Open it by inserting a Robertson No. 2 screwdriver into the narrow slot just above the hinge and then rotating the screwdriver half a turn counterclockwise.

Start with a Plan

A clearly written instruction contains four main compartments, as shown in Figure 8-2. These compartments contain the following information:

- A **Summary Statement** that outlines briefly what has to be done:

  The 28 Vancourt Model AL-8 LCD projectors in rooms A4 through A32 are to be bolted to their projection tables...

- The **Purpose,** which explains why the work is necessary:

  ...to reduce the current high damage rate caused by projectors being accidentally knocked onto the floor.

  (A technician who understands *why* a job is necessary will much more readily follow an instruction.)

- The **Tools and Materials** identify what is needed to perform the task:

  To carry out the modification you will require:

  Modification kit LCD-4, comprising

  1 template, LCD-4T

  4 bolts, flat head, 50 mm long, 3 mm dia

  4 washers, 25 mm dia, with 4 mm dia central hole

  A 6 mm drill with a 3.5 mm drill bit

  A Phillips No. 2 screwdriver

  A slot-head No. 3 screwdriver

  A sharp pencil

  Some manufacturers list the assembly tools on the outside of the shipping carton

- The **Steps** tell readers step-by-step what they must do:

  Proceed as follows:

  1. Disconnect the projector's power cord from the wall socket, then take the projector to a table and turn it on its side.

Figure 8-2   Writing plan for an instruction.

2. Use a slot-head No. 3 screwdriver to unscrew the four bolts that hold the feet onto the base of the projector. Remove, but retain, the bolts and feet for future use.

Number the steps: show there is a sequence

3. Place template LCD-4T onto the projection table and position it where the projector is to stand. Using a sharp pencil, mark the table through each of the four holes in the template.

4. Drill four 3.5 mm dia holes through the table top at the places marked in step 3.

5. Place the LCD projector on the table with the lens assembly facing the screen. Align the four screwholes identified in step 2 with the four holes drilled in the table top.

6. From beneath the table, place a washer under each hole and insert a 50 mm flat-head bolt up through the washer and hole until it engages the corresponding hole in the projector base. Tighten the four bolts in place, using a Phillips No. 2 screwdriver.

Use this writing plan and the suggestions below to write clear, direct, and convincing instructions.

Give Your Reader Confidence

A well-written technical instruction automatically instills confidence in its readers. They feel they have the ability to do the work even though it may be new to them and highly complex. Consider these examples:

Vague	Before the trap is set, it is a good idea to place a small piece of cheese on the bait pan. If it is too small it may fall off and if it is too big it might not fit under the serrated edge, so make sure you get the right size.
Clear and Concise	Cut a 0.62 m length of 10-gauge wire and strip 20 mm of insulation from each end. Solder one end of the wire to terminal 7 and the other end to pin 49.

An instruction is not the place for weak, wishy-washy words

The first excerpt is too ambiguous. It only suggests what should be done, it hints where it should instruct, and despite using 31 explanatory words, it fails to define the size of a "small" piece of cheese. The second excerpt is assertive and keeps strictly to the point. The verbs *cut*, *strip*, and *solder* make readers feel the writer is confident. Clear commands convince them of the accuracy and validity of the steps.

The best way to be authoritative is to write in the imperative mood. This means beginning each step with a strong verb, so that your instructions are commands:

Ignite the mixture…	*Connect* the green wire…
Mount the transit on its tripod…	*Excavate* 1.4 metres down…
Apply the voltage to…	*Measure* the current at…
Cut a 40 mm wide strip of…	*Insert* the USB cord…

Sometimes, however, the verb may be preceded by an introductory or conditional clause:

Before connecting the meter to the power source, *set* all the switches to "zero."

The imperative mood in the clear, concise excerpt quoted above keeps the instruction taut and definite. The vague excerpt would have been equally effective (and much shorter) if it had also been written in the imperative mood:

> Before setting the trap, wedge an 8 mm cube of cheese firmly under the serrated edge of the bait pan.

(Note how the vague word "place" has been replaced by the image-conveying verb–adverb combination "wedge...firmly.")

The following two statements clearly show the difference between an instruction written in the imperative mood and one that is not:

A. Disengage the gear, then start the engine. (***Definite: uses strong verbs***)

B. The gear should be disengaged before starting the engine. (***Indefinite: uses weaker verbs***)

Make each step a command, not a broad statement of intent

Avoid Ambiguity

There is no room for ambiguity in technical instructions. You have to assume that the person following your instructions cannot ask questions, so you must never write anything that could be interpreted more than one way. The following statement is open to misinterpretation:

> Align the trace so that it is inclined approximately 30° to the horizontal.

Each technician will align the trace with a different degree of accuracy, depending on his or her interpretation of "approximately." The reader may also question the technical validity of the whole instruction. Replace such vague references with clearly stated tolerances:

> Align the trace so that it is inclined 30° (±2°) to the horizontal.

Never leave a statement open to misinterpretation

More subtle, but equally open to misinterpretation, is this statement:

> Adjust the capstan handle until the rotating head is close to the base.

Here the offending word is "close," and needs to be replaced by a specific distance:

> Adjust the capstan handle until the distance between the rotating head and the base is 2.5 mm.

Similarly, replace vague references such as "*relatively* high," "*near* the top," and "*an adequate* supply" with clearly stated measurements, tolerances, and quantities.

Write specific details; never generalize

Avoid weak words such as "should," "could," "would," "might," and "may," because they weaken the authority of an instruction and reduce the reader's confidence in the writer. For example:

> Set the meter to the +300 V range. The needle should indicate 120 V (±2 V).

Here "should" implies that the voltage reading is not essential. The writer has also forgotten the cardinal rule of instruction writing: *Tell* the reader to *do* something. To be authoritative, the instruction needs very few changes:

> Set the meter to the +300 V range, then check that its needle indicates 120 V (±2 V).

The instructions in Figure 8-3 show steps that are clear, concise, and definite. You need not be a specialist in the subject to recognize that they would be easy to follow.

Keep diagrams uncluttered...

...and shown from the reader's point of view

Figure 8-3 Excerpts from an instruction manual. (Courtesy the Heath Company, Mississauga, Ont.)

Write Short Steps

You can help technicians who work in tight, crowded conditions by writing short paragraphs, each containing only one main step. If a step is complicated and its paragraph grows too long, divide it into a major step and a series of substeps, numbering the paragraphs and subparagraphs:

3. List the supporting documents in block J of Form 658. Check that blocks A to G have been completed correctly, then sign the form and distribute copies as follows:

   3.1 Attach the supporting documents to Copies 1 and 2 and mail them to the Chief Recording Clerk, Room 217, Civic Centre, Thompson, Manitoba.
   3.2 Mail Copy 3 to the Computer Data Centre, using one of the special pre-addressed envelopes.
   3.3 File Copy 4 in the "Hold—Pending Receipt" file.
   3.4 When Copy 2 is returned by the Chief Recording Clerk, attach it to Copy 4 and file both in the "Action Complete" file.

Offer short pieces of information

Insert Precautions

Insert precautionary comments into instructions whenever you need to warn readers of dangerous conditions, or of damage that may occur if they do not exercise care. There are two recognized notices you can use:

Warning: To alert readers to an element of personal danger (such as unprotected high voltage terminals).

Caution: To tell readers when care is needed to prevent equipment damage.

Draw attention to a precautionary comment by placing it in a box in the middle of the text, indenting the box from both margins. Precede the cautionary note with the single word WARNING or CAUTION.

Use simple design techniques to create a noticeable warning

> ### WARNING
> ### Disconnect the power source
> ### before removing the cover plate.

Ensure that every precautionary comment *precedes* the step to which it refers. This will prevent a reader from acting before reading the warning.

Use warnings and cautions sparingly. A single warning will catch a reader's attention. Too many will cause a reader to treat them all as comments rather than as important protective devices.

Insist on an Operational Check

Usability testing is an essential part of instruction writing. To obtain an objective check, give the instruction to someone roughly equal to the people who will eventually be using it, and observe how well that person performs the task (but do not interrupt or guide them!)

Usability Testing on documents
http://jerz.setonhill.edu/ design/usability/ intro.htm
This document suggests some ways you might conduct tests to measure the usability of your technical documents. It covers the kind of data you should collect, how many test subjects you need, and how you should treat those subjects.

Make a note every time the user hesitates or has difficulty; then when the task is completed, ask if any steps need clarification. Rewrite ambiguous steps and then recheck your instruction with another person. Repeat these steps until you are confident your readers will be able to follow your instruction easily.

Project 8.1:   Performing a Task Analysis

Think of a product you use often. It might be an iPod, a cellphone, a vacuum cleaner, or anything else you are familiar with. Perform a task analysis for the product and then group and label the topics. Remember to use "ing" words to indicate the user's perspective. List the tasks, then group and label them.

Project 8.2:   Writing Instructions for a Familiar Product or Process

Find a product or process you are familiar with and write user-focused instructions for it. It will help if you perform a task analysis first. Remember to keep your audience and their skill level in mind.

Use visuals to instruct

Project 8.3:   Writing Instructions Using Pictures

Design the instructions for a cooking recipe or how to use a webcam using *only* pictures.

Project 8.4:   Installing a Mini-Minder

You are employed in the construction department of Midprovince Telephone System, and you have been asked to write an installation instruction sheet to be shipped with the "Mini-Minder" (an electronic intrusion detection device developed by Midprovince's engineering department). The Mini-Minder is a security monitor that is mounted above windows, doors, or any other entries, where it automatically detects movement and transmits an alarm signal to a central unit. The central unit is concealed within the building and, when activated, sounds an audible alarm and sends a message to police headquarters.

The Mini-Minder is shown in Figure 8-4. It is fixed to the wall above the door or window by removing the backplate and screwing the plate to the wall. The unit is then snapped onto the backplate (removing the unit from the backplate also sounds the alarm). The unit is battery-operated.

All materials and hardware are supplied with the Mini-Minder, but the installer will need an electric drill with a 5 mm masonry drill bit, a Robertson No. 2 screwdriver, and a sharp pencil to do the job. The sequence in which the installation should occur is shown by the circled numbers in Figure 8-4.

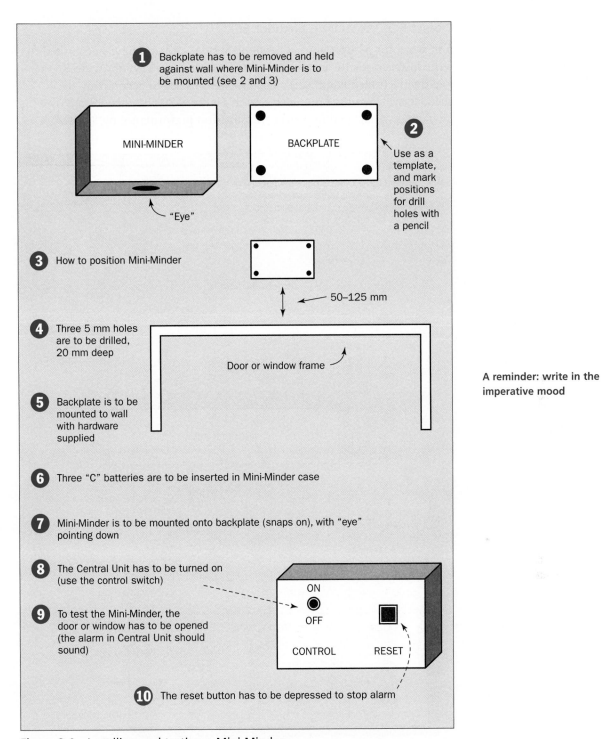

1 Backplate has to be removed and held against wall where Mini-Minder is to be mounted (see 2 and 3)

MINI-MINDER

BACKPLATE

2 Use as a template, and mark positions for drill holes with a pencil

"Eye"

3 How to position Mini-Minder

50–125 mm

4 Three 5 mm holes are to be drilled, 20 mm deep

Door or window frame

A reminder: write in the imperative mood

5 Backplate is to be mounted to wall with hardware supplied

6 Three "C" batteries are to be inserted in Mini-Minder case

7 Mini-Minder is to be mounted onto backplate (snaps on), with "eye" pointing down

8 The Central Unit has to be turned on (use the control switch)

ON
OFF
CONTROL   RESET

9 To test the Mini-Minder, the door or window has to be opened (the alarm in Central Unit should sound)

10 The reset button has to be depressed to stop alarm

Figure 8-4   Installing and testing a Mini-Minder.

Project 8.5: Installing Encoder EC7

You will have to extract pertinent points from the illustration

You work for Midprovince Telephone System and you have been asked to write instructions for installing an EC7 encoder at all Midprovince's microwave transmission sites. The instructions are to accompany the encoder, which is the box illustrated in Figure 8-5. The encoder removes unwanted signals and improves transmission performance by 8–10%.

Consider writing in the active voice

Figure 8-5 Mounting and connecting Encoder EC7.

In your instructions, tell the site technicians to find a suitable location for the encoder at the bottom right of the control panel (see Figure 8-5), drill two holes for mounting the encoder, and connect the encoder with four wires (the connections are shown on the diagram). All materials (such as mounting hardware and wire) are supplied with each encoder but the technician will need a soldering iron, some Ersin 60/40 resin core solder, a drill with a 5 mm bit, and a Robertson No. 2 screwdriver to carry out the work. The circled numbers on the diagram show the sequence in which the installation is to be carried out.

When the installation is complete, remind the technician to turn on the power to the control panel.

Chapter 9
Illustrating Technical Documents

Many people are visual learners, and to accommodate their needs technical report writers must incorporate graphics, illustrations, charts, tables, and photos into documents. This chapter discusses the illustrations seen most often in technical reports, indicates the overlaps that exist among illustration types, suggests occasions when they can be used most beneficially, and provides guidelines for preparing them. This information is only an overview. Many books and resources are devoted entirely to illustrations. We encourage you to investigate them.

Primary Guidelines

The criterion for any illustration is that it should help to explain the narrative—the narrative should *never* have to explain an illustration. Hence, an illustration must be simple enough for readers to understand quickly and easily. If an illustration immediately captures readers' interest, they are encouraged to read the article.

To help readers readily understand the illustrations you insert into your reports, follow these guidelines:

1. Before selecting or designing an illustration, first consider the audience for whom you are writing, and what you want your readers to learn from each illustration.

2. Keep each illustration simple and uncluttered.

3. Let each illustration depict only one main point.

4. Position each illustration as near as possible to the narrative it supports (see "Positioning the Illustrations" on page 213).

5. Label each illustration clearly with a number and a title. The number and title belong *beneath* a figure or chart, and *above* a table. See the samples in this chapter.

6. If necessary, add a caption (that is, comments or remarks) beneath a figure title, to draw attention to significant aspects of the illustration.

7. Refer to every illustration at least once in the report narrative. This helps integrate the text and the visual.

8. Identify the original source of the illustration or image if it is not your original work.

Good illustrations attract readers

Computer-Designed Graphs and Charts

Computer software programs will help you create illustrations and graphics. Software programs allow a report writer to enter the quantities of each function and then choose the type of graph or chart. It is possible to view the same information in several formats, for example, as a line graph, a bar chart, or a histogram. The following sections describe the different types of graphs and charts available. Understanding the benefits of each type will help you decide which is best for your information and audience.

Computer-designed graphics still need to follow the above guidelines. In addition, you need to be aware of how the computer truncates and positions the labels, because the results may make a chart incomprehensible.

Computer software makes it easy to prepare graphs and charts

Graphs

Graphs are a simple way to show a change in one function in relation to a change in another. Time is a function used frequently in such comparisons. The other function may be temperature, erosion, wear, speed, strength, or any factors that vary over time.

Table 9-1 shows readings that are part of a study engineering echnologist John Greene is undertaking into the cooling rate of different components. The information will also be used by the production department to establish how long manometer cases must cool before assemblers can start working on them with bare hands (the maximum bare-hand temperature has been established by management/union negotiation to be 38C).

A quick inspection of this table shows that the temperature of the manometer case drops continuously, is within 8.3° of the ambient temperature after 10 minutes (*ambient* means "surrounding environment"), and

Table 9-1 Cooling rate, manometer case MM-7.

Time Elapsed (min:sec)	Temperature (°C)	Time Elapsed (min:sec)	Temperature (°C)
:30	152.9	5:30	43.9
1:00	123.4	6:00	41.1
1:30	106.7	6:30	38.9
2:00	91.2	7:00	37.2
2:30	77.8	7:30	35.6
3:00	69.5	8:00	34.5
3:30	61.7	8:30	33.4
4:00	55.6	9:00	32.8
4:30	51.5	9:30	31.7
5:00	47.3	10:00	31.1
Ambient temperature 22.8°C		Oven temperature 180°C	

A table provides specific details

is down to the bare-hand temperature after 7 minutes. A closer examination identifies that the temperature drops rapidly at first, then progressively more slowly as time passes.

Single Curve

A graph translates the details into an easily understood form

John can make the data he has recorded in Table 9-1 easier to understand if he converts it into the graph in Figure 9-1. Now it is immediately evident that the temperature drops rapidly at first, then slows down until the rate of change is almost negligible. He chose a single curve graph because he had only one measurement over one function (time).

Multiple Curves

In Table 9-2, John compares the temperature readings he has recorded for the cooling manometer case with measurements he has taken under similar conditions for a cover plate and a panel board. This time, however, he

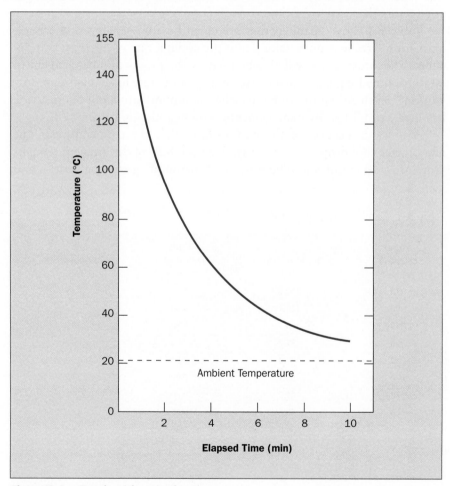

Figure 9-1 Graph with a single curve.

Table 9-2 Cooling rates for three components.

Time Elapsed (minutes)	Temperature (°C)		
	Cover Plate	Panel Board	Manometer Case
0:30	154.5	145.1	152.9
1	136.7	97.3	123.4
2	112.3	67.8	91.2
3	95.1	51.7	69.5
4	82.3	42.3	55.6
5	71.7	36.1	47.3
6	63.9	32.2	41.1
7	55.6	29.5	37.2
8	49.5	27.2	34.5
9	43.4	26.1	32.8
10	38.9	25.0	31.1

A multi-factor table can be even more difficult to interpret

simplifies the table slightly by showing the temperatures at one-minute intervals.

What can we assess from this table? The most obvious conclusion is that in 10 minutes the panel board has cooled down the most, then the manometer case, then the cover plate. We can also see that the initial rate at which the components cooled varied considerably, but it is difficult to assess whether there were any *changes in the rate of cooling* as time progressed.

Again, this data can be shown more effectively in a graph, which John has plotted in Figure 9-2, this time with three curves. The rapid initial drop in temperature is evident from the initial steepness of the three curves, with each curve flattening out to a slower rate of cooling after two to four minutes. The difference in cooling rates for the three components is much more obvious from the curves than in the table. (The lines in Figures 9-1 and 9-2 are commonly referred to as curves, even though in some cases they may be straight lines or a series of short straight lines joining points plotted on the graph.)

Eventually John will have to present this data in a report. If he plans to present only a general description of temperature trends, his narrative can be accompanied by graphs like these. But if he also wants to discuss exact temperatures at specific times for each material, then the narrative and graphs will have to be supported by numbers similar to those in Table 9-2.

Technical Illustration
http://www.arcm.com/ illustra.html
This site contains a discussion of the purpose of technical illustrations and has a link to descriptions and samples of product renderings, exploded diagrams, and cutaway views.

Graph Scales

The two functions to be compared in the graph are entered on two scales: a horizontal scale along the bottom and a vertical scale along the left side. (On large graphs the vertical scale is sometimes repeated on the right side to simplify interpretation.) The scales meet at the bottom left corner, which normally—but not always—is designated as the zero point for both.

Both functions may be variable, but only one depends on the other

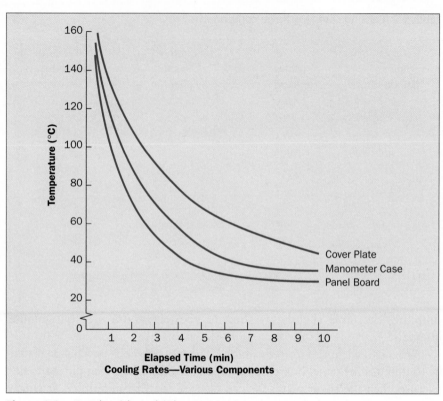

Figure 9-2   Graph with multiple curves.

The two functions are commonly known as the dependent and independent variables, so named because a change in the dependent variable *depends* on a change in the independent variable. For example, if we want to show how the fuel consumption of a car increases with speed, we will enter speed as the independent variable along the bottom scale, and fuel consumption as the dependent variable along the left side, as in Figure 9-3. (Fuel consumption *depends* on speed; speed does not depend on fuel consumption.) The same applies to John's temperature measurement graphs: temperature is the dependent variable because it depends on *the time that has elapsed* since the components came out of the oven (the independent variable).

When you construct a graph, the first step is to identify which function should form the horizontal scale and which the vertical scale. Table 9-3 lists some typical situations that show that the same function (e.g. temperature) can be an independent variable in one situation and a dependent variable in another. Selection of the independent variable depends on which function can be more easily identified as influencing the other function.

The second factor to consider is scale interval. Poorly selected scale intervals, particularly scale intervals that are not balanced between the two variables, can defeat the purpose of a graph by distorting the story it conveys. Suppose John had made the vertical scale interval of his graph

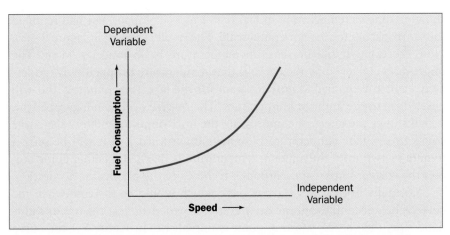

Figure 9-3   The dependent variable depends on the independent variable.

Table 9-3   Identifying dependent and independent variables.

Graph Illustrates	Dependent Variable (vertical scale)	Independent Variable (horizontal scale)
1. How attendance at a ball game varies with temperature	Attendance	Temperature
2. How much a motor's speed affects the noise it produces	Noise	Speed
3. The changes in temperature brought about by changes in pressure	Temperature	Pressure
4. How much an increase in payload reduces an aircraft's range by limiting the amount of fuel it can carry	Aircraft range (or fuel load)	Payload
5. How much increasing the fuel load of an aircraft to achieve greater range reduces its effective payload	Payload	Fuel load (or aircraft range)

Note: A function can be either dependent or independent, depending on its role in the comparison (see temperature in Examples 1 and 3, and both functions in Examples 4 and 5).

showing time vs temperature in Figure 9-1 more compact, but had retained the same spacing for the horizontal scale. The result is shown in Figure 9-4(a). Now the rapid initial decrease in temperature is no longer evident. The impression conveyed by the curve is that temperature dropped only moderately at first, remained almost constant for the last three minutes, and will never drop to the ambient temperature. The reverse occurs in Figure 9-4(b), which shows the effect of compressing the horizontal scale. Now the curve seems to say that temperature plummets downward and it will be only a minute or two until the ambient temperature is reached. Neither curve creates the correct impression, although technically the graphs are accurate.

Normally both scales start at zero, which would be the case when the curve is balanced in the graph area. If it is crowded against the top or right-hand side, then a zero starting point is unrealistic. In Figure 9-1 the curve occupies the top 75% of the graph area. Since no points will ever be plotted below the ambient temperature (which will hover around 23°C), the bottom portion of the vertical scale is unnecessary. This can be corrected by starting the vertical scale at a higher value (say 20°, as in Figure 9-5), or by breaking the scale to indicate that some scale values have been omitted (Figures 9-2 and 9-6).

Adjust a scale's starting point to centre the curve(s)

(a) Effect of compressed vertical scale.

(b) Effect of compressed horizontal scale.

Figure 9-4 Poorly chosen scales can create an inaccurate image.

Figure 9-5   A correctly centred curve.

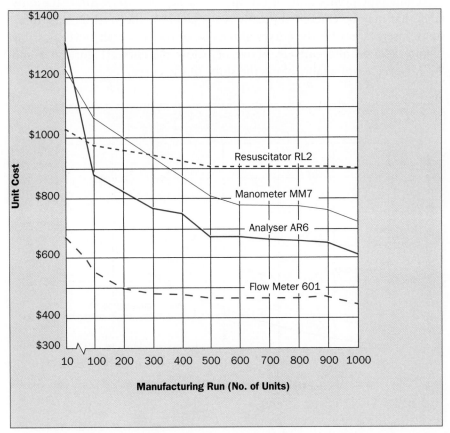

Avoid confusion: limit
the number of curves

Figure 9-6   Bolder lines draw attention to the most important curve (those showing maximum benefit from quantity manufacturing). The grid permits readers to draw reasonably accurate data from the graph.

Multiple-curve graphs should have no more than four curves, otherwise they will be difficult to interpret (particularly if the curves cross one another). You can help a reader identify the most important curve by making it heavier than the others (Figure 9-6), and can differentiate among curves that cross by creating different line types (Figure 9-7). Avoid using coloured lines because many copiers and printers will reproduce all the lines in one colour (usually black).

Simplicity

Simplicity is important in graph construction. If a graph illustrates only trends or comparisons, and the reader is not expected to extract specific data from it, then you may omit the grid as in Figure 9-5. But if the reader wants to extrapolate quantities, you should include a grid as in Figures 9-6 and 9-7. Note that Figure 9-1 has an *implied* grid that only suggests the grid pattern for the occasional reader who may want to draw in a grid. Note also that you may omit the top and right-hand borders on graphs without grids, as in Figures 9-2 and 9-3.

Omit plot points and ensure that all labels are *horizontal* (the only label that may be entered vertically is the label for the vertical scale function). Insert labels for the curves at the end of the curve whenever possible (Figure 9-2) or, alternatively, above or below the curve (Figures 9-6 and 9–7). Never write a label along the slope of the curve.

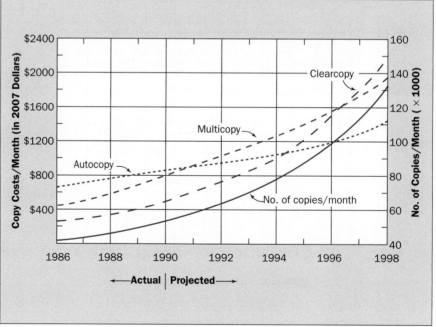

Figure 9-7 Different line types distinguish between curves showing current and projected copying costs for three copiers. Note the two vertical scales, which permit three functions to be shown on one graph.

Charts

Most charts show trends or compare only general quantities. They include bar charts, histograms, and pie charts.

Bar Charts

You can use bar charts to compare functions that do not necessarily vary continuously. In the graph in Figure 9-1, John plotted a curve to show how temperature decreased continuously with time. He could do this because both functions were varying continuously (time was passing and temperature was decreasing). For the production department, however, he has to prepare a report on how long it takes various components coming from the oven to cool to a safe temperature for bare-hand work. He prepares a bar chart to depict this because he knows the report will be read by both management and union representatives, and some of the readers may need easier-to-interpret data. He also has only one continuous variable to plot: elapsed time. The other variable is noncontinuous because it represents the various components he has tested. In this case elapsed time is the dependent variable, and the components are the independent variable. The bar chart John constructs is shown in Figure 9-8.

Illustrating Tech Documents http://www. incrediblecharts.com/ technical/chart_types.htm This website shows the different charts that can be created for technical purposes.

Use horizontal bar charts to depict elapsed time

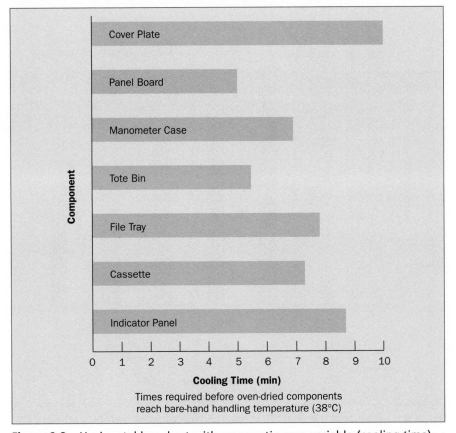

Figure 9-8   Horizontal bar chart with one continuous variable (cooling time).

Scales for a bar chart can be made up of such diverse functions as time, age groups, heat resistance, employment categories, percentages of population, types of soil, and quantities (of products manufactured, components sold, software programs used, and so on). Charts can be arranged with either vertical or horizontal bars depending on the type of information they portray; when time is one of the variables, it is usually plotted along the horizontal axis, as in Figure 9-8. The bars are normally separated by a space, which can be as wide as each of the bars, but more often is less wide.

Some computer software provides only a narrow space between the bars

In a complex bar chart, the bars may be shaded to indicate comparisons within each factor being considered. The vertical bar chart in Figure 9-9 uses two shades to describe two factors on the one chart; individual bars can also be shaded to show proportional content, as has been done in Figure 9-10, in which case a legend must be inserted beside or below the graph to show readers what each shading represents. Alternatively, each segment may be labelled as in Figure 9-11. A 3-D vertical bar graph showing the same information as presented in Figures 9-10 and 9-11 is shown in Figure 9-12.

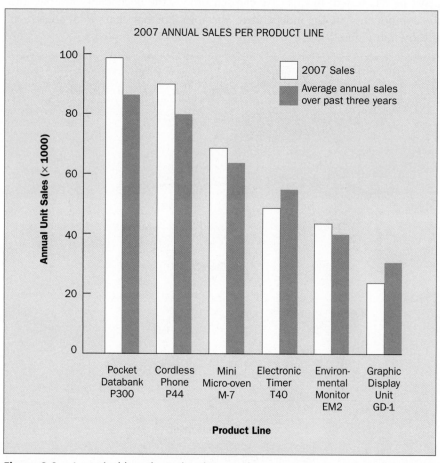

Figure 9-9   A vertical bar chart that lets readers compare current statistics with past statistics, and so determine trends.

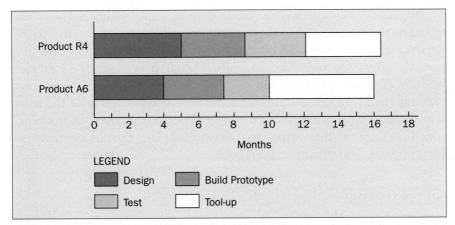

Insert a key or legend to help identify the factors

Figure 9-10   The bars in this chart show development times for proposed new products. The legend is included with the chart.

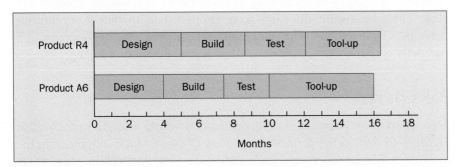

Figure 9-11   A segmented bar chart with internal labelling.

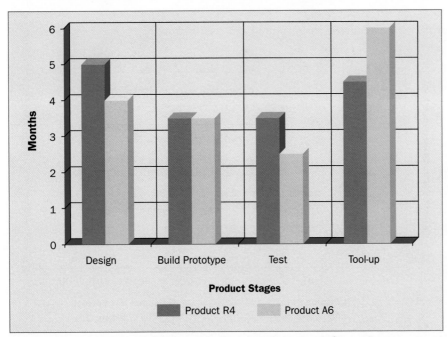

Figure 9-12   A 3-D vertical bar graph showing the same information as presented in Figures 9-10 and 9-11.

Horizontal bar charts can be used in an unconventional way by arranging the bars on either side of a zero line. This can be done, for example, to compare negative and positive quantities, satisfactory and defective products, or passed and failed students. The chart in Figure 9-13 divides products returned for repair into two groups: those that are covered by warranty, and those that are not. Each bar represents 100% of the total number of items repaired in a particular product age group and is positioned at about the zero line depending on the percentage of warranty and nonwarranty repairs.

Histograms

Although seen rarely, histograms are useful when there is only limited data

A histogram looks like a bar chart, but functionally it is similar to a graph because it deals with two continuous variables (functions that can be shown on a scale to be increasing or decreasing). It is usually plotted like a bar chart because it does not have enough data to plot a continuous curve (see Figure 9-14). The major difference between a histogram and a bar chart is that there are no spaces between the bars of a histogram.

Pie Charts

Probably the most widely recognized and readily understood

A pie chart shows approximate divisions of a whole unit. The pie chart in Figure 9-15 depicts the percentage of work done by Macro Engineering Inc in eight major product or service categories. Figure 9-16 is a pie chart showing the stages of product development.

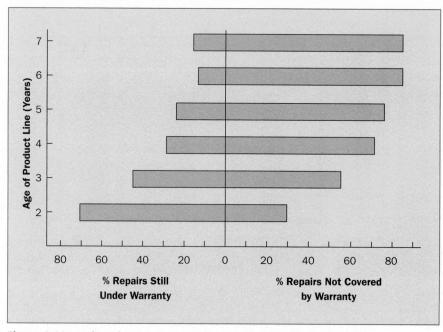

Figure 9-13   A bar chart constructed on both sides of a zero point.

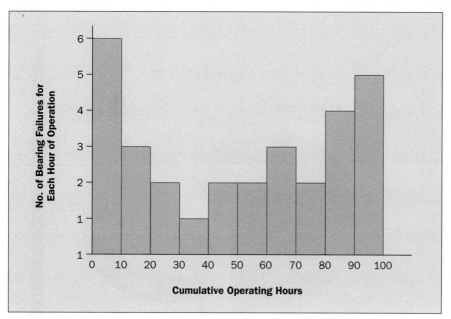

Figure 9-14 This histogram shows the number of bearing failures for every 10 hours of operation. Considerably more data would have been required to construct a curve.

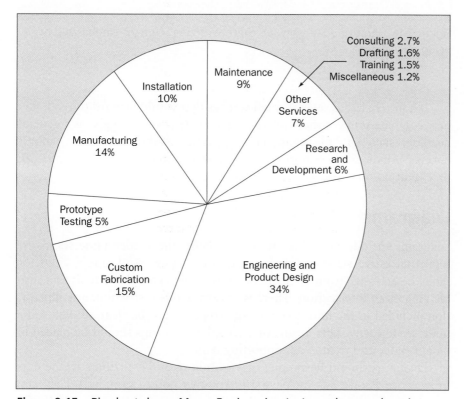

Figure 9-15 Pie chart shows Macro Engineering Inc's products and services. "Slices" add up to 100%.

Illustration Samples from NASA's Glenn's Graphics Group http://grcpublishing. grc.nasa.gov/graphics/ samillus.cfm **Several examples of detailed illustrations from NASA's Glenn's Graphics Group are available at this site. A contact address is included for readers who want more information about the preparation of technical illustrations.**

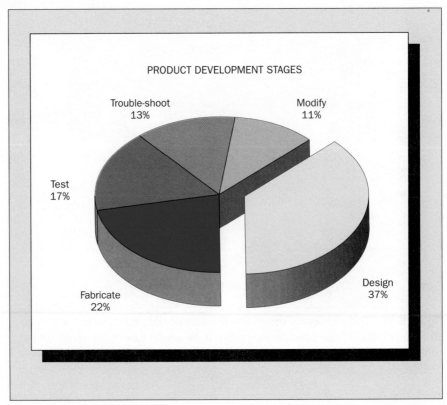

The pie chart particularly adapts to 3-D presentation

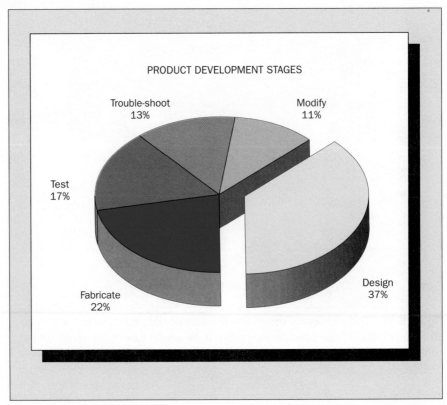

Figure 9-16 An exploded-view pie chart, with one segment emphasized by being pulled partly away.

If a pie chart has several small wedges that would be hard to read, you may combine some of them into a larger single wedge and give it a general heading, such as "miscellaneous expenses," "other uses," or "minor effects." All the wedges must add up to a whole unit, such as 100%, $1.00, or 1 (unity).

Diagrams

A diagram must be readily understood; it should rarely need to be explained

Diagrams include any illustration that helps the reader understand the report narrative yet does not fall within the category of graph, chart, or table. It can range from a schematic drawing of a complex circuit to a simple plan of an intersection. There is, however, one restriction: any illustration included in the narrative part of a report must be clear enough to be understood easily. This means that complex drawings should be placed in an appendix and treated as supporting data.

Diagrams should be simple, easy to follow, and contribute to the narrative. (See Figure 8-3 on page 190 for two good examples.) They can comprise organizational charts, flow diagrams, site plans (Figure 9-17), and sketches.

Figure 9-17 A site plan that illustrates where college facilities are to be located. (Courtesy Smith, Carter, Searle—W L Wardrop & Associates Ltd, Winnipeg, Man.)

Photos

A photo helps a reader visualize shape, appearance, complexity, or size. The criterion when selecting a photo is that it be clear and contain no extraneous information that might distract the reader. For example, if you are trying to show damage to a building's foundation, the picture should be a close-up of the area, showing cracks in the cement. You should remove any garbage cans, bicycles, car parts or other items that have nothing to do with what you are trying to demonstrate.

Digital equipment (scanners and cameras) makes taking pictures easy even for novice photographers. There are some things you need to consider, though. The minimum acceptable quality for an image created by a scanner or camera is 150 pixels. (A pixel is the tiny dot that forms digital images.) This ensures that the eye cannot see the individual dots. Your output device

With digital equipment, it's easier to use photos

(normally a printer) should be set for a minimum of 300 dpi (dots per inch). A higher dpi will result in better image quality, so if you are preparing a report for an external client on glossy paper you should consider an even higher dpi.

Pay attention to the contrast and lighting in a photo. You can use image-editing software to manipulate the contrast (the difference in brightness between the light and dark areas of a picture) of an image. This is particularly important if you know the report will be photocopied, since photocopiers inherently add contrast in the copying process. You'll want the image to be of less contrast (a little darker). Always test it yourself by making several photocopies and paying attention to the image quality.

Often reports are distributed electronically, which means that including images and photographs may increase the file to an unmanageable size. Save your photos as JPG files (a compressed format for encoding graphic images) to retain the image quality. If, however, you are capturing computer screen images, you'll need to save them as GIF files (graphic interchange format) because the compression of the JPG format deteriorates the screen image.

Digital Clip Art

We now have access to extensive libraries of free (and sometimes *not* free) generic graphic images. This simple artwork can add variation to your page design and create reader interest, but make sure the image is professional and relevant to your content. Use these generic images sparingly. Too many basic designs may create an amateur image of you and your content.

Tables

A table may be a collection of technical data, as in Tables 9-1 and 9-2, or a series of short narrative statements, as in Table 9-3. Whether you insert a table into the report narrative or place it in an attachment or appendix depends on three factors:

1. If the table is short (i.e. less than half a page) and readers need to refer to it as they read the report, then include it as part of the report narrative (i.e. in the discussion), preferably on the same page as the text that refers to it.

2. If readers can understand the discussion without referring to the table as they read the report, but may want to consult the table later, then place the table in an attachment or appendix.

3. If readers need to refer to a table but the data you have will occupy a full page or more, then

- summarize the table's key points in a short table to be inserted into the report narrative, and
- place the full table in an attachment or appendix.

Use tables for words as well as numbers

There are four additional guidelines that apply to tables, particularly if the tables contain columns of numerical data:

1. Keep a table simple by limiting it only to data the readers will *really* need, and create as few columns as possible.

2. Insert units of measurement, such as decibels, bolts, kilograms, or seconds, at the head of each column rather than after each column entry (see the "min:sec" and "°C" entries at the top of the columns in Table 9-1).

3. Insert a table number and an appropriate title above the table.

4. Draw readers' attention to a table by referring to it in the report narrative and commenting on a specific inference to be drawn from the table. For example:

The voltage fluctuations were recorded at 10-minute intervals and entered in column 3 of Table 7, which shows that fluctuations were most marked between 8:15 and 11:20 a.m.

Positioning the Illustrations

Whenever possible, place each illustration on the same page as or facing the narrative it supports. A reader who has to keep flipping pages back and forth between narrative and illustrations will soon tire, and your reasons for including the illustrations will be defeated.

Consider illustrations as an integral part of a document, not just an "add on"

When reports are printed on only one side of the paper, full-page illustrations can be difficult to position. Try to limit the size of illustrations so that they can be placed beside, above, or below the words.

When an illustration is too large to fit on a normal page, or is going to be referred to frequently, consider printing it on a fold-out sheet and inserting it at the back of the report (see Figure 9-18). If the illustration is printed only on the extension panels of the foldout, the page can be left opened for continual reference while the report is being read. This technique is particularly suitable for circuit diagrams and flow charts.

Position horizontal full-page illustrations sideways on a page so the top of the diagram is at the left-hand side of the page (see Figure 9-19).

So that the reader can refer to any figures or tables from your report, we suggest you add a list of figures and tables right after your table of contents. List the figure or table number, the title or caption, and the page number.

(a) Fold-out sheet opened out for reading

(b) Sheet folds neatly into report

(c) Typical panel dimensions

Figure 9-18 Large illustrations can be placed on a fold-out sheet at the back of the report.

You align horizontal illustrations this way, even if some words appear to be upside down

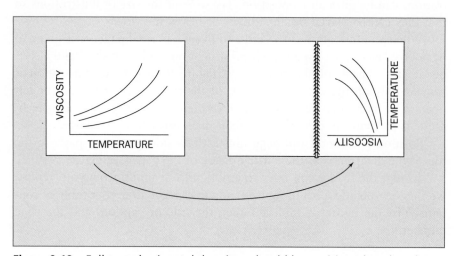

Figure 9-19 Full page horizontal drawings should be positioned so that the top of the diagram is at the left-hand side of the page.

Project 9.1:   Who Buys "Planit"?

You work for a very successful software company that publishes a monthly user magazine. The company's most successful software has been *Planit*, a program for organizing a user's business operations.

Part 1

The editor of the user magazine asks you to provide an illustration showing the breakdown of buyers by user groups for last year, when there were 14 236 sales, and suggests you keep the illustration simple. The buyers were:

You have to illustrate a consumer survey

Hospitals	1588
Small businesses	1011
Public utilities	2165
Consultants	233
Manufacturers	3176
Architects	217
Writers/editors	116
Land surveyors	245
Sales representatives	866
City/town planners	1155
Engineers	1732
Miscellaneous	433
Radio and television stations	1299

Part 2

When you give your illustration to the editor, the response is: "I like that. But I'd also like another one comparing last year's buyers with those of four years ago, which was the first year we marketed *Planit*."

The sales of *Planit* four years ago were:

Hospitals	174
Small businesses	1393
Public utilities	1132
Consultants	174
Manufacturers	2351
Sales representatives	958
City/town planners	1306
Engineers	784
Miscellaneous	261
Radio and television stations	174

Project 9.2: Comparing Electricity Costs

Your company markets heat pumps, and wants to demonstrate to electricity users that a heat pump can significantly reduce their electricity bills. Prepare an illustration based on the following actual monthly bills for four different dwellings last year. The residences are identical five-room homes built at the same time and in the same block on Margusson Avenue. The only differences are that No. 216 and 234 do not have air-conditioning (marked "No AC" in the table), while No. 227 and 248 do (marked "+AC"), and No. 234 and 248 each have a heat pump.

Use these figures to create an easy-to-read illustration

	Monthly Electricity Bills			
	Actual Bills No Heat Pump		Amount Saved With Heat Pump	
	216	227	234	248
	No AC	+AC	No AC	+AC
January	$ 48.07	$ 49.23	$ 12.06	$ 11.59
February	45.15	46.01	11.68	11.86
March	43.20	42.86	10.90	11.13
April	41.11	42.20	4.15	3.80
May	38.37	42.15	0.36	3.48
June	35.20	48.16	—	6.10
July	33.06	57.19	—	18.26
August	32.87	56.80	—	17.44
September	34.11	47.10	2.64	7.21
October	38.62	39.20	7.85	8.60
November	41.67	41.10	9.62	10.51
December	43.20	42.89	11.58	11.77

Chapter 10
Technically-Speak!

This chapter covers the oral report, sometimes called the technical briefing, delivered to a client, one's colleagues, or a professional meeting of scientific or engineering-oriented people. It also describes how to present information at and contribute effectively to office meetings.

The Technical Briefing

Your department head approaches your desk and says:

> "We've had a call from the RAFAC Corporation. They're sending in some representatives next Tuesday. I'd like you to give them a rundown on the project you're working on."

Every day engineers and technicians are being called upon to stand up and say a few words about their work. On paper, this sounds straightforward, but to those who have to make the presentation it can be a traumatic experience. Much of their nervousness can be reduced (it can seldom be entirely eliminated, as any experienced speaker will tell you) if they learn a few simple public speaking techniques.

Many people fear having to stand up and speak, even more than they fear sky diving

Establish the Circumstances

Your first step is to establish the circumstances affecting your presentation. Ask the person arranging the event four questions:

1. **Who Will Be in My Audience?**
   To focus your presentation properly and use appropriate terminology, you need to know whether your audience contains technical people who have experience in your field, managers with only a general appreciation of the subject, or laypersons with very little or no technical knowledge.

2. **What Will They Know Already?**
   If you are to avoid boring your listeners by repeating information they already know, or confusing them by omitting essential background details, you need to find out how much they know now about your subject, or will have been told before you address them.

It's just like writing a report: first, identify your audience

3. How Long Do You Want Me to Talk?

Find out if you are to describe the project in detail or simply touch on the highlights. The answer will directly influence how deeply you cover the topic.

4. Where Is the Presentation Taking Place?

Identify whether you are to make your presentation in your company's conference room or training room, at a client's premises, or at a technical society meeting. Within your own company you can easily identify what audio-visual facilities are available and where your audience will be seated in relation to you. If you will be speaking at an outside location you should ask for a description of the facilities or, even better, be able to view them in advance.

Now you can start making your notes. Jot down the topics you intend to discuss, and arrange them in an interesting, logical order.

Determine Your Audience's Needs

We have all sat through boring, long-winded presentations that seem to have no direction. We are in the audience and wonder, "What does this have to do with me?" Yet there are other presentations that seem to be tailored specifically to the group. How does the speaker do this?

The major problem with many presentations is that the content is speaker-focused rather than audience-focused. This is an easy trap to fall into. When asked to give a presentation, most inexperienced speakers jot down everything *they* know about the subject. This is a big mistake. What happens then is that the presentation becomes just that: everything *they know about the subject* and not what the audience needs to know about the subject.

List Audience Questions

The best way to make your presentation audience-focused is to start by identifying your audience (this is similar to the way you determine your reader in a written document). You need to know the types of people who will attend your presentation, the level of knowledge and interest they have in your topic, and what they will do with your information.

Once you know your audience, list as many questions as you can that may be asked about the topic. Try to list at least 15 questions. This will help you identify the areas to address and the audience's concerns before you prepare your content. Now you can answer the audience's questions before they are even asked. This turns your presentation from a speaker-focused presentation *("This is everything I know about this topic.")* into an audience-focused presentation *("Here are the answers to your questions on this topic.")*

Most audience questions evolve from fears or concerns. Here are some examples:

- How will we do this?
- Will it be expensive?
- Who will be responsible for what?
- How long will it take?
- What needs to be done to complete the task?
- What experience do you have in this field?

Organize Your Information

Once you have identified your audience and listed their questions and concerns, you are ready to start structuring your presentation content.

In their book *The Short Road to Great Presentations*,[*1] Peter and Cheryl Reimold introduce a formula for structuring a presentation. They call it the Universal Presentation Structure, which is shown in Figure 10-1.

This Universal Presentation Structure is especially helpful for technical professionals who relate well to formulas.

Tell Your Story Three Times

Another way to view this structure is the TELL—TELL—TELL method. You have to tell your audience what you have to say three different times and in three different ways.

Tell 1:	Tell your readers what they most need to hear: the key points. Then outline very briefly the main topics you will cover.
Tell 2:	Now provide all the details, in the same order you mentioned them in *Tell 1*.
Tell 3:	Sum up by very briefly repeating the key points, and possibly offering a recommendation.

Capture the Audience's Attention

In your first TELL, the Introduction, you must accomplish four goals:

1. Establish **Rapport** with your audience
2. Grab the audience's **Attention**
3. State your **Main Message**
4. Outline your **Plan**

Preparing Outstanding Presentations
http://www.cs.utexas.edu/users/ethics/Other/presentation1.html
This is a series of articles from Cheryl Reimold's "Tools of the Trade" column. Preparing Outstanding Presentations includes sections on understanding your audience; basic presentation structure; the introduction, body, and summary of a presentation; effective visuals; and making visuals memorable.

Start by telling your audience where you plan to take them...

...end by telling them where they have been

Introduction:	**1 to 2 minutes**
Body:	**3 to 5 key points**
Conclusion:	**1 minute**

Figure 10-1   The Reimolds' Universal Presentation Structure formula.

The Reimolds define this as your **RAMP** and allow you *only* 1 to 2 minutes. This is when you have your audience's full attention. Don't waste the opportunity by reciting dull information such as your name, the title of your presentation, or your purpose. You can let an opening slide provide that information.

Building **Rapport** is as easy as smiling, connecting with your audience by telling them you are excited to be with them, or greeting them at the door when they come in. This warms them up to you and encourages them to listen to you.

Use an **Attention**-getter that relates to your main message. A joke, an apology, or a thank-you is dull and you risk offending someone. Instead, try a statistic, a photo, or a word of caution. You need to find something that relates to your main message and grabs the audience's attention. In the example shown in the next section, the speaker pulled out an actual mousetrap. That image stuck with the audience long after the presentation was over and it symbolized the products designed in their firm.

Make sure your **Main Message** is direct. This isn't a time to be wishy-washy. If you have a plan that can reduce costs by 40%, then say that. If your proposal shows you can alleviate the stormwater issues in a new commercial area, then state that right up front. Your audience will appreciate this and pay more attention to your presentation now that they know what your purpose is and what the topic has to do with them.

End your Introduction with a **Plan**. This is your road map for your presentation. It shows your audience that you are organized and what they can expect next. It also reminds you of your own structure and helps you stay on track. We encourage you to add a slide into your presentation showing your plan (or write it on a chart or board) and also to speak it.

Using the RAMP in the Introduction is the best way to establish yourself as a confident, interesting speaker.

Open with a RAMP

Grab your listeners' attention by offering an *interesting* start: tell your audience immediately where you are going to take them, and why you are going to take them there. Here are two examples:

A dull start:	"Today, I want to tell you about the effects of poor quality control when manufacturing electrical products. This happened in the fall of 2006, at our plant in Montreal. The problem began when a supplier failed to monitor production quality adequately…"
Get off to a flying start! *An exciting start:*	"Have you, in your company, ever built a better mousetrap? A product that significantly outclasses the competition? Well, we did, in the spring of 2006. It was an immediate success and we had to start a second production line to keep up with the demand. But five months later we had a disaster on our hands: warranty returns were reaching an unprecedented 30%!! The reason: poor quality control at one of our suppliers' plants. In the next 20 minutes I will explain to you what we did to reverse that trend, how we established criteria for evaluating suppliers, and what results we expect from our efforts."

Select Key Points

In your second TELL, the Body, you identify three to five key points to address. These evolve from the list of questions you predict your audience may have. Although you may have identified 15 to 20 potential questions, you'll see a pattern form and be able to group several questions under one key point. For example, *How much will this cost?*, *Is this expensive?*, and *What is our budget for the project?* all can be addressed under the key point Cost Factors.

Figure 10-2 shows how to use the pyramid technique to structure each key point. State your key point and follow it with supporting information. Remember that to be convincing you need to provide facts and evidence.

Vary the number of key points you present based on the amount of time you have to speak. If it is just a short 10-minute presentation, stick to only three points. If you have more time, stretch it to five points. Don't be tempted to add more than five points if you are given a longer amount of time. Rather than overloading your listeners with too many points, you can go into greater detail and depth about the five selected points.

Wrap It Up with a Conclusion

The third TELL is your Conclusion. This is your chance to summarize what you have just told your audience. In *The Short Road to Great Presentations*, the Reimolds suggest you say the words *To summarize* or *In conclusion* to pique audience attention. Your listeners may have dosed off in the middle of your presentation and this is your clue that you are almost finished. In just one minute, you briefly restate your main message and key points. Don't add in any more details, and never go over one minute. When you signal the conclusion, you have the full attention of your audience and they expect you to finish. Don't drag it out.

Prepare to Speak

Make Speaking Notes

Prepare your speaking notes on cards no smaller than 150 × 100 mm. Write in large, bold letters that you can see at a glance, and use brief headings to

Figure 10-2   Use the pyramid technique to organize each key point.

develop the information in sufficient detail. A sample note card is shown in Figure 10-3. Avoid using a full sheet of paper for your notes. If you are nervous, your hand may quiver and the paper will shake. You also may be tempted to include far too much information on it and end up reading from the paper.

The amount of information you include will depend on the subject, your familiarity with it, and your previous speaking experience. Your notes should not be so detailed that you cannot quickly pick out points, nor so skimpy that you have to rely too much on your memory. This may cause you to stumble.

Prepare Visual Aids

Visual aids help clarify and explain your concepts. They are especially important when discussing complex, technical information. Some people are visual learners and need to *see* the information as well as *hear* it. Examples of visual aids are *PowerPoint* slides, poster boards, physical props, equipment, and hand-drawn diagrams.

Here are some tips for creating effective visuals:

- Strive for simplicity: let each visual make just one point. A visual aid should support your spoken narrative; you should rarely have to explain it.
- Use large, bold letters that will be visible from the back of the room. Use upper and lower case letters rather than all capitals.
- Use colour to accentuate key words or parts, but in moderation. Some colours, such as green and blue or red and orange, are difficult to tell apart from a distance.
- Place a short title or heading above or below each slide.

To prepare *PowerPoint* slides, follow these guidelines:

- Select a design that is appealing and provides good contrast between the background colour and the colour of the text.

Visual Aids in Presentations
http://www.adm.
uwaterloo.ca/infotrac/
tips/usingvisualaids.pdf
This document, from TRACE tip sheets at the University of Waterloo, contains a summary of the use of visual aids in presentations.

Let each visual provide just one message

Write in bold letters that can be read from an arm's length away

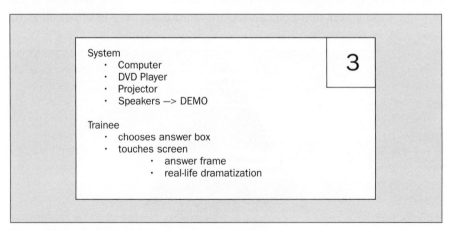

Figure 10-3 Note card for an oral presentation.

- Avoid dazzling transitions that tend to take attention away from your message. Choose transitions that make a smooth, effective, but conservative change between each item and each slide. Maintain continuity by using similar transitions throughout the presentation.

- Create a natural progression from one slide to the next. If you are presenting, say, four bulleted points on a slide, bring in each point one at a time. This allows you to discuss each item before showing the next one. As you bring in a new point, show it in dark, bold type, and dim the previous points.

- Print copies of your slides onto 8 1/2 × 11 inch sheets, four or six slides to a page. You can use these as a prompt when presenting the slides, or as a handout for your audience.

Resist the temptation to use fancy transitions!

Chapter 9 contains additional suggestions for preparing visual aids such as graphs, charts, and diagrams.

Practise working with your visual aids, first on their own and then as part of the whole presentation. This gives you a chance to check whether you have inserted them in the correct places, and whether the entries in your notes allow you to switch from speech to a visual aid without losing continuity.

Don't overlook the practical aspects of the presentation. If you have equipment to demonstrate, consider the sequence of your presentation and when you want to show the demo. Make sure you are comfortable with the demonstration and have practised your body positioning with any equipment. Avoid walking in front of the display, obstructing it from the audience's view. And to avoid any distractions, keep your demo short and place any visuals or equipment out of sight until you are ready to use them.

Practise, Practise, Practise

Take a tip from experienced speakers: practise your talk. Run through it several times, working entirely from your prompt cards, until you can speak without hesitating or stumbling over awkward words. If the cards are too hard to follow, or contain too much detail, adjust them. Then ask a colleague to sit through your presentation and give critical comments.

Practise...practise... practise

Modify your notes after each practice reading. Where necessary, insert more information; in other places, delete unneeded words. As you grow familiar with the notes, you will find that your confidence increases and certain sentences and phrases will come to you at the sight of a single word or topic heading; this will help you to maintain continuity.

Time yourself. Aim to speak for slightly less time than allowed; for example, plan to speak for 17 or 18 minutes for a talk scheduled to last 20 minutes. This will give you time to include some previously unanticipated remarks, if you need to at the last minute.

Prepare Handout Notes

During the planning stages, you need to decide whether to provide printed handouts for your listeners. If so, you will also have to decide whether they should be copies of your *PowerPoint* slides or a specially prepared narrative-style report of the main topics.

There is a trend today for speakers to provide only copies of their slides, which are much simpler to make. However, we recommend you prepare a summary of your presentation which, although it may take longer, will provide your listeners with a useful resource when, in future months, they want to refresh their memories about the topic you presented.

Make Your Presentation

Control Your Nervousness

Prepare well in advance; then relax, knowing you are ready

There are very few people who are not at least a little nervous when the time comes to stand up and speak before an audience. Some nervous tension is perfectly normal and can even help a speaker give a better performance. You will find that, once you start speaking, your nervousness will gradually decrease. A lot depends on the quality of your speaking notes: if you have done a thorough job preparing them, know they are reliable, and have practised using them, you will find that the familiar phrases and sentences form easily. Then you will begin to relax and so speak with even greater confidence, which will help you relax even more.

Here are some additional tips to help calm your nerves:

Crossing a Bridge of Shyness: Public Speaking for Communicators http://www.eeicom.com/eye/shyness.html Diane Ullius, the author of this article published in *The Editorial Eye*, teaches oral and written communication skills at Editorial Experts Inc and at Georgetown University. She offers practical advice about getting over the fear of speaking in public.

- Visit the room before you speak. Check the equipment and become comfortable with your surroundings.

- Find a quiet space to project your voice and warm it up. During your presentation, you need to talk louder than you normally do and, for some, the first few words are uncomfortable. Experience these words alone, in private if possible.

- Avoid looking at your notes and rehearsing just minutes before the presentation. It's too late now, and last-minute preparation will only make you more nervous.

- Take a few deep breaths and roll your ankles and shoulders to help you relax any tight muscles.

- If a question arises and you don't know the answer, don't bluff. You can (and should) say you don't know the answer but will follow up on it. And then do so!

- Know that your listeners are there to learn something from you and *you* are the authority. If you have done your research and have prepared well, it *will* show.

Sharpen Your Platform Manner

Knowing some elementary platform techniques can help improve your performance:

- Arrive early and check that the projector, computer, and microphone work. Identify the light switches you will need to control, if you have to dim the lights at any time when presenting.

- Appear businesslike and cheerful.

- Speak from notes. You will lose contact with your audience if you read from a prepared speech.

- Let your enthusiasm *show*. If you present your information with passion, your audience will see that you really enjoy talking about your subject and will listen more attentively.

Be an energetic, enthusiastic speaker

- Vary your voice to create interest: louder, softer, faster, slower.

- Look at your audience. Try to speak to individuals in turn, rather than the group as a whole. Pick out someone in one part of the room and talk to that person for a few moments, then turn to someone in another part of the room. Let each listener feel he or she is being addressed personally.

- Use humour sparingly, and only if it fits naturally into your presentation. Never insert a joke to "warm up" an audience. If you do use humour, make sure your audience is laughing *with* you, not *at* you.

- Speak at a moderate speed. We recommend 120 to 140 words per minute. This will feel a little slower than a normal conversational rate.

- Speak up. If possible try speaking without a microphone, since this gives you much greater freedom of movement and tonal flexibility. If the room is large and you have to use one, try to obtain a lavaliere (travelling) microphone that clips onto your clothing and is wireless.

- Pause occasionally to study your speaker's notes. Never be afraid to stop speaking for a few moments to gather your thoughts and establish that you have covered every major topic.

Watch your body language; make it work for you, not against you

- Avoid distracting habits that divert audience attention. For example, avoid pacing back and forth or balancing precariously on the edge of the platform (the audience will be far more interested in seeing whether you fall off than in following your topic). Also avoid nervous behaviour, such as jingling keys or coins in your pocket (put them in a back pocket, out of reach), playing with objects on the speaker's table (remove them before you start speaking), or cracking your knuckles.

Distribute Your Handouts

When is the best time to give your listeners your handout materials? There are three approaches:

1. If your handouts are simply copies of your slides, then hand them out right at the start of your presentation so listeners can make notes on them while you speak.

2. If you have charts or diagrams you want your listeners to refer to as you speak, hand them out at the appropriate moment during your talk.

3. If your handouts are a detailed narrative-style description of the points you will be making, rather than copies of your slides, and the audience

does not need to refer to them as you speak, then we recommend you hand them out toward the end or immediately after your presentation. (If you hand them out at the start, your listeners will tend to leaf through them to identify "where you are" in your talk, and create a disturbance for their neighbours.)

Reach Out to Your Audience

Although good pre-platform preparation and knowledge of platform techniques can give you confidence, they are not sufficient in themselves to break down the initial barrier between speaker and audience. Successful speakers develop a well-rounded personality they use continuously and unconsciously to establish a sound speaker–audience relationship. When you speak to an audience only once, and then only briefly, probably the most important attributes to develop are enthusiasm and sincerity: enthusiasm about your topic, and sincerity in wanting to help your audience learn about it.

The time and effort you invest in preparing for a talk will depend on your confidence as a speaker and your familiarity with the subject. No one expects you to give a fully professional briefing at your first attempt, but your listeners (and your employer) will appreciate your efforts when they see that you have prepared your talk carefully and are presenting it in an interesting way.

Taking Part in Meetings

The chairperson may run the meeting, but the participants control its progress

We all occasionally attend meetings. In industry, you may be asked to sit on a committee set up for a multitude of reasons, from resolving technical problems that are tying up production to organizing the company's annual picnic. The effectiveness of such meetings is entirely controlled by those taking part. Meetings attended by people *aware of their role* as participants can move quickly and achieve good results; those attended by individuals who seize the opportunity to air personal complaints can be dull and can cripple action.

Meetings can be either structured or unstructured, depending on their purpose. A structured meeting follows a predetermined pattern: its chairperson prepares an agenda that defines the purpose and objectives of the meeting and the topics to be covered. The meeting then proceeds logically from point to point. An unstructured meeting uses a conceptual approach to derive new ideas. Only its purpose is defined, since its participants are expected to introduce suggestions and comments that may generate new concepts (this approach is frequently called "brainstorming"). We will discuss the structured meeting here, because you are much more likely to encounter it in industry.

A meeting is composed of a chairperson and two or more meeting participants, one of whom often is appointed to be secretary for that particular meeting. The secretary makes notes of what happens during the meeting and, after the meeting, writes the "minutes," or meeting record. Each person's role is discussed here.

The Chairperson's Role

A good chairperson controls the direction of a meeting yet leaves ample room for the participants to feel they are making the major contribution to the meeting. The chairperson must be a good organizer, an effective administrator, and a diplomat (to smooth ruffled feathers if opinions differ widely). Much of the success of a meeting will result from the chairperson's preparation before the meeting starts and ability to maintain control as it proceeds.

Prepare an Agenda

Approximately two days before the meeting the chairperson prepares an agenda of topics to be discussed and circulates it to all meeting participants. The agenda identifies three things:

- The date, time, place, and purpose of the meeting.
- The topics that will be discussed (numbered, and in the sequence they will be addressed), divided into two groups:

  1. Decision Items
  2. Discussion Items

  This arrangement ensures that participants deal with the most important items early in the meeting.

- The person who is delegated to record the meeting's minutes (the secretary).

A typical agenda is shown in Figure 10-4.

Place the most important points at the top of the agenda

Run the Meeting

The chairperson's first responsibility is to start the meeting on time: a person with a reputation for being slow in getting meetings started will encourage latecomers. The chairperson must also keep the meeting as short as possible without seeming to "railroad" decisions and must maintain control of the meeting.

The meeting should be run roughly according to the rules of parliamentary procedure. Since most in-house meetings are relatively informal, full parliamentary procedure would be too cumbersome. (For more information about these procedures, refer to *Robert's Rules of Order*. You can find this guide in most libraries.) The chairperson introduces each topic on the agenda in turn, invites the person specializing in the topic to present a report, then opens the topic for discussion. The discussion offers the greatest challenge for the chairperson, who must

- permit a good debate among the members, yet steer a member who digresses back to the main topic,
- sense when a discussion on a subject has gone on for long enough, then be ready to break in and ask for a decision, and

An effective chairperson encourages reluctant contributors, dampens over-enthusiastic ones

MACRO
ENGINEERING INC.

600 Deepdale Drive, Toronto ON M5W 4R9

To: Members, E-Learning Research Committee

The monthly meeting of the E-Learning Research Committee will be held in conference room B at 3 p.m. on Friday, September 19, 2008. The agenda will be:

Decision Items:
1.   Accelerated completion of the e-learning program for the DPS-2A ultra-narrowbeam system installation. (R Taylor)
2.   Purchase of off-the-shelf e-learning software. (W Frayne)
3.   Proposals for papers: 2009 International E-Learning Conference and Symposium, Vancouver, BC. (D Thomashewski)

Name the person who will speak about each particular topic

Discussion Items:
4.   Report on investigation into significance of streaming e-learners according to their ability. (C Bundt)
5.   Proposal for beta-testing completed e-learning modules. (R Mohammed)
6.   Plans for Annual Research Division banquet. (C Tripp; J Kosty)
7.   Other business: (Please send topics to me by 10 a.m. Thursday, September 18.)

This month's meeting secretary: J Kosty.

Daniel K Thomashewski

Daniel K Thomashewski
Chairperson, ELR Committee
September 16, 2008

Figure 10-4   An agenda for a meeting.

- know when strong opinions are likely to block resolution of a difficult problem, and assign one person or a small subcommittee to investigate further and present the results at the next meeting.

Sum Up

Before proceeding from one topic to the next, the chairperson summarizes the outcome of the discussion on the first topic. The outcome may be a general conclusion, a consensus of members' opinions, a decision, or a statement of action defining who is to do what, and when. In this way all members are aware of the outcome, and the secretary knows what to enter into the minutes.

Effective "summing up" helps the secretary identify what should be recorded in the minutes

The chairperson also sums up at the end of the meeting, this time reviewing major issues that were discussed and the main results. At the same time, the chairperson points the way forward by mentioning any important actions to be taken and the time, date, and place of the next meeting (presuming there is to be one).

The best way to learn to be a good chairperson is to watch others undertake the role. Study those who get a lot of business done without appearing to intrude too much in the decision making. Learn what you should *not* do from those whose meetings tend to wander from topic to topic before a decision is made, allow many "contributors" to all speak at the same time, and last far too long.

The Participants' Role

You can contribute most to a meeting by arriving prepared, stating clearly your facts, ideas, and opinions when called on, and keeping quiet the remainder of the time. If you observe the following three basic rules you will help speed up the meeting.

Come Prepared

If a meeting is scheduled to start at 3:00 p.m., do not wait until 2:30 to gather the information you need. Arriving with a sheaf of papers in your hand and shuffling through them for the first 15 minutes creates a disturbance and causes you (and those around you) to miss much of what is being said. Start gathering information as soon as the agenda arrives, sort your information to identify the specific items you need, then jot down topic headings.

Plan your presentation like a technical briefing

Preparation becomes even more important if you have been researching data on a particular topic and will be expected to present your findings at the meeting. Start by dividing your information into two compartments:

1. Facts your listeners *must* have if they are to fully understand the case you are making and reach a decision (if, for example, you are requesting their approval to take a specific course of action). These become "Need-to-Know" facts.

2. Details your listeners only *may* be interested in, and do not necessarily need to understand your case or reach a decision. These are "Nice-to-Know" facts.

Plan to present only the "Need-to-Know" facts in your prepared presentation, but have the "Nice-to-Know" facts ready in case one of the listeners asks questions about them.

Then examine the "Need-to-Know" facts to identify the one or two pieces of information your listeners will *most* need to hear. This will become your Main Message, or Summary Statement.

The three compartments form a pyramid-style speaking plan, as illustrated in Figure 10-5.

Be Brief

In your opening remarks summarize what your listeners most need to hear from you (your Main Message), and then follow immediately with facts and details from the "Need-to-Know" compartment. If you have statistical data to offer, either project the prepared tables onto a screen or print copies and distribute them when you begin to speak. If you have a lot of information to distribute, print copies ahead of the meeting and ask the chairperson to distribute them with the agenda, so that everyone can examine your data before coming to the meeting.

Keep your cool; defend your point logically and rationally

At the end of your presentation, invite questions from the meeting participants. For your answers, draw on the data you have prepared for the "Nice-to-Know" compartment. If some listeners seem to resist your ideas, try to avoid becoming defensive. Say that you can see their point of view, and then explain why your approach is sound or offers a better alternative than the one they may be suggesting. In particular, avoid getting into a personal confrontation with one or more of the meeting participants. And when the chairperson calls on the members to indicate whether they accept your ideas or will approve your proposal, if they respond negatively be ready to accept their decision gracefully.

Structure your information like a written report or proposal

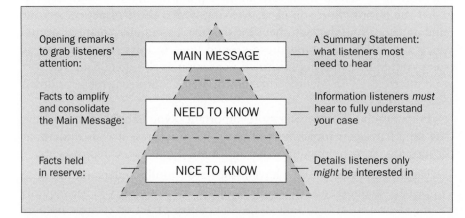

Figure 10-5 Plan for presenting information at a meeting.

Contribute Constructively

Many parts of a meeting require you to be only an interested observer. At these times keep quiet unless you have a relevant question, additional information to contribute, or an educated opinion to offer. Discussion of a topic should be a one-to-one conversation between you and the chairperson, or sometimes between you and the topic specialist. It should never become a free-for-all with each person arguing a point with his or her neighbour.

When you have a comment to make, raise your hand and look at the chairperson, then wait for the chairperson to call on you to present your opinion.

The Secretary's Role

Sometimes an administrative assistant is brought in to record the minutes of a meeting, but more often the chairperson appoints one of the participants to take minutes. If you happen to be selected, you need to know how to go about it.

Recording minutes does not mean writing down everything that is said. Minutes should be brief, so there is room to mention only the highlights of each topic discussed. Items that must be recorded are

- main conclusions reached,
- decisions made (with, if necessary, the name[s] of the person[s] who made them, or the results of a vote),
- what is to be done next, who is to do it, and by when, and
- the exact wording of any policy statements derived during the meeting.

The best way to get this information quickly is to write the agenda topics on a lined sheet of paper, spacing them about two inches apart vertically. In these spaces jot down the highlights in note form, leaving room to write in more information from memory immediately after the meeting.

The completed minutes should be distributed to everyone present, preferably within 24 hours. They become a permanent record on which the chairperson can base the agenda for the next meeting, and which participants can use as a reminder of what they are supposed to do. The format shown in Figure 10-6 also provides an "action" column to draw participants' attention to their particular responsibilities.

Write the minutes while the events are still fresh in your mind

MACRO
ENGINEERING INC.
600 Deepdale Drive, Toronto ON M5W 4R9

E-Learning Research Committee

Minutes of Meeting

Friday, September 19, 2008, 3:00 p.m.

In Attendance:	C Bundt	R Mohammed
	W Feldman	R Taylor
	W Frayne	D Thomashewski (Chair)
	J Kosty (Secretary)	C Tripp
Regrets:	D Wilton	

Minutes	*Action*

Decision Items:

1. The e-learning program for the DPS-2A ultra-narrowbeam system is incomplete. Changes had to be made to the storyboard to reflect learning difficulties experienced during usability testing of module 4. The program is now scheduled for completion on October 16. — *R Taylor*

2. The committee approved W Frayne's proposal to purchase three copies of the Telesat software Version 4.3 at a total cost of $2200. The cost will be drawn equally from the E-Learning Research and the Operating budgets. — *W Frayne* / *R Mohammed*

3. Three papers are to be submitted to the program committee for next year's International E-Learning Conference and Symposium. Deadline for proposals is November 30. — *C Bundt* / *W Feldman* / *J Tripp*

Discussion Items:

4. C Bundt completed Phase 1 of the investigation into streaming e-learners on September 12. She estimates Phase 2 will be complete on October 2.

6. The Research Division banquet will be held in collaboration with the annual Awards Dinner on March 13, 2009. The banquet committee will establish a joint plan with the Awards Committee. — *C Tripp* / *J Kosty*

J Kosty
_____
J Kosty, Secretary

Minutes should reflect key outcomes, not describe what everybody said

Figure 10-6 Minutes of a meeting. Note the "Action" column, which draws individuals' attention to their post-meeting responsibilities. (The dotted line indicates a break between two pages and some omitted information.)

Speaking situations you are likely to encounter in industry will develop from projects on which you are working. Hence, assignments for this chapter are assumed to grow naturally out of the writing assignments presented in other chapters.

Project 10.1: Speaking Situations Evolving from Other Projects

You have to attend a meeting to present the results of a study or investigation you have carried out, at which you will brief managers or a client on your findings and recommendations. In each of the following instances, which are drawn from projects in Chapters 3, 4, 5, 6, and 7, list in point form the information you would convey

- as your "Main Message," and
- as your "Need-to-Know" details.

In some projects—mainly in Chapters 3 and 4—you will be able to draw on the details provided in the assignment instructions without first doing the report writing project itself. In others—primarily in Chapters 5 and 6—it will help if you have first completed the study and written the report.

Be ready to present this information orally.

1. Project 3.9

Two government representatives involved with Environmental Studies Contract WM-23357 are to visit Manfred Industries Ltd next week. Your manager asks you to return to the office to attend a meeting with them to explain that the two-week delay in completing the lake-level measurement program has been caused by faulty manufacture of the water stage manometer's spring and drive assembly, not by poor operation or slow work.

2. Project 4.2

When you return to your office after checking the damaged crates with Noella Redovich, there is a request from manager Vern Rogers among your email messages: "Please come in as soon as it's convenient and describe your findings."

3. Project 4.4

You drive back to the office to pick up a van to replace the one that was damaged during your drive to the Mooswa River construction site. Your manager—M B Corrigan—telephones and asks you to see him before you return to Mooswa River. "Please describe the incident to me," he says when you enter his office. "I need the details for when I talk to Meadows Electronics (where you rented the video camera) and the insurance company."

4. Project 5.1

Robert Delorme telephones you and asks, "Have you finished the Quillicom landfill study?" You tell him you have, but you have not yet written the report. "Then I want you to go to the Quillicom Town Council meeting at 7:30 p.m. tonight. The councillors want to hear what recommendations you will be making."

5. Project 5.2

Paullette Machon (vice-president of operations at Baldur Agri-Chemicals—BAC) telephones to say she will be coming to your office tomorrow and bringing BAC's manager of human resources with her. Rather than wait for your report to reach them, they want you to brief them on your findings about BAC's power house problems, and then they want to discuss the implications with you.

6. Project 6.1

Highways engineer Morris Hordern asks you to brief his highway engineers on the results of your highway paint study.

7. Project 6.2, Part 3

When you deliver your sound-level study to Wendy Partridge, you tell her there is a problem at Mirabel Realty and it's going to cost a fair sum to remedy it. She telephones you two days later. "Three people from head office will be here next week on a routine visit. I'd appreciate it if you could come in one afternoon to describe your findings to them. You'll do a better job than me, because you know the study better than I do."

8. Project 7.1

You have written the proposal for purchasing handheld computers and you handed it to Tracey Harcourt three days ago. Today she emails you with this message: "I want you to present your idea to purchase handheld computers in person at next week's Capital Budget meeting. The committee may want to know specifically which model you are recommending and why it is your preferred choice."

9. Project 7.3

The project manager from Terrapin Control Systems flies in to your city a few days after the power outage that caused you to discard the electronic switches in Batches 87H and 84C. Your manager—John Grayson—asks you to join him and the Terrapin project manager for a 2 p.m. meeting at which you are to describe the cause of the problem and what steps you will be taking to prevent a recurrence. "It's essential we assure him there will be no further work stoppages," Grayson says. "We've been told privately that Terrapin Control Systems is issuing an even bigger contract to us, so we must be sure they understand we have taken positive action to prevent further delays."

10. Project 7.4

When you deliver your proposal to Student Council president Sharon Gilchrist, she says: "It's a good idea. I'd like you to come to the next meeting and present the proposal in person."

Project 10.2: Informing Technicians of a New Manufacturing Material, Product, or Process

You are to research information on a topic related to your technology and then prepare it for both written and oral presentation. The topic may be a new manufacturing material, product, or process. The written and spoken presentations must

1. introduce the topic,
2. state why it is worth evaluating,
3. describe the material, method, or process,
4. discuss its uniqueness and usefulness, and
5. show how it can be applied in your particular field.

To obtain data for your topic, you will have to research current literature and probably talk to industrial users, manufacturers, and suppliers. Typical examples of topics are: a new oil that can be used at very low temperatures, a method for supporting the deck of a bridge during concrete-pouring by building up a base on compacted fill, a new paint for use on concrete surfaces, a new materials-handling system, and a recently developed computer software program. Assume that both your readers and your audience are technicians to whom the topic will be entirely new.

Make an in-depth presentation to unknowledgeable listeners

Part 1

On a sheet of paper write brief notes in point form identifying what you will say under each of the following topic headings:

- Summary Statement
- Purpose (of product, material, or process)
- Details (what it does and why it is unique)
- Conclusions

Part 2

Create your visuals.

Part 3

Deliver your presentation.

REFERENCES

1. Peter and Cheryl Reimold, *The Short Road to Great Presentations: How to Reach Any Audience Through Focused Preparation, Inspired Delivery, and Smart Use of Technology* (IEEE Press and Wiley-Interscience, 2003).

Chapter 11
Communicating with Prospective Employers

This chapter describes the various stages of the job-seeking process, and the careful steps that you, as an applicant, must take if you want employers you contact to consider you as a potential employee. The process starts with preparing a personal data record, then proceeds through preparing a resume, writing an application letter, completing an application form, attending interviews, and accepting or declining a job offer.

The Employment-Seeking Process

Figure 11-1 illustrates the five steps a *successful* applicant has to take before being employed. Depending on the firm or organization, some of these steps may be eliminated or combined.

These steps are outlined below. At each step you have to present a confident, positive image of yourself if you are to proceed to the next step.

The image you convey —on paper or online— has a major impact on a potential employer

1. **Initial Contact.** Your first step as a job seeker is to approach a prospective employer and ask to be considered for employment, either by responding to an advertisement or by approaching the employer

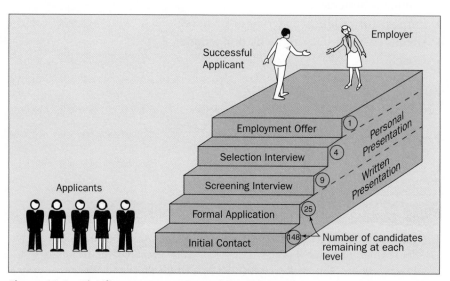

Figure 11-1   The five stages or steps of the job-seeking process.

"cold" (in the hope that the employer either has or shortly will have an opening). You may make this initial contact by presenting yourself at the employer's door, by writing a letter or email message, or by telephoning. The personal visit and the letter or email are better, because they let you *place your resume in the employer's hands.*

A resume may be submitted electronically

2. **Formal Application.** Often the employer will ask you to complete a company application so that all applicants are documented in the same way.

3. **Screening Interview.** The first interview you attend helps the employer identify which applicants have the strongest potential. In a large firm, the screening interview may be conducted by only one person, usually the employment manager or an employment representative.

4. **Selection Interview.** The most promising candidates are asked to attend a second interview. This time the manager of the department where the successful applicant will work is also present, and is sometimes accompanied by technical specialists.

5. **Employment Offer.** The employer makes a formal offer of employment to the successful applicant, often by telephone first and then by letter. The applicant responds, also by telephone and letter, to confirm his or her acceptance.

Using the Internet in Your Job Search

The internet offers vast opportunities and possibilities to people seeking employment. It provides an efficient way for employers and potential employees to meet and learn about each other.

You can use the internet to research information about companies, search for job postings, or enter your electronic resume into a database. Both large and small companies are using their websites to distribute employment opportunities and provide company information, so if you are looking for details about a particular company, its history, its corporate structure, and its beliefs and philosophies, check its websites. This will help prepare you for an interview or help you decide if you would like to work for that company.

You research corporate information online...

You can also use the internet to place an online international, domestic, or local classified advertisement. Online job ad services and electronic employer databases allow job hunters to quickly compile a list of prospects.

...or announce your availability as a potential employee

Companies from around the world in all types of industries use the internet to advertise employment opportunities. Search capabilities allow you to narrow your criteria to specific locations or job requirements. There are also a number of commercially run internet services that specialize in matching people to positions, and nonprofit Bulletin Board networks that allow anyone to list or look at job openings.

Another way to use the internet in your job search is to post your resume so potential employers can find you. It is not only a quick and effective way of transmitting your credentials, but also demonstrates your understanding of and ability with technology.

Start by contacting an internet resume specialist

Consider using an internet resume service that specializes in organizing, indexing, and distributing resumes (see the section "Electronic Resume Formats" later in this chapter for suggestions on preparing this type of resume). Independent database services are companies that match people with jobs.

A word of caution about the internet: it is just as easy for a potential employer to find information about you on the internet as it is for you to find information about them. Be careful about the persona and language you present online, in various networking areas. Make sure you are comfortable having a hiring manager view the information and potentially ask you questions about it.

Developing a Personal Data Record

Start a databank: store your history electronically

There are three ways you can go about writing a resume: you can rely solely on your memory; you can dust off and update a previous resume; or you can create a new resume from information you store in your own permanent personal data record (PDR). Using a PDR is best, because it provides a much broader information base for you to draw on.

A PDR becomes particularly useful in later years, when our ability to recall names, addresses, dates, and specific details of earlier employment diminishes. It can also be invaluable if, when calling initially on a potential employer, you are asked to complete an application form on the premises.

If you do not already have a PDR, prepare one now. You may find it's a pain to start, but it's not difficult to update and keep current. You will need to record details (and update them approximately once a year) for four topic areas:

Writing in the Job Search
http://owl.english.
purdue.edu/handouts/
pw/#sub2
The Online Writing Lab
at Purdue University has
a section devoted to
writing job search
materials, including
applications, resumes,
cover letters, acceptance
letters, references, and
personal statements.

- Education
- Work Experience
- Extracurricular Activities
- References

Remember, this is not a resume. You will draw from this information when you begin to organize your resume. As you progress in your career you will need to remove older, unrelated experience and add newer, more relevant information.

Education

List the schools, colleges, and universities you have attended or are attending. Start at high school and record the name of each school, the address and telephone number, and the dates you were there, your graduation date and your area of specialization. For college and university, list courses taken, major studies, and the full name of the degree, diploma, or certificate you were awarded. Include grades or at least a grade point average

(GPA) for each year. List any additional courses or seminars you completed and the date attended. Don't forget about courses taken while working for an organization or during school breaks.

Work Experience

For each job you have held in the past—and, if you are currently employed, the job you now hold—list

- the full name, address, telephone number, and website of the company or organization, and the full name, title, and email address of each supervisor you worked for,
- the dates you started and finished employment and, if you held several positions within the company, the name of the position and the date you were appointed to it,
- your job title, or titles if you held several positions,
- your specific responsibilities and duties for each position, paying particular attention to the supervisory aspects and responsibilities of any job that you carried out without supervision,
- any special skills you learned on the job,
- special awards or words of praise you received, or results you achieved, and
- projects you were involved in, including the type of technology you learned or used.

Be as detailed as possible: don't rely on your memory

Extracurricular Activities

List your activities in organizations that were not necessarily part of the jobs you have held or your education, but which show your participation and leadership qualities. These help identify you as a well-rounded, balanced person. For example:

- Membership in a club, society, or group, particularly noting your responsibilities as an active participator or committee member. (For example, member of sports committee or secretary of administrative committee.)
- Participation in community activities such as the Big Brother or Sister Organizations, YMCA or YWCA, 4-H Club, Parent–Teacher Association (PTA), or local community club. In particular, describe any executive or administrative positions you held, with special responsibilities and dates.
- Involvement in a technical society on a local or national level, with particular mention of any conferences you attended or papers you presented or published.
- Participation on a sports team, with special mention of your role as a team leader or coach.

Don't overlook your
personal attributes and
life experience

- Involvement in hobby activities—for example, stock car racing or rebuilding, a computer club, or dog breeding.
- Awards you have received for any activities you have been involved in.

For each activity, include the dates of your involvement and the name, address, telephone number, and email address of a person who can vouch for your participation. Make sure you indicate whether you were elected to the position or were doing the work voluntarily.

References

List the names of people you feel are best fitted to speak on your behalf. They fall into two groups: those who can vouch for your *capabilities* (as an employee, student, or committee member), and those who can speak for your *character*. Always contact these people first and ask if you may list them as a reference. Then, for each person write down

Be thorough: you cannot
tell in advance who you
may want to use as a
reference

- full name, professional title (such as Plant Engineer), place of employment, and job position,
- employer's address, telephone number, and website,
- home address, email address, and telephone number, and
- how long you have known them.

(If a reference has changed jobs, list details of both the previous and current employer.)

For each person you worked with in an extracurricular activity, also list

- the name of the organization you both were involved with, and the reference's position within that organization, and
- whether the person prefers to be called, or written to, at home or at work.

Preparing a Resume

A resume contains key information about yourself, carefully assembled and presented so that prospective employers will be impressed not only by your qualifications but also by your ability to present yourself effectively. (The correct spelling is "résumé," but common usage has made the accentless "resume" acceptable. In some countries it's called a *curriculum vitae*, or CV.)

Technical people tend to be conservative when they write their resumes, yet today's employment environment demands they be *competitive*. If a resume is to capture an employer's attention, it must display its writer's capabilities completely. The resume is a sales tool and the writer is the product.

There are no specific rules about the "right" way to prepare a resume. A resume is a very personal document and should show your personality. However, there are generally accepted guidelines of what employers expect to see and the type of information they require when evaluating you as a prospective employee. This section discusses three different formats for a paper resume. Later in this chapter we discuss the various types of electronic resumes and present some guidelines for submitting resumes electronically. You can submit your resume either electronically or on paper. It really depends on what the employer or job search agency has asked for. Don't fall into the trap of creating just one version of your resume and using it both electronically and on paper. The designs are very different.

Resume Formats

Of the three resumes presented on the following pages, you will have to decide which style will best present your qualifications and suit the position you are applying for. These examples are designed as paper resumes and do not follow the guidelines for electronic resumes.

For ease of reference, we will refer to the three styles as the traditional resume, the focused resume, and the functional resume. All three open with a summary statement, often called an Objective, that (1) describes the applicant's strongest qualifications from the *employer's* point of view, and (2) identifies that the writer is seeking work in a particular field. They are presented in a short paragraph of no more than two or three sentences.

Your resume style must fit your personality...

Objective
I have four years of experience supervising the installation and testing of wire and fibre optic telephone communication systems, and a recent MSc in electrical engineering with a major in fibre optics. I am now seeking employment where I can apply my knowledge and experience in fibre optics engineering.

An assertive statement such as this at the start of a resume draws the employer's attention rapidly to the applicant's primary experience and education, and to the employment direction the applicant wants to pursue. If the resume "hits the mark," the employer automatically reads further to learn more about the applicant.

To be of most value, the opening statement is focused to suit the needs of a particular employer, which means you have to carefully tailor each resume you submit.

...and that of the particular employer you are contacting

Job Star Central
http://jobstar.org/ tools/resume/index.php
Job Star Central gives you all the information you need to write your resume, with sample cover letters, resume resources on the web, and samples of different kinds of resumes.

The Traditional Resume

For decades the most widely recognized approach to resume writing has been to divide a job applicant's information into five parts, each preceded by an appropriate heading:

Objective
Education
Experience
Extracurricular Activities
References

The traditional resume is particularly suitable for recent university or college graduates who have limited work experience, or for students who expect to graduate shortly. Alison Witney is a biological sciences undergraduate who has held two previous jobs, totalling three years of full-time employment. Her resume is shown in Figure 11-2. Comments on the resume, plus guidelines you can use to write a resume of your own in the traditional format, are presented here.

A short, concise, directed resume is welcomed by employers!

1 Job applicants with only limited work experience should try to keep their resumes down to one page.

2 Each line of Alison's name, address, telephone number, and email address is centred to give the top of the resume a balanced appearance.

3 There is no need for Alison to list all the primary and secondary schools she attended; it is enough to state the name of her high school and the year she graduated. She should then list each college or university she attended, plus the type of course enrolled in, the diploma or degree received, and her year of graduation (or expected graduation). Alison has decided to include her grade point average (GPA) because it is high. This is optional, but if you do include it be sure to include it for all schools.

4 Experience is usually presented in reverse order, with the most recent work experience appearing first. You should provide more details about recent experience (as Alison has done), and about earlier work that is similar to that of the position you are seeking, than for less-related work. Quote dates as whole years for long periods of employment, but as month and year for short periods; for example, Jun 2007–Feb 2008.

5 For each employer, state the name of the company or organization first, emphasize it with bold type, and then identify the city and province in which it is located. Then describe the position held (give the job title), and what the work involved. Particularly draw attention to the *responsibilities* of the job rather than merely listing the duties you performed. Use words that create strong images of your confidence, such as:

Let the words you use convey a positive impression

coordinated	organized
monitored	implemented
presented	supervised
planned	directed

(Note that Alison uses "responsible for," "administering," "coordinating," and "teaching.")

①

Alison V Witney
1670 Fulham Boulevard
Truro NS B2N 6C4

②

Tel: (902) 474-6318
email: avwitney@nsonline.net

OBJECTIVE
To work in a position related to Animal Biology or Health Science, where I can use to good advantage both my Diploma in Biological Science and my experience as a veterinary assistant.

③

EDUCATION AND TRAINING
- Will graduate with a Diploma in Biological Science from Amiento Technical College, June, 2008 (GPA to date: 3.7).
- Graduate of Morton Stanley High School, Corisand, Nova Scotia, 2004 (avg: 92.3%)

WORK EXPERIENCE

2006 to date **Animal Treatment Centre**, Amiento, NS. Veterinary assistant,

④

responsible for reception, grooming, and exercising of animals, assisting veterinarian during operations, changing dressings, administering injections and anaesthetics, and

⑤

performing administrative duties such as accounting and ordering of supplies. (One year full-time, two years part-time.)

2004 to 2006 **Remick Airlines**, Fredericton, NB. Accounts clerk in air freight department; coordinating billings, preparing

⑥

invoices, following up lost shipments, assisting clients, and writing monthly reports. For nine months assisted in payroll preparation.

1998 to date **Bar None Riding Stables**, Corisand, NS. Part-time employment teaching the care and handling of horses, and basic riding techniques, to young riders. Assisted in grooming, cleaning, feeding, and saddling-up.

⑦

ADDITIONAL INFORMATION
- Winner of two educational awards: Morton Stanley Science Scholarship (2003) and Amiento Technical College Biology Scholarship (2008).
- Active at Truro Recreational Centre since 1998, where I teach swimming and lifesaving
- Interests: horseback riding and jumping, swimming, and water skiing

⑧

REFERENCES
The following people have agreed to supply references on my behalf:

Dr Alex Gavin
Veterinary Surgeon
Animal Treatment Centre
2230 Wolverine Drive
Amiento NS B3R 2G1
Tel: 474-1260
Fax: 474-1355
email: a.gavin@atlantic.vet.net

Mr Charles Devereaux
Owner-Manager
Bar None Riding Stables
2881 Westshore Drive
Corisand NS B4L 3A2
Tel: 632-2292
Fax: 631-3105
email: bar.none@nst.ns.ca

An appealing, uncrowded appearance, coupled with good words, will catch an employer's attention

Figure 11-2 A traditional resume or biography of experience.

If you have held several short part-time jobs, describe them together and draw attention to the most important, like this: "Several after-school jobs, primarily as a stock clerk in a small grocery store."

6 The two-column arrangement of dates and work experience is important because it gives a less crowded appearance to the page. If the job descriptions were carried to the left—under the dates—the job details would appear as heavy, less visually appealing blocks of information.

An employer wants to see the "whole picture"

7 Information on your hobbies, interests, and participation in sports and community activities tells prospective employers that you recognize your role in society, are not too rigid or too narrow, and adapt well to your environment. Employers reason that such an applicant will make an interesting, active employee who will not only contribute to the company, but also take part in social and sports functions. Outside activities represent a balanced lifestyle and provide outlets for stress.

8 Try to draw your list of references from a cross-section of people you have worked for, been taught by, or served with on committees, and ensure that their relevance is apparent (their connection to one of your previous jobs or activities must be clear). Before including them in your list, check that each is willing to act as a reference. We suggest you always provide references on your resume. Resumes that list "References Available on Request" make the reader take one more step. By providing them in advance you are making the selection committee's work easier and shorter.

Figure 11-3 shows an alternative way that Alison could prepare the Work Experience part of her resume, in which she shows the strengths she will bring to the job as a series of bulleted points divided into relevant experience and other experience. The reader can scan this quickly and then obtain details from the now shorter descriptions of her employment history. This is similar to the way Reid Qually offers his key points in the functional resume in Figure 11-5 (pages 251 to 252). You can choose which you feel is most appropriate for the Work Experience section of your resume.

The Focused Resume

Focus your resume to match the employer's primary interest

Job applicants who have more extensive experience to describe do better if they focus an employer's attention on their particular strengths and aims. This means asking themselves what a prospective employer is *most likely to want to know* after reading their opening statement. (Probably it will be: "What have you done that specifically qualifies you to achieve the objective you have presented?") To answer, applicants must focus on their work experience rather than their education, particularly on work that is

Specific Experience Working with Animals
- Assisting veterinarian during operations; administering injections and anaesthetics; grooming and exercising
- Horseback riding and jumping; daily care and grooming; teaching

Other Experience
- Training: teaching young people swimming, life saving, horseback riding
- Administration: accounting, invoicing; payroll preparation, general office management, report writing

Employment History

2006 to date	**Animal Treatment Centre**, Amiento, NS. Veterinary assistant to Dr Alex Gavin (1 year full-time, 2 years part-time)
2004 to 2006	**Remick Airlines**, Fredericton, NB. Accounts clerk in air freight department, coordinating shipments and billing (3 years full-time)
1998 to date	**Bar None Riding Stables**, Corisand, NS. Teaching care and handling of horses, and basic riding techniques (10 years part-time)

Figure 11-3 An alternative way to present experience that could replace the Work Experience section of Alison Witney's resume in Figure 11-2.

relevant to the position they are seeking (which means they must first research information about the company).

If their experience is sufficiently varied, then they can go one step further and divide the Work Experience section of their resume into two parts: (1) work related to the position they are seeking; and (2) work in unrelated areas. They must place all of this information *ahead* of the "Education" section, so that there is a natural flow from their Objective to their Related Experience. Thus, the parts of a focused resume are:

Objective (or Aim)
Related Experience
Other Experience
Education
Extracurricular Activities
References

Colin Farrow's two-page resume in Figure 11-4 adopts this sequence. The circled numbers beside the resume refer to the following comments.

1 Colin has sufficient information to warrant preparing a two-page resume, but he should not run over onto a third page. A third page can be used, however, if an applicant has published papers and articles or has obtained patents for new inventions, which can be listed on a separate sheet and identified as an attachment. A separate page can also be used to list references.

2 Colin's objective clearly shows his thrust toward structural engineering and his desire to obtain employment in that field.

Colin R Farrow, P.Eng

408 Medwin Street
Brandon MB R7C 0B3
Tel: (204) 548-1612
email: c.farrow@mbonline.com

OBJECTIVE

After four years of comprehensive experience as an engineering technologist installing and testing transmission line towers in Northern Canada, I returned to university where I obtained a B.Sc in Structural Engineering. Now I am seeking employment where I can use my experience and education to research and test tower anchors and grouts in permafrost areas.

Immediately announce your strengths and show how they can be used by the employer

RELATED WORK EXPERIENCE

June 2006 to October 2008	**Fairborne and Warren Associates,** Consulting Engineers, Brandon, Manitoba. Project engineer managing construction of microwave transmission towers and associated structures between Brandon and The Pas, Manitoba, for Manitoba Telephone System. Wrote specifications, coordinated and monitored contractors' work, prepared progress reports, and maintained liaison with client.
June 1998 to August 2002	**Northwestern Steel Constructors Ltd.** Winnipeg, Manitoba. Crew chief, supervising team installing high-voltage transmission line towers between Flin Flon, Manitoba, and Minnowin Point, N.W.T. After 30 months was assigned to assist project engineers of Ebby, Little and Company, testing concretes and grouts installed in discontinuous permafrost (10 months). For final year, appointed installation coordinator, responsible for scheduling and supervising installation crews. Resigned to attend university.

OTHER WORK EXPERIENCE

January 1993 to February 1997	**Canadian Forces**, Construction and Maintenance Directorate. For first two years, member of crew installing communication systems (buildings and towers) at CF bases between Armstrong, Ontario, and Prince George, BC. For final two years, antenna installation and maintenance technician at CFB Comox, Vancouver Island. Attained rank of corporal.
September 1993 to December 1997	**Bowlands Stores**. Stock clerk in Store No. 26, St. Boniface, Manitoba. (One year part-time while at high school, 1 1/4 years full-time.)

/2...

Figure 11-4 A focused resume for a job applicant with a varied background.

Colin R Farrow – page 2

EDUCATION

6
- B.Sc in Structural Engineering, University of Manitoba, 2005.
- Diploma in Civil Engineering Technology, Red River Community College, Winnipeg, Manitoba, June 1998.
- Graduate (Grade 12), Dakota Collegiate, St Vital, Manitoba, 1991.

ADDITIONAL ACTIVITIES/INFORMATION

- Member, Association of Professional Engineers and Geoscientists of Manitoba (APEGM).
- Member, Certified Technicians and Technologists Association of Manitoba (CTTAM).

7
- Awarded Orton R Smith Scholarship for proficiency in applied mathematics, Red River Community College, 1997.
- Courses attended in Canadian Forces:
    * Construction Techniques, 1993.
    * Supervisory Skills Development, 1995.
    * First Aid and Safety Methods (various courses), 1994 to 1996.
- Junior Leader, St Vital YMCA, 1989 to 1992, teaching swimming and aquatic activities to boys and girls age 9 to 15. Awarded Red Cross Bronze Medallion, 1990. Lifeguard at Grand Beach, Manitoba, summers of 1990 and 1991.

REFERENCES

8
The following have agreed to provide information regarding my qualifications and work capabilities:

Martin G Warren, M.Sc	Philip G Karlowsky
Projects Coordinator	Contracts Manager
Fairborne and Warren Associates	Northwestern Steel Constructors Ltd
360 Rosser Avenue	3335 Notre Dame Avenue
Brandon, Manitoba R7A 0K2	Winnipeg, Manitoba R3H 2J4
Tel: (204) 544-1687	Tel: (204) 632-1450
Fax: (204) 544-1628	Fax: (204) 632-2177
email: mgw13@aol.com	email: p.karlowsk@norsteel.mb.ca

If applying to an educational institution, consider placing the Education section ahead of Work Experience

We recommend including two references, rather than writing "References available on request"

Divide your work
experience into "directly
related" and "less
related" compartments

3 The positions described within each Experience section should be listed in reverse order, the most recent experience being described first. The most recent and most relevant experience should be described in greater depth than early or unrelated experience (compare the descriptions of Colin's Northwestern Steel Constructors' experience with his Bowlands Stores' experience).

4 As in the traditional resume, each employer's name is listed first (in boldface type) and followed by the city and province. The applicant's position or job title is identified next, and then a description of what the job involved. If several positions have been held within the same firm, each is named and its duration stated so that the applicant's progress within the firm is clear. Each position should draw particular attention to the personal responsibilities and supervisory aspects of the job, rather than just listing specific duties. Verbs should be chosen carefully, so they make the position sound as comprehensive and self-directed as possible. If the paragraph grows too long, it can be broken into a list like this:

...appointed crew chief responsible for
- installing interconnection and distribution systems
- hiring, training, and supervising local labour
- ordering and monitoring delivery of parts and materials
- arranging and supervising subcontract work
- preparing progress and job completion reports.

Notice how the verbs are all in the same format.

5 Single-spaced typing should be used as much as possible to keep the resume compact, but use a reasonable amount of white space on each side and between major paragraphs to avoid a crowded effect. Although we normally recommend setting the right margin "ragged right," for Colin's resume a justified right margin does not seem too rigid. See the "Electronic Resume Formats" section starting on page 253 if you are submitting your resume electronically. The guidelines are different.

6 Education can be listed either in chronological or reverse sequence. Identify the city and province of each educational institution attended, the name, and the type of diploma or degree earned.

7 Employers are *interested* in a job applicant's accomplishments and extracurricular activities, particularly those describing community involvement and awards or commendations. This part of a resume can be preceded by a heading such as "Extracurricular Activities."

8 Both people Colin has chosen as references can be cross-referenced to his previous work experience. Telephone numbers and email addresses are important, because they are the fastest way to communicate.

The Functional Resume

Of the three paper-based resumes discussed here, the functional resume goes furthest in *marketing* a job applicant's attributes. For some employers its approach may seem too assertive or pushy; for others, particularly employers seeking someone for a technical sales position, its approach helps demonstrate that the applicant has strong capabilities.

The functional resume is the only one to offer *opinions*: its objective identifies in general terms what the applicant believes he or she can do to improve the quality of the employer's products or service, and then follows immediately with the applicant's key qualifications—the capabilities the applicant believes best demonstrate that he or she is qualified to do what the Objective proclaims.

The functional resume is not for everyone, yet for certain people and jobs its direct approach is ideal

To prove that the applicant's opinions are valid, the third section establishes—with clear facts and figures—what he or she has done for previous employers or organizations. This results in a revised arrangement of the resume's parts:

Objective
Qualifications
Major Achievements
Employment Experience
Education
Awards/Other Activities
References

The intent of this arrangement is to target the resume not just for a particular employer but also for a particular position. It is especially useful under two circumstances: for job applicants who have experience in marketing and want to be employed in technical sales; and for applicants who have a lean educational background but have proven practical experience that can be of value to a specific employer.

The resume in Figure 11-5 shows how Reid Qually uses the functional method to capture the attention of the marketing manager of a company engaged in selling cellular telephone services. The circled numbers beside his resume relate to the following comments.

1 Reid has positioned his name in the top right corner of the page because, in a pile of resumes, his name will stand out just where the person's hand is placed to flip through the pages. The line underneath his name helps draw the reader's eye to it. Reid has also

Use subtle marketing techniques to promote yourself

saved a few lines by putting his contact address all on one line. If you are gong to submit your resume electronically or if you know it will be scanned, the techniques are different. See the "Electronic Resume Formats" section starting on page 253.

2 Reid has written his Objective with a specific employer in mind. He discovered that King Cell—a relatively new West Coast player in the cellular telecommunications field—is planning to expand and hopes to become a major provider of cellular telephone services across the continent. By echoing the company's philosophy, he is almost certain to catch management's attention.

3 Reid is aware that, as soon as the personnel manager at King Cell has read his Objective, he or she is likely to think: "You have told me what you want to do; now tell me *why* you think you can do it." So he immediately offers five reasons, each demonstrating that he can handle the job. Note particularly that

Opinions must be supported by solid evidence

- each is short, so that the reader assimilates the information quickly,
- each starts with a strong "action" verb (i.e. *identify, create, establish*), which creates a strong, definite image, and
- each is an opinion. (Although not recommended for other types of resumes, opinions can be used here because Reid will follow immediately with *evidence* to support his assertions.)

4 Reid's evidence provides *facts*, which demonstrate he has already established a solid track record. Reid keeps each piece of evidence short and offers definitive details (i.e. percentages, names, and dates) which add credibility to his statements.

5 Reid can keep details of his work experience short because he has already identified his major accomplishments. For each employer he provides

An unusual yet conservative appearance can help "sell" you as a strong, imaginative applicant...

- start and finish dates (by month),
- employer's name (emphasized, in bold or italic letters),
- employer's location (city and province), and
- his job title and major responsibilities.

To maintain continuity, he lists his employment experience in reverse sequence.

... but these techniques cannot be applied if you send your resume electronically

6 Reid has only limited formal education, so he draws attention to his high grade point average (GPA) on returning to school after a long absence. (Comments continue after Figure 11-5.)

Reid G Qually

7 - 2617 East 38th Avenue • Vancouver, BC • V5R 2T9 • Tel: 604-263-4250 • email: qually@interex.net

Reid sets the scene with a commanding, professional approach

Objective

To use my proven marketing skills to increase market share for a Canadian company providing cellular telephone services and systems continent-wide.

Qualifications

I have proven capability to

- Identify special-interest client groups and develop innovative marketing strategies.
- Create results-oriented proposals and focus them to meet specific client needs.
- Follow through with clients, both before and after a sale.
- Supervise and coordinate the efforts of small groups.
- Establish strong interpersonal relations with clients, management, and sales staff.

Major Achievements

For previous employers and organizations I have

- Devised an innovative lease/purchase marketing plan for first-time customers, resulting in a 34% increase in lease agreements and a 23% increase in follow-on sales over a 12-month period (for Morton Sales and Leasing, in 2005).
- Increased sales of BlackBerry message devices by 31% over a nine-month period (for Advent Communications Limited, in 2007–2008).
- Received a company-wide "Salesperson of the Year" award (from Provo Department Stores, in 2002).
- Advised and coordinated Electronic/Computer Technology students who won a nationwide IEEE "Carillon Communication Award" (for Pacific Rim Community College, 2007).

Achievements must be stated strongly and supported with specific details

/2...

Figure 11-5 A functional resume identifies in detail what an applicant feels he or she can do for a particular employer.

Employment Experience

(5)

June 2007
to the present

Advent Communications Limited, Vancouver, BC. Assistant Marketing Manager, responsible for coordinating four representatives selling BlackBerry and other mobile devices to commercial customers.

November 2003
to June 2007

Morton Sales and Leasing, New Westminster, BC. Sales representative marketing office furniture and equipment to business accounts and private customers.

July 2000
to October 2003

Provo Department Stores, Store No. 17, Calgary, Alberta. Sales representative in Home Electronics Department. Responsible for over-the-counter sales of computers and home entertainment centres.

Education

(6)

June 2007

Certificate in Commercial and Industrial Sales, Pacific Rim Community College, Vancouver, BC (placed 2nd in course with GPA of 3.84).

2002 to 2006

Various courses in theoretical and applied electronics, at Pacific Rim Community College, Extension Division (partial credit toward electronics technician certificate).

June 2000

Graduated from Rosemount High School, Port Coquitlam, BC.

Awards and Other Activities

(7)

October 2006 and
November 2007

Coordinator, IEEE "Papers Night," Pacific Rim Community College, at which students of Electronics and Computer Technology presented term projects.

2004 to present

Associate Member, Institute of Electrical and Electronics Engineers Inc (IEEE).

2003 to present

Member, British Columbia Sales and Advertising Association; currently vice-president.

Information in a functional resume must be easy to find

References

(8)

Two people will provide immediate references; other names are available.

James B Morton
President, Morton Sales & Leasing
330 Pruden Avenue
New Westminster BC V3J 1J5
Tel: (604) 475-3166
Fax: (604) 475-2807
email: j.morton@bconline.com

Dr Fergus Radji
(Chairman, Burnaby Section, IEEE)
Pacific West HV Power Consultants
1920 – 784 Thurlow Street
Vancouver BC V6E 1V9
Tel: (604) 488-1066
Fax: (604) 489-2722
email: radji@pacwest.bc.ca

7 In a functional resume, the "other activities" section provides additional information to support statements in the Qualifications and Major Achievements sections.

8 Reid has asked several people to act as references but lists only two, partly because they are best able to speak about his qualifications, and partly to keep his resume down to two pages.

Reid's use of bullets on page 1 and a two-column format with dates on the left of page 2 provide variety in his resume's overall layout yet continuity within each page. The bulleted items on page 1 can be read easily—Reid wants his readers to learn quickly about him—while the facts on page 2 can be examined in more detail.

The functional resume is an effective way for a job applicant like Reid to present himself to a particular employer, but it *must* be done well if it is to create the right impact. Ideally, an applicant should use it only if he or she is confident that the employer will not be "turned off" by its nontraditional approach.

Never be afraid to use a display technique for your resume that will enhance its professional quality and make it stand out among other resumes. (We do not mean you should make your resume "flashy," because an overdone appearance can evoke a negative reaction from a reader.) Remember, your resume is selling you. Make it stand out from the others by using good design techniques.

Electronic Resume Formats

In today's competitive workplace there are more people looking for fewer jobs, which means that Human Resources departments are often flooded with far too many resumes for the jobs they have available. (The Human Resources staff may even hesitate to advertise a position because they fear the overwhelming response they might get!) Instead they tend to maximize their hiring time by using automated computer systems that narrow the search for them. Often, instead of posting a job and seeing who applies, they first go into the databases and see who is out there.

If you submit electronically, be aware of the different requirements

The paper resume is *not* obsolete: you just have more options. You will still need to carry a resume to the interview. Even a scanned resume that has been key worded and indexed for a computerized retrieval system may end up being viewed or downloaded, once it has been flagged as a possible match. With this in mind, your word choice is still critical since it presents an image of you.

Smart job seekers use every avenue to get their resume "out there"

All three types of resumes described earlier will work as an electronic resume. There are, however, some additional factors you need to consider when preparing an electronic resume.

There are several variations of an electronic resume and each has its own purpose:

If you are sending your resume...	We suggest this format...
As part of an email message	ASCII plain text
To post to a database	ASCII plain text with key word summaries
As an attachment to an email message	A word-processed document in ASCII rich text format (RTF) or converted to PDF
To be scanned into a database	Follow the guidelines listed below

It never hurts to follow-up with a paper copy of your resume

This section provides general information on creating e-resumes. There are many excellent websites that give detailed tutorials on how to develop and submit a resume electronically.

Plain Text Resumes

Although plain ASCII text is not very appealing to look at, it is the safest way to transfer electronic information to guarantee your document converts properly. Special formatting, boldface, italic, indents, and bullets, for example, are not used. Figure 11-6 shows the resume Susan Jenkins emailed to an agency knowing it would be posted to their database.

You can use any word-processing program to create your ASCII plain text document. After you have typed your resume (using formatting with bullets, bold, etc), follow these steps:

1. Select all of the text and change it to a non-proportional font, such as Courier 12. This will give you 65 characters per line, which will accommodate most email programs.

2. Save your resume as "Plain text (*.txt)," (an option listed in the document types of your Save As dialog box), then choose "Insert line breaks." This will insert a hard return at the end of each line. If the agency or person you are sending your resume to has requested you use hard returns only at the end of each paragraph, save as plain text but don't choose the option "Insert line breaks." This instructs the software to break the lines whenever it needs and forces a break where you have entered one.

3. Use a text editor, such as Notepad, to open your new resume. This is what your recipient will see when you email your resume. The text editor will show you any characters that are not ASCII characters, such as bullets or bold. Replace all unsupported characters with an ASCII equivalent. (You can use any character that you can find on a standard keyboard as a replacement.) For example, bullets appear as a question mark when opened in Notepad. They can be replaced with asterisks or hyphens since those are easier to understand than a question mark.

4. Now you can copy and paste this ASCII plain text resume into the body of an email message. Use the same technique to create a short cover letter and paste it into the email message above the resume text.

We suggest that before you send it to the agency or employer, you send yourself or a friend a copy of the message to make sure it displays properly.

```
SUSAN R JENKINS
517-210 Olivia Crescent
London ON N5Z 3E9
Tel: (519) 438-0761    email: s.jenkins@interact.on.ca

KEY WORD SUMMARY
Engineering firm. Computer services. Computer systems design. Computer maintenance. Computer
specialist. Computer integration. Computer engineering. BSc Computer Science. UWO. Manager.
Website design. Consulting. UNIX. C++, C, SQL. HP-UX.

OBJECTIVES
To obtain a position as a computer services consultant/coordinator for a major engineering
firm, so I may use my expertise in computer system maintenance and design.

QUALIFICATIONS SUMMARY
Five years of experience in designing, installing, and troubleshooting computing systems; a
proven track record in identifying problems and developing innovative solutions.

TECHNICAL SKILLS
* PROGRAMMING: C, C++, Visual BASIC, SQL, OSF/Motif, UNIX Shell Script, and JAVA scripting.
* OPERATING SYSTEMS: UNIX, MS Windows, MS DOS, MS Windows NT, Solaris, and HP-UX.
* NETWORKING: TCP/IP, OSI, Microsoft LAN Manager, and Novell Netware.
* APPLICATIONS: Microsoft Office, Microsoft Access, Microsoft Visual C++, Microsoft Project,
Microsoft Publisher, Lotus 123, Lotus Freelance, and others.

PROFESSIONAL EXPERIENCE
Information Technologist
Superior Manufacturing Systems, Cambridge, ON.  May 2007 to Present
* Responsible for upgrading software, configuring new systems and managing computer accounts
and server space for a research and development lab of 138 employees.

Independent Consultant
Jenkins Communication Services, London, ON.  April 2005 to Present
* Part-time business designing and developing websites for small businesses and organizations.

Computer Specialist
Woolland Computer Services, London, ON.  June 2002 to 2005
* One year full-time, after high school graduation; two years part-time while attending
university. Duties included
* direct sales of computers and software
* onsite servicing of computers and training of users

EDUCATION
* BSc in Computer Science, University of Western Ontario, London, ON, 2007: GPA 3.8
Senior Project: Developed a hypertext information system for athletic department.
* East Elms High School, Stratford, ON, 2002: 84.6%

EXTRACURRICULAR ACTIVITIES
Westferry Ski Club, London, ON.  2002 to present
* Received ski instructor certification in 1993, served as club secretary 2006 - present

Theatre for Youth, Stratford, ON.  2000 to 2006
* Actor-in-training for one year, then as electrical/computer technician for five years,
responsible for designing and implementing computer-generated dramatic effects.

SPECIAL AWARDS
* Recipient of Miller Foundation scholarship in Computer Science, UWO, 2006
* Awarded Maitland Trophy for best overall performance, East Elms High School, 2001

REFERENCES
Margaret Ferbrache, Owner/Manager
Woolland Computer Services
313 Oak Street, London ON N2R B6J
519-323-6647  email: ferbrache@woollcom.on.ca

David Singh, Program Director
Theatre for Youth
PO Box 212, Stratford ON N6A 7M3
519-717-6690  email: d.singh@players.net
```

Figure 11-6   Resume saved in ASCII plain text format.

Key Word Summary Resumes

Effective key words are the key to getting noticed!

The resumes that get listed first as the result of a search are the ones that have matched the most key words. So, when developing an electronic resume, you need to think like a Human Resources Manager and include as many key words as possible.

A key word is usually a noun, not an action verb. This is a change from how we recommend you write paper resumes, using strong action verbs like *managing*, *implementing*, *installing*. The Human Resources Manager will search for words that describe the qualities or skills needed for a particular position, words like *account manager*, *CAD skills*, *member IEEE*. The search often includes other company names, particular tools or technologies, schools, degrees, universities, years experience, and responsibilities.

The key words *Computer Specialist*, *three years experience*, *web pages*, *website design*, and *manager* were used to look for someone to fill a Computer Services Manager position. And the search found Susan's resume. You can see her key word summary in the resume shown in Figure 11-6.

Scanned Resumes

Sometimes an agency or employer will scan a paper resume and convert it to an electronic format. It may then be posted to a database or entered into a resume tracking system. With this in mind, it is imperative that you include key words as described in the previous section. If you know your resume will be scanned by a service there are certain guidelines you should follow to make sure your paper resume scans well.

Always send an original resume printed from a laser jet. Ink jet printers can smear the text. Photocopies or faxed copies do not scan well. The best paper to use is light-coloured, standard-sized 8 1/2 × 11 inch, printed on one side only. Pick a simple, easy to read sans-serif font such as Arial. Avoid complex formatting like graphics, shading, italics, bold, parentheses and brackets or horizontal and vertical lines. Make sure there are no folds or staple marks in your original. Your resume may appear very bland and generic visually, but it will scan better and be more useful to your potential employer.

Web Portfolios or Resumes

The more global and technical our society becomes the more competitive the job market becomes. Many technical professionals are using the internet to advertise their capabilities. You can do this too, by creating your own web portfolio or resume. This is an HTML version of your resume with a URL to point to it.

Susan Jenkins used a basic menu structure with links to additional information. The first page of her web portfolio is shown in Figure 11-7.

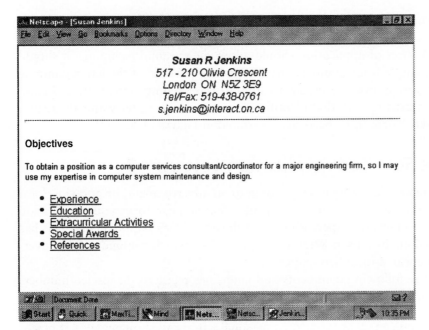

Figure 11-7   An HTML-coded web portfolio.

An employer accessing this home page clicks on a particular bulleted heading to bring specific details onscreen

Unlike for ASCII plain text resumes or scanned resumes, using backgrounds, graphics, and special fonts and characters enhances HTML resumes. Be careful though: you still want your words to describe you and your capabilities. The danger is that you may get carried away designing your web page and the only quality you will demonstrate is your programming skills. Remember, this is still your resume and it needs to sell you.

A major difference between electronic resumes posted to a database service and a web portfolio is how people access them. If you create a web portfolio it is your responsibility to attract people to it. When you post your resume to a database, people go there by themselves to search for it.

Most word-processing packages today have tools to help you develop HTML pages. If you need additional help, search the web for a tutorial or find a book on simple HTML coding.

Writing a Letter of Application

Although some resumes may be delivered personally, the majority are mailed or submitted electronically, both with a covering letter. Because potential employers will probably read the letter first, it must do more than simply introduce the resume. The letter needs to state your purpose for writing (that you are applying for a job) and demonstrate that you have some very useful qualifications that the reader should take the time to consider. It should never simply repeat what your resume says.

An assertive, interesting, and well-planned application letter can encourage employers to place your letter and resume in the pile to interview. Conversely, a dull, unemphatic letter may cause the same employers

Write using a firm yet personable style

to drop your application on a pile of "not nows" because its approach and style seem to imply you are a dull, unemphatic person.

A letter of application should adopt the pyramid technique: it should open with a brief summary that defines the purpose of the letter, continue with strong, positive details to support the opening statement, and close with a brief remark that identifies what action the writer wants the reader to take. These three parts are illustrated in Figure 11-8.

The Solicited Application Letter

The main advantage in responding to an advertisement, or applying for a position that you know to be open, is that you can focus your application letter on facts that specifically meet the employer's requirements. This has been done by Alison Witney in Figure 11-9, which responds to an advertisement in a local newspaper.

The following comments and guidelines relate to the circled numbers beside Alison's letter.

1 You can create your own personal letterhead showing your contact information. Include your name, address, telephone number and email address. Some people have the information all on one line like Reid Qually did with his resume (Figure 11-5 on page 251) and others centre the information, with each item on a separate line.

2 Whenever possible, personalize an application letter by addressing it by name to the personnel manager or the person named in the advertisement. This gives you an edge over applicants who address theirs impersonally to the "Personnel Manager" or "Chief Engineer." If the job advertisement does not give the person's name, invest in a telephone call to the advertiser and ask the receptionist for the person's name and complete title. (You may have to decide whether to send your letter and resume to someone in the personnel department or to a technical manager who is more likely to be aware of the quality of your qualifications and how you could fit into the organization.)

Never write "Dear Sir or Madam" or "To Whom It May Concern"

Keep your letter to one page and no more than four paragraphs

Figure 11-8 Writing plan for a job application letter.

Alison V Witney
1670 Fulham Boulevard
Truro NS B2N 6C4
Tel: (902) 474-6318
email: avwitney@nsonline.net

March 23, 2008

Dr Eugene Cartwright
Animal Science Experimental Institute
Mount Ashburn University
Three Hills NB E4K 1A7

Dear Dr Cartwright

I am applying for the position of Research Technician (Animal Sciences) advertised in the March 18, 2008, issue of the *Amiento County Herald*. I have been involved with animals and their care and treatment for many years, and shortly will receive my Diploma in Biological Science.

My interest in animals dates back 12 years, to when I first learned to care for, groom, and ride horses. I now teach horseback riding in my spare time. For the past three years my employer has been Dr Alex Gavin, veterinary surgeon at the Amiento County Animal Treatment Centre, where I assist in the medical treatment of small animals. It was my interest in horses, plus Dr Gavin's influence, that led to my enrolment in the two-year Biological Sciences course at Amiento Technical College, from which I will graduate in early June. The attached biographical details provide further information on my education, employment background, and work experience.

I will be visiting your research station from April 21 to 23, as part of my college term research project. May I call on you then, while I am at Three Hills?

Regards

Alison V Witney

Alison V Witney
enc

Figure 11-9 A solicited letter of application prepared by an undergraduate.

3 This is the **Initial Contact**, in which Alison summarizes key points about herself that she believes will most interest her reader and states that she is applying for the advertised position. Note particularly that she creates a purposeful image by stating confidently "I am applying…." This is much better than writing "I wish to apply…," "I would like to apply…," or "I am interested in applying…," all of which create weak, wishy-washy images because they imply she is only interested rather than purposefully applying for the job. An equally confident opening is "Please accept my application for…."

Draw on key information in your resume to support your opening statement

4 The **Evidence** section starts here. It should offer facts drawn from the resume and expand on the statements made in the first paragraph. Avoid broad generalizations such as "I have 13 years of experience in a metrology laboratory," replacing them with shorter descriptions that describe your exact role and responsibilities, and stress the supervisory aspects of each position. The name of a person for whom you worked on a particular project can be usefully inserted here because it adds credibility to the role and responsibilities you are describing.

5 The **Evidence** section covers the key points an employer is likely to be interested in and draws the reader's attention to the attached resume. If the paragraph grows too long, divide it into two shorter paragraphs (as Colin Farrow has done in Figure 11-10).

6 This paragraph is Alison Witney's **Action Statement**, in which she effectively opens the door to an interview by drawing attention to her upcoming visit to the advertiser's premises. She avoids using dull, routine remarks such as "I look forward to hearing from you at your earliest convenience" or "I would appreciate an interview in the near future," both of which tend to close rather than open the door to the next step.

7 Contemporary business letters end with a single-word closing such as "Regards" or "Sincerely," rather than the less meaningful "Yours truly."

The Unsolicited Application Letter

An unsolicited application letter (Figure 11-10) has the same three main parts as a solicited letter and looks much the same to the reader. To the writer, however, there is a subtle but important difference: it cannot be focused to fit the requirements of a particular position an employer needs to fill. This means the job applicant has to make the letter sound both positive and directed.

December 15, 2007

The letter's appearance
and sans-serif type
create a crisp,
professional impression

Vern A Rogers, P.Eng
Branch Manager
H L Winman and Associates
574 Reston Avenue
Winnipeg MB R3C 4G2

Dear Mr Rogers

As a Structural Engineer who has specialized in constructing and maintaining
transmission line towers and associated buildings for 10 years, and who has particular experience working in permafrost, I am applying for a position with
H L Winman and Associates.

My experience evolves from three periods of employment. For four years I
installed and maintained communications systems with the Canadian Forces.
Subsequently I became a crew chief and installation coordinator with the
Northwestern Steel Construction Company, where for four years I was responsible
for erecting and testing high-voltage transmission line towers between Flin Flon,
Manitoba, and the Northwest Territories. For the past two years I have been a
project engineer supervising the construction and installation of microwave
towers on Manitoba Telephone System's Brandon–The Pas extension.

The enclosed resume describes my responsibilities in greater detail and my particular involvement in testing structures erected on discontinuous permafrost. I
hold a Diploma in Civil Engineering Technology from Red River College in
Winnipeg, and a B.Sc in Structural Engineering from the University of Manitoba. I
am eager to return to the north and the challenge of building on unstable soil.

I welcome the opportunity to meet you and learn more about your project at
Winterton Lake. Because I travel frequently between Brandon and Winnipeg, I will
call you when I next expect to be in your city.

Sincerely

Colin R. Farrow

Colin R Farrow
enc

Figure 11-10   An unsolicited letter of application prepared by an experienced engineer.

Here are some guidelines:

- Make a particular point of addressing your letter to the person, by name and title, who will most likely be interested in you. This may mean selecting a particular department or project head who will immediately recognize your qualifications and how you would fit into the organization, rather than applying to the personnel manager. Never address an unsolicited letter to a general title such as "Manager, Human Resources" because, if the company does not use such a title and you have not used a personal name, it will likely be the mail clerk who decides who should receive your letter.

Start your research with the company's website

- Try to find out enough information about a firm so that you can visualize the type of work it does and how you and your qualifications would fit the company's needs. This will enable you to focus your letter on factors likely to be of most interest to the employer.

- Try to make your initial contact positive and interesting even though you are not applying for a particular position, as Colin Farrow has done in his unsolicited letter in Figure 11-10.

Completing a Company Application Form

Jobfind.ca
http://www.jobfind.ca/
Jobfind.ca contains links to more than a thousand Canadian employment-related sites, including job and resume banks, employer sites, and related internet sites.

Filling in company application forms (online and on paper) can become a boring and repetitive task, yet any carelessness on an applicant's part can draw a negative reaction from readers. Each company or organization usually uses its own specially designed form that, although asking for generally the same basic information, may vary in detail. Consequently the suggestions below apply primarily to the *approach* you should take rather than suggest what you should write:

- When visiting prospective employers, always carry your personal data record with you so you can readily search for details such as dates, telephone numbers, and names of supervisors.

- Treat every application form as though it is the *first* one you are completing—write carefully, neatly, and legibly. Never let an untidy application form subconsciously prepare an employer to meet an untidy worker.

Take care: èvery word you write conveys an image of how you approach a task

- Complete *every* space on the form, entering N/A (not applicable), Not Known, or a short horizontal line in spaces that do not apply to you or for which you genuinely do not have information. This will prevent an employer from thinking that you carelessly (or, worse, intentionally) omitted answering the question.

- Take care that your familiarity with your city and street names does not cause you to abbreviate or omit them. If you write "Wpg" for Winnipeg or omit the "St," "Ave," or "Crescent" from your street name (because you *know* it is a street, avenue, or crescent), you may create the impression that your approach to work is to take shortcuts whenever possible.

- Use words that describe the responsibility and supervisory aspects of each job you have held (as you would for a resume) rather than list only the duties you performed.

- Particularly describe extracurricular activities that show your involvement in the community, or activities in which you held a teaching or coaching role.

- Pay particular attention if there is a section on the form that asks you to comment on how your education and past experience have prepared you for the position. Think this through very carefully before you write so that what you say shows a natural progression from past experience to the job you are applying for. If you can, and if they fit naturally, add a few words to demonstrate how the position fits your overall career plan. This can be a particularly difficult section to write.

The most difficult part to write! You should prepare in advance for such a question

Attending an Interview

This is the third step in the job application process and might be the first time you meet a prospective employer (or, more often, the employer's representative) face to face.

Prepare for the Interview

The key to a good interview is thorough preparation. If you have prepared yourself well, the interview will likely run smoothly and you will present yourself confidently.

As soon as you are invited to attend an interview—or, better still, before you are called—start researching facts about the company (or organization, if it is a government establishment). Presumably, you will have done some research before submitting your letter of application. Now you need to identify additional information, such as the number of people the company employs, specific fields in which it is involved, work for which it is particularly well known, its major products and services, important contracts it has received (news of which has been released to the media), locations of branch offices, and the company's involvement in community activities. Such knowledge can be extremely useful during the interview, because it permits you to ask intelligent questions at appropriate places—questions that indicate to the interviewer that you have done your homework.

Attending an interview can create as much anxiety as speaking before an audience

You also need to prepare for difficult questions an interviewer may pose. You may be asked:

- *Why do you want to join our organization?*
- *How do you think you can contribute to our company?*
- *Why do you want to leave your present employer?* (Asked only of persons who are already employed.)

- *Why did you leave such-and-such company on such-and-such date?* (Asked of persons whose resumes show no explanation for a previous employment termination.)
- *What do you expect to be doing in five years? Ten years?*
- *What salary do you expect?*

Lack of preparation will show up in your body language and how you answer questions

If you have not prepared for such questions, and hesitate before answering, an interviewer may interpret your hesitation to mean that you find a question difficult to answer or that there are factors you would rather conceal. In either case, you may give an entirely misleading impression of yourself.

An interviewer who asks what salary you expect is partly testing your preparation for the interview and partly assessing how accurately you value yourself. For an undergraduate at a university or college, the question is largely academic: undergraduates compare notes and quickly learn what starting salaries are being offered. Plus the campus career centre can provide guidance. But for a person who recently has been or is currently employed, the question is more difficult.

Decide what salary you think the position can command and also what you feel your experience is worth. Websites that offer career counselling will help you determine a figure. Avoid quoting a salary range, such as "between 42 and 44 thousand dollars," because it indicates unsureness. Quote a definite figure, such as $43 000, and you will sound much more confident. If you fear that the salary you want to quote may be too high, you can always add the qualification "...depending, of course, on the opportunities for advancement and the fringe benefits your company offers."

An interview is like a two-way street: traffic should flow in both directions

You also should be prepared to ask questions during the interview. The interviewer wants to acquire information about you, but you should also learn about the company and the opportunities it can offer. Consider what questions you would like answered, jot them onto a small card, and store the card in a pocket or purse. Then when the interviewer asks, "Now, do you have any questions?" you can pull out the card.

Remember, too, that the quality of your questions will demonstrate how carefully you have thought about the interview. If necessary, take the time to write down the answer.

Create a Good Initial Impression

Remember that you are being evaluated from the moment you step into the interview room. Consequently,

- walk in briskly and cheerfully,
- shake hands firmly, because a limp handshake creates an image of a limp, indefinite applicant,
- repeat the person's name as you are introduced and look him or her directly in the eye, and

- sit when invited to do so, pushing yourself well back in the chair, making yourself comfortable, and avoiding folding your arms across your chest (which psychologically suggests you are resisting questions).

Participate Throughout the Interview

An interview normally falls into three parts. The first is an exchange of general information during which you may be asked questions on topics you can answer easily, such as a major news item or something from the hobbies and interests section in your resume. This part of the interview normally is short.

An experienced interviewer will try to ease your nervousness

The middle part of the interview is much longer. The interviewer will want to hear your opinions and have you demonstrate your knowledge of certain topics. Although the interviewer will want to control the direction the interview takes, you will be expected to develop your answers and to comment on each topic in sufficient depth to establish that you have real knowledge and experience, backed up by well-thought-out opinions.

The closing portion of the interview is also short. The interviewer will ask if you have any questions and will discuss details about the company and employment with it. By this stage the interviewer should have a good impression of you, and you should know whether you want to be employed by the company.

An effective interviewer will pose questions from one discussion point to the next and automatically encourage you to provide comprehensive answers. If, however, you face an inexperienced or unprepared interviewer, the responsibility to develop your answers in greater depth may become yours.

Be ready to offer information, but don't monopolize the conversation!

For example, the interviewer may ask, "How long did you work in a mobile calibration lab?"

You might be tempted to reply "Three years," and then sit back and wait for the next question. You will do better to reply: "For three years total. The first year and a half I was one of four technicians on the North Bay to Sioux Lookout circuit. And then for the next year and a half I was the lab supervisor on the Dana, Saskatchewan, to Prince George route." An answer developed in this depth often provides the link for the interviewer to formulate the next question.

Sometimes you will face a single interviewer, while at other times you may face an interview board of several people. In a single-interviewer situation you will naturally direct your replies to the interviewer and establish eye contact from time to time. However, in a multiple-interviewer situation,

- direct most of your questions, and your responses to general questions, to the chairperson (but if an answer is long, occasionally look briefly at and talk momentarily to other board members),

- if a particular board member asks you a specific question, address your response to that person, and
- if a board member has been identified as a specialist in a particular discipline, direct your questions to that board member if they especially apply to that field.

Be prepared for questions that challenge your thinking or your ethics

In certain interviews—often when applicants are being interviewed for a high-stress position—you may be presented with a stress question. A stress question is designed to place you in a predicament to which there may be two or even more answers or courses of action that could be taken. You are expected to think *briefly* about the situation presented to you and then to select what you believe is the best answer or course of action. Often you will be challenged and expected to defend the position you have taken.

The secret is not to let yourself be rattled and to defend your answer rationally and reasonably even though the questioner's challenging may seem harsh or unreasonable. Remember that the interviewer is probably more interested in seeing how you cope in the stress situation than in hearing you identify the correct answer.

Here are seven additional factors to consider:

- Use your voice to show confidence; make sure everyone can hear you, speak at a moderate speed (think out your answers before speaking) and, where appropriate, let your enthusiasm *show*.
- Be ready to ask questions, but have a clear idea of what you want to ask before you pose them. The interviewer will recognize a good question and the clarity of thought behind it.
- If you do not know the answer to a question, say you don't know rather than try bluffing your way through it.
- If you do not understand the question, again don't bluff. Either say you do not understand or, if you think you know what the interviewer is driving at, rephrase the question and ask if you have interpreted it correctly. (Never imply that the interviewer posed the question poorly.)
- Use humour with great care. What to you may be extremely funny may not match the interviewer's sense of humour.
- Bring demonstration materials to the interview if you wish (such as a technical proposal or report you have written, or a drawing of a complex circuit you designed) but be aware that you may not have an opportunity to display them. If the topic they support comes up during the interview, introduce them naturally into your response to a question. But remember that the interviewer does not have time to read your work, so the point you are trying to make must be readily identifiable. Never force demonstration materials on an interviewer.

Above all, present an image of "the real you"

Finally, try to be yourself. Remember that interviewers want to see the kind of person you really are. If you relax and answer questions comfortably and purposefully, they will gain a good impression of you. If you try too hard to be the kind of person you think the interviewers want you to be, or to give the kind of answers you think they want rather than the answers you really believe in, they may detect it and judge you accordingly.

Accepting a Job Offer

The telephone rings and the personnel representative you met during your interview tells you that the company is offering you employment at a salary of $xx xxx. You accept the offer! And then she asks when you can start work. (Employers recognize that if you are attending college there will be a waiting period until you are finished and have graduated; similarly, an employed professional has to resign from their current position, normally giving either two weeks or one month notice.) You quote a starting date to the personnel representative, which she agrees to. She then says she will confirm the offer in writing. She also asks you to write a letter confirming your acceptance of the position.

The two letters become, in effect, a contractual agreement: the employer offers you work under certain conditions, which you agree to. The letters can also prevent any misunderstandings from developing, which can occur if arrangements are made only by telephone. Consequently your acceptance letter should:

- announce that you are accepting the offer of employment,
- repeat any important details, such as the agreed salary and starting date, and
- thank the employer for selecting you.

The following acceptance letter conforms to this pattern:

Dear Ms Tataryn

I am confirming my telephone acceptance of your May 19 offer of employment as an engineering technologist in the controls department. I understand that I am to join the company on June 15 and that my salary will be $36 500 annually.

Thank you for selecting me for this position. I very much look forward to working for Magnum Electronics.

Sincerely

Sometimes an applicant may receive two offers of employment at the same time and will have to decline one. The letter declining employment should follow roughly the same pattern:

- decline the offer,
- briefly explain why, and
- thank the employer.

Accept a job offer *in writing,* like sealing a contract

Also decline a job offer in writing, with a smile on your face

Here is an example:

Dear Mr Genser

I regret that I will be unable to accept your offer of employment. Since my interview with you I have been offered employment elsewhere and have a commitment to the other company. Thank you for considering me for this position.

Regards

Declining a job offer pleasantly and formally in a carefully worded letter like this is insurance for the future: one day you may want to work for that employer!

ASSIGNMENTS

Project 11.1:   Preparing a Resume

You are to prepare a resume describing your background, education, work experience, extracurricular activities, and other interests. Do it in three parts.

Part 1

If you do not already have one, prepare a personal data record (PDR).

Part 2

Write down the following information:

- The name of a real employer for whom you would like to work at the end of your course.
- The type of position you would be qualified to hold with that particular employer.
- The type of resume that would be most effective to use.

Part 3

Create a resume

Prepare the resume (assume that you will be graduating from your course in two months). You can decide which format: paper or a particular electronic format.

Project 11.2:   Applying for a Locally Advertised Position

From your campus student employment centre or your local newspaper, identify a company currently advertising a position that you could apply for at the end of your course.

Part 1

Write a letter applying for the position (assume that you will be graduating in six weeks). Also assume that you are attaching a resume to your letter. If you are replying to a newspaper advertisement, attach a copy of the advertisement to your letter.

Part 2

Assume that the company you wrote to in Part 1 sends you an application form. Obtain a standard application form from your campus student employment centre and complete it as though it is the advertiser's form. If it is an electronic form, print a copy.

Rehearse applying for a real position

Part 3

Now assume that the company has telephoned and asked you to attend an interview next Tuesday. Prepare five questions you will ask during the interview. After each question explain why the question is important and what answer it might elicit from the interviewer.

Project 11.3: Unsolicited Application for Summer Employment

Assume that you are looking for summer employment but few summer jobs have been advertised. Write to H L Winman and Associates or Macro Engineering Inc, asking for a summer job. Use your knowledge of the companies, plus your actual background, to write an interesting letter.

Address your letter to the attention of Tanys Young in Calgary or George Dunn in Toronto.

Project 11.4: Preparing Different Versions of Your Resume

Assume you have identified a large, multi-location company you want to work for after graduation and have decided to send your information to them even though they are not advertising any open positions. You have talked to the Human Resources Manager who has told you she needs an electronic resume to post in their internal database. She also requested you send her a paper version.

Part 1

Prepare a paper version of your resume and convert it to a format appropriate for posting to the company's resume database.

Part 2

Besides sending the paper and electronic resumes to the Human Resources Manager, you decide to also send the URL of your personal web portfolio. Create a web portfolio that resembles your paper resume but also has professional-looking graphics and additional details about your experience. Remember, this is a reflection of you and it should encourage the visitor to want to hire you.

Project 11.5: Replying to Other Advertisers

This project assumes that you are seeking permanent employment at the end of a technical or engineering-oriented educational program. Reply to any one of the following advertisements, using your present situation and actual background. If it is still early in your studies, assume that it is now two months before your graduation date. In each case enclose a resume and an application letter.

Apply for one of these positions

(Advertisement in your local newspaper, last week)

(Advertisement on college notice board)

Chapter 12
The Technique of Technical Writing

This chapter concentrates on techniques that will help you write quickly and efficiently. It will show you how to create a whole document, structure paragraphs, write individual sentences, use descriptive words, and establish a comfortable writing style. At the end of the chapter you will find several exercises that will test your ability to write well.

We assume you are already proficient in grammar and can recognize and correct basic writing problems. If you need practice, we suggest you refer to a textbook such as *The Brief Penguin Handbook,* first Canadian edition.[1] You can also refer to the Glossary of Technical Usage (see page 317) for information on how to form abbreviations and compound adjectives, spell problem words, and use numerals or spell out numbers in narrative.

The Whole Document

Three factors affect the whole document: the tone you set, the writing style you adopt, and how you arrange the information on the page. Tone is by far the least tangible: a reader is less likely to be aware of the tone you establish than the writing techniques you use and the arrangement of paragraphs and headings.

Tone

You need to know your reader if you are to set the right tone

Whether your writing should be formal or informal depends on the situation and how well you know your reader. Formal reports normally adopt a formal tone, yet the tone still is natural and comfortable, even though you may know much more about the subject than your reader does. On the other hand, most business correspondence is less formal. For example, a management-level letter proposing a joint venture on a major defence project would be formal, whereas letters between engineers discussing mutual technical problems would be informal, and email would be very informal. A memo report also can be informal, since normally it would be an in-plant document written between people who know each other.

How tone can vary is evident in the following extracts from three separate documents, all written on the same subject.

1. **Extract from a Memo.** John Wood's materials testing laboratory has compression-tested samples of concrete for Karen Woodford of the civil engineering department at H L Winman and Associates. In an email to her, reporting the test results, John writes:

Informal Tone   I have tested the samples of concrete you took from the sixth floor of Tarryton House and none of them meets the 33.25 MPa you specified. The first failed at 28.08 MPa; the second at 26.84 MPa; and the third at 27.95 MPa. Do you want me to send these figures over to the architect, or will you?

2. **Extract from a Letter Report.** Karen Woodford conveys this information to the architect in a brief letter report:

Semiformal Tone   Our tests of three samples taken from the sixth floor of Tarryton House show that the concrete at 52 days still was 5.63 MPa below your specification of 33.25 MPa. We doubt whether further curing will increase the strength of this concrete more than another 1.10 MPa. We suggest, however, that you examine the design specifications before embarking on an expensive and time-consuming remedy.

3. **Extract from a Formal Report.** The architect rechecked the design specifications and decided that 28.50 to 29.00 MPa still would not satisfy the design requirements. He then requested that H L Winman and Associates prepare a formal report he could present to the general contractor and the concrete supplier. Karen Woodford's report said, in part:

Formal Tone   At the request of the architect we cut three 0.3 x 0.15 metre diameter cores from the sixth floor of Tarryton House 52 days after the floor had been poured. These cores were subjected to a standard compression test with the following results (detailed calculations are attached at Appendix A):

Imagine you are speaking personally to the reader and adjust your tone accordingly

Core No.	Location	Failed at:
1	0.46 m W of col 18S	28.08 MPa
2	0.84 m N of col 22E	26.84 MPa
3	1.42 m N of col 46E	27.95 Mpa

The average of 27.62 MPa for the three cores is 5.63 MPa below the design specification of 33.25 MPa. Since further curing will increase the strength of the concrete by no more than 1.10 MPa, we recommend rejecting this concrete pour.

The sequence in which you write longer reports also affects the tone. To set the right tone, try writing *in reverse order*, starting with all the technical details that will appear in the major discussion, and then working forward to the brief statements you write in the Summary. The comments on Karen Woodhouse's formal report in Chapter 6 explain how she did this (see pages 129 to 130, 146). They recommend the following writing sequence:

Deal with all the details before you start writing

Step 1   Assemble and document all the details and technical data. These will become the appendices to your report.

Step 2	Write the Discussion, or full development. Direct it to the type of technical reader who will use or analyse your report in depth.
Step 3	Write the Introduction, Conclusions, and Recommendations. Keep them brief and direct them to a semitechnical reader or person in a supervisory or managerial position.
Step 4	Write the Summary. Direct it to a nontechnical reader who has absolutely no knowledge of the project or the contents of your report.

Style

Style is affected by the complexity of the subject you are describing and the technical level of the reader(s) to whom you are writing. Consequently you need to "tailor" your writing style to suit each situation, following these guidelines:

Adjust sentence length to suit the subject and the reader's familiarity with it

1. When presenting low-complexity background information, and descriptions of nontechnical or easy-to-understand processes, write in an easygoing style that tells readers they are encountering information that does not require total concentration. Use slightly longer paragraphs and sentences, and insert colourful adjectives and adverbs to enhance the descriptions and make them more interesting.

2. For important or complex data, use short paragraphs and sentences. Present one item of information at a time. Develop it carefully to make sure it will be fully understood before proceeding to the next item. Use simple words. The more punchy style will warn readers that the information demands their full attention.

3. When describing a step-by-step process, start with a narrative-type opening paragraph that introduces the topic and presents any information that the readers should know or would find interesting. Follow it with a series of subparagraphs, each describing a separate step, choosing between two alternative styles:

Style A: Integrated Lead-in Line

Precede subparagraphs with bullets or sequential numbers

In this style the lead-in line becomes part of each subparagraph that follows it, as in this example:

Let each subparagraph
- develop only one item or aspect of the process,
- be short, and
- be parallel in construction (the importance of parallelism is discussed later in this chapter).

Here, the lead-in words (*Let each subparagraph*) do not form a complete sentence and so do not end with a colon. Consequently the bulleted items each start with a lower case letter and end with a comma (except the last item), because the lead-in words and the bulleted items really make one long, complete sentence.

Style B: Separate Lead-in Line
In this style the lead-in line stands alone, like this:

> If you use subparagraphs to present a series of points, follow these guidelines:
>
> 1. Indent each subparagraph as a complete unit of information, to show your readers how you are subordinating your ideas.
>
> 2. Precede each subparagraph with either a bullet (as in style A) or a sequential number (as in style B).
>
> 3. Number the subparagraphs if you want to identify that the information is presented in a prescribed sequence or in decreasing order of importance, or if you want to refer to the subparagraph later in your letter or report. At all other times use bullets.

Here, the lead-in words (*If you use…follow these guidelines:*) create a complete sentence. Consequently the lead-in words end with a colon, and the subparagraphs each start with a capital letter and end with a period. Ideally, leave a 3 pt or 6 pt space between the subparagraphs to make them visually more appealing.

Appearance

If you incorporate Information Design techniques into your writing you can help your readers understand and access information more readily. Information Design can be applied to letters, memos, reports, proposals, instructions, newsletters, and many other documents.

Insert Headings as Signposts
In longer documents, you can help your reader by inserting headings. Each heading must be short yet informative, summarizing clearly what is covered in the paragraphs that follow. Here are some guidelines:

Make your headings contribute *to the overall appearance*

- Use upper and lower case letters rather than all capital letters.
- Use boldface type rather than underlining the headings.
- Keep headings in the same font (typeface) as the main text.
- Use larger point sizes for the principal headings, and progressively smaller point size for each level of subsidiary heading.

Figure 12-1 illustrates how this can be done.

Insert Paragraph Numbers
In some documents—particularly specifications, technical instructions, and military reports—the paragraphs and subparagraphs are numbered. A simple paragraph numbering system starts at 1 and continues consecutively to the end of the document. More complex systems combine numbers, decimals, and letters to allow for subparagraphing, as shown in Figure 12-2. (Note that Roman numerals are *not* used.)

Guidelines for Integrating Paragraphs and Headings

Set the main centre heading (above) in a larger boldface type than all other headings in the document. You may use a different typeface, such as Arial, for this heading.

Using Subparagraphs Without Paragraph Numbers
If you use a subsidiary centre heading, as done immediately above, set it in the same type as the body text, or slightly larger, and in boldface. (The body text here is Times New Roman, 12 pt.)

Side Headings
A side heading introduces a new section of text. Set it, and the paragraphs that follow, flush against the left margin. In technical writing, the first line normally is not indented.

Inserting Subparagraph Headings and Subparagraphs
Indent subparagraph headings, and the paragraphs that follow, about 1 cm from the original left margin. Type each subparagraph as a solid indented block, so your readers can see how you have subordinated your ideas.

Creating Secondary Subparagraphs
If further subparagraphing is necessary, indent each heading and the text that follows it a further 1 cm to the right.

Building a Heading into a Paragraph. If you use a paragraph heading, continue writing the text immediately after the heading. Usually, this type of heading is followed by only one paragraph of text.

Figure 12-1   Guidelines for integrating paragraphs and headings.

For headings, vary font size and use boldface type rather than underlining the words

Pick Only One Font

The availability of numerous type styles is not an invitation to mix and match

A font such as Century OldStyle or Helvetica is a set of printing type. Some fonts are called serif (they have a slight finishing stroke—T) and some are called sans serif (they don't have a finishing stroke—T). The font you choose will project an image of you, your company and your document. Statistics show that a serif font like Times New Roman or Garamond is easier to read because the serifs lead the eye from letter to letter, and so are more suitable for longer documents. This text is printed in a serif type called Sabon; the examples in Figures 12-1 and 12-2 are in Times New Roman, except for the main heading, which in each case is in Arial. Although sans-serif fonts like Arial, Helvetica, or **Franklin Gothic** are clean

Guidelines for Combining Headings
and Paragraph Numbers

If your main centre heading runs into two lines, always ensure the second line is shorter than the first.

1. Side Headings

You may use one brief unnumbered paragraph immediately following a side heading, without giving it a number.

1.1 You can also use the brief introductory paragraph (above) to introduce a series of points, each in a numbered paragraph.

1.2 When there is more than one paragraph, assign each a consecutive number (1.1, 1.2, etc), as has been done here. Indent the paragraph number so that it is flush with the start of the heading above it.

1.3 **Subparagraph Headings and Subparagraphing**

Limit the use of paragraph numbers to only one decimal point (as shown above). If you have subparagraphs, assign each a lower case letter:

a. This will be the first subparagraph.

b. This will be the second subparagraph.

c. You can also subdivide a subparagraph into a series of very short points, using a number enclosed within brackets before each:

(1) Here is a secondary subparagraph.

(2) Limit each secondary subparagraph to only one sentence.

Figure 12-2 Guidelines for integrating a paragraph-numbering system.

and clear, and portray a neat and modern image, they are not as easy to read. Consequently they are suitable only for short documents and electronic mail.

For example, Daniel Thomashewski chose a sans-serif font to type the agenda for the E-Learning Research Committee meeting in Figure 10-4 on page 228. Morley Wozniak, however, used a serif font for his report evaluating proposed landfill sites in Figure 5-5 on page 94.

We recommend using 11 pt or 12 pt type for serif fonts, and 10 pt for sans-serif fonts.

Select character size to suit font style and readers' visual acuity

Justify Only on the Left

Word processors make it easy to justify both the left and right margins, which permits you to create lines of exactly the same length. Yet research has shown that it is better to justify only the left margin and leave the right margin "ragged." Otherwise, your computer will generate spaces between words and characters to force the right margin to be straight, which can create uneven spacing between words from line to line.

Sometimes a writer may use a justified right margin to create a particular impression for a report, as Karen Woodhouse has done in her formal report on radiant heating in Figure 6-6 (see pages 132 to 145).

Use Two Columns

Let careful use of white space focus readers' attention

Many people hesitate to change the standard settings that come with word-processing programs, which normally provide a single 155 mm (6 in.) typing line, yet sometimes it can be advantageous to create two columns, one for headings and one for the text. Figure 12-3 compares (a) normal headings and paragraphs with (b) two columns containing the headings on the left and the text on the right. The latter takes more space, but it makes its information much more accessible. A suitable guideline is to have a 45 mm (1.75 in.) column for the headings and a 110 mm (4.25 in.) column for the text.

Use Subparagraphs to Present Ideas

We recommend using bulleted lists to break up text and make it visually more appealing. Morley Wozniak's use of white space in his report evaluating proposed landfill sites (see Figure 5-5 on page 94), and particularly the "chunks" of information on its fourth page, provide an effective example. Here is an excerpt from another report that is not effective:

Shaping your information can encourage readers to keep reading

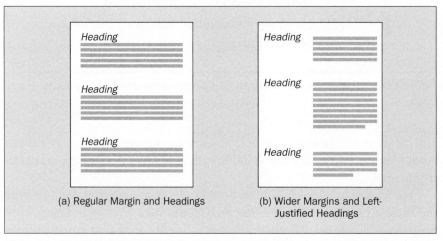

(a) Regular Margin and Headings

(b) Wider Margins and Left-Justified Headings

Figure 12-3   Using (a) standard margins and (b) columns to provide a wide left margin for inserting headings.

I have analysed our present capabilities and estimate that we can increase our commercial business from $20 000 to $30 000 per month. But to meet this objective we will have to shift the emphasis from purely local customers to clients in major centres. To increase business from local customers alone will require extensive sales effort for only a small increase in revenue, whereas a similar sales effort in a major centre will attract a 30% to 40% increase in revenue. We will also have to increase our staff and manufacturing facilities. The cost of additional personnel and new equipment will in turn have to be offset by an even larger increase in business. Properly administered, such a program should result in an ever-increasing workload. And, third, we will have to create a separate department for handling commercial business. If we remove the department from the existing production organization it will carry a lower overhead, which will result in products that are more competitively priced.

L-o-n-g paragraphs build reader resistance

If this writer had broken up the second long sentence by inserting *take three steps* and a colon after *steps*, and then made a numbered list of the actions to be taken, the information would have been much easier to read and understand.

I have analysed our present capabilities and estimate that we can increase our commercial business from $20 000 to $30 000 per month. But to meet this objective we will have to take three steps:

1. Shift the emphasis from purely local customers to clients in major centres. To increase business from local customers alone will require extensive sales effort for only a small increase in revenue, whereas a similar sales effort in a major centre will attract a 30% to 40% increase in revenue.

2. Increase our staff and manufacturing facilities. The cost of additional personnel and new equipment will in turn have to be offset by an even larger increase in business. Properly administered, such a program should result in an ever-increasing workload.

3. Create a separate department for handling commercial business. If we remove the department from the existing production organization it will carry a lower overhead, which will result in products that are more competitively priced.

Short paragraphs build reader acceptance

Use Tables to Capture Information

Tables can be used to present more than just numerical data. We suggest using a table to present text when it is convenient to compartmentalize your information into easy-to-find chunks, as shown in Figure 12-4. There is another example in Table 9-3 on page 201.

Use Good Language

It hardly seems necessary to tell you to use good language, but in this case we mean language that you know your readers will understand. Use only technical terms and abbreviations they will recognize immediately. If you are in doubt, define the term or abbreviation, or replace it with a simpler expression. Pages 299 to 300 provide special guidelines for abbreviating technical and nontechnical terms.

Instructions for Completing Travel Expense Forms

Expense	Guidelines	Receipts Required
Air Travel	• Book with Haynes Travel Services • Charge to Account A78641	• Haynes's invoice • Ticket stub
Accommodation	• Request corporate rate (quote file 2120) • Pay with company VISA card	• Hotel/motel receipt
Meals	• Per diem rate is $30	• Receipt not required unless meal cost is over $25 (excluding tip)

Figure 12-4   Using a table to present written information.

Paragraphs

The role of the paragraph is complex. It has to stand alone but normally is not expected to. It has to contribute to the whole document, yet it must not be obtrusive (except when called on to emphasize a specific point). And it has to convey only one idea, although made up of several sentences each containing a separate thought.

Good paragraph writing depends on three elements:

> **Unity**
> **Coherence**
> **Adequate Development**

These elements cannot stand alone. All three must be present if a paragraph is to be useful to its reader.

Unity Within the Paragraph

To have unity, each paragraph must be built entirely around a central idea. This idea is expressed in a topic sentence—often the first sentence—and developed in supporting sentences. This is like the pyramid technique, with the topic sentence taking the place of the summary and the supporting sentences representing the full development (see Figure 12-5).

Although the topic sentence does not always have to be the first sentence in a paragraph, for technical writing we recommend that you consistently place it there.

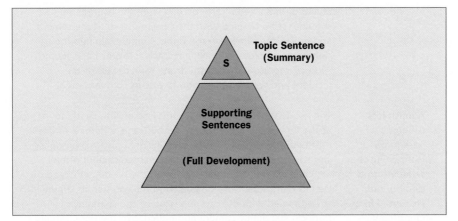

Figure 12-5 Pyramid technique applied to the paragraph.

Every supporting sentence must amplify or evolve from the topic sentence

The following paragraph has the topic sentence right up front. It has strong unity because its topic is clearly expressed and the supporting sentences develop it fully.

> Content reuse means writing content once and reusing it many times. Traditional documents are written in files that consist of sections. Reusable content is written as objects or elements, not documents. Documents are therefore made up of content objects that can be mixed and matched to meet specific information needs. For example, a product description (paragraph) could be used in a brochure, on the web, in a parts catalogue, in product support documentation, or even on a package.[2]

Coherence in the Paragraph

To be coherent, a paragraph must be assembled into a solid, logical, well-organized block of information. A coherent paragraph is abundantly clear to its readers; they can easily follow your line of reasoning and have no problem progressing from one thought to the next. However, simply summarizing a paragraph in the topic sentence and then following it with a series of supporting sentences does not necessarily make a coherent paragraph. The sentences must be arranged in an identifiable order, following a pattern that helps the reader to understand what is being said.

Good sequencing and effective transitions help create coherent paragraphs

Sequential Patterns

You can write narrative-type paragraphs to describe a sequence of steps or events. The past-present-future pattern of a progress report or occurrence report, such as Bob Walton's incident report in Figure 4-5 (see page 59), is a typical example. The pattern should be clearly evident, as in two of the following three paragraphs:

> **A coherent paragraph (in chronological order)** The accident occurred when Dennis Friesen was checking in at the Remick Airlines counter. He placed the company's Nabuchi 300 digital camera on the counter while he completed flight boarding procedure. When the passenger

ahead of him lifted a carry-on bag from the counter, its shoulder strap tangled with the carrying strap of the camera and pulled the camera to the floor. Dennis examined the camera and discovered a 40 mm crack across its back. Remick Airlines' representative Kathy Trane took details of the incident and will be calling you to discuss compensation.

Two treatments of the same information

A much less coherent paragraph (containing the same information but not presented in an identifiable pattern)

The accident occurred when Dennis Friesen was checking in at the Remick Airlines counter. Kathy Trane, a Remick Airlines representative, took details of the incident and will be calling you to discuss compensation. The damaged camera received a 40 mm crack across the back. When the passenger ahead of Dennis removed a carry-on bag from the counter, its shoulder strap tangled with the carrying strap of the company's Nabuchi 300 digital camera and pulled it to the floor. Dennis had placed the camera on the counter while he completed flight boarding procedure.

A coherent paragraph (tracing events from evidence to conclusion)

We noticed a mild shimmy at speeds above 80 km/h about 10 days after the new tires had been installed. A visual check of all four wheels revealed no obvious defects, so we rotated the four wheels to different positions on the vehicle. This did not eliminate the shimmy but did change its point of origin. To pin down the cause we replaced each wheel in turn with the spare wheel, and found that the shimmy disappeared when the spare was in the left front position. We removed the wheel from that position, tested it, and found that it had been incorrectly balanced.

Descriptive Patterns

You can write descriptive paragraphs to describe scenes, buildings, equipment, and any subject having physical features. This pattern can be defined by the shape of the subject, the order in which parts are operated, the arrangement of parts from smallest to largest, or the importance of the various parts. For example:

The topic sentence sets the scene

Excerpt from paragraph (features in order of importance)

The most important control on the bomb aimer's panel is the firing button, which when not in use is held in the black retaining clip at the bottom left-hand corner. Next in importance is the fusing switch at the top right of the panel; when in the "OFF" position it prevents the bombs from being dropped live. Two safety switches, one immediately above the firing button retaining clip and the other to the right of the bank of selector switches, prevent the firing button from being withdrawn from its clip unless both are in the "LIVE" (up) position.

Continuity

A fully coherent paragraph must also have smooth transitions between its sentences. Smooth transitions make your readers feel comfortable. As they finish one sentence, there is a logical bridge to the next. This can be accomplished by using linking words and by referring back to what has already been said. In the example just quoted, there is a natural flow from "The most important…" in the first sentence to "Next in importance…" in the second. The third sentence then refers back to the firing button and so relates the newly introduced safety switches to the previous information. The transitions are equally good in the first paragraph describing damage to a digital camera, each sentence containing a component that is a development from one of the previous sentences. This is not true of the second camera-damage paragraph, in which each new sentence introduces a new subject with no reference to what has already been said.

Paragraph Development

Paragraph development demands good judgment. You must identify your readers clearly enough so that you can look at each paragraph from their point of view. Only then can you establish whether your supporting sentences amplify the topic sentence in sufficient detail to satisfy their interest.

You want to say enough, but not ramble on, and on, and on…

Simply inserting additional supporting sentences does not mean a paragraph has better development. The supporting sentences must contain just the right amount of pertinent information, all directed to a particular reader. There must never be too little or too much. Too little results in fragmented paragraphs that offer snippets of information that arouse readers' interest but do not satisfy their curiosity. Too much information can lead to long, repetitious paragraphs that annoy readers. Compare the following paragraphs, all describing the result of exploration crews' first venture with machinery across the Peel Plateau in the Yukon, intended for a reader who is interested in the problems of working in northern Canada, but who has never seen what the terrain is like.

Inadequate development	Trails left by tractors look like long narrow scars cut in the plateau. Many of them have been there for years. All have been caused by permafrost melting. They will stay like this until the vegetation grows in again.
Adequate development	To the visitor viewing this far northern terrain from the air, the trails left by tractors clearing undergrowth for roads across the plateau look like long, narrow scars. Even those that have been there for as long as 28 years are still clearly defined. All have been caused by melting of the permafrost, which started when the surface moss and vegetation were removed and will continue until the vegetation grows in again—perhaps in another 30 years.
Over-development	To conservationists, whose main interest is the protection of the environment, viewing this far northern terrain from the air is a heartrending sight. To them, the trails left by tractors clearing undergrowth for roads across the plateau look like long, narrow scars. The tractors were making way for the first roads to be built by man over an area that until now had been trodden only by Inuit indigenous to the area, and the occasional

Each paragraph has a good topic sentence…

…but the development is erratic

trapper. Some of these trappers had journeyed from Quebec to seek new sources of revenue for their trade. But now, in the very short time span of 28 years, man has defiled the terrain. With his machines he has cut and gouged his way, thoughtlessly creating havoc that will be visible to those that follow for many decades. Those that preceded him for centuries had trodden carefully on the permafrost, leaving no trace of their presence. The new trails, even those that have been there for 28 years, are visible almost as though they had been cut yesterday. And all were caused by melting of the permafrost...

The above paragraphs shift from one extreme to the other:

- The first paragraph leaves the reader with questions: What were the tractors doing? How many years? How soon will the vegetation grow in again?

- The second paragraph develops the topic sentence in just enough detail; it explains why the tractors left semipermanent scars and predicts how long they will remain.

- The third paragraph, although interesting, is filled with irrelevant information (e.g. where the trappers come from) and repetitive statements that detract from the main theme. It might be suitable for a novel but not for a technical report.

Correct Length

We recommend that, for a 6 in. (152 mm) typing line, you try to limit paragraph length to no more than 8 printed lines. But also keep these points in mind:

If your work will be printed in narrow, newspaper-like columns, write shorter paragraphs

- You can adjust paragraph length to suit the complexity of the topic and the technical level of the reader. Generally, complex topics demand short paragraphs containing small portions of information, while general topics can be covered in longer paragraphs.

- Variety in paragraph length has a lively visual effect. Conversely, if you write a series of equal-length paragraphs you may create an impression of dullness.

- Readers attach importance to a paragraph that is clearly longer or shorter than those surrounding it. A very short paragraph among several longer paragraphs particularly attracts attention.

- If you write too many short paragraphs close together, your readers may feel you are providing them with incomplete snippets of information. Conversely, if you write a succession of very long paragraphs, your readers may feel they are facing "heavy going" reading.

Sentences

Although sentences normally form an integral part of a larger unit—the paragraph—they still must be able to stand alone. Three elements apply to their construction:

> **Unity**
> **Coherence**
> **Emphasis**

Unity and coherence perform a function in the sentence similar to their role in a well-written paragraph.

Unity Within the Sentence

A unified sentence presents and develops a single thought. It can be a simple statement:

> We completed the installation on May 28.

Or it can be more complex, containing a primary clause plus one or more subsidiary clauses that enlarge on the primary clause:

> We completed the installation on May 28, which comprised assembling a template for each unit and then bolting down and aligning the components.

Compare these two sentences:

A unified sentence that expresses one main thought	The Amron Building will make an ideal manufacturing plant because of its convenient location, single-level floor, good access roads, and low rent.
A complicated sentence that tries to express two thoughts	The copier should never have been placed in the general office, where those using it interrupt the work being done by the administrative staff, who have been consistently over-worked since the beginning of the year.

The first sentence has unity because everything it says relates to only one topic: that the Amron Building will make a good manufacturing plant. The second sentence fails to have unity because readers cannot tell whether they are supposed to be agreeing that the copier should have been placed elsewhere, or sympathizing that the administrative staff have been over-worked.

> Every subordinate clause must either develop or actively support what has been said in the primary clause.

Coherence Within the Sentence

Coherent sentences are continuously clear, even though they may have numerous subordinate clauses. This requires arranging the clauses in logical sequence, linking them through direct or indirect reference to the primary clause, and writing them in the same grammatical form. Parallelism, discussed at the end of this chapter, plays an important role here.

The unified sentence describing the Amron Building (on the previous page) has good coherence because its purpose is continuously clear and each of its subordinate clauses links comfortably back to the lead-in statement (through the phrase "because of its..."). The clauses are written in parallel form (i.e. they have the same grammatical pattern), which is the best way to carry the reader smoothly from point to point.

The first sentence below lacks coherence because there is no logic to the arrangement or form of the subordinate clauses. Compare it with the second sentence, which despite its greater length is still coherent because it continuously develops the thought of "late" and "damaged" expressed in the primary clause.

An incoherent sentence	The Amron Building will make an ideal manufacturing plant because of its convenient location, which also should have good access roads, the advantage of its one-level floor, and it commands a low rent. **(34 incoherent words)**
A coherent sentence	Many of the 61 samples shipped in December either arrived late or were damaged in transit, even though they were shipped one week earlier than usual to avoid the Christmas mail tie-up, and were packed in polyurethane as an extra precaution against rough handling. **(45 coherent words)**

Emphasis Within the Sentence

Properly placed emphasis helps readers identify a sentence's important parts. You can attach importance to the whole sentence, to a clause or phrase, or even to a single word.

Emphasis on the Whole Sentence

You should aim for variety in sentence length, although there may be times when you will need to adjust the length of a particular sentence to give it greater emphasis. Readers will attach importance to a short sentence placed among several longer sentences, or to a long sentence among predominantly short ones. They will also detect a sense of urgency in a series of short sentences that carry them quickly from point to point. This technique is used effectively by story tellers:

The prisoner huddled against the wall, alone in the dark. He listed intently. He could hear the guards, stomping and muttering. Cursing the cold, probably.

In technical writing we have little occasion to write very short sentences, except perhaps to impart urgency to a warning of a potentially dangerous situation:

Dangerously high voltages are present on exposed terminals. Before opening the doors,

1. set the master control switch to "OFF," and
2. hang the red "NO" flag on the operator's panel.

Never cheat the interlocks.

Neither must we err in the opposite direction and write overly long sentences that are confusing. Adjust sentence length to suit the complexity of the topic and the technical level of the reader. If your sentences tend to exceed 22 words, they are probably too long.

Similarity of shape can signify that all parts of a sentence are of equal importance. Clauses separated by a coordinate conjunction (mainly *and*, *or*, *but*, and sometimes a comma) tell a reader that they have equal emphasis. The following sentences are "balanced" in this way:

> Eight test instruments were used for the rehabilitation project *and* were supplied free of charge by the Dere Instrument Company.

> The gas pipeline will be 420 km shorter than the oil pipeline *but* will have to cross much more difficult terrain.

> The upper knob adjusts the instrument in the vertical plane, *and* the lower knob adjusts it in the horizontal plane.

Keep sentence parts parallel, particularly the verbs

Emphasis on Part of a Sentence

Coordination means giving equal weight to all parts of a sentence; subordination means emphasizing a specific part and deemphasizing all other parts. It is effected by placing the most important information in the primary clause and placing less important information in subordinate clauses. In each of the following sentences, the main thought is italicized to identify the primary clause:

> When the technician momentarily released his grip, *the control slipped out of reach.*

> *The bridge over the underpass was built on a compacted gravel base*, partly to save time, partly to save money, and partly because materials were available on site.

> *He lost control of the vehicle* when the wasp stung him.

> When the wasp stung him, *he lost control of the vehicle.*

Emphasis on Specific Words

Where we place individual words in a sentence has a direct bearing on their emphasis. Readers automatically tend to place emphasis on the first and last words in a sentence. If we place unimportant words in either of these impact-bearing positions, they can rob a sentence of its emphasis:

Emphasis misplaced	Such matters as equipment calibration will be handled by the standards laboratory however.
Emphasis restored	Equipment calibration, however, will be handled by the standards laboratory.
Emphasis misplaced	Change the oil every six days at least.
Emphasis restored	Change the oil at least every six days.

Let a noun have the last word!

Passive Voice	Active Voice
Elapsed time is indicated by a pointer.	A pointer indicates elapsed time.
The project was completed by the installation crew on May 2.	The installation crew completed the project on May 2.
It is suggested that meter readings be recorded once every hour.	I suggest you record meter readings once every hour.
The samples were passed to quality control for inspection, and then to the shipping department where they were packed in polyurethane.	Quality control inspected the samples and then the shipping department packed them in polyurethane.

Figure 12-6 Comparison of passive and active voice.

The verbs we use have a powerful influence on emphasis. Strong verbs attract the reader's attention, whereas weak verbs tend to divert it. Verbs in the active voice are strong because they tell *who did what*. Verbs in the passive voice are weak because they merely pass along information; they describe *what was done by whom*. The sentences in Figure 12-6 are written using both active and passive voice; those written in the active voice are consistently shorter and more direct.

There are occasions when you will choose to use the passive voice, because you are reporting an event without knowing who took the action, or prefer not to name a person. For instance, you may prefer to write:

> The strain gauge should have been read at 10-minute intervals.

rather than:

> Kevin McCaughan should have read the strain gauge at 10-minute intervals.

Completeness

Every day we see examples of incomplete sentences—on television, in magazines, and especially in advertising. Media writers use them to create a crisp, intentionally choppy effect:

> SHEER COMFORT!
>
> 8200 metres high. Wide seats, just like your living room.
> Tempting meals. Complimentary refreshments.
> Only on Remick Airlines. Our Business Class. Try us!

But if we do the same in our business letters and reports, our sentences are likely to be read with raised eyebrows.

Avoid Writing Sentence Fragments

It's easy to form a sentence fragment. Normally you correct it later, when you are checking what you have written, but sometimes your familiarity with the information may cause you not to notice it. Consider these two pieces of information:

- The meeting achieved its objective. Even though three members were absent.
- The staff were allowed to leave at 3 p.m. Seeing the air conditioning had failed.

The first sentence in each of these examples is complete (it has a subject-verb-object construction), but the two second sentences are incomplete because each depends on information in the first sentence.

A useful way to check whether or not a sentence is complete is to read it aloud entirely on its own. If it contains a complete thought it will be understood just as it stands. For example, *The meeting achieved its objective* is a complete thought because you do not need additional information to understand it. *The staff were allowed to leave at 3 p.m.* is also complete. But you cannot say the same when you read these aloud:

- Even though three members were absent.
- Seeing the air conditioning had failed.

In most cases a sentence fragment can be corrected by removing the period that separates it from the sentence it depends on, inserting a comma in place of the period, and adding a conjunction or connecting word such as *and, but, which, who,* or *because*:

- The meeting achieved its objective, even though three members were absent.
- The staff were allowed to leave at 3 p.m. *because* the air conditioning had failed. (*"Seeing"* has been changed to *"because."*)

Here are two others:

- Staff will have to bring bag lunches or go out for lunch from October 6 to 10. While the lunchroom is being renovated. (*Change the period to a comma.*)
- All 20-year employees are to be presented with long-service awards. Including three who retired earlier in the year. At the company's annual banquet. (*Change both periods to commas.*)

In particular, check sentences that start with a word that ends in "-ing" (e.g. refer*ring*, answer*ing*, be*ing*) or an expression that ends in "to" (e.g. with reference *to*):

- With reference to your letter of June 6. We have considered your request and will be sending you a cheque. (*Change the period to a comma.*)
- Referring to the problem of vandalism to employees' automobiles in the parking lot. We will be hiring a security guard to patrol the area from 8 a.m. to 6 p.m., Monday through Friday. (*Although the period could be changed to a comma, a better sentence could be formed by reconstructing the fragment:*)
- To resolve the problem of vandalism to employees' automobiles in the parking lot, we will be hiring...

Avoid Forming Run-on Sentences

A similar sentence error occurs if you link two separate thoughts in a single sentence, joining them with only a comma or even no punctuation. The effect can jar a reader uncomfortably. For example:

Your reader will know
what you are saying, but
will feel uncomfortable
reading your words

- Ms Solvason has been selected for the word-processing seminar on March 11, she is eager to attend.

This awkward construction is known as a run-on sentence. It can be corrected by

- replacing the comma with a period, to form two complete sentences:

  ...on March 11. She is eager to attend.

- or retaining the comma and following it with *which* or *and*:

  ...on March 11, which she is...
  ...on March 11, and she is...

A run-on sentence with no punctuation is even more noticeable:

  The customer said he never received an invoice I made up a new one.

Either a period, or a comma and a linking word, must be inserted between the words *invoice* and *I*:

  ...an invoice. I made up...
  ...an invoice, so I made up...

Position End Punctuation Correctly

There are particular rules for inserting punctuation after quotation marks and closing brackets:

- If a sentence ends with a quotation mark, place the period *inside* the quotation mark:

  "That's the information we need," the chief engineer remarked.
  "Now we can start the project." ↑
                              ↑

(The above example also shows that when a comma ends an introductory statement, it is also placed *inside* the closing quotation mark.)

These are North
American rules; they
differ in Great Britain

- If a sentence ends with a closing bracket, place the period *outside* the bracket if the words within the bracket do not form a complete sentence:

  Sound levels measured in the laboratory exceeded the tolerance specification (as shown in Table 2).
                                        ↑

- However, if the opening bracket is preceded by a period, and the words within the bracket create a complete sentence, then place the period *inside* the bracket:

  Sound levels measured in the laboratory exceeded the tolerance specification. (They were above 82 dBA for more than two hours per day.)
            ↑

Words

The right words in the right place at the right moment can greatly influence your readers. A heavy, ponderous word will slow them down; an overused expression will make them doubt your sincerity; a complex word they do not recognize will annoy them; and a weak or vague word will make them think of you as indefinite. But the right word—short, clear, specific, and necessary—will help them understand your message quickly and easily.

The key word here is "specific"

Words That Tell a Story

Words should convey images. We have many strong, descriptive words in our individual vocabularies, but most of the time we are too lazy to use them because the same old routine words spring easily to mind. We write "put" when we would do better to write "position," "insert," "drop," "slide," or any one of the numerous descriptive verbs that better describe the action, as shown in Figure 12-7. One descriptive word that defines size, shape, colour, smell, texture, or taste is much more valuable than a dozen words that only generalize.

Analogies can offer a useful means for describing an unfamiliar item in terms a nontechnical reader will recognize:

Relate a complex concept to a well-known idea or fact

> A resistor is a piece of ceramic-covered carbon about the size of a cribbage peg, with a 50 mm length of wire protruding from each end.

Specific words tell the reader that you are a definite, purposeful individual. Vague generalities imply that you are unsure of yourself. For example:

> It is considered that a fair percentage of the samples received from one of our suppliers during the preceding months contained a contaminant.

Whenever possible, insert specific words rather than generalizations

Vague Words	Descriptive Words
While the crew was in town they *got* some spare parts.	*Replace "got" with* bought purchased borrowed requisitioned
I have *contacted* the site.	*Replace "contacted" with* telephoned visited written to emailed faxed
The project will *take a long time*.	*Replace "take a long time" with* last four months require 300 work hours employ two installers for three weeks

Figure 12-7 Replacing non-descriptive words with descriptive words.

This sentence gives a reader four opportunities to wonder whether the writer really knows much about the topic:

1. "It is considered"   Who has voiced this opinion?
2. "a fair percentage"   How many?
3. "one of our suppliers"   Who? One in how many?
4. "contained a contaminant" What contaminant? In how strong a concentration?

All these generalizations can be avoided in a shorter, more specific sentence:

We estimate that 60% of the samples received from RamSort Chemicals in June were contaminated with 0.5% to 0.8% mercuric chloride.

Combining Words into Compound Terms

The trend is to compound multiword expressions into a single word

One of the biggest problems for technical writers is knowing whether multiword expressions should be compounded fully, joined by hyphens, or allowed to stand as two or more separate words. For example, should you write

cross check, cross-check, or crosscheck?

counter clockwise, counter-clockwise, or counterclockwise?

change over, change-over, or changeover?

The tendency today is to compound a multiword expression into a single term. But this bare statement cannot be applied as a general rule because there are too many variations, some of which appear in the glossary.

Most multiword expressions are compound adjectives. When two words combine to form an adjective they are either joined by a hyphen or compounded to form one word. They are usually joined by a hyphen if they are formed from an adjective-noun expression:

Adjective + Noun	*As a Compound Adjective*
heavy water	heavy-water production
four channels	four-channel receiver
high frequency	high-frequency oscillator

But when one of the combining words is a verb, they often combine into a one-word adjective. Under these conditions they will normally also compound into a single-word noun:

Two Words	As a Noun	As an Adjective
lock out	lockout	lockout voltage
shake down	shakedown	shakedown test
cross over	crossover	crossover network

Refer to the Glossary for the more common multiword expressions

Three or more words that combine to form an adjective in most cases are joined by hyphens. For example, *lock test pulse* becomes *lock-test-pulse generator*. Occasionally, however, they are compounded into a single term, as in *counterelectromotive force*. Specific examples are listed in the Glossary.

Obviously, these "rules" cannot be taken at full face value because there are occasions when they do not apply. Useful guides for doubtful combinations are contained in many dictionaries, and in *The Brief Penguin Handbook* referenced earlier.

Spelling "Canadian Style"

English-speaking Canadians have inherited a spelling problem. Should we continue to spell words such as "theatre" and "labour" as they are traditionally spelled in Britain? Or should we spell them "theater" and "labor," as they are spelled by our neighbours (or *neighbors*) in the United States?

Unfortunately, there are no clearcut guidelines for the correct spelling of such words in Canada, which means that each of us must decide individually whether we want to spell according to contemporary British usage, or align ourselves with the standards current in the United States.

Do you write "metre" or "meter"?; "harbor" or "harbour"?

If almost all of your business correspondence is to people and organizations in Canada, and if your reports are seldom read in the US, then you can safely adopt the British spellings. But if you correspond frequently with people in the US, and write reports that will be read on both sides of the border, then you probably should adopt US spelling as your "standard."

You need a good dictionary to guide you. We recommend *The Canadian Oxford Dictionary*[3] if you prefer the traditional British spelling style, and the *Webster's New Collegiate Dictionary*[4] if you choose the American spelling style. These dictionaries show both the preferred and the alternative spellings of words that can be spelled more than one way. For example, the *Oxford* dictionary lists

theatre, *theater (the asterisk means "chiefly US")

whereas the *Webster's* dictionary lists

theater or theatre.

The first word in each case is the preferred spelling for the country in which the dictionary has been published, and the second spelling is an alternative, much less common, spelling for that country. (Few people in Britain would write *theater*, and even fewer Americans would write *theatre*.)

A third choice is *Funk & Wagnalls Canadian College Dictionary*,[5] which tends to lean toward American spelling style.

We have chosen to use a widely respected Canadian guideline as our authority for most spellings, both throughout previous chapters and in the Glossary. This is *The Canadian Press Stylebook*[6] and its companion booklet *Caps and Spelling*.[7]

We use the *CP Stylebook* as our style guide

Two features of the *Stylebook* are its preference for the "re" spelling for words such as "centre" and "theatre," and the "our" spelling for words such as "honour" and "favour." This is reflected throughout the Glossary of Technical Usage in this book and is reinforced on page 7 of CP's *Caps and Spelling*:

> The Canadian Oxford Dictionary is the authority for Canadian Press spelling…(so) CP style is our, not or, for labour, honour and other such words of more than one syllable in which the "u" is not pronounced.

Where there is a spelling choice, the Glossary describes the alternatives and then identifies which spelling we recommend for use in Canada, like this:

favo(u)r   *favour* pref in Br and rec in Can.; *favor* pref in US
(pref = preferred; rec = recommended; Can. = Canada)

Note that the emphasis is on the word "recommend": we only *recommend* which spelling we believe to be preferable; the ultimate choice is yours.

Long Versus Short Words

Avoid using an 89-cent word when an equally suitable 25-cent word is available

Big words create a barrier between writer and reader. There are many long scientific words that we have to use in technical writing; we should surround them with short words whenever possible so our writing will not become ponderous and overly complex.

Low-Information-Content Expressions

Words and expressions of low information content (LIC) contribute little to a sentence. Remove them and the sentence says just as much! Consider this paragraph:

Vague and Wordy   Pursuant to the client's original suggestion, Mr Richards is of the opinion that the structure planned for the client would be most suitable for erection on the site until recently occupied by the old established costume manufacturer known as Garrick Garments. In accordance with the client's anticipated approval of this site, Mr Richards has taken great pains to design a multi-level building that will use the property to an optimum extent.

"Waffle" describes such cumbersome writing. By eliminating unnecessary expressions (such as *pursuant to*; *of the opinion that*; *for erection on*; *in accordance with*; *to an optimum extent*), we can cut the original 71 words to a much more effective 40 words:

Clear and Direct   Mr Richards believes the building planned for the client should be erected on the site previously occupied by Garrick Garments. He has assumed the client will approve this site, and has designed a multi-level building that fully develops the property.

Low-information-content words are untidy lodgers

Table 12-1 contains some of the words and phrases you should delete from your writing. They are difficult to identify because they often sound like good prose. In the following sentences, the LIC words have been italicized; they should be either deleted or replaced, as indicated by the notes in brackets.

- Flow is controlled by *means of* No. 3 valve. (**delete** *means of*) Or: No. 3 valve controls the flow. (**active voice**)
- Adjust the control *as necessary* to obtain maximum deflection. (**delete** *as necessary*)
- Tests were run for *a period of* three weeks. (**delete** *a period of*)

Table 12-1 Examples of low-information-content (LIC) words and phrases.

The LIC words and phrases in this partial list are followed by an expression in brackets (to illustrate a better way to write the phrase) or by an (X), which means that it should be dropped entirely.

actually (X)
a majority of (most)
a number of (many; several)
as a means of (for; to)
as a result (so)
as necessary (X)
at present (X)
at the rate of (at)
at the same time as (while)
at this time (X)
bring to a conclusion (conclude)
by means of (by)
by use of (by)
communicate with (talk to; telephone; write to)
connected together (connected)
contact (talk to; telephone; write to)
due to the fact that (because)
during the course of, during the time that (while)
end result (result)
exhibit a tendency (tend)
for a period of (for)
for the purpose of (for; to)
for this reason (because)
in all probability (probably)
in an area where (where)
in an effort to (to)
in close proximity to (close to; near)

in colour, in length, in number, in size (X)
in connection with (about)
in fact, in point of fact (X)
in order to (to)
in such a manner as to (to)
in terms of (in; for)
in the course of (during)
in the direction of (toward)
in the event that (if)
in the form of (as)
in the light of (X)
in the neighbourhood of; in the vicinity of (about; approximately; near)
involves the use of (employs; uses)
involves the necessity of (demands; requires)
is a person who (X)
is designed to be (is)
it can be seen that (thus; so)
it is considered desirable (I or we want to)
it will be necessary to (I, you, or we must)
of considerable magnitude (large)
on account of (because)
previous to, prior to (before)
subsequent to (after)
with the aid of (with; assisted by)
with the result that (so, therefore)

Note: Many of these phrases start and end with words such as *as, at, by, for, in, is, it, of, to,* and *with.* This knowledge can help you identify LIC words and phrases in your writing.

This is only a partial list; there are many more LIC expressions

- By Wednesday we had a backlog of 632 units, *and for this reason* we adopted a two-shift operation. **(replace** *and for this reason* **with** *so***)**

Clichés and wordy expressions are similar to LIC words and phrases. If you refer to yourself as "the writer," start and end letters with overworked phrases such as "We are in acknowledgment of..." and "...please feel free to call me," or use semilegal jargon such as "the aforementioned discussion," you will be a wordy writer. Further examples are listed in Table 12-2.

Table 12-2   Typical clichés and wordy expressions.

all things being equal	in the foreseeable future
a matter of concern	in the long run
and/or	in the matter of
as a matter of fact	last but not least
as per	many and diverse
attached hereto	needless to say
at this point in time	please feel free to
enclosed herewith	pursuant to your request
for your information (as an introductory phrase)	regarding the matter of
	this will acknowledge
if and when	we are pleased to advise
in our opinion	we wish to state
in reference to	with reference to
in short supply	you are hereby advised

Some Fine Points
Using Parallelism to Good Effect

Good parallelism has a subtle, mostly hidden effect on readers

Parallelism in writing means "similarity of shape." Good parallelism makes readers feel comfortable, so that even in long or complex sentences they never lose their way. Its ability to help readers through difficult passages makes parallelism particularly applicable to technical writing.

The Grammatical Aspects

If you keep your verb forms similar throughout a sentence in which all parts are of equal importance (i.e. in which the sentence has coordination, or is balanced), you will have taken a major step toward preserving parallelism. For example, if you write "unable to predict" in the early part of a sentence, you should write "able to convince" rather than "successful in convincing" later in the sentence:

Readers feel uncomfortable when parallelism is violated

Parallelism violated	Mr Johnson was *unable to predict* the job completion date, but was *successful in convincing* management that the job was under control.
Parallelism restored (A)	Mr Johnson was *unable to predict* the job completion date, but was *able to convince* management that the job was under control.
Parallelism restored (B) (more direct alternative)	Mr Johnson *predicted* no completion date, but *convinced* management that the job was under control.

Here are two other examples:

Parallelism violated	Pete Hansk likes surveying airports and to study new construction techniques.

Parallelism restored	Pete Hansk likes to survey airports and to study new construction techniques.
	or
	Pete Hansk likes surveying airports and studying new construction techniques.

| Parallelism violated | Following graduation, you will be able to find employment in environmental resources management or in developing research tools. |

Parallelism restored	Following graduation, you will be able to find employment in environmental resources management or in research tools development.
	or
	Following graduation, you will be able to find employment managing environmental resources or developing research tools.

Parallelism is particularly important when you are joining sentence parts with the coordinating conjunctions *and*, *or*, and *but* (as in the examples above), with a comma, or with correlatives such as

either...or
neither...nor

Each part of a correlative must be followed by an expression in the same grammatical form. That is, if *either* is followed by a verb, then *or* must also be followed by the same form of verb:

Be particularly careful when using the expression *Not only...but also*

| Parallelism violated | You may either repair the test set or it may be replaced under the warranty agreement. |

| Parallelism restored | You may either *repair* the test set or *replace* it under the warranty agreement. |

Application to Technical Writing

When building sentences that have a series of clauses, you can help your reader see the connection between the different parts by writing them in the same shape throughout the sentence. There is complete loss of continuity in the following sentence because it lacks parallelism:

| Parallelism violated | We inadvertently omitted listing the 7 lathes in room B101, 5 milling machines in room B117, and from the next room, B118, we also forgot to include 16 shapers. |

You can restore the clarity by rewriting the sentence so that its parts all have a similar shape:

| Parallelism restored | We inadvertently omitted listing 7 lathes in room B101, 5 milling machines in room B117, and 16 shapers in room B118. |

Maintain similarity of shape within each sentence...

Within the paragraph, parallelism has to be applied more carefully, because if it is too obvious the similarity in construction can be dull and repetitive. The verbs are often the key: keep them generally in the same mood and they will help bind the paragraph into one cohesive unit. This paragraph has good parallelism:

...and within each paragraph

> The effects of sound are difficult to measure. What to some people is simply background noise, to others may be ear-shattering, peace-destroying drumming. The roar of a jet engine, the squeal of tires, the clatter of machinery, the hiss of air conditioning, the chatter of children, and even the repetitive squeak of an unoiled door hinge can seriously affect them and create a distinct feeling of uneasiness.

Similarity of shape is most obvious in the third sentence, with its rhythmic use of "sound" words:

roar of a jet engine	*hiss* of air conditioning
squeal of tires	*chatter* of children
clatter of machinery	*squeak* of an unoiled door hinge

Here we have words that paint strong images. They not only have the same grammatical form but are also bound together because they relate to the same sense: hearing.

Even if the subject has less noticeable impact, you should still try to use parallelism to carry your reader smoothly through your description, as in this description of a surveyor's transit:

Very technical, yet the rhythm binds the parts together

> Two sets of clamps and tangent screws are used to adjust the levelling head. The upper clamp fastens the upper and lower plates together, while the upper tangent screw permits a small differential movement between them. The lower clamp fastens the lower plate to the socket, while the lower tangent screw turns the plate through a small angle. When the upper and lower plates are clamped together they can be moved freely as a unit; but when both the upper and lower clamps are tightened the plates cannot be moved in any plane.

Application to Subparagraphing

Subparagraphing seldom occurs in literature, but is used frequently in technical writing to separate events or steps, describe an operation or procedure, or list parts or components. Subparagraphing always demands good parallelism, which is *not* present in the following example:

> Three tests were conducted to isolate the fault:
> 1. A matrix was imposed upon the video screen to provide greater clarity.
> 2. Voltage was measured between terminals 4 and 9 to check for line losses.
> 3. To provide additional monitoring, a continuity tester was connected to the unit.

It's when writing point form that parallelism becomes particularly important

The third subparagraph is not parallel with the first two. To be parallel it should first say what was done and then explain why:

> 4. A continuity tester was connected to the unit to provide additional monitoring.

An alternative is to use active verbs together with parallelism to build a strong, emphatic description:

A running lead-in line and imperative-mood verbs create a convincing effect

> To isolate the fault we
> 1. *imposed* a matrix upon ...
> 2. *measured* voltage between...
> 3. *connected* a continuity tester to ...

To change from the first person to the third person, only the lead-in sentence has to be rewritten:

In tests conducted to isolate the fault, the laboratory
1. *imposed...*
2. *measured...*
3. *connected...*

See pages 274 to 277 for more information on inserting bullets and paragraph numbers.

Abbreviating Technical and Nontechnical Terms

You may abbreviate any term you like, and in any form you like, providing you indicate clearly to the reader how you intend to abbreviate it. The first time you use the term, write it out in full and then follow it with its abbreviation enclosed within brackets. For example:

In technical narrative, spell out single-digit numbers (sdn). However, when inserting an sdn into a series of single- and multiple-digit numbers, write it in numeral form.

When forming abbreviations, observe these three basic rules:

These guidelines are recognized worldwide

1. **Use lower case letters,** unless the abbreviation is formed from a person's name:

centimetre	cm
kilogram	kg
approximately	approx
decibel	dB (the *B* represents *Bell* [Alexander Graham Bell])

2. **Omit all periods,** unless the abbreviation forms another word:

horsepower	hp
cubic centimetre	cm^3
cathode-ray tube	crt
metre	m
pascal	Pa
number	no. (also often abbreviated as *No.*)

3. **Write plural abbreviations in the same form as the singular abbreviation:**

28 metres	28 m
7.2 pascals	7.2 Pa
11 kilograms	11 kg
3 hours	3 h *or* hr

There are, however, exceptions which, through continued use, have been generally accepted as the correct form. For example:

for example *(exempli gratia)*	e.g.	*(There is a slowly growing trend*
that is *(id est)*	i.e.	*to write these as* eg *and* ie)

morning *(ante meridiem)*	a.m.
afternoon *(post meridiem)*	p.m.
inside diameter	ID

The Glossary of Technical Usage offers a reasonably comprehensive list of standard abbreviations and some technical abbreviations. For specific technical terms, you may need to refer to a list of abbreviations compiled by a technical society in your discipline.

Writing Numbers in Narrative

The conventions that dictate whether a number should be written out or expressed as numerals differ between ordinary writing and technical writing. In technical writing you are much more likely to express numbers in numeral form.

The rules listed below are intended mainly as a guide. They will apply most of the time, but there will be occasions when you will have to make a decision between two rules that conflict. Your decision should then be based on three criteria:

- Which method will be most readable.
- Which method will be simplest to type.
- Which method you used previously, under similar circumstances.

Numerals are more common than spelled-out numbers in most technical narrative

Good judgment and a desire to be consistent will help you select the best method each time.

The basic rule for writing numbers in technical narrative is

- spell out single-digit numbers (one to nine inclusive), and
- use numerals for multiple-digit numbers (10 and above).

However, there are exceptions to this rule, as shown in Table 12-3.

There are also five additional general rules:

- Spell out one of the numbers when two numbers are written consecutively and are not separated by punctuation: 36 fifty-watt amplifiers or thirty-six 50-watt amplifiers. (Generally, spell out whichever number will result in the simplest or shortest expression.)

Always place a "0" in front of an open decimal

- Insert a zero before the decimal point of numbers less than one: 0.75; 0.0037.
- Use decimals rather than fractions (they are easier to type), except when writing numbers that are customarily written as fractions: $^3/_4$ in. plywood.
- Insert spaces in large numbers containing five or more digits: 1 275 000; 27 291; 4056. (Insert a space in four-digit numbers only when they appear as part of a column of numbers.) We recommend using spaces rather than commas, because in many European countries the comma is used to represent a decimal point.

Table 12-3 Guidelines for writing numbers in narrative.

Guideline	Example *(where applicable)*
Always use numerals for the following:	
• Specific technical information, such as test results, dimensions, tolerances, temperatures, statistics, and quotations from tabular data.	
• Any number that precedes a unit of measurement.	3 mm; 7 kg; 121.5 MHz
• A series of both large and small numbers in one passage.	On May 28 we tested 7 transmitters, 49 receivers, and 38 power supplies.
• Section, chapter, page, figure (illustration), and table numbers.	Chapter 7; Figure 4; page 219
• Numbers that contain fractions or decimals.	7½; 3.25
• Percentages.	3% gain; 6% GST
• Years, dates, and times.	At 3 p.m. on January 9, 2008; 08:17; 20 Feb 08
• Sums of money.	$2000; $28.50; 27 cents or $0.27
• A person's age.	Nearly 8 years old
Always spell out the number for the following:	
• Round numbers that stand alone.	about five hundred; approximately forty thousand
• Fractions that stand alone.	Repairs were made in less than three-quarters of an hour.
• Numbers that start a sentence. *(Or, better, revise the sentence so the number is not at the beginning.)*	

- Write numbers that denote position in a sequence as 1st, 2nd, 3rd, 4th...31st...42nd...103rd...124th...

When writing and abbreviating numerical prefixes such as "giga" and "kilo," follow the guidelines in Table 12-4.

Writing Metric Units and Symbols (SI)

The Glossary of Technical Usage includes terms and symbols prescribed by the International System of Units (SI). The trend toward worldwide adoption of metric units of measurement means that for some time both the imperial inch/pound system and the metric (SI) system will be in use. The terms and symbols introduced here are those you are most likely to encounter.

The acronym "SI" represents the name "Système International d'Unités." Both the acronym and the name were adopted for universal usage in 1960 by the eleventh Conférence Générale des Poids et Mesures (CGPM), which is the international authority on metrication. Since then, many of the metric terms the conference established have become part of our language. *Hertz*, the unit of frequency measurement, which replaced *cycles per second* in 1960, is a typical example, as are the following:

	non-SI	SI
Temperature:	degrees Fahrenheit	degrees Celsius
Length:	miles, yards, feet, inches	kilometres, metres, millimetres
Weight:	tons, pounds, ounces	tonnes, kilograms, grams, milligrams
Liquid volume:	gallons, quarts	kilolitres, litres

The "-re" spelling is correct for *litre* and *metre*, although only the "-er" spelling is recognized in the US

There are nine general guidelines for writing SI symbols, which must be written, typed, or printed as listed below:

1. In upright type, even if the surrounding type slopes or is in italic letters.

2. In lower case letters, except when the name of the unit is derived from a person's name (e.g. the symbol F for *farad* is derived from *Faraday*), in which case the first letter of the symbol is capitalized (e.g. Wb for *weber*).

3. With a space between the last numeral and the first letter of the symbol: **355 V, 27 km** (*not* 355V, 27km).

4. With no space between the letters forming the symbol: **3.6 kg, 150 mm, 960 kHz**.

5. With no "s" added to a plural: **1 g, 236 kg**.

6. With no period after the symbol, unless it forms the last word in a sentence.

7. With a solidus (oblique stroke: /) to represent the word *per*: **m/s** (metres per second). There can be only one solidus in each expression.

8. With a dot at midletter height (·) to represent that symbols are multiplied: **lm·s** (lumen second).

The abbreviation for *litre* is L, because a lower case letter l looks like the numeral 1

9. Always as a symbol when a number is used with the SI unit (e.g. "the tank holds 400 L"), but spelled out when no number is used with the unit (e.g "capacity is measured in litres" [*not* "capacity is measured in L"]).

This guideline is also recognized worldwide

Table 12-4 Numerical prefixes and abbreviations.

Multiple/ Submultiple	Prefix	Symbol	Multiple/ Submultiple	Prefix	Symbol
10^{24}	yotta	Y	10^{-1}	deci	d
10^{21}	zetta	Z	10^{-2}	centi	c
10^{18}	exa	E	10^{-3}	milli	m
10^{15}	peta	P	10^{-6}	micro	μ
10^{12}	tera	T	10^{-9}	nano	n
10^{9}	giga	G	10^{-12}	pico	p
10^{6}	mega	M	10^{-15}	femto	f
10^{3}	kilo	k	10^{-18}	atto	a
10^{2}	hecto	h	10^{-21}	zepto	z
10	deca	da	10^{-24}	yocta	y

Writing Non-Gender-Specific Language

History has provided us with a scenario in which men were the warriors and hunters, and subsequently the breadwinners, and women were the home bodies who cooked meals and reared children and catered to their men's needs. Today, all that has changed and it is universally recognized in developed countries that women and men are equal and can for the most part have equal occupations and equal roles. Consequently, we now see men as administrative assistants, nurses, and child care workers, and women as airline captains, engineers, truck drivers, and backhoe operators.

Unfortunately, our language has not kept pace and we still see some people who write like this:

> A secretary will be brought in to record the minutes of the client/contractor project meeting. *She* will be responsible for making travel arrangements for all meeting participants.

> After much deliberation, the committee decided to hire an engineer to look into the problem. *He* will evaluate the extent of erosion that occurred when the river overflowed its banks.

Awareness is the key to writing non-gender-specific language

Neither of these writers knew whether the secretary and the engineer were going to be male or female, yet *they automatically assumed* that the secretary would be a woman and the engineer would be a man. Traditionally, that was what they and their parents, and their grandparents, and their parents before them, were accustomed to.

It's our job to eradicate such gender-specific references from our writing:

> A secretary will be brought in to record the minutes of the client/contractor project meeting, and to make travel arrangements for all meeting participants.

> After much deliberation, the committee decided to hire an engineer to evaluate the extent of erosion that occurred when the river overflowed its banks.

Interestingly, these examples are shorter than the original sentences

Eliminate Masculine Pronouns

When describing engineers, scientists, architects, managers, supervisors, technical people, and even accountants and lawyers, historically our language has abounded with masculine pronouns. Here is an excerpt from a company's operating procedures:

> **17.3 Senior Systems Engineer.** *His* primary role is to plan, schedule, manage, and coordinate the activities of the engineers within the Systems Engineering Department. *He* also is responsible for preparing budgets and maintaining fiscal control of operations performed by the department, and for maintaining liaison with and reporting progress to clients.

There are several ways you can remove the male pronouns:

1. Repeat the job title, and abbreviate it:

> **17.3 Senior Systems Engineer (SSE).** The SSE's primary role is to plan, schedule, manage, and coordinate the activities of the engineers within the Systems Engineering Department. The SSE also is responsible for preparing budgets

and maintaining fiscal control of operations performed by the department, and for maintaining liaison with and reporting progress to clients.

2. Use a bulleted list:

This is probably the clearest and most comfortable revision

17.3 **Senior Systems Engineer.** The Senior Systems Engineer is responsible for

- planning, scheduling, managing, and coordinating the activities of the engineers within the Systems Engineering Department,
- preparing budgets and maintaining fiscal control of operations performed by the department, and
- maintaining liaison with and reporting progress to clients.

3. Create a table:

17.3 **Senior Systems Engineer**

This revision employs good information design principles

Primary Responsibility	Secondary Responsibilities
To plan, schedule, manage, and coordinate the activities of the engineers within the Systems Engineering Department.	To prepare budgets and maintain fiscal control of operations performed by the department. To maintain liaison with and report progress to clients.

4. Replace the male pronoun with "you" and "your":

17.3 **Senior Systems Engineer.** *Your* primary role is to plan, schedule, manage, and coordinate the activities of the engineers within the Systems Engineering Department. *You* also are responsible for preparing budgets and maintaining fiscal control of operations performed by the department, and for maintaining liaison with and reporting progress to clients.

(Note: If you use "you" in one part of a document, be consistent and use it throughout the document. Avoid bouncing back and forth between "you" and "he" or "she".)

5. Change singular pronouns to plural pronouns:

Suggestions 4 and 5 are less comfortable revisions

17.3 **Senior Systems Engineers.** *Their* primary role is to plan, schedule, manage, and coordinate the activities of the engineers within the Systems Engineering Department. *They* also are responsible for preparing budgets and maintaining fiscal control of operations performed by the department, and for maintaining liaison with and reporting progress to clients.

(Note: This method can be used only when the description lends itself to using plural nouns and pronouns; i.e. there must be more than one Senior Systems Engineer.)

We do not recommend using the expressions "he or she," "he/she," or "s/he."

Replace Gender-Specific Nouns

Each province in Canada has its Workers' Compensation Board, an organization that provides financial help to employees who are injured at work. Yet, not many years ago, all Workers' Compensation Boards in Canada were known as *Workmen's* Compensation Boards. The previous title seemed to imply that the board provided help *only* to male workers, which was not true. Similarly, until about 15 years ago, flight attendants on airlines were known as stewardesses, implying that the job was held only by females. Again, particularly today, this is plainly inaccurate.

Many other job titles are gender-specific and predominantly male-oriented. Table 12-5 shows some that have been replaced in recent years.

Be Consistent When Referring to Men and Women

Men throughout recent history have been given the courtesy title *Mr* before their names. Until 20 years ago, women had two courtesy titles, to denote whether they were married or single: *Mrs* and *Miss*. Today, a woman's marital status is *never* implied in her title: always address a woman as *Ms*.

Be particularly careful when addressing letters and writing the salutation

Writing for an International Audience

People in many European and Asian countries are much more formal in their correspondence than we tend to be in North America. Where a Manitoban writing to Paul Villeneuve in Quebec would write *Dear Paul* quite early in an exchange of letters, an Italian or Norwegian (for example) would continue to write *Dear Mr Villeneuve* for much longer.

In a growing global economy, we have to be aware of and adapt to cultural differences

Table 12-5   Preferred names for gender-specific titles.

If you are tempted to write:	Consider replacing it with:
actor; actress	actor (for both sexes)
chairman	chairperson (*or* chair)
cowboy	cattle rancher
fireman	firefighter
foreman	supervisor
man-hours	work-hours or staff hours
Miss or Mrs	Ms
newsman	reporter
policeman; policewoman	police officer
postman	letter (*or* mail) carrier
repairman	service technician
salesman	sales representative
spokesman	spokesperson
workman	worker; employee
waiter; waitress	server (or "waiter" for both sexes)

Titles such as *fireman, foreman,* and *salesman* are deeply entrenched, and so are difficult to eradicate

This formality extends to how you use the letter-writing pyramid described in Chapter 3, particularly for countries in Eastern Europe and Asia. Rather than discard the pyramid, you will need to insert two additional writing compartments, one at the beginning and one at the end, as shown in Figure 12-8. The opening compartment often will contain a greeting and polite remarks about the reader's family, and their health and happiness. The closing compartment will also contain polite remarks, perhaps wishing the reader continuing good health and prosperity in the months and years ahead.

However, changing the focus is not the only part of a message to an Eastern or Asian country that requires attention. When you write in English to readers who normally speak another language—German, French, Italian, Spanish, Malayan, or Chinese, for example—you have to choose words that will be clearly understood. This also holds true for different cultures who speak the same language. In Great Britain, for instance, the word "fortnight" is commonly used to mean "two weeks," yet in the United States and even in much of Canada it would not be understood. Similarly, the word "presently" means "shortly" in Great Britain but "right away" in the US.

Here are some guidelines to follow:

- Avoid long, complex sentences.
- Avoid long, complex words. If you have a choice between two or more words or expressions that have roughly the same meaning, choose the simpler one. For example, write "pay" rather than "salary" or "remuneration."

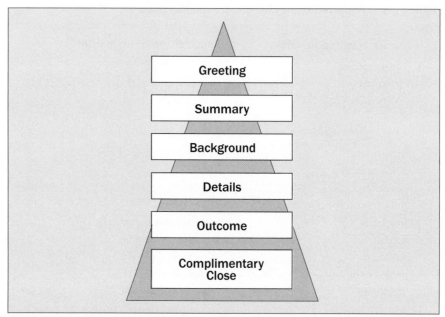

Figure 12-8 "Adapted" pyramid for a letter to an Eastern European or Asian reader.

- Use the same word to describe the same action or product consistently throughout your letter. Decide, for example, whether you will refer to money in the bank as *funds, currency, deposits, capital,* or *money.*

- Always use a word in the same sense. You would confuse a foreign-language reader if you were to write "It would not be *appropriate* to transfer funds from Account A to Account B" (meaning it would not be suitable to do it), and then in another sentence write "We had insufficient capital to *appropriate* Company A" (meaning to take over Company A, or buy it out).

Two sources for more information about writing to and observing the communication culture of different countries can be obtained through the Society for Technical Communication (STC), which has a Special Interest Group concentrating on global communication (www.stc.org), and from a book by Nancy L Hoft titled *International Technical Communication.*[8]

ASSIGNMENTS

Exercise 12.1
The following sentences and short passages lack compactness, simplicity, or clarity, and particularly contain low-information-content (LIC) expressions. Improve them by deleting unnecessary words, or by partial or complete rewriting.

1. New identity badges will be introduced as a means of improving security.

2. An electrical storm was the cause of last night's power disruption lasting for a period of two hours.

3. Before making any attempt to close the valve, be sure as a first step to check that the master control is in the up (OFF) position.

4. The end result of rotating the control clockwise will be in the form of an increase in flow.

5. There will be little or no advantage at this point in time in carrying out any further tests.

6. Please do not hesitate to call this office at any time in the future if you experience problems with the heater.

7. Check the voltage between terminals X7 and Y12 with the use of a Vancourt 272 meter.

8. If it is your intention to put in an application for the supervisor's position, then it is my opinion that you should do so by at the very latest March 31.

Simple ideas confused
by wordy, rambling
sentences

9. It is indeed a possibility that the equipment was damaged at some point while in transit.

10. For your information, the Mayerling report on the permafrost study conducted in the region of Lac La Biche will be readily available in the company library with effect from October 24.

11. It is a point of considerable concern to us, that since 2005 there is evidence of higher levels of toxicity in the waters of Lake Winnipeg.

12. The road traffic study to be conducted on the bypass around the region of the town of Corrigan will last for a period of two weeks starting on or about May 16.

13. During the time of the spring audit, the auditors identified an accounting error in the amount of $130 000.

14. The purchase of any software upgrade is permitted without pre-authorization providing the price is not in excess of $235 per item.

15. It is entirely within the realm of possibility that the Prometheus Project may be divided between two contractors.

16. In an effort to increase reliability of our products, the Quality Assurance Department will conduct random checks during the stage of module assembly.

17. In response to a decision made at the May meeting, a supplementary budget of $60 000 will actually be prepared in June for the purpose of providing extra funding for the Wildwood Project.

18. The final phase of testing planned for October will bring the installation project to a conclusion.

19. For the balance of the current year, it is expected that the company will be in the process of hiring seven additional technicians.

20. When a contractor is inspecting underwater bridge structures, it is a Labour Department specification that the contractor is required to provide a minimum of two or more divers who will be connected together by a cable of no more than 3 metres in length.

Exercise 12.2

The following sentences offer choices between words that sound similar or are frequently misused. Select the correct word in each case.

1. The technician reported that the flywheel became (stationary/stationery) 127 seconds after power was cut off.

2. (Preventive/Preventative) maintenance has to be performed on the engine after 800 hours of (continual/continuous) non-stop operation.

3. In his welcoming speech to staff, the newly appointed director (implied/inferred) there would be no lay-offs for at least 18 months.

4. The proposed change will be difficult to (affect/effect) because over 80% of the employees will be (affected/effected).

5. On reception, signals are separated into two (discreet/discrete) channels.

6. No (farther/further) payments have been made to the outstanding account.

7. Because the storm has cut off power to site 17, you will be unable to (elicit/illicit) a response from the site for 48 hours.

8. The inspection team (is/are) experiencing difficulty and will be unable to complete (its/it's/their) investigation of the equipment until May 17.

9. The (amount/number) of installations we will be able to undertake in 2008 will decrease by 27% from the 2007 total, because we will have 24 (fewer/less) staff to carry out the work.

10. It is essential to carry out (a disinterested/an uninterested) personal evaluation when considering an employee for promotion.

11. From the technician's report, telephoned to me on June 10, it (appears/seems) unlikely the project will be completed on schedule.

12. No work will be done on the project between December 23 (and/to) January 3.

13. Over 70% of the repairs will be carried out by December 31; the (balance/remainder) will be completed in the following year.

14. Although the data (has/have) been evaluated, (its/it's) unlikely the results will be available before October 12.

15. Before taking any measurements, check that the pointer on the rotating ring has been (oriented/orientated) to point at exactly 216°.

16. When the transformer blew out, we had to choose an (alternate/alternative) power source from our neighbouring provinces.

17. The agenda (was/were) too detailed to handle in a single meeting.

18. Forty-eight hours after the concrete was poured on the second floor of the new parking structure, we took seven drill cores to ensure the pour was (free from/free of) flaws.

19. The number of hirings in 2008 showed a 20% increase compared (to/with) the hirings in 2007.

20. Our (principal/principle) reasons for including this exercise in the seventh edition of *Technically-Write!* (is/are) to draw your attention to the Glossary of Technical Usage at the end of the book.

Some words are so similar it can be difficult to choose between them

Exercise 12.3

Rewrite the following sentences to make them more emphatic (in many cases, change them from the passive to active voice). Create a "doer" if one is not identified.

1. The supply of natural gas was cut off for a period of 18 hours by a fracture in the pipeline near Snow Lake.

2. In the interest of public safety, it is recommended by the Workplace Health and Safety Committee that hard hats be worn by all visitors to the site.

3. It is our considered opinion that entrance to the lab on the night of June 15 was gained by a thief who used a duplicate set of keys.

4. It was agreed the meeting should run until 6:30 p.m., in order for all topics on the agenda to be covered in a single day.

5. On a recommendation by the Chief of Quality Assurance, the seven Meteor calibrators used by our lab technicians have been replaced by two Vancourt model 370 multi-function calibrators.

6. The pH level in the city's three swimming pools has been reduced by 3.5%, in order to meet the requirements stipulated by the Health Inspector in her August 12 report.

7. It is company policy that a cell phone must be carried by all drivers travelling outside the city limits during winter months.

8. Before departure, it is a further requirement that it is the responsibility of the driver to ensure the cellphone's battery is in a fully charged condition.

9. Before the drugs could be shipped, a release certificate had to be signed by the health inspector that they were in conformance with the requirements of specification A1637/2.

10. Over $80 000 in damage was sustained by equipment in the laboratory, when a fire was caused by an overloaded electrical power circuit.

11. As reported in the *Examiner*, our local newspaper, the top marks achieved by student Janet Raulston's project in the inter-high-school science fair, means that her science project has been selected by the newspaper for funding at the inter-provincial science fair in Toronto on May 8.

12. It was not expected by the local authorities in southern Ontario, that damage would be caused by any hurricanes that drift northeast along the eastern seaboard from South Carolina to Nova Scotia.

13. Yet there were many reports by the local media—both print and electronic—that many trees were uprooted and power lines were brought down along the northern shore of Lake Ontario by tropical storm Ernesto in September 2006.

14. It is essential that the chlorine and pH levels of the campus swimming pool be tested on a daily basis and, if an imbalance occurs, for corrective action to be taken immediately by the resident technician.

A passive-voice sentence is longer than an active-voice sentence

15. If the rated low fuel consumption is to be achieved in a gasoline/electric hybrid automobile, the key is for only a light foot to be applied to the gas pedal.

16. The tendency, as exhibited by some drivers, to consistently make a fast get-away when a stop light turns from red to green, has been shown by a prominent consumer analysis to be the major cause of high fuel consumption.

Exercise 12.4

Improve the parallelism in the following sentences.

1. Our price for a one-dozen pack of blank Conroy special-issue DVDs is $15.95, however the price will drop to $12.95 a pack if you choose to purchase three one-dozen packs as a single order.

2. We faxed a purchase order for three Nabuchi 700 computers to the supplier on May 13, but there was a delay until 24 May before they were able to deliver the units.

3. To apply for the Vancourt Supervisory Management seminar, click on www.vancourtsupmgtsem.com and

   - fill in your personal details in Part 1,
   - respond to the questions about your previous supervisory experience in Part 2, and
   - in Part 3, tell us in a 300-word summary why you should be accepted for the seminar.

4. There is severe vibration at flywheel speeds between 3200 and 3800 rpm but, surprisingly, above 4500 rpm the vibration disappears completely.

5. Technician Wendy Roberts was assigned to site 17 at Weekaskasing Narrows from 22 January to 10 February for three reasons: (1) to evaluate the performance, under sub-zero conditions, of the remote sensing system AQR-6; (2) as an assistant for Carl Jorgenson in the workshop while technician Sandy Weismann was on medical leave from January 25 to February 5; and (3) to assess the need for repairs to the fence along the western perimeter of the site.

6. It will take 12 days to carry out the survey, which we can accept, but it is not acceptable that it will take a further 18 days to process the results.

7. The new software has not only reduced project downtime but also errors in transferring data to the mainframe computer have been eliminated.

Keep the ideas—like trains—on parallel tracks

8. When the Waverley Avenue branch closed, we transferred three of the six-member staff to the downtown office, offered an early-retirement package to one who was approaching 60, but two of the staff chose to resign and seek employment elsewhere.

9. We recorded sound levels on the east side of the lab at 68.6 dB, but they decreased to only 47.5 dB on the west side of the room.

10. We are dissatisfied with the reliability of the industrial paper cutter we purchased from you 18 months ago. The first failure occurred after only 13 months, when the drive assembly failed and had to be replaced at a cost of $167.50. The second failure occurred just three months later and cost us $89.90 to replace a sheared lower cutter blade. And now we are facing another $167.50 repair cost, for today the drive assembly has failed again.

Exercise 12.5

Improve the punctuation in the following sentences.

1. I am in receipt of your letter of Nov 17 you'll be glad to hear the damage to your equipment will be repaired at no cost to you.

2. Parts for your Nabuchi model 370 printer will be hard to get locally, I phoned around but no one has any, next I went direct to the manufacturer. In Japan; they've got what you need.

3. We propose building a 24 inch culvert from the east end of the parking lot at Richmond Mall, the whole lot slopes down toward the east end. A drop in grade of 0.89 metre overall.

4. We measured sound levels in the new lab, they were 1.45 dB higher at the north end of the room; compared to the south end.

5. I will telephone you immediately when the parts for your printer come in. But it won't be for at least fifteen days. Maybe three weeks.

6. Follows is the revised procedure for filing expense claims from the field.

   • When you are travelling, file your expenses weekly from Sunday through to Saturday. No later than noon on Tuesday of the following week.

   • Download the claim form from www.multind.ca/accounts, its a template and you can complete it online.

   • Send it electronically to the Accounting Department's address; its on the form.

   • Send the supporting receipts by regular mail, use priority mail. Or scan your receipts if you have a scanner available and send them by email. As an attachment to the claim form.

7. You will be assigned to the northern office for six months starting on September 30. As it will be winter from November 1 for the next five months you will be entitled to a northern allowance of $11.50 per day; additional to your regular pay.

8. Please schedule a meeting for 2 p.m. on May 22, this confirms my telephone call of May 3 and all staff engaged in the Romulus project

if on site are to attend with no exceptions, please send me a list of those who are scheduled to be off site on that date by May 18.

9. Repairs to the heating system will cost $1735.00, $335 more than we had estimated in our proposal of January 20. Corrosion in the pipes above the shipping area was the main problem, also rust in the furnace blower unit.

10. Notice to all staff, the last one leaving at night is to turn the thermostat down to 15C, the first one in the following a.m. or following a weekend is to turn the thermostat back up to 22C.

11. When you fly into Churchill Manitoba, you will be met by Sandy Wilkins, he's the plant operations manager, who will brief you on the repair work he has ready for you, it should take about 10 days total. But I wouldn't book my return flight if I were you until you have had at least four days on site if not more to assess the extent of the damage and can assess what spare parts need to be shipped in. And how long it will take for them to reach you.

12. I am referring to job lot 2180 received on July 20 which appears to have been damaged in transit alternatively the packing materials may have been insufficient to withstand the stress of shipping by snowmobile across the tundra, five of the eight modules were damaged and are unusable.

Exercise 12.6

Correct any quantities, abbreviations, or numbers that are presented incorrectly in the following sentences. Also correct improperly spelled words or improperly used punctuation.

1. The distance between the two measurement points is exactly .2576 metres.

2. With affect from February 1st, radio station DMLZ's radio frequencies will be moving from 101.37 khz to 103.6 khz on the A.M. band and from 98.7 MHZ to 95.7 MHZ on the F.M. band.

3. We will be flying to Abbotsford, B.C. on the evening of 07/06/08, arriving at 09.17, and returning on the 14th of the next month (Jly), departing at 10.32 am.

4. Each bottle contains one-and-one-half litres (1.5 l) of triple-filtered water, which it is essential that at all times should be kept above freezing point (either 32C or zero F).

5. Please prepare a checque for two hundred and eighty-seven dollars and fifty cents payable to Multiple Industries Inc, cross-reference it to there purchase order 2,817, and send it by Express Post.

6. The high sound level's of 69 db and 72 db (decibels) measured at two points beside the west wall are caused by a packaging machine

in the ajoining room, situated only 1.2 metres from the dividing wall that seperates the two rooms.

7. 34 tanks were filled during the week ending May twenty-first, which was thirteen percent more than were filled during the week ending May 14th.

8. For further information, turn to paragraph two on page seven.

9. To connect the 2 sites will mean stringing a decimal five five milli-metre cable between the poles for approximately three kms.

10. We estimate the cost to repair your company's delivery van will be three thousand, four hundred and sixty dollars ($3,460).

11. Thirteen model six-four-six transmitters bearing thirteen consecutive serial Nos. between 11728 and 11730 have been shipped to Site Seven.

12. We will need to instal a three km long, twentyfour inch Diameter pipe to handle the runoff from the new developement site beside Highway 276, three point 6 Kilometres west of the city.

Exercise 12.7
Select the correctly spelled words among the choices offered below.

1. The (computer/computor) is supplied with a built-in 99-year (calendar/calender).

2. A (coarse/course)-grained (aggregate/agreggate) is used as a base before pouring the concrete.

3. Profits in the (forth/fourth) quarter increased by (forty/fourty) percent.

4. The (affluent/effluent) produced by the paper mill is (enviromentally/ environmentaly/environmentally) sound.

5. The preface to a book or report is sometimes called a (forward/ foreward/foreword).

6. The (cite/site) is (inaccessable/inaccessible) except by helicopter.

7. Version 6.0 of *4Tell for Windows 05* (supercedes, supersedes) version 5.5.

8. The tests show that the materials have (similar/similiar) properties.

9. To a young business owner seeking a cash flow loan, the (colatteral/collatteral/collateral) demanded by the bank may seem (exhorbitant/exorbitant).

10. When Multiple Industries bought all the outstanding shares of Torrance Electronics, the latter company became a (wholely/wholly)-owned subsidiary.

Well? How good are you at spelling?

11. It's better to edit your own writing on (hard copy/hardcopy) rather than (online/on line).

12. Silica gel is a drying agent, or (desiccant/dessiccant/dessicant), that is packed with electronic equipment before shipment.

13. Software designers who have (entepreneurial/entrepeneurial/entrepreneurial) drive do not (necessarily/neccessarily) have good management expertise.

14. After (lengthy/lengthly) deliberation, the executive committee admitted that Ken Wynne's innovative design was indeed (ingenious/ingenuous).

15. After we have (accumulated/accummulated) all the results from product tests, we will (prescribe/proscribe) definitive purchase specifications.

16. An (auxiliary/auxilliary) heater cuts in when temperature drops below 3°C.

17. The (eigth/eighth) test demonstrated that the process is (feasable/feasible).

18. The incandescent lamps have been replaced with (flourescent/fluorescent/fluourescent) lamps.

19. The sales manager was (embarassed/embarrassed/embarrased) that customers were being (harassed/harrassed/harrased) by overly zealous sales staff.

20. Well? How many words did you (mispell/misspell)?

All these words are in the Glossary

Exercise 12.8

Improve the following passages so they contain no gender-specific language and (where appropriate) are better conveyors of information:

1. Memo to all lab technicians:

   The Department of Defence has informed us that a D.O.D. inspector will visit our calibration lab on May 17. He will be evaluating our equipment and calibration hierarchy to determine whether our lab meets MIL-STD-202 specifications. Please extend him every courtesy and your cooperation.

2. To: Andy Rittman:

   Please inform each field technician that from April 1 he will be covered by company-sponsored travel insurance arranged through ManSask Assurance Corporation. They won't have to pay for it, but belonging to the scheme won't be automatic, they have to apply for it. I suggest you write a personal memo to each technician and enclose a copy of the enclosed application form and explanatory brochure. In each case be sure to remind him to apply by March 25, otherwise he'll have to wait until May 1 for his coverage to start.

3. To all staff:

   Construction will start shortly in room B101, which is to become a child day care centre that will accommodate 20 children ages 1 to 5. If you have pre-schoolers and would like to take advantage of this service, have your wife call Rick Davis in Personnel and ask for form CCC01.

Correcting gender-specific terms can be more subtle than is immediately evident

Additionally, we will be hiring three experienced child care workers to man the facility. If you or your spouse knows of someone who might be suitable, ask her (the child care worker) to telephone Rick for an application form.

4. From a company notice board:

Christmas Cheer Is About to Start!

Are you planning to attend the Christmas Party? Tell your most significant other it will be at O'Halloran's on December 15 and to expect a royal feast!

Line up a babysitter today and tell her to expect to stay late…!

Call Dave Michaelson at extension 207 if you want to announce your intentions or to reserve a table, or if you want more information.

REFERENCES

1. Lester Faigley, Roger Graves and Heather Graves, *The Brief Penguin Handbook*, 1st Canadian ed (Toronto: Pearson Longman, 2007).

2. Ann Rockley, *Managing Enterprise Content: A Unified Strategy* (Indianapolis, Indiana: New Riders, 2003), p 17.

3. *The Canadian Oxford Dictionary*, 2nd ed, Katherine Barber, ed (Don Mills, Ontario: Oxford University Press), 2004.

4. *Webster's New Collegiate Dictionary*, 9th ed (Springfield, Massachusetts: G & C Merriam Company, 1989).

5. *Funk & Wagnalls Canadian College Dictionary* (Markham, Ontario: Fitzhenry & Whiteside, 1986).

6. *The Canadian Press Stylebook*, 12th ed (Toronto: The Canadian Press, 2002).

7. *Caps and Spelling*, 17th ed (Toronto: The Canadian Press, 2005).

8. Nancy L Hoft, *International Technical Communication: How to Export Information About High Technology* (New York: John Wiley & Sons, Inc, 1995).

Glossary of Technical Usage

A standard glossary of usage contains rules for combining words into compound terms, for forming abbreviations, for capitalizing, and for spelling unusual or difficult words. The glossary in *Technically-Write!* also offers suggestions for handling many of the technical terms peculiar to industry. Hence, it is oriented toward the technical rather than the literary writer.

The entries in the glossary are arranged alphabetically. Among them are words that are likely to be misused or misspelled, such as

- words that are similar and frequently confused with one another, such as *imply* and *infer*, *diplex* and *duplex*, *principal* and *principle*,
- common minor errors of grammar, such as *comprised of* (should be *comprises*), *most unique* (*unique* should not be compared), *liaise* (an unnatural verb formed from *liaison*), and
- words that are particularly prone to misspelling, such as *desiccant, oriented,* and *immitance,* and words for which there may be more than one "correct" spelling, (e.g. *program* or *programme*; *center* or *centre*)

Where two spellings of a word are in general use (e.g. *symposiums* and *symposia*), the glossary lists both and states which is preferred.

Definitions have been included when they will help you select the correct word for a given purpose, or to differentiate between similar words having different meanings. These definitions are intentionally brief and are intended only as a guide; for more comprehensive definitions, consult one of the authoritative dictionaries we recommend in Chapter 12 (pages 293 and 294).

All entries in the glossary are in lower case letters. Capital letters are used where capitals are recommended for a specific word, phrase, or abbreviation. Similarly, periods have been eliminated except where they form part of a specific entry. For example, the abbreviation for "inch" is *in.*, and the period that follows it is inserted intentionally to distinguish it from the word "in".

Finally, think of the glossary as a guide rather than a collection of hard and fast rules. Our language is continually changing, so that what was fashionable yesterday may seem pedantic today and a cliché tomorrow. We expect that in some cases your views will differ from ours. Where they do, we hope that the comments and suggestions we offer will help you to choose the right expression, word, abbreviation, or symbol, and that you will be able to do so both consistently and logically.

Occasionally you will see an abbreviation or spelling that does not conform exactly to the guidelines spelled out in Chapter 12. These anomalies are caused when an expression has become commonly accepted in the discipline in which the expression is used. The periods after B.Sc. are an example.

For further information on how to form compound terms, see page 292.

A further reference is available on the web, provided by the International Organization for Standardization (commonly abbreviated to **ISO**), in ICS Fields 01.120 and 01.140.

The Glossary

General abbreviations used throughout the glossary:

abbr	abbreviate(d); abbreviation	pl	plural
adj	adjective	pref	prefer; preferred; preference
Br	Britain; British	rec	recommend(ed)
Can.	Canada; Canadian	SI	International System of Units
def	definition	US	United States
lc	lower case	v	verb
n	noun		

A

a; an use *an* before words that begin with a silent *h* or a vowel; use *a* when the *h* is sounded or if the vowel is sounded as *w* or *y*; *an hour* but *a hotel, an onion* but *a European*

aberration

above- as a prefix, *above-* combines erratically: *aboveboard, above-cited, aboveground*

above-mentioned avoid using this expression in technical writing

abrasion

abscess

abscissa

absence

absolute abbr: **abs**

absorb(ent); adsorb(ent) *absorb* means to swallow up completely (as a sponge absorbs moisture); *adsorb* means to hold on the surface, as if by adhesion

abut; abutted; abutting; abutment

ac abbr for alternating current

accelerate; accelerator; accelerometer

accept; except *accept* means to receive (normally willingly), as in *he accepted the company's offer of employment*; *except* generally means exclude: *the night crew completed all the repairs except rewiring of the control panel*

access; accessed; accessible

accessory; accessories abbr: **accy**

accidental(ly)

accommodate; accommodation

account abbr: **acct**

accumulate; accumulator

acetaminophen

achieve means to conclude successfully, usually after considerable effort; avoid using *achieve* when the intended meaning is simply to reach or to get

acknowledg(e)ment *acknowledgment* pref in US, rec in Can.; *acknowledgement* pref in Br

acquiesce def: agree to

acquire; acquisition

across not *accross*

actually omit this word: it is seldom necessary in technical writing

actuator

adapt; adept; adopt *adapt* means to adjust to; *adept* means clever, proficient; *adopt* means to acquire and use

adapter; adaptor *adapter* pref

adaptation pref spelling; *adaption* also used in US but less common

addendum pl: *addenda*

adhere to never use *adhere by*

ad hoc def: set up for one occasion

adjective (compound) two or more words that combine to form an adjective are either joined by a hyphen or compounded into a single word; see p 292; abbr: **adj**

adsorb(ent) see **absorb**

advanced power manager abbr: **apm** (pref) or **APM**

advantageous

adverse; averse *adverse* means unsatisfactory or unsuitable, as in *driving speed was adversely affected by the 20 cm of snow on the highway*; *averse* means in opposition to, as in *the staff were averse to working overtime* (they did not want to)

advice; advise use *advice* as a noun and *advise* as a verb: *the engineer's advice was sound; the technician had to advise the driver to take an alternative route*; spell: **adviser, advisable**

ae; e *ae* is pref in Br and common in Can., as in *aesthetic* and *anaemic*; *e* is pref in US and rec in Can., as in *esthetic* and *anemic*

aerate

aerial see **antenna**

aero- a prefix meaning *of the air*; it combines to form one word: *aerodynamics, aeronautical*; in some instances it has been replaced by *air*: *airplane, aircraft*

aesthetic; esthetic *esthetic* pref; see **ae**

affect; effect *affect* is used only as a verb, never as a noun; it means to produce an effect upon or to influence (*the potential difference affects the transit time*); *effect* can be used either as a verb or as a noun; as a verb it means to cause or to accomplish (*to effect a change*); as a noun it means the consequences or result of an occurrence (as in *the detrimental effect upon the environment*), or it refers to property, such as *personal effects*

aforementioned; aforesaid avoid using these ambiguous expressions

after- as a prefix, usually combines to form one word: *afteracceleration, afterburner, afterglow, afterheat, afterimage;* but *after-hours*

agenda although plural, *agenda* is generally treated as singular; *the agenda is complete;* pl *agendas* also is acceptable

aggravate the correct definition of *aggravate* is to increase or intensify (worsen) a situation; try not to use it when the meaning is *annoy* or *irritate*

aggregate

aging; ageing *aging* pref in US, rec in Can.; *ageing* pref in Br

agree to; agree with to be correct, you should *agree to* a suggestion or proposal, but *agree with* another person

air- as a prefix, normally combines to form one word: *airborne, airfield, airflow, airlift, airmail;* exceptions: *air-condition(ed) (er) (ing), air-cool(ed) (ing), air strike*

air horsepower abbr: **ahp**

airline; air line an *airline* provides aviation services; an *air line* is a line or pipe that carries air

algae

algorithm

alkali; alkaline pl: *alkalis* (pref) or *alkalies*

allot(ted)

all ready; already *all ready* means that all (everyone or everything) is ready: *already* means by this time: *the samples are all ready to be tested; the samples have already been tested*

all right def: everything is satisfactory; never use *alright*

all together; altogether *all together* means all collectively, as a group; *altogether* means completely, entirely: *the samples have been gathered all together, ready for testing; the samples are altogether useless*

allude; elude *allude* means refer to; *elude* means avoid

almost never contract *almost* to *most;* it is correct to write *most of the software has been tested,* but wrong to write *the software is most ready*

alphanumeric def: in alphabetical, then numerical, sequence

alternate; alternative *alternate(ly)* means by turn and turn about: *the inspector alternated between the two construction sites; alternative(ly)* offers a choice between two or more things: *the alternative is to find a replacement speaker, change the meeting into a workshop, or cancel the event*

alternating current abbr: **ac**

alternator

altitude abbr: **alt**

AM abbr for audio modulation

a.m. def: before noon (*ante meridiem*)

amateur

ambience; ambient abbr: **amb**

ambiguous; ambiguity

American standard code for information exchange abbr: **ASCII**

American Wire Gauge abbr: **AWG**

among; between use *among* when referring to three or more items; use *between* when referring to only two; avoid using *amongst*

amount; number use *amount* to refer to a general quantity: *the amount of time taken as sick leave has decreased;* use *number* to refer to items that can be counted: *the number of applicants to be interviewed was reduced to six*

ampere(s) abbr: **A** (pref) or **amp**; other abbr: **kA, mA, µA, nA, pA, A/m** (amperes per minute)

ampere-hour(s) abbr: **Ah** (pref) or **amp-hr** (more common)

amplitude modulation abbr: **AM**

an see **a**

anaemic; anemic *anemic* pref; see **ae**

anaesthetic; anesthetic *anesthetic* pref; see **ae**

analog(ue) *analog* pref in US; *analogue* pref in Br, rec in Can. (except in electronics and computers, as in *an analog cellphone*)

analogous

analogy

analyse; analyze *analyse* pref in Br, rec in Can.; *analyze* pref in US; also: **analyser; analysing**

analysis pl: *analyses*

anesthetic; anesthesia see **ae**

AND-gate

and/or avoid using this term; in most cases it can be replaced by either *and* or *or*

anemia; anemic see **ae**

angle def: an angular unit of measurement; an *angel* has wings

ångström abbr: **A**

anion def: negative ion

anneal; annealed; annealing

annihilate; annihilated; annihilation

anomaly pl: *anomalies*

anonymous

ANSI abbr for American National Standards Institute

antarctic see **arctic**

ante- a prefix that means before; combines to form one word: *antecedent, anteroom*

ante meridiem def: before noon; abbr: **a.m.**; can also be written as *antemeridian*

antenna the proper plural in the technical sense is *antennas*; use *antennae* for zoology; *antenna* has generally replaced the obsolescent *aerial*

anti- a prefix meaning opposite or contradictory to; generally combines to form one word: *antiaircraft, antiastigmatism, anticapacitance, anticoincidence, antisymmetric;* if combining word starts with i or is a proper noun, insert a hyphen: *anti-icing, anti-American*

antimeridian def: the opposite of meridian (of longitude); e.g. the antimeridian of 96°30′W is 83°30′E

anybody; any body *anybody* means any person; *any body* means any object: *anybody can attend; discard the batch if you find any body containing foreign matter*

anyone; any one *anyone* means any person; *any one* means any single item: *you may take anyone with you; you may take any one of the samples*

anyway; any way *anyway* means in any case or in any event; *any way* means in any manner: *the results may not be as good as you expect, but we want to keep them anyway; the work may be done in any way you wish*

AOL

apm abbr for advanced power manager

apparatus; apparatuses

apparent; apparently

appear(s); seem(s) use *appears* to describe a condition that can be seen: *the equipment appears to be new*; use *seems* to describe a condition that cannot be seen: *the temperature seems to be low*

appendix def: the part of a report that contains supporting data; pl: *appendices* (pref in Br and Can.) or *appendixes* (pref in US)

applets def: JAVA computer programs

approximate(ly) abbr: **approx**; but *about* is a better word

aquarium(s)

arbitrary

arc; arced; arcing

archeology; archeologist; archeological

Archie

architect; architecture

arctic capitalize when referring to a specific area: *beyond the Arctic Circle*; otherwise use lc letters: *in the arctic*; never omit the first *c*

area the SI unit for area is the *hectare* (abbr: **ha**)

areal def: having area

around def: on all sides, surrounding, encircling

arrester, arrestor *arrester* pref

article

artifact

artwork

as avoid using when the intended meaning is *since* or *because*; to write *he could not open his desk as he left his keys at home* is incorrect (replace *as* with *because*)

ASCII abbr for American standard code for information exchange

as per avoid using this hackneyed expression, except in specifications

asphalt *asfalt* also used in US, but less pref

assembly; assemblies abbr: **assy**

assure means to state with confidence that something has been or will be made certain; it is sometimes confused with *ensure* and *insure*, which it does not replace; see **ensure**

asthma; asthmatic

as well as avoid using when the meaning is *and*

asymmetric; asymmetrical

asynchronous

atmosphere abbr: **atm**

atomic weight abbr: **at. wt**

attenuator

atto def: 10^{-18}; abbr: **a**

audible; audibility

audio frequency abbr: **af** (pref) or **a-f**

audiovisual

audit; auditor

auger; augur an *auger* is a tool; *augur* means to sense something

aural def: that which is heard; avoid confusing with *oral*, which means that which is spoken

author; writer avoid referring to yourself as *the author* or *the writer*; use *I*, *me*, or *my*

authoritative

authorize; authorise *authorize* pref

auto- a prefix meaning self; combines to form one word: *autoalarm, autoconduction, autogyro, autoionization, autoloading, automation, automaton, autotransformer, autoworker*

automatic frequency control abbr: **afc** (pref) or **AFC**

automatic volume control abbr: **avc** (pref) or **AVC**

auxiliary abbr: **aux**; pl: **auxiliaries**

average see **mean**

averse def: reluctant; see **adverse**

avocation def: an interest or hobby; avoid confusing with *vocation*

ax; axe *axe* pref in Br, rec in Can.; *ax* pref in US; pl: *axes*

axis the plural also is *axes*

azimuth abbr: **az**

B

bachelor of science abbr: B.Sc.

bacillus pl: **bacilli**

back- as a prefix in n form normally combines into one word: *backboard,* *backdate(d), backlog, backup*; but *back burner* (two words)

bacterium pl: **bacteria**

balance; remainder use *balance* to describe a state of equilibrium (as in *discontinuous permafrost is frozen soil delicately balanced between the frozen and unfrozen state*), or as an accounting term; use *remainder* when the meaning is the rest of: *the remainder of the shipment will be delivered next week*

balk(ed)/baulk(ed) *balk* pref in US; *baulk* pref in Br, rec in Can.

ball bearing

bandwidth

bare; bear *bare* means barren or exposed; *bear* means to withstand or to carry (or a wild animal)

barometer abbr: **bar.**

barrel; barrel(l)ed; barrel(l)ing *ll* pref in Br, rec in Can., single *l* pref in US; the abbr of *barrel(s)* is **bbl**

barretter

barring def: preventing, excepting

bases this is the plural of both *base* and *basis*

basically

basic input/output system abbr: **bios** (pref) or **BIOS**

baud; baud rate

baulk see **balk**

because; for use *because* when the clause it introduces identifies the cause of a result: *he could not open his desk because he left his keys at home*; use *for* when the clause introduces something less tangible: *he failed to complete the project on schedule, for reasons he preferred not to divulge*

becquerel def: a unit of activity of radionuclides (SI); abbr: **Bq**; other abbr: **PBq, TBq, GBq, kBq**

behavior/behaviour *behaviour* pref in Br and rec for Can.; *behavior* pref in US

benefit; benefit(t)ed; benefit(t)ing single *t* pref

beside; besides *beside* means alongside, at the side of; *besides* means as well as

between see **among**

bi- a prefix meaning two or twice; combines to form one word: *biangular, bicultural, bidirectional, bifilar, bilateral, bilingual, bimetallic, bizonal*

biannual(ly); biennial(ly) *biannual(ly)* means twice a year; *biennial(ly)* means every two years

bias; biased; biases; biasing

billion def: 10^9 (Can. and US); 10^{12} (Br)

billion electron volts although the pref abbr is **GEV**, *beV* and *bev* are more commonly used

Bill of Materials abbr: **BOM**

bimonthly def: every two months

binary

binaural

bioelectronics

bionics def: application of biological techniques to electronic design

bios basic input/ouput system: a program that starts the computer and manages data flow between the operating system and the hard disk, video adapter, keyboard, mouse, printer, etc

bird's-eye (view)

bit; kilobit abbr: **b; kb** (pref) or **kbit**

Bitnet

bits per second abbr: **bps**

biweekly def: every two weeks

blow- as a prefix, combines to form one word as a noun: *blowhole, blowoff, blowout*

blueprint

blur; blurred; blurring; blurry

board feet abbr: **fbm** (derived from *foot board measure*)

boiling point abbr: **bp**

boldface (type)

bookkeeper

boot *to boot* means the operating system is being loaded into the computer; also *reboot*

borderline

bps bits per second

brakedrum; brake lining; brakeshoe

brake horsepower; brake horsepower-hour abbr: **bhp, bhp-hr**

brand-new

break- when used as a prefix to form a compound noun or adj, *break* combines into one word: *breakaway, breakdown, breakup*; in the verb form it retains its single-word identity: *it was time to break up the meeting*

bridging

Brinell hardness number abbr: **Bhn**

British thermal unit abbr: **BTU**

B.Sc. abbr for Bachelor of Science

budget; budgeted; budgeting

build- compounds as one word in n or adj form, as in *corrosive buildup*; use two words in v form, as in *to build up our resources, we have...*

buoy; buoyant

burned; burnt *burned* pref in Can. and US; *burnt* pref in Br

bur(r) *burr* pref

buses; bused; busing; bus bar

business; businesslike; businessperson avoid using *businessman* or *businesswoman* unless referring to a specific male or female person

by- as a prefix, *by-* normally combines to form one word: *bylaw, byline, bypass, byproduct*

byte abbr: **kbyte** and **Mbyte** (pref), or **kB** and **MB**

B2B abbr for business-to-business (or **e-biz**); the exchange of products, services or information between businesses

B2G abbr for business-to-government; permits businesses and government agencies to use central websites to exchange information and do business with each other

C

cache memory

calendar; calender; colander a *calendar* is the arrangement of the days in a year; *calender* is the finish on paper or cloth; a *colander* is a sieve

calibre; caliber *calibre* pref in Br and rec in Can.; *caliber* pref in US

calk/caulk *caulk, caulked, caulking* pref in Br, rec for Can.; *calk* pref in US

cal(l)iper *caliper* pref

calorie abbr: **cal**

calorimeter; colourimeter a *calorimeter* measures quantity of heat; a *colourimeter* measures colour

cancel(l)ed; cancel(l)ing *ll* pref in Br, rec in Can.; single *l* pref in US; **cancel** always has single *l*; **cancellation** always has *ll*

candela def: unit of luminous intensity (replaces *candle*); abbr: **cd**; recommended abbr for candela per square foot and square metre are **cd/ft²** and **cd/m²**

candlepower; candlehour(s) abbr: **cp, c-hr**

candoluminescence

cannot one word pref; avoid using *can't* in technical writing

canvas; canvass *canvas* is a coarse cloth used for tents; *canvass* means to solicit

capacitor

capacity for never use *capacity to* or *capacity of*

capillary

capital letters abbr: **caps.**

car- as a prefix normally combines to form one word: *carload, carlot, carpool, carwash*

carburet(t)or *carburetor* pref; a third, seldom used spelling is *carburetter*; also: **carburetion**

carcino- as a prefix combines to form one word

cartilage

case- as a prefix normally combines to form one word: *casebook, caseharden, casework(er)*; exceptions: *case history, case study*

cassette

caster; castor use *caster* when the meaning is to swivel freely, and *castor* when referring to castor oil, etc

catalog(ue) *catalogue(d)* and *cataloguing* pref in Can. and Br; *catalog(ed)* and *cataloging* pref in US

catalyst; catalytic

cathode-ray tube abbr: **crt** (pref) or **CRT** (commonly used)

cation def: positive ion

caulk pref spelling; also see **calk**

CD-ROM

-ceed; -cede; -sede only one word ends in *-sede*: *supersede*; only three words end in *-ceed*: *exceed, proceed, succeed*; all others end in *-cede*: e.g. *precede, concede*

cellphone abbr: **cell**; called *mobile* in Br

Celsius abbr: **C**; see **temperature**

cement; concrete *cement* is the powder used to make concrete; *concrete* is the hard, finished product

central processing unit abbr: **cpu** (pref) or **CPU**

centre; center *centre, centred, centring, central* pref in Br, rec in Can.; *center, centered, centering, central* pref in US

centreline abbr: $\mathcal{C}$(pref) or **CL**

centre-to-centre abbr: **c-c**

centi- def: 10^{-2}; as a prefix combines to form one word: *centiampere, centigram*; abbr: **c**; other abbr:

centigram	**cg**
centilitre	**cL**
centimetre	**cm**
centimetre-gram-second	**cgs**
centimetres per second	**cm/s**
square centimetre	**cm²**

centigrade abbr: **C**; in SI, *centigrade* has been replaced by *Celsius*; see **temperature**

centri- a prefix meaning centre; combines to form one word: *centrifugal, centripetal*

cga colour/graphics adapter

chairperson avoid using *chairman* or *chairwoman*

chamfer

changeable; changeover (n and adj); **change over** (v)

channel(l)ed; channel(l)ing *ll* pref in Br, rec in Can.; single *l* pref in US

chargeable

chassis both singular and plural are spelled the same

chat room a website, part of a website, or an online service in which users with a common interest can communicate in real time (see **real time**)

check- as a prefix combines to form one word: *checklist, checkoff, checkpoint* and *checkup* are one word as n or adj, but two words in v form

checksum def: a term used in computer technology

cheque in US, spelled *check*

chisel(l)ed; chisel(l)ing *ll* pref in Br, rec in Can., single *l* pref in US

chlorophyll

chrominance

chromosome

chunk; chunking

cipher in Br also spelled *cypher*

circuit abbr: **cct**; also: **circuitous; circuit breaker**

cite def: to quote; see **site**

cleanup (n and adj); **clean up** (v)

climate avoid confusing *climate* with *weather*: *climate* is the average type of weather, determined over a number of years, experienced at a particular place; *weather* is the state of the atmospheric conditions at a specific place at a specific time

clockwise (turn) abbr: **CW**

cmc computer-mediated communication

cmos complementary metal-oxide conductor

co- as a prefix, *co-* generally means jointly or together; it usually combines to form one word: *coexist, coequal, cooperate, coordinate, coplanar* (*co-worker* is an exception); it is also used as the abbr for *complement of* (an arc or angle) as in *codeclination* and *colatitude*

coalesce; coalescent

coarse; course *coarse* means rough in texture or of poor quality; *course* implies movement or passage of time; *a coarse granular material; the technical writing course*

coaxial abbr: **coax.**

Cobol def: common business-oriented language

coefficient abbr: **coef**

coerce; coercion

collaborate; collaborator avoid writing *collaborate together* (delete *together*)

collapsible

collateral

collide use *collide* to describe two moving objects that bang or crash into one another; use *drove into* or *bumped into* if one object is stationary

cologarithm abbr: **colog**

colon when a colon is inserted in the middle of a sentence to introduce an example or short statement, the first word following the colon is not capitalized; see guidelines on p 274 for inserting a colon at, or omitting it from, the end of a sentence that introduces a list or subparagraphs; a hyphen should not be inserted after a colon

colo(u)r *color* pref in US; *colour* pref in Br, rec in Can.

colour/graphics adapter abbr: **cga** (pref) or **CGA**

colourimeter see **calorimeter**

column abbr: **col.**

combustible

comma a comma normally need not be used immediately before *and, but,* and *or*, but may be inserted if to do so will increase understanding or avoid ambiguity

commence in technical writing, replace *commence* with the more direct *begin* or *start*

commit; commitment; committed; committing

committee

communicate it is vague to write *I communicated the results to the client*; use a clearer verb: *I emailed/faxed/wrote/telephoned*

compare; comparable; comparison; comparative use *compared to* when suggesting a general likeness; use *compared with* when making a definite comparison

compatible; compatibility

complement; compliment *complement* means the balance required to make up a full quantity or a complete set; to *compliment* means to praise; *in a right angle, the complement of 60° is 30°; Mr Perchanski complimented Janet Rudman for writing a good report*

complementary metal-oxide conductor abbr: **cmos** (pref) or **CMOS**

composed of; comprising; consists of all three terms mean "made up of" (specific items); if any one of these terms is followed by a list of items, it implies that the list is complete; if the list is not complete, the term should be replaced by *includes* or *including*

compound terms two or more words that combine to form a compound term are joined by a hyphen or are written as one word, depending on accepted usage and whether they form a verb, noun, or adjective; the trend is toward one-word compounds (see p 292)

comprise; comprised; comprising to write *comprised of* is incorrect, because the verb comprise includes the preposition *of*

CompuServe

computer-mediated communication abbr: cmc (pref) or CMC

concrete the hard, rock-like substance used to make roads, bridges and buildings; avoid confusing with *cement*

concur; concurred; concurrent; concurring

condenser

conductor

config.sys a text file containing DOS commands that tells the operating system how the computer is set up

conform use *conform to* when the meaning is to abide by; use *conform with* when the meaning is to agree with

connection; connexion *connection* pref in Can. and US; *connexion* is alternative spelling in Br

conscience; conscientious

conscious

consensus means a general agreement of opinion; hence to write *consensus of opinion* is incorrect; e.g. write: *the consensus was that a further series of tests would be necessary*

consistent with never *consistent of*

consists of; consisting of see composed of

contact *contact* should not be used as a verb when *email*, *write*, *visit*, *speak*, *fax*, or *telephone* better describes the action taken

continual; continuous *continual(ly)* means happens frequently but not all the time: *the generator is continually being overloaded* (is frequently overloaded); *continuous(ly)* means goes on and on without stopping: *the noise level is continuously at or above 100 dB* (it never drops below 100 dB)

continue(d) abbr: cont

continuous wave abbr: cw

contra- as a prefix normally combines into a single word

contrast when used as a verb, *contrast* is followed by *with*; when used as a noun, it may be followed by either *to* or *with* (*with* pref)

control; controlled; controlling; controller

convenor

conversant with never *conversant of*

converter; convertible

conveyor

cooperate

coordinate; coordinator

copyright not *copywrite*

corollary

correlate

correspond *to correspond to* suggests a resemblance; *to correspond with* means to communicate in writing

corroborate

corrode; corridible; corrosive

cosecant abbr: csc (pref) or cosec

cosine abbr: cos

cotangent abbr: cot

coulomb def: a quantity of electricity, electric charge (SI); abbr: C; other abbr: kC, mC, μC, nC, pC, C/m^2

counter- a prefix meaning opposite or reciprocal; combines to form one word: *counteract, counterbalance, counterflow, counterweight*

counterclockwise (turn) abbr: CCW

counterelectromotive force abbr: cemf; also known as *back emf*

counts per minute abbr: cpm

course see coarse

cpu; CPU central processing unit; see microprocessor

criteria; criterion the singular is *criterion*, the plural is *criteria*: e.g. *one criterion; seven criteria*

criticism; criticize; critique

cross- as a prefix combines erratically: *cross-border, cross-check, cross-examine, crosshatch, crosstalk, cross-purpose, cross section*

cross-refer(ence) abbr: x-ref

crt abbr for cathode-ray tube

cryogenic

cryptic

crystal abbr: xtal

crystalline; crystallize

cubic abbr: cu or ^{3}; other abbr:

cubic centimetre(s)	cm^3 (pref); cc
cubic decimetre(s)	dm^3
cubic foot (feet)	ft^3 (pref); cu ft
cubic feet per minute	cfm (pref); ft^3/min
cubic feet per second	cfs (pref); ft^3/sec
cubic inch(es)	in.^{3} (pref); cu in.
cubic metre(s)	m^3
cubic millimetre(s)	mm^3
cubic yard(s)	yd^3 (pref); cu yd

curb; kerb *curb* pref in Can. and US; *kerb* pref in Br

curie abbr: Ci; other abbr: mCi, μCi; in SI the *curie* is replaced by the *becquerel* (Bq)

current; currant *current* refers to a flow (of water, electricity); a *currant* is a dried fruit

curriculum pl: *curriculums* (pref) or *curricula*

cursor

cw continuous wave

cyberspace

cycles per minute abbr: cpm

cycles per second abbr: cps; although occasionally used, this term has been replaced by *hertz*

cylinder; cylindrical abbr: cyl

D

daraf def: the unit of elastance

data def: gathered facts; although *data* is plural (derived from the singular *datum*, which is rarely used), it is more acceptable to use it as a singular noun: *when all the data has been received, the analysis will begin*

database

dateline

date(s) avoid vague statements such as "last month" and "next year" because they soon become indefinite; write a specific date, using day (in numerals), month (spelled out), and year (in numerals): *January 27, 2008*, or *27 January 2008* (the latter form has no punctuation); to abbreviate, reduce month to first three letters and year to last two digits: *Jan 27, 08* or *27 Jan 08*; "th" is unnecessary after the "27"

day- as a prefix, generally combines to form one word: *daybook, daylight, daytime, daywork*

days days of the week are capitalized: *Monday, Tuesday*

dc direct current

de- a prefix that generally combines to form one word: *deaccentuate, deactivate, decentralize, decode, decompress, deemphasize, deenergize, derate, destagger;* exceptions are *de-ionize* and *de-ice*

dead- as a prefix combines erratically: *deadbeat, dead centre, dead end, deadline, deadweight, deadwood*

debug; debugged; debugging

decelerate def: to slow down; never use *deaccelerate*

decibel abbr: **dB**; the abbr for decibel referred to 1 mW is **dBm**

decimals for values less than unity (one), place a zero before the decimal point: *0.17, 0.0017*

decimate def: to reduce by one-tenth; can also mean to destroy much of

decimetre abbr: **dm**

declination abbr: **dec**

deductible

defective; deficient *defective* means unserviceable or damaged (generally lacking in quality); *deficient* means lacking in quantity (it is derived from *deficit*), and in the military sense incomplete: *a short circuit resulted in a defective transmitter; the installation was completed on schedule except for a deficient rotary coupler that will not be delivered until June 10*

defence; defense *defence* pref in Can. and Br; *defense* pref in US; **defensive** always has an *s*

defer; deferred; deferring; deferrable; deference

definite; definitive *definite* means exact, precise; *definitive* means conclusive, fully evolved; e.g. *a definite price* is a firm price; *a definitive statement* concerns a topic that has been thoroughly considered and evaluated

defuse; diffuse *defuse* means to ease tension; *diffuse* means scattered

degree(s) abbr: **deg** (pref in narrative) or ° (following numerals); see **temperature**

demarcation

demi- a little-used prefix meaning half (generally replaced by *semi-*); combines to form one word: *demivolt*

demonstrate; demonstrator; demonstrable not *demonstratable*

depend; dependence; dependent (adj); **dependant** (n); **dependable**

deprecate; depreciate *deprecate* means to disapprove of; *depreciate* means to reduce the value of: *the use of "as per" in technical writing is deprecated; the vehicle's value depreciated by 50% the first year and 20% the second year*

depth

desiccant, desiccate(d)

desirable

desktop

desktop publishing abbr: **dtp** (pref) or **DTP**

desktop video conference abbr: **dtv** (pref) or **DTV**

deter; deterred; deterrence; deterrent; deterring

deteriorate

develop not *develope*

device; devise the noun is *device*, the verb is *devise*: *a unique device; he devised a new software program*

dext(e)rous *dexterous* pref

diagnose; diagnosis pl: *diagnoses*

diagram(m)ed; diagram(m)ing *mm* pref in Can. and Br; single *m* pref in US; **diagram** always has a single *m*; **diagrammatically** always has *mm*

dial(l)ed; dial(l)ing *ll* pref in Br, rec in Can.; single *l* pref in US

dialog(ue) *dialogue* pref

dialysis

diameter abbr: **dia**

diaphragm

diazo

didn't never use this contraction in technical writing; use *did not*

die; dye; dying *die* means to end life; *dye* means a change of colour

dielectric

diesel; diesel-electric

dietitian

differ use *differ from* to demonstrate a difference; use *differ with* to describe a difference of opinion

different *different from* is preferred; *different to* is sometimes used; *different than* should never be used

diffraction

diffusion; diffusible

digital library a collection of documents organized electronically on the internet or CD-ROM

dilemma means to be faced with a choice between two unhappy alternatives; should not be used as a synonym for *difficulty*

diplex; duplex *diplex operation* means the simultaneous transmissions of two signals using a single feature, e.g. an antenna; *duplex operation* means that both ends can transmit and receive simultaneously

direct current abbr: **dc**

directly def: immediately; do not use when the meaning is *as soon as*

disassemble; dissemble *disassemble* means to take apart; *dissemble* means to conceal facts or put on a false appearance

disassociate see **dissociate**

disc; disk *disc* pref in Br, rec in Can. (except in computer technology, where *disk* is more common); *disk* pref in US

discernible

discolo(u)r *discolour* pref in UK, rec in Can.; *discolor* pref in US

discreet; discrete *discreet* means prudent or discerning: *his answer was discreet*; *discrete* means individually distinctive and separate: *discrete channels*; **discretion** is formed from *discreet*, not from *discrete*

disinterested; uninterested *disinterested* means unbiased, impartial; *uninterested* means not interested

disk cache

disk operating system abbr: **DOS**

dispatch; despatch *dispatch* pref

dispel; dispelled

disseminate

dissimilar

dissipate

dissociate; disassociate *dissociate* pref

distil(l) *distil* pref in Can. and Br; *distill* pref in US; **distillate, distillation, distilled** and **distiller** always have *ll*

distribute; distributor

don't; doesn't such contractions should not appear in technical writing

donut; doughnut for electronics/nucleonics, use *donut*

doppler capitalize only when referring to the Doppler principle

DOS disk operating system

double- as a prefix combines erratically: *double-barrelled, doublecheck, doublecross, double-duty, double entry, doublefaced, doubletalk*

down- as a prefix combines into one word: *downgrade, downrange, downtime, downwind*

dozen abbr: *doz*

drafting; draftsperson avoid writing *draftsman* or *draftswoman*

drawing(s) abbr: *dwg*

drier; dryer the adjective is always *drier*; the pref noun is *dryer* in Can. and US, and *drier* in Br: *this material is drier; place the others back in the dryer*

drop; droppable; dropped; dropping

dtp desktop publishing

dtv desktop video conferencing

due to an overused expression; *because of* pref

duo- a prefix meaning two; combines to form one word: *duocone, duodiode, duophase*

duplex see **diplex**

duplicator

dye; dying

dynamic data exchange an operating system function which allows information to be shared between programs

dysfunction not *disfunction*

E

each abbr: *ea*

east capitalize only if *east* is part of the name of a specific location: *East Africa*; otherwise use lc letters: *the east coast of Canada*; abbr: *E*; the abbr for *east-west* (control, movement) is *E-W*; *eastbound* and *eastward* are written as one word

e-Bay

e-biz abbr for business conducted electronically

eccentric; eccentricity

echo; echoes

ecommerce electronic commerce, or EC; the buying or selling of goods and services on the internet; also called **e-business**

economic; economical use *economical* to describe economy (of funds, effort, time); use *economic* when writing about economics: *an economical operation* (it did not cost much); *an economic disaster* (it will have a major effect on the economy)

EDI Electronic Data Interchange; a standard format for exchanging business data

effect see **affect**

efficacy; efficiency *efficacy* means effectiveness, ability to do a job; *efficiency* is a measurement of capability, the ratio of work done to energy expended: *we hired a consultant to assess the efficacy of our training methods; the power house is to have a high-efficiency boiler*

e.g. def: *for example*; avoid confusing with **i.e.**; no comma is necessary after *e.g.*; may also be abbr **eg**

ega enhanced graphics adapter; abbr also **EGA**

eighth

electric(al) if in doubt, use *electric*; generally, *electric* means produces or carries electricity, whereas *electrical* means related to the generation or carrying of electricity; abbr: *elec*

electro- a prefix generally meaning pertaining to electricity; it normally combines to form one word: *electroacoustic, electroanalysis, electrodeposition, electromechanical, electroplate*; if the combining word starts with *o*, insert a hyphen: *electro-optics, electro-osmosis*

e-learning

electromagnetic units abbr: **emu**

electromotive force abbr: **emf**

electronic(s) use *electronic* as an adjective, *electronics* as a noun: *electronic countermeasures; your career in electronics*

electronic mail abbr: **email**

electron volt(s) abbr: **eV** (pref) or **ev**

electrostatic units abbr: **esu**

elicit; illicit *elicit* means to obtain or identify; *illicit* means illegal

eligible; illegible *eligible* means "meets the required conditions"; also: *eligibility*; *illegible* means unreadable

ellipse; ellipsis pl: *ellipses*

email

embarrass; embarrassed; embarrassing; embarrassment

embedded

embryo; embryos

emf abbr for electromotive force

emigrate; immigrate *emigrate* means to go away from; *immigrate* means to come into

emit; emitter; emittance; emission; emissivity

emu abbr for electromagnetic units

emulate; emulation

enamel(l)ed; enamel(l)ing *ll* pref in Br, rec in Can.; single *l* pref in US

encase; incase *encase* pref

encipher

enclose; inclose *enclose* pref; *inclose* is used mainly as a legal term

endeavo(u)r *endeavour* pref in Br, rec for Can.; *endeavor* pref in US

enforce not *inforce*

engineer; engineered; engineering

enhanced graphics adapter abbr: **ega** (pref) or **EGA**

enquire; inquire *enquire* pref

enrol; enroll both are correct, but *enrol* pref; universal usage prefers *ll* for **enrolled** and **enrolling,** but a single *l* for **enrolment**

en route def: on the road, on the way; never use *on route*

ensure; insure; assure use *ensure* when the meaning is to make certain of: *the new meter will ensure accurate calibration*; use *insure* when the meaning is to protect against financial loss: *we insured all our drivers*; use *assure* when the meaning is to state with confidence that something has been or will be made certain: *he assured the meeting that production would increase by 8%*

entrepreneur; entrepreneurial

entrust; intrust *entrust* pref

envelop; envelope *envelop* is a verb that means to surround or cover completely; *envelope* is a noun that means a wrapper or a covering

environment; environmental; environmentally

EPROM def: abbr for erasable programmable read-only memory; can also be abbr as **eprom**

equal; equal(l)ed; equal(l)ing *equal, equality, equalize* always have single *l*; *equaled, equaling* pref in US, rec in Can.; *equalled, equalling* pref in Br; *equalize* can be spelled *equalise* in Br

equi- a prefix that means equality; combines to form one word: *equiphase, equipotential, equisignal*

equilibrium; equilibriums

equip; equipped; equipping; equipment

equivalent abbr: **equiv**

erase; erasable

errata although *errata* is plural (from the singular *erratum*, which is seldom used), it can be used as a singular or plural noun: both *the errata are ready* and *the errata is complete* are acceptable

erratic

erroneous

escalator

esker

especially; specially *specially* pref when it refers to an adjective, as in: *a specially trained crew; especially* should introduce a phrase, as in: *they were well trained, especially the computer technicians*

esthetic see **ae**

esu abbr for electrostatic unit

et al. def: and others; now rarely used

et cetera def: and so forth, and so on; abbr: **etc**; use with care in technical writing: *etc* can create an impression of vagueness or unsureness: *the transmitters, etc, were tested* sounds much less definite than *the transmitter, modulator, and power supply were tested* (or, if to restate all the equipment is too repetitious, *the transmitting equipment was tested*)

euro European currency; abbr: **EUR**

everybody; every body *everybody* means every person, or all the persons; *every body* means every single body: *everybody was present; every body was examined for gun-powder scars*

everyone; every one *everyone* means every person, or all the persons; *every one* means every single item: *everyone is insured; every one of the samples had to be tested in a saline solution*

exa def: 10^{18}; abbr: **E**

exaggerate

exceed

excel; excelled; excellent; excelling

except def: to exclude; see **accept**

exhaust

exhibit; exhibitor

exorbitant

expedite; expediter (pref) or **expeditor**

explicit; implicit *explicit* means clearly stated, exact; *implicit* means implied (the meaning has to be inferred from the words): *the supervisor gave explicit instructions* (they were clear); *that the manager was angry was implicit in the words he used*

extemporaneous

extracurricular

extranet a private network that uses the internet to securely share part of a business's information with users outside an organization

extraordinary

extremely high frequency abbr: **ehf**

eye- as a prefix, normally combines into one word: *eyeball, eyesight, eyewitness*; also: **eyed**

F

face- as a prefix normally combines to form one word: *facedown, facelift, faceplate*; exceptions: *face-saver, face-saving*

Fahrenheit abbr: **F**; see **temperature**

fail-safe

fallout one word as n; two words as v

familiarize; familiarization

farad def: a unit of electric capacitance; abbr: **F**; other abbr: **µF, nF, pF**

farfetched; far-out; far-reaching; farseeing; farsighted

farther; further *farther* means greater distance: *he travelled farther than the other salespeople; further* means a continuation of (as an adjective) or to advance (as a verb): *the promotion was a further step in her career plan*, and *to further his education, he took a part-time course in industrial drafting*

fasten; fastener

faultfinder; faultfinding

favo(u)r *favour* pref in Br and rec in Can.; *favor* pref in US; also *favourite* in Br and Can.

feasible; feasibility

February

feet; foot abbr: **ft**; other abbr: foot board measure

(board feet)	**fbm**
feet per minute	**fpm**
feet per second	**fps**
foot-candle(s)	**fc** (pref); **ft-c**
foot-pound(s)	**fp** (pref); **ft-lb**
foot-pound-second (system)	**fps** system

femto def: 10^{-15}; abbr: **f**; other abbr:

femtoampere(s)	**fA**
femtovolt(s)	**fV**

ferri- a prefix meaning contains iron in the ferric state; combines to form one word: *ferricyanide, ferrimagnetic*

ferro- a prefix meaning contains iron in the ferrous state; combines to form one word: *ferroelectric, ferromagnetic, ferrometer*

ferrule; ferule a *ferrule* is a metal cap or lid; a *ferule* is a ruler

fewer; less use *fewer* to refer to items that can be counted: *fewer technicians than we predicted have been assigned to the project*; use *less* to refer to general quantities: *there was less water than predicted*

fibre; fiber; fibrous *fibre, fibreglass, fibreoptic* pref in Br, rec in Can.; *fiber, fiberglass, fiberoptic* pref in US; *Fiberglas* is a US trade name

field- as a prefix normally does not combine into a single word or hyphenated form: *field glasses, field test, field trip*; but: *fieldwork(er)*

figure numbers in text, spell out the word *Figure* in full, or abbr it to **Fig.**: *the circuit diagram in Figure 26* and *for details, see Fig. 7*; use the abbreviated form beneath the illustration; always use numerals for the figure number

file transfer protocol abbr: **ftp** (pref) or **FTP**

final; finally; finalize

fire- as a prefix combines erratically: *firearm, fire alarm, firebreak, fire drill, fire escape, fire extinguisher, firefighter, firepower, fireproof, fire sale, fire wall*

firmware

first to write *the first two…* (or three, etc) is better than to write *the two first…*; never use *firstly*; as a prefix, *first-* combines erratically: *first-class, firsthand, first-rate*

fix in technical usage, *fix* means to firm up or establish as a permanent fact; avoid using it when the meaning is to repair

flameout; flameproof

flammable def: easily ignited; see **inflammable**

flatcar

flavo(u)r *flavour* pref in Br, rec in Can.; *flavor* pref in US

flexible

flight- usually combines to form two words: *flight control, flight deck, flight plan*

flip-flop

floe floating ice

flotation this is the correct spelling for describing an item that floats: *flotation gear*

flowchart

fluid abbr: **fl**; the abbr for fluid ounces is **fl oz**

fluorescence; fluorescent

fluorine; fluoridation; fluorite; fluorocarbon; fluoroscope

flyer not *flier*

FM abbr for frequency modulation

focus; focused; focusing; focuses pl: *focuses* (pref in Can. and US) or *foci* (pref in Br)

followup one word as n or adj; two words as v: **follow up**

foot- as a prefix normally combines into one word: *footbridge, footcandle, foothold, footnote, footwork*; also see **feet**

for see **because**

forceful; forcible use *forceful* to describe a person's character; use *forcible* to describe physical force

fore- def: that which goes before; as a prefix normally combines into one word: *foreclose, forefront, foreground, foreknowledge, foremost, foresee, forestall, forethought, forewarn*

forecast this spelling is correct for present and past tense

forego; forgo *forego* means to go before; *forgo* means to go without

foreman avoid using in a general sense, except when referring to a person specifically, as in *John Hayward, the foreman*; never use *forewoman* (a better word is *supervisor*)

foresee; foreseeable

forestall

foreword; forward a *foreword* is a preface or preamble to a book; *forward* means onward: *the scope is defined in the foreword to the book; he requested that we move forward*

for example abbr: **e.g.** (pref) or **eg**

former; first use *former* to refer to the first of only two things; use *first* if there are more than two

formula pl: *formulas* (pref in Can. and US) or *formulae* (pref in Br)

Fortran def: formula translation

forty def: 40; it is not spelled *fourty*

fourth def: 4th; it is not spelled *forth*

fractions when writing fractions that are less than unity, spell them out in descriptive narrative: *by the end of the heat run, nine-tenths of the installation had been completed*; for technical details use decimals rather than fractions, as in *a flat case 0.75 m wide by 0.060 m deep*, except when a quantity is normally stated as a fraction (such as *3/8 in. plywood*)

free- as a prefix normally combines into one word: *freehand, freehold, freestanding, freeway, freewheel*

free from use *free from* rather than *free of*: *he is free from prejudice*

free on board abbr: **fob** (pref), **f.o.b.** (commonly used), or **FOB**

frequency abbr: **freq**

frequency modulation abbr: **FM**

ftp file transfer protocol

fulfil(l) *fulfil, fulfilment* pref in Br, rec in Can.; *fulfill, fulfillment* pref in US; fulfilled and fulfilling always have *ll*

fungus pl: *fungi*

funnel(l)ed; funnel(l)ing single *l* pref

further see **farther**

fuse as a verb, means join together or weld; as a noun, means a circuit protection device or (in Br) a detonation initiation device

fuselage

fuze def: a detonation initiation device

G

gadget; gadgetry

gage US alternative spelling of *gauge*

gallon gallons differ between US (3.785 dm^3) and Br (4.546 dm^3); abbr: **gal**; other abbr:

gallons per day	**gpd**
gallons per hour	**gph**
gallons per minute	**gpm**
gallons per second	**gps**

gang; ganged; ganging

gas; gases; gassed; gassing; gaseous; gassy

gauge *gauging* does not retain the *e*

gearbox; gearshift

geiger (counter)

gelatin(e) *gelatin* pref

genealogy; genealogist

geo- a prefix meaning of the earth; combines to form one word; *geocentric, geodesic, geomagnetic, geophysics*

giga def: 10^9, abbr: **G**; other abbr:

gigabecquerel(s)	**GBq**
gigahertz	**GHz**
gigajoule(s)	**GJ**
gigaohm(s)	**GΩ; Gohm**
gigapascal(s)	**GPa**
gigavolt(s)	**GV**

gimbal

glue; glueing; gluey

glycerin(e) *glycerine* pref in Br, rec in Can.; *glycerin* pref in US

gnd abbr for *ground*

Gopher def: an internet search tool

government capitalize when referring to a specific government either directly or by implication; use lc if the meaning is government generally: *the Canadian Government; the Government specifications; no government would sanction such restrictions*

gram abbr: **g**; abbr for **gram-calorie** is **g-cal**

grammar; grammatical(ly)

grateful not *greatful*

gray def: absorbed dose of ionizing radiation (SI); abbr: **Gy**; other abbr: **mGy, μGy**; in SI, the *gray* replaces the *rad*

Greenwich mean time abbr: **GMT**

grey; gray def: a colour; *grey* pref in Br, rec in Can.; *gray* pref in US

grill(e) when the meaning is a loudspeaker covering or a grating, *grille* pref; when referring to cooking, use *grill*

ground (electrical) abbr: **gnd**; *groundcrew; ground floor*

GST abbr for goods and services tax (Canada)

guage wrongly spelled; the correct spelling is *gauge*

guarantee never *guaranty*; also *guarantor*

guesstimate

GUI a graphical (rather than textual) user interface to a computer; pronounced *goo-ee*

guideline

gyroscope abbr: **gyro**

H

half; halved; halves; halving as a prefix, *half* combines erratically; some common compounds are *half-hourly, half-life, half-monthly, halftone, halfwave*; for others, consult your dictionary

hand- as a prefix normally combines to form one word: *handbill, handbook, handful, handfuls, handhold, handmade, handpicked, handset, handshake*

hangar; hanger a *hangar* is a large building for housing aircraft; a *hanger* is a supporting bracket

harass; harassed; harassment

harbo(u)r *harbour* pref in Br, rec in Can.; *harbor* pref in US

hard- as a prefix normally combines into one word: *hardbound, hardhanded, hardhat, hardware*; exceptions: *hard-earned, hard-hitting*

haversine abbr: **hav**

H-beam

head- as a prefix normally combines into one word: *headfirst, headquarters, headset, headstart, headway*

heat- as a prefix, *heat* combines erratically; some typical compounds are: *heatresistant, heat-run, heatsink, heat-treat, heat wave*; for others, consult your dictionary

heavy-duty

hectare def: a large unit of area, used in surveying and agriculture; in SI, *hectare* replaces *acre*; abbr: **ha**

height (not *heighth*) abbr: **ht**; also: *heighten, heightfinder, heightfinding*

helix pl: *helixes* (pref) or *helices*

hemi- a prefix meaning half; combines to form one word: *hemisphere, hemitropic*

hemophilia; hemorrhage see **ae**

henry def: a unit of inductance; abbr: **H**; other abbr: **mH, μH, nH, pH**

here- whenever possible avoid using *here-* words that sound like legal terms, such as *hereby, herein, hereinafter, hereof*; they make a writer sound pompous; as a prefix, *here-* combines to form one word

hertz def: a unit of frequency measurement (similar to *cycles per second*, which it replaces); abbr: **Hz**; other abbr: **THz, GHz, MHz, kHz**

heterodyne

heterogeneous; homogeneous *heterogeneous* means of the opposite kind; *homogeneous* means of the same kind

hexadecimal

high- as a prefix either combines into one word or the two words are joined by a hyphen: *highhanded, highlight*; as compound adj: *high-frequency, high-power, high-priced, high-speed*

high frequency abbr: **hf** (pref) or **HF**

high-pressure (as an adjective) abbr: **h-p**

high voltage abbr: **hv** (pref) or **HV**

hinge; hinged; hinging

homogeneous see **heterogenous**

hono(u)r *honour* pref in Br, rec in Can.; *honor* pref in US

horizontal abbr: **hor**

horsepower abbr: **hp**; the abbr for horse-power-hour is **hp-hr**

hotkey

hovercraft

hour(s) abbr: **hr** or **h** (SI)

HTML hypertext markup language

http Hypertext Transfer Protocol; rules for exchanging files on the world wide web

humo(u)r *humour* pref in Br, rec in Can.; *humor* pref in US; but **humorous** and **humorist** each have only one *u*

hundred abbr: **C**

hundredweight def: 112 lb; abbr: **cwt**

hybrid

hydro- a prefix meaning *of water*; combines to form one word: *hydroacoustic, hydroelectric, hydromagnetic, hydrometer*

hyper- a prefix meaning *over*; combines to form one word: *hyperacidity, hypercritical*

hyperbola the plural is *hyperbolas* (pref) or *hyperbolae*

hyperbole def: an exaggerated statement

hyperbolic cosine, sine, tangent abbr: **cosh, sinh, tanh**

hyperlink

hypertext information organized into related chunks or units; the web is a massive set of hypertext information

hypertext markup language abbr: **html** (pref) or **HTML**

hyphen in compound terms you may omit hyphens unlesss they need to be inserted to avoid ambiguity or to conform to accepted usage; e.g. *preemptive* is preferred without a hyphen, but *photo-offset* and *re-cover* (when the meaning is *to cover again*) both require one; refer to individual entries in this glossary

hypothesis pl: *hypotheses*

I

I-beam

ibid. def: Latin abbr for *ibidem*, meaning in the same place; used in footnoting, but becoming obsolete

icon

ID card

i.e. def: *that is*; avoid confusing with **e.g.**; no comma is necessary after *i.e.*; may also be abbr **ie**

ignition abbr: **ign**

ill- as a prefix combines into a hyphenated expression: *ill-advised, ill-defined, ill-timed*

illegible def: not readable; also see *eligible*

im- see in-

imbalance this term should be restricted for use in accounting and medical terminology; use *unbalance* in other technical fields

immalleable

immaterial

immeasurable

immigrate see emigrate

immittance

immovable

impasse

impel; impelled; impelling; impeller

imperceptible

impermeable

impinge; impinging

imply; infer speakers and writers can *imply* something; listeners and readers *infer* from what they hear or read: *in his closing remarks, Mr Smith implied that further studies were in order; the technician inferred from the report that no further changes were necessary*

impracticable; impractical *impracticable* means not feasible; *impractical* means not practical; a less-preferred alternative for impractical is *unpractical*

in; into *in* is a passive word; *into* implies action; *ride in the car; step into the car*

in-; im-; un- all three prefixes mean not; all combine to form one word: *ineligible, impossible, unintelligible*; if

you are not sure whether you should use *in-, im-,* or *un-,* use *not*

inaccessible

inaccuracy

inadmissible

inadvertent

inadvisable; unadvisable *inadvisable* pref

inasmuch as a better word is *since*

inaudible

incalculable not *incalculatable*

incandescence; incandescent

incase *encase* pref

inch(es) abbr: **in.**; other abbr:
inches per second **ips**
inch-pound(s)   **in.-lb**

inclose see enclose

includes; including abbr: **incl**; when followed by a list of items, *includes* implies that the list is not complete; if the list is complete, use *comprises* or *consists of*

incomparable

incompatible

incur; incurred; incurring

index pl: *indexes* pref, except in mathematics (where *indices* is common)

indicated horsepower abbr: **ihp**; the abbr for indicated horsepower-hour is **ihp-hr**

indifferent to never use *indifferent of*

indiscreet; indiscrete *indiscreet* means imprudent; *indiscrete* means not divided into separate parts

indispensable

indorse *endorse* pref

industrywide

ineligible

inequitable

inessential; unessential both are correct; *unessential* pref

inexhaustible

inexplicable

infallible

infer; inferred; inferring; inference also see imply

infinitesimal

inflammable def: easily ignited (derived from *inflame*); *flammable* is a better word: it prevents readers from

mistakenly thinking the *in* of *inflammable* means *not*

inflexible

infrared

infrastructure

ingenious; ingenuous *ingenious* means clever, innovative; *ingenuous* means innocent, naive; *ingenuity* is a noun derived from ingenious

in-house

inoculate

inoperable not *inoperatable*

input/output abbr: **I/O**

inquire; enquire *enquire* pref in Br, rec in Can.; *inquire* pref in US; also: *enquiry*

insanitary; unsanitary both are correct; *insanitary* pref

inseparable

inside diameter abbr: **ID**

in situ def: in the normal position

instal(l) *install, installed, installer, installing, installation* pref; but *instalment* pref in Br, rec in Can.; *installment* pref in US

instantaneous

instil; instilled

instrument

insure the pref def is to protect against financial loss; can also mean make certain of (particularly in US); see **ensure**

integer

integral; integrate; integrator

intelligence quotient abbr: **IQ**

intelligible

inter- a prefix meaning among or between; normally combines to form one word: *interact, intercarrier, interdependence, interdigital, interface, intermodulation, interoffice*

intermediate-pressure (as an adjective) abbr: **i-p**

intermittent

internal abbr: **int**

internet a worldwide computer network of networks that allows users at one computer to access information from another computer

internet relay chart abbr: **irc** or **IRC** (pref)

interrupt

into see **in**

intra- a prefix meaning within; normally combines to form one word: *intranet, intranuclear*; if combining word starts with *a*, insert a hyphen: *intra-atomic*

intranet an organization's private internet network, used to share company information and computing resources among employees

intrust *entrust* pref

I/O input/output

IQ

irc internet relay chat

irrational

irregardless never use this expression; use *regardless*

irrelevant frequently misspelled as *irrevelant*

irreparable also see repairable

irreversible

irritate also see *aggravate*

ISO International Organization for Standardization

iso- a prefix meaning the same, of equal size; normally combines to form one word: *isoelectronic, isometric, isotropic*; if combining word starts with *o*, insert a hyphen: *iso-octane*

its; it's *its* means belonging to; *it's* is an abbr for it is: *the transmitter and its modulator; if the fault is not in the remote equipment, then it's most likely in master control*; in technical writing *it's* should seldom be used: replace with *it is*

J

jackhammer

jobholder; jobseeker; job lot

joule def: a unit of energy, work, or quantity of heat (SI); abbr: **J**; other abbr: **TJ, GJ, MJ, kJ, mJ, J/m³, J/K** (joule(s) per kelvin), **J/kg, J/mol** (joule(s) per mole)

journey; journeys

judg(e)ment *judgment* pref in US and Can.; *judgement* pref in Br

judicial; judicious *judicial* means related to the law; *judicious* means sensible, discerning

K

kelvin def: the SI unit for thermo-dynamic temperature; abbr: **K**

kerb Br equivalent of *curb* (road edge)

key- as a prefix normally combines to form one word: *keyboard, keypunch, keying, keynote, keystroke*; but *key word*

kilo def: 10^3, abbr: **k**; other abbr:

kiloampere(s)	**kA**
kilobecquerel(s)	**kBq**
kilobyte(s)	**kbyte** (pref) or **kb**
kilocalorie(s)	**kcal**
kilocoulomb(s)	**kC**
kilogram(s) (see **kilogram**)	**kg**
kilohertz	**kHz**
kilohm(s)	**kΩ**; kohm
kilojoule(s)	**kJ**
kilolitre(s)	**kL**
kilometre(s)	**km**
kilometres per hour	**km/h**
kilomole(s)	**kmol**
kilonewton(s)	**kN**
kilopascal(s)	**kPa**
kilosecond(s)	**ks** (pref); **ksec**
kilosiemens	**kS**
kilovolt(s)	**kV**
kilovolt-ampere(s)	**kVA**
kilovolt-ampere(s) reactive	**kVAr**
kilowatt(s)	**kW**
kilowatthour(s)	**kWh** (pref); **kw-hr**

avoid writing *kilo* in text as an abbr for *kilogram* or *kilometre*

kilogram def: the SI unit for mass; abbr: **kg**; other typical abbr: **Mg, g, mg, µg**; also:

kilogram-calorie(s)	**kg-cal**
kilogram(s) per metre	**kg/m**
kilogram(s) per square metre	**kg/m²**
kilogram(s) per cubic metre	**kg/m³**

kilogram metre(s) per second   **kg·m/s**

knockout as noun or adjective, one word

knot abbr: **kn**

know-how (n); **know how** (v)

knowledge; knowledgeable

L

label(l)ed; label(l)ing single *l* pref

laboratory abbr: **lab**

labo(u)r *labour* pref in Br, rec in Can.; *labor* pref in US; also: *laboursaving*

lacquer

lambert abbr: **L**; use the abbr L with care: it is also the SI abbr for *litre*

lampholder

laptop (computer)

large scale integration abbr: **LSI**

laser light amplification by stimulated emission of radiation

last; latest; latter *last* means final; *latest* means most recent; *latter* refers to the second of only two things (if more than two, use *last*); it is better to write *the last two* (or *three*, etc) than *the two last*

lath; lathe a *lath* is a strip of wood; a *lathe* is a machine

latitude abbr: **lat** or ∅

lay- as a prefix generally combines to form one word (as noun or adj): *layoff, layout, layover*

LCD liquid crystal display

lead; led as a n, *lead* is a metal; as a v, *lead* means to show the way, as a leader would; the past of the v is *led: a lead-filled pipe; he was asked to lead the project team; he led the project team*

learned; learnt *learned* pref

LED light emitting diode

leeway

left-hand(ed) abbr: **LH**

length the SI unit of length is the *metre*, expressed in multiples and submultiples of *kilometres* (**km**), *metres* (**m**), and *millimetres* (**mm**)

lengthy not *lengthly*

less see **fewer**

letter- as a prefix combines erratically: *letterhead, letter-perfect, letter writer*

letter of intent; letter of transmittal pl: *letters of intent, letters of transmittal*

level(l)ed; level(l)er; level(l)ing *ll* pref in Br, rec in Can.; single *l* pref in US

liable to means under obligation to; avoid using as a synonym for *apt to* or *likely to*

liaison liaison is a noun; it is sometimes used uncomfortably as a verb: *to liaise*

libel(l)ed; libel(l)ing *ll* pref in Br, rec in Can.; single *l* pref in US

library

licence; license in Can. and Br, the noun is *licence* and the verb is *license*; in US, *license* is pref for both noun and verb

life- as a prefix combines erratically: *lifebelt, lifeboat, life cycle, lifeless, lifelong, life-size, lifespan, lifetime*

light- as a prefix *light-* generally combines to form one word: *lightface* (type), *lightweight*; but *light-year*; the past tense is *lighted*, but *lit* is common in Can. and Br

light emitting diode abbr: **LED**

lightening; lightning *lightening* means to make lighter; *lightning* is an atmospheric discharge of electricity

likable not *likeable*

linear abbr: **lin**; the abbr for lineal foot is **lin ft**

lines of communication not *line of communications*

liquefy; liquefiers; liquefaction

liquid abbr: **liq**

liquid crystal display abbr: **LCD**

listserv

litre; liter the SI spelling is **litre** (pref in Can. and Br), but in US *liter* is more common; abbr: **L**; other abbr: **kL, mL, µL**; the abbr for *litre(s) per day/hour/minute/second* are **L/d, L/h, L/m, L/s**

lock- as a prefix combines into a single word: *locknut, lockout* (n), *locksmith, lockstep, lockup, lockwasher*; but two words as a v: *lock out; lock up*

locus pl: *loci*

logarithm abbr: (common) **log**; (natural) **ln**

logbook

logistic(s) use *logistic* as an adj, *logistics* as a n: *logistic control; the logistics of the move*

long- as a prefix normally combines into a single word or is hyphenated: *long-distance, longhand, longplaying, long-range, long-term, long-winded*; but *long shot*

longitude abbr: **long.** or λ

loophole

looseleaf

loran abbr for long-range air navigation system

lose; loose *lose* is a verb that refers to a loss; *loose* is an adjective or a noun that means free or not secured: *three loose nuts caused us to lose a wheel*

louvre; louver *louvre* pref in Can. and Br; *louver* pref in US

low frequency abbr: **lf** (pref) or **LF**

low-pressure (as an adjective) abbr: **l-p**

LSI large scale integration

lubricate; lubrication abbr: **lub**

lumbar; lumber *lumbar* is the lower back; *lumber* is wood

lumen def: a unit of luminous flux (SI); abbr: **lm**; other abbr:

lumen-hour(s)	**lm-h** (pref); **lm-hr**
lumens per square foot	**lm/ft^2**
lumens per square metre	**lm/m^2**
lumens per watt	**lm/W**
lumen-second(s)	**lm·s**
microlumen(s)	**µlm**
millilumen(s)	**mlm**

luminance; luminescence; luminosity; luminous

lux def: a unit of illuminance (SI); abbr: **lx**; other abbr: **klx**

M

Mach

macro- a prefix meaning very large; combines to form one word: *macroscopic; macroview*

magneto pl: *magnetos*; as a prefix normally combines to form one word: *magnetoelectronics, magnetohydrodynamics, magnetostriction*; if combining word starts with *o* or *io*, insert a hyphen: *magneto-optics, magneto-ionization*

magneton; magnetron a *magneton* is a unit of magnetic moment; a *magnetron* is an electronic device controlled by an external magnetic field

maintain; maintained; maintenance

majority use *majority* mainly to refer to a number, as in a *majority of 27*; avoid using it as a synonym for many or most; e.g. do not write *the majority of technicians* when the intended meaning is *most*

make- as a prefix normally combines to form one word as a n or adj: *makeshift, makeover, makeup*; as a v, use two words: *make over, make up*

malfunction

malleable

manage; managed; manageable; managing

manoeuvre; maneuver *manoeuvre, manoeuvred, manoeuvring* pref in Br, rec in Can.; *maneuver, maneuvered, maneuvering* pref in US

manufacturer abbr: **mfr**

marketplace

marshal; marshal(l)ed; marshal(l)er; marshal(l)ing *ll* pref in Br, rec in Can.; single *l* pref in US

mass see **kilogram**

Master of Science abbr: **M.Sc.**

mat; matt a *mat* is a covering; *matt* is a dull finish

material; materiel *material* is the substance or goods out of which an item is made; when used in the plural, it describes items of a like kind, such as *writing materials*; *materiel* are all the equipment and supplies necessary to support a project or undertaking (a term commonly used in military operational support)

matrix *matrixes* pref in US, rec in Can.; *matrices* pref in Br

maximum pl: *maximums* (pref) or *maxima*; abbr: **max**; like *minimize, maximize* can be used as a verb

maybe; may be *maybe* means "perhaps": *maybe there is a second supplier*; the verb form *may be* means "perhaps it will be" or "possibly there is": e.g. *there may be a second supplier*

mda monochrome display adapter; also **MDA**

meagre not *meager*

mean; median the *mean* is the average of a number of quantities; the *median* is the midpoint of a sequence of numbers; e.g. in the sequence of five numbers 1, 2, 3, 7, 8, the mean is 4.2 and the median is 3

mean effective pressure abbr: **mep**

mean sea level abbr: **msl** (pref) or **MSL**

mediocre

medium when *medium* is used to mean substances, liquids, materials, or communication or advertising, the pref plural is *media*; in all other senses the pref plural is *mediums*

mega def: 10^6, abbr: **M**; other abbr:

megabyte(s)	**Mbyte** (pref) or **Mb**
megacoulomb(s)	**MC**
Megaelectronvolt(s)	**MeV**
megahertz	**MHz**
megajoule(s)	**MJ**
meganewton(s)	**MN**
megaohm(s	**MΩ**; Mohm
megapascal(s)	**MPa**
megavolt(s)	**MV**
megawatt(s)	**MW**

memorandum pl: *memorandums* (pref in US, rec in Can.) or *memoranda* (pref in Br); abbr: **memo** (singular); the pl is **memos**

memory the electronic holding place for instructions and data that a computer's microprocessor can reach quickly

merit; merited; meriting

metal(l)ed; metal(l)ing *ll* pref in Br, rec in Can.; single *l* pref in US; **metallic** and **metallurgy** always have *ll*

meteorology; metrology *meteorology* pertains to the weather; *metrology* pertains to weights, measures, and calibration

meter def: a measuring instrument (n) or to measure out (v)

metre; meter def: metric unit of length; the SI spelling is *metre* (pref in Can. and Br), but in US *meter* is more common; abbr: **m**; other typical abbr:

square metre(s)	**m²**
cubic metre(s)	**m³**
metres per second	**m/s**
newton-metre(s)	**N·m**
newtons per square metre	**N/m²**
kilogram(s) per cubic metre	**kg/m³**

metrication

micro def: 10^{-6}; abbr: **μ** (pref) or **u**; other abbr:

microampere(s)	**μA**
microcoulomb(s)	**μC**
microfarad(s)	**μF**
microgram(s)	**μg**
microgray(s)	**μGy**
microhenry(s)	**μH**
microhm(s)	**μΩ**; μohm
microlumen(s)	**μlm**
micromho(s)	**μmho**
micrometre(s)	**μm**
micromole(s)	**μmol**
micronewton(s)	**μN**
micropascal(s)	**μPa**
microsecond(s)	**μs** (pref); **μsec**
microsiemens	**μS**
microtesla(s)	**μT**
microvolt(s)	**μV**
microwatt(s)	**μW**

micro- as a prefix meaning very small, normally combines to form one word: *microammeter, microcomputer, micrometre, microprocessor, microswitch, microview, microwave*; but *micro-organism*

microchip a logic chip; often called an integrated circuit in computer circuitry

microphone abbr: **MIC** (pref) or **mike**

microprocessor a computer processor on a microchip; the "engine" that runs a computer; previously called the CPU

Microsoft disk operating system abbr: **MS-DOS**

mid- a prefix that means in the middle of; generally combines into one word: *midday, midpoint, midweek*; if used with a proper noun, insert a hyphen: *mid-Atlantic*

mile the word mile is generally understood to mean a statute mile of 5280 ft (1609 m), so the statement *I drove 326 miles* implies statute miles; when referring to the *nautical mile* (6080 ft; 1853 m), always identify it as such: *the flight distance was 4210 nautical miles* (or 4210 *nmi*); abbr:

statute mile(s)	**mi**
nautical mile(s)	**nmi** (pref) or **n.m.**
miles per gallon	**mpg**
miles per hour	**mph**

mileage; milage *mileage* pref

milli def: 10^{-3}; abbr: **m**; other abbr:

milliampere(s)	**mA**
millicoulomb(s)	**mC**
millicurie(s)	**mCi**
millifarad(s)	**mF**
milligram(s)	**mg**
milligray(s)	**mGy**
millihenry(s)	**mH**
millijoule(s)	**mJ**
millikelvin(s)	**mK**
millilitre(s)	**mL**
millilumen(s)	**mlm**
millimetre(s)	**mm**
millimho(s)	**mmho**
millimole(s)	**mmol**
millinewton(s)	**mN**
milliohm(s)	**mΩ**; mohm
millipascal(s)	**mPa**
milliroentgen(s)	**mR**
millisecond(s)	**ms** (pref); **msec**
millisiemens	**mS**
millitesla(s)	**mT**
millivolt(s)	**mV**
milliwatt(s)	**mW**
milliweber(s)	**mWb**

milli- as a prefix, combines to form one word: *milliammeter, milligram, millimicron*

millibar def: a unit of pressure (= 100 Pa); abbr: **mbar**

mini- as a prefix combines to form one word: *minicomputer, minireport*

miniature; miniaturization

minimum pl: *minimums* (pref) or *minima*; abbr: **min**; also **minimize**

minority use mainly to refer to a number, as in *a minority by 2*; avoid using it as a synonym for several or a few; to write *a minority of the technicians* is incorrect when the intended meaning is *a few technicians*

minuscule not *miniscule*; def: very small

minute abbr:

time	**min**
angular measure	'

mis- a prefix meaning wrong(ly) or bad(ly); combines to form one word: *misalign, misfired, mismatched, misshapen*

miscellaneous

miscible

misspelled; misspelt *misspelled* pref (note double *s*)

mitre; miter *mitre* pref in Br, rec in Can.; *miter* pref in US

mnemonic

model(l)ed; model(l)er; model(l)ing *ll* pref in Br, rec in Can.: single *l* pref in US

mole def: the SI unit for amount of substance; abbr: **mol**; other abbr: **kmol, mmol, µmol, mol/m³**

momentary; momentarily both mean *for a moment*, not *in a moment*

money- as a prefix normally combines to form one word: *moneymaking*

monitor

mono- a prefix meaning one or single; combines to form one word: *monopulse, monorail, monoscope*

monochrome display adapter abbr: **mda** (pref) or **MDA**

months the months of the year are always capitalized: *January, February*, etc; if abbr, use only the first three letters: *Jan, Feb*, etc; the abbr for *month* is **mo**

mortice; mortise *mortise* pref

mosaic

most never use as a short form for *almost*; to say *most everyone is here* is incorrect

motherboard

mo(u)ld *mould* pref in Br, rec in Can.; *mold* pref in US

movable; moveable *movable* pref

Mr; Ms address men as *Mr* and women as *Ms*; use *Miss* or *Mrs* only if you know the person prefers to be so addressed; the period (punctuation) may be inserted after *Mr* and *Ms*

M.Sc. abbr for Master of Science

MS-DOS Microsoft disk operating system

msl abbr for mean sea level; also **MSL**

mucous

multi- a prefix meaning many; combines to form one word: *multiaddress, multicavity, multielectrode, multimedia, multistate*

municipal; municipality

myself often used wrongly; write "Peter and I...", not "Peter and myself"

N

NAND-gate

nano def: 10^{-9}; abbr: **n**; other abbr:

nanoampere(s)	**nA**
nanocoulomb(s)	**nC**
nanofarad(s)	**nF**
nanohenry(s)	**nH**
nanometre(s)	**nm**
nanosecond(s)	**ns** (pref); **nsec**
nanotesla(s)	**nT**
nanovolt(s)	**nV**
nanowatt(s)	**nW**

naphtha(lene)

national information infrastructure abbr: **NII**

nationwide

nautical mile def: 1853 m (6080 ft); abbr: **nmi** (pref) or **n.m.**; see **mile**

navigate; navigator; navigable

NB means note well, and is the abbr for *nota bene*; it is more common to use the word **Note**

NC abbr for *normally closed* (contacts)

nebula pl: *nebulae* (pref in Br, rec in Can.) or *nebulas* (pref in US)

negative abbr: neg

negligible

neighbo(u)r *neighbour* pref in Br, rec in Can.; *neighbor* pref in US; also: **neighbourhood**

nevertheless

newsgroup

newton def: a unit of force (SI); abbr: **N**; other abbr: **MN, kN, mN, µN, N·m** (newton metre), **N/m** (newtons per metre)

next write the *next two* (or *next three*, etc) rather than *the two next* (etc)

nickel

night never use *nite*; write *nighttime* as one word

NII national information infrastructure

nineteen; ninety; ninth all three are frequently misspelled

nitroglycerine

NO abbr for *normally open* (contacts)

No. abbr for **number**; omit *s* when writing a series, as in *No. 30 to 36*; see **number**

noise-cancel(l)ing *ll* pref; see **cancel**

nomenclature

nomogram; nomograph *nomogram* pref

non- as a prefix meaning not or negative, normally combines to form one word: *nonconductor, nondirectional, nonnegotiable, nonlinear, nonstop*; if combining word is a proper noun, insert a hyphen: *non-Canadian*; avoid forming a new word with *non-* when a similar word that serves the same purpose already exists (i.e. you should not form *nonaudible* because *inaudible* already exists)

none when the meaning is "not one," treat as singular; when the meaning is "not any," treat as plural: *none* (not one) *of the sites meets our needs*; *none* (not any) *of the receivers were repaired*

no one two words

NOR-gate

norm def: the average or normal (distribution, situation, or condition)

normalize

normally closed; normally open (contacts); abbr: **NC, NO**

normal to def: at right angles to

north abbr: **N**; other abbr:

northeast	**NE**
northwest	**NW**
north-south (control, movement)	**N-S**

northbound and *northward* are written as one word; for rule on capitalization, see **east**

notable

not applicable abbr: **N/A**

note well abbr: **NB** (derived from *nota bene*), but *Note* is more common

NOT-gate

notice; noticeable; notification

not to exceed an overworked phrase that should be used only in specifications; in all other cases use *not more than*

nth (harmonic, etc)

nuclear frequently misspelled

nucleus the plural is *nuclei* (pref) or *nucleuses*

null

number although **no.** would appear to be the logical abbr for number (and is pref), **No.** is much more common (the symbol # is no longer used as an abbr for number); the abbr *no.* or *No.* must always be followed by a quantity in numerals: it is incorrect to write *we have received a No. of shipments*; for the difference in usage between *amount* and *number*, see **amount**

numbers in narrative, as a general rule spell out up to and including nine, and use numerals for 10 and above; for specific rules, see pp 300 to 302

O

oblique; obliquity

obsolete; obsolescent

obstacle

obtain; secure use *obtain* when the meaning is simply to get; use *secure* when the meaning is to make safe or to take possession of (possibly after some difficulty); *we obtained four additional samples; we secured space in the prime display area*

occasional; occasionally

occur; occurred; occurrence; occurring

o'clock avoid using; see **time**

OCR optical character recognition

odo(u)r *odour* pref in Br, rec in Can.; *odor* pref in US; *odorous* has only one *u*

off- as a prefix *either* combines into one word, or a hyphen is inserted: *offset, offshoot, off-centre(d), off-scale, off-the-shelf*

offence; offense *offence* pref in Can. and Br; *offense* pref in US; *offensive* always has an *s*

offline

off of an awkward construction; omit the word *of*

ohm def: a unit of electric resistance; abbr: Ω or **ohm**; other abbr: GΩ, Gohm, MΩ, Mohm, kΩ, kohm, mΩ, mohm, μΩ, uohm; abbr for ohm-centimetre(s) is **ohm-cm**; *ohmmeter* has *mm*

oilfield; oil-filled; oilsands

omit; omitted; omission

omni- a prefix meaning all or in all ways; combines to form one word: *omnibearing, omnidirectional, omnirange*

on; onto *on* means positioned generally; *onto* implies action or movement: *the report is on Mr Cord's desk; the speaker stepped onto the platform*

one- as a prefix mostly combines with a hyphen: *one-piece, one-sided, one-to-one, one-way*; but *oneself* and *onetime*

online

onward(s) *onward* pref

opaque; opacity

op. cit. def: Latin abbr for *opere citato*, meaning the work cited; used in footnoting; now obsolescent

operate; operator; operable not *operatable*

optical character recognition abbr: **OCR**

optimum pl: *optima* (pref) or *optimums*; also: **optimal**

oral def: spoken; avoid confusing with *aural*, which refers to hearing

orbit; orbital; orbited; orbiting

organize; organizer; organization

OR-gate

orient; orientation the noun form is *orientation*; the pref verb form is *orient, oriented, orienting*

orifice

origin; original; originally

oscillate

oscilloscope slang abbr: **scope**

ounce(s) abbr: **oz**; other abbr:

ounce-foot	**oz-ft**
ounce-inch	**oz-in.**

out- as a prefix normally combines to form one word: *outbreak, outcome, outdistance*; when *out-* is followed by *of*, insert hyphens if used as a compound adjective (as in *an out-of-date list*), but treat as separate words when used in place of a noun (as in *the printing schedule is out of phase*)

outside diameter abbr: **OD**

outward(s) *outward* pref

over- as a prefix meaning above or beyond, normally combines to form one word: *overbunching, overcurrent, overdriven, overexcited, overrun*; avoid using as a synonym for *more than*, particularly when referring to quantities: *more than 17 were serviceable* is better than *over 17 were serviceable*

overage means either too many or too old

overall an overworked word; as an adjective it often gives unnecessary additional emphasis (as in *overall impression*) and should be deleted; avoid using as a synonym for *altogether, average, general,* or *total*

oxidation; oxidization *oxidation* pref in US, rec in Can.; *oxidization* pref in Br; also: **oxidize**

oxyacetylene

P

pacemaker; pacesetter

page; pages abbr: **p; pp**

paid not *payed*, when the meaning is to spend

pair(s) abbr: **pr**

pamphlet

panel(l)ed; panel(l)ing *ll* pref in Br, rec in Can.; single *l* pref in US

paper- as a prefix mostly combines to form one word: *paperback, paperbound, paperwork*; but *paper-covered, paper-thin*

parabola; parabolas; parabolic; paraboloid

paragraph(s) abbr: **para**

parallax

parallel; paralleled; paralleling; parallelism; parallelogram both *parallel to* and *parallel with* are correct

paralysis pl: *paralyses*; also: **paralyse** pref in Br, rec in Can.; **paralyze** pref in US

parameter; perimeter *parameter* means a guideline; *perimeter* means a border or edge

paraplegic

paraprofessional

parenthesis pl: *parentheses*; in Can., the term **bracket(s)** is more common

parity

particles

partly; partially use *partly* when the meaning is "a part" or "in part"; use *partially* when the meaning is "to a certain extent," or when preference or bias is implied

parts per million abbr: **ppm**

part-time

pascal def: a unit of pressure (SI); abbr: **Pa**; other abbr: **Gpa, Mpa, kPa, mPa, μPa, pPa, Pa·s** (pascal second)

pass- as a prefix normally combines to form one word: *passbook, passkey, passport, password*

passed; past as a general rule, use *passed* as a verb and *past* as an adjective or noun: *the test equipment has passed quality control inspection; past experience has demonstrated a tendency to fail at low temperature; in the past…*

pay- as a prefix normally combines to form one word: *paycheque, payload, payroll*; but *pay day*

pcb printed circuit board

PCMCIA Personal Computer Memory Card International Association

PDF abbr for portable document format

pel

pencil(l)ed; pencil(l)ing *ll* pref in Br, rec in Can.; single *l* pref in US

pendulum pl: *pendulums*

penultimate def: the next to last

P.Eng abbr for Professional Engineer

people; persons *people* pref: *all the people were present*; use *persons* to refer only to small numbers of people: *one person was interviewed; seven people failed the test*

per in technical writing it is acceptable to use *per* to mean either *by, a*, or *an*, as in *per diem* (by the day) and *miles per hour*; avoid using *as per* in all writing

percent abbr: **%**; use **%** only after numerals: 42%; use *percent* after a spelled-out number: *about forty percent*; avoid using the expression *a percentage of* as a synonym for *a part of* or *a small part*; also: **percentage** and **percentile**

perceptible

peripheral

permafrost

permeable; permeameter; permeance

permissible

permit; permitted; permitting; permittivity; permit-holder

perpendicular abbr: **perp**

persevere; perseverance

persistent; persistence; persistency

personal; personnel *personal* means concerning one person; *personnel* means the members of a group, or the staff: *a personal affair; the personnel in the power house*

Personal Computer Memory Card International Association abbr: **PCMCIA**

peta def: 10^{15}; abbr: **P**; other abbr: **PBq** (petabecquerel)

petrochemical

pharmacy; pharmacist; pharmaceutical

phase in the nonelectric sense, *phase* means a stage of transmission or development; it should not be used as a synonym for aspect; it is used correctly in *the second phase called for a detailed cost breakdown*

phase-in; phaseout but use two words for the verb forms: *to phase in, to phase out*

Ph.D. abbr for Doctor of Philosophy

phenolic

phenomenon pl: *phenomena*

photo- as a prefix, normally combines to form one word: *photoelectric, photogrammetry, photoionization, photomultiplier*; if combining word starts with *o*, insert a hyphen: *photo-offset*

pico def: 10^{-12}, abbr: **p**; other abbr:

picoampere(s)	**pA**
picocoulomb(s)	**pC**
picofarad(s)	**pF**
picohenry(s)	**pH**
picosecond(s)	**ps** (pref); **psec**
picowatt(s)	**pW**

piecemeal; piecework

piezoelectric; piezo-oscillator

pilot; piloted; piloting

pipeline

pixel

plagiarism def: to copy without acknowledging the original source

plateau pl: *plateaus* (pref in US, rec in Can.) or *plateaux* (pref in Br)

platform the underlying operating system of a computer, on which application programs can run

plug; plugged; plugging

plumbbob; plumb line

p.m. def: after noon (post meridiem)

pneumatic

polarize; polarizing; polarization

poly- a prefix meaning many; combines to form one word: *polydirectional, polyethylene, polyphase*

polyvinyl chloride abbr: **pvc**

pop-up window

portable document format abbr: **PDF**

positive abbr: **pos**

post- a prefix meaning after or behind; mostly combines to form one word: *postacceleration, postdated, postgraduate, postpaid*; but *post-mortem, post office, post-secondary*

post meridiem def: after noon; abbr: **p.m.**; can also be written as *post-meridian* (less pref)

potentiometer abbr: **pot.**

pound(s) (weight) abbr: **lb** (singular and pl); other abbr:

pound-foot	**lb-ft**
pound-inch	**lb-in.**

pounds per square foot	**psf** (pref); **lb/ft²**
pounds per square inch	**psi** (pref); **lb/in²**
pounds per square inch, absolute	**psia**

power factor abbr: **pf** or spell out

power house; power line; powerpack

practicable; practical these words have similar meanings but different applications that sometimes are hard to differentiate; *practicable* means feasible to do: *it was difficult to find a practicable solution* (one that could reasonably be implemented); *practical* means handy, suitable, able to be carried out in practice: *a practical solution would be to combine the two departments*

practice; practise the noun always is *practice*; the verb is *practise* (pref in Br, rec in Can.), but can also be *practice* (pref in US)

pre- a prefix meaning before or prior; normally combines to form one word: *preamplifier, predetermined, preemphasis, preignite, preset*; if combining word is a proper noun, insert a hyphen; *pre-Roman*

precede; proceed *precede* means to go before; *proceed* generally means to carry on or continue: *a brief business meeting preceded the dinner* (the meeting occurred first); *after dinner, we proceeded with the annual presentation of awards*; see **proceed**

precedence; precedent *precedence* means priority (of position, time, etc): *the pressure test has precedence* (it must be done first); a *precedent* is an example that is or will be followed by others: *we may set a precedent if we grant his request* (others will expect similar treatment)

précis

predominate; predominant; predominantly

prefer; preferred; preference; preferable avoid overstating *preferable*, as in *more preferable* and *highly preferable*

prescribe; proscribe *prescribe* means to state as a rule or requirement; *proscribe* means to deny permission or forbid

presently use with care; in US *presently* means now; in Br *presently* means soon

or in good time; a better word is *immediately* (US) or *shortly* (Br and Can.)

pressure-sensitive

prestigious

pretence; pretense *pretence* pref in Can. and Br; *pretense* pref in US

prevalent; prevalence

preventive; preventative *preventive* pref

previous def: earlier, that which went before; avoid writing *previous to* (use *before*); see **prior**

principal; principle as a noun, *principal* means (1) the first one in importance, the leader; or (2) a sum of money on which interest is paid: *one of the firm's principals is Martin Dawes; the invested principal of $10 000 earned $950 in interest last year*; as an adjective, *principal* means most important or chief: *the principal reason for selecting the Arrow microprocessor was its low capital cost*; *principle* means a strong guiding rule, a code of conduct, a fundamental or primary source (of information, etc): *his principles prevented him from taking advantage of the error*

printed circuit board abbr: **pcb**

printout (n and adj form only)

prior; previous use only as adjectives meaning earlier: *he had a prior appointment*, or *a previous commitment prevented Mr Perchanski from attending the meeting*; write *before* rather than *prior to* or *previous to*

proceed; proceeding; procedure use *proceed to* when the meaning is to start something new; use *proceed with* when the meaning is to continue something that was started previously

processor

producible

Professional Engineer abbr: **P.Eng**

program(me) single *m* pref in US, rec in Can.; *mm* pref in Br; **programmed, programmer, programming** always have *mm* in Can. and Br, and usually in US (where single *m* also is used but is less pref)

prohibit use *prohibit from*; never *prohibit to*

prominent; prominence

proofread

propel; propelled; propelling; propellant (noun); **propellent** (adjective); **propeller**

prophecy; prophesy use *prophecy* only as a noun, *prophesy* only as a verb

proposition in its proper sense, *proposition* means a suggestion put forward for argument; it should not be used as a synonym for *plan, project*, or *proposal*

pro rata def: assign proportionally; sometimes used in the verb form as **prorate**: *I want you to prorate the cost over two years*

prospectus; prospectuses

protein

protocol a term used in information technology to describe a special set of rules used to make telecommunication connections

proved; proven use *proven* only as an adjective or in the legal sense; otherwise use *proved*: *he has been proven guilty; he proved his case*

provincewide

psycho- as a prefix normally combines to form one word: *psychoanalysis, psychopathic, psychosis*; if combining word starts with *o*, insert a hyphen: *psycho-organic*

purge; purging

pursuant to avoid using this wordy expression

Q

quality control abbr: **QC**

quantity; quantitative the abbr of quantity is **qty**

quart abbr: **qt**

quasi- a prefix meaning seemingly or almost; insert a hyphen between the prefix and the combining word: *quasi-active, quasi-bistable, quasi-linear*

question mark insert a question mark after a direct question: *how many booklets will you require?*; omit the question mark when the question posed is really a demand: *may I have your decision by noon on Monday*

questionnaire

quick- as a prefix normally combines with a hyphen: *quick-acting, quick-freeze, quick-tempered*; exceptions: *quicklime, quicksilver*

quiescent; quiescence

R

rack-mounted

racon def: a radar beacon

radian def: a unit of angular measurement; abbr: **rad**

radiator

radio- as a prefix, combines to form one word: *radioactive, radiobiology, radioisotope, radioluminescence*; if combining word starts with *o*, omit one *o*: *radiology, radiopaque*; in other instances *radio* may be either combined or treated as a separate word, depending on accepted usage; examples are *radio compass, radio countermeasures, radio direction-finder, radio frequency* (as a noun), *radio-frequency* (as an adj), *radio range, radiosonde, radiotelephone*

radio frequency abbr: **rf**

radio frequency interference abbr: **rfi** (pref) or **RFI**

radius pl: *radii* (pref) or *radiuses*

radix pl: *radices* (pref) or *radixes*

rain- as a prefix normally combines to form one word: *raincoat, rainproof, rainwear*; exception: *rain check*

rally; rallied; rallying

RAM abbr for random access memory

ramdrive

R and D abbr for research and development

range; ranging; rangefinder; range marker

rare; rarely; rarity; rarefy; rarefaction

ratemeter

ratio; ratios

rational; rationale *rational* means reasonable, clear-sighted: *John had a rational explanation for the error*; *rationale* means an underlying reason: *Tricia explained the company's rationale for diversifying the product line*

re def: a Latin word meaning in the case of; avoid using *re* in technical writing, particularly as an abbr for *regarding, concerning, with reference to*

re- a prefix meaning to do again, to repeat; normally combines to form one word: *reactivate, rediscover, reemphasize, reentrant, reignition, reorganize, rerun, reset, reunite*; if the compound term

forms an existing word that has a different meaning, insert a hyphen to identify it as a compound term, as in *re-cover* (to cover again)

reaction use *reaction* to describe chemical or mechanical processes, not as a synonym for *opinion* or *impression*

reactive kilovolt-ampere abbr: **kVAr**; the abbr for **reactive volt-ampere** is **VAr**

readability

read-only memory abbr: **ROM**

readout (noun and adj form)

realize; realization

real time defines computer responsiveness in a human rather than a machine sense of time; insert a hyphen when two words are combined into a compound adj; also: **real-time chat; real-time transmission**

reboot reload the operating system; see **boot**

recede

receive; receiver; receiving; receivable

rechargeable

recipe; receipt often confused; *recipe* means cooking instructions; *receipt* means a written record that something has been received

recommend; recommendation

reconcile; reconcilable

reconnaissance

recover; re-cover *recover* means to get back, to regain; *re-cover* means to cover again

recur; recurred; recurring; recurrence these are the correct spellings; never write *reoccur* (etc)

recycle; recyclable

reducible

reenforce; reinforce *reenforce* means to enforce again; *reinforce* means to strengthen: *Rick Davis reenforced his original instructions by circulating a second memorandum; The Artmo Building required 34 750 tonnes of reinforced concrete*

refer; referred; referring; referral; referee; reference

referendum Br and US dictionaries list *referenda* as the pref pl, but *referendums* is much more commonly used and rec by CP

refuel; refuelled

reiterate def: to say again

relaid; relayed *relaid* means laid again, like a carpet; *relayed* means to send on, as a message would be relayed from one person to another

remit; remitted; remitting; remitter; remittance

remodel; remodelled; remodelling see **model**

removable

rent-a-car

reoccur(rence) never use; see **recur**

repairable; reparable both words mean in need of repair and capable of being repaired; *reparable* also implies that the cost to repair the item has been taken into account and it is economically worthwhile to effect repairs

repel; repellent; repeller

replaceable

reproducible

rescind

research and development abbr: **R and D**

reservoir

reset; resetting; resettability

resin; rosin these words have become almost synonymous, with a preference for *resin*; use *resin* to describe a gluey substance used in adhesives, and *rosin* to describe a solder flux-core

respective(ly) this overworked word is not needed in sentences that differentiate between two or more items; e.g. it should be deleted from a sentence such as: *pins 4, 5, and 7 are marked R, S, and V respectively*

restart

resume def: a personal biography; the correct spelling is *résumé* (with two accents), but the single accent (*résume*) or no accent has become standard

retrieve; retrieval

retro- a prefix meaning to take place before, or backward; normally combines to form one word: *retroactive, retrofit, retrogression*; if combining word starts with *o*, insert a hyphen: *retro-operative*

reverse; reverser; reversal; reversible

revolutions per minute; revolutions per second abbr: **rpm; rps**

rfi radio frequency interference

rheostat

rhombus pl: *rhombuses* (pref) or *rhombi*

rhythm; rhythmic; rhythmically

ricochet; ricocheted; ricocheting

right-hand(ed) abbr: **RH**

rigo(u)r *rigour* pref in Br, rec in Can.; *rigor* pref in US; *rigorous* is standard spelling in Can., US, and Br

RISC

rivet; riveted; riveter; riveting

road- as a prefix normally combines to form one word: *roadblock, roadmap, roadside*

roentgen abbr: **R**

role; roll a *role* is a person's function or the part that he or she plays (in an organization, project, or play); a *roll*, as a technical noun, is a cylinder; as a verb, it means to rotate: *the technician's role was to make the samples roll toward the magnet*

rollover one word as a n or adj; two words as a v

ROM def: read-only memory

root mean square abbr: **rms**

rosin see **resin**

rotate; rotator; rotatable; rotary

round def: circular; in Br, *round* is commonly used in place of *around*, but this is not rec in Can.

ruggedize

rumo(u)r *rumour* pref in Br, rec in Can.; *rumor* pref in US

run-off insert a hyphen when used as n or adj; use two words as a v

rustproof; rust-resistant

S

salvageable

same avoid using *same* as a pronoun; to write *we have repaired your receiver and tested same* is awkward; instead, write *we have repaired and tested your receiver*

satellite

saturate; saturation; saturable

save; savable

sawtooth; saw-toothed

scalar; scaler *scalar* is a quantity that has magnitude only; *scaler* is a measuring device

scarce; scarcity

sceptic(al); skeptic(al) *sceptic(al)* pref in Br; *skeptic(al)* pref in US, rec in Can.; also **skepticism**

schedule

schematic although really an adjective (as in *schematic diagram*), in technical terminology *schematic* can be used as a noun (meaning a *schematic drawing*)

science; scientific(ally); scientist

screwdriver; screw-driven

seam-weld

seasonal; seasonable *seasonal* means affected by or dependent on the season; *seasonable* means appropriate or suited to the time of year; *a seasonal activity; seasonable weather*

seasons the seasons are not capitalized: *spring, summer, autumn* or *fall, winter*

secant abbr: **sec**

secede; secession

second (position) as a prefix, *second-* combines erratically: *second-class, second-guess, secondhand, second-rate, second sight*

second (time) abbr: **s** (pref as part of a symbol) or **sec** (in narrative)

second (angular measure) abbr: **″**

secure see **obtain**

-sede *supersede* is the only word to end with *-sede*; others end with *-cede* or *-ceed*

seem(s) see **appear(s)**

self- insert a hyphen when used as a prefix to form a compound term: *self-absorption, self-bias, self-excited, self-locking, self-setting*; but there are exceptions: *selfless, selfsame*

semi- a prefix meaning half; normally combines to form one word: *semiactive, semiannually* (every six months), *semiconductor, semimonthly* (half-monthly), *semiremote, semiweekly* (half-weekly); if combining word starts with *i*, insert a hyphen: *semi-idle, semi-immersed*

separate; separable; separator; separation all are frequently misspelled

sequence; sequential

serial input/output abbr: **SIO**

serial number abbr: **ser no.** or **S/N**

series-parallel

serrated

serviceable

serviceperson avoid using *serviceman* or *servicewoman*

servo- as a prefix, combines to form one word: *servoamplifier, servocontrol, servosystem*; as a noun, *servo* is an abbr for *servomotor* or *servomechanism*

sewage; sewerage *sewage* is waste matter; *sewerage* is the drainage system that carries away the waste matter

SGML abbr for standard generalized markup language

shall *shall* is rarely used in technical writing (*will* is pref), except in specifications when its use implies that the specified action is mandatory

short- as a prefix, may combine with a hyphen, as in *short-circuit, short-form* (report), *short-lived, short-term*; in some cases it may combine into one word, as in *shorthand* (writing), *shorthanded, shortcoming, shortsighted, shortwave*

shrivel(l)ed; shrivel(l)ing *ll* pref in Br, rec in Can.; single *l* pref in US

sic a Latin word which means a quotation has been copied exactly, even though there was an error in the original; e.g. *the report stated: "Our participation will be an issential (sic) requirement."*

siemens def: a unit of electric conductance (SI); abbr: **S**; other abbr: **kS, mS, μS**

signal(l)ed; signal(l)er; signal(l)ing *ll* pref in Br, rec in Can.; single *l* pref in US

signal-to-noise (ratio)

silhouette

silverplate; silver-plate use *silverplate* as a noun or adjective; *silver-plate* as a verb

similar not *similiar*

sine abbr: **sin**

singe; singeing the *e* must be retained to avoid confusion with *singing*

singlehanded

siphon not *syphon*

sirup; syrup *syrup* pref

site; sight; cite three words that often are misspelled; a *site* is a location: *the construction site; sight* implies the ability to see: *mud up to the axles became a familiar sight; cite* means quote: *I cite the May 17 progress report as an example of good writing*

siz(e)able *sizable* pref in US, rec in Can.; *sizeable* pref in Br

skeptic(al) pref spelling; see **sceptic(al)**

skil(l)ful *skilful* pref in Br, rec in Can.; *skillful* pref in US; note that this is contradictory to most *l* and *ll* situations listed in this glossary

slip- usually combines into a single word: *slippage, slipshod, slipstream;* but *slip ring(s)*

smelled; smelt *smelled* pref in Can. and US; *smelt* pref in Br

smo(u)lder *smoulder* pref in Br and Can.; *smolder* pref in US

soft key; software

solder

solely

soluble

someone; some one *someone* is correct when the meaning is any one person; *some one* is seldom used

some time; sometimes *some time* means an indefinite time: *some time ago; sometimes* means occasionally: *he sometimes works until after midnight*

sound- combines irregularly: *sound-absorbent, sound-absorbing, sound-powered, soundproof, sound track, sound wave*

south abbr: S; other abbr:

southeast	**SE**
southwest	**SW**

southbound and *southward* are written as one word; for rule on capitalization, see **east**

space- as a prefix normally combines to form one word: *spacecraft, spaceflight*

spare(s) can be used as a noun meaning spare part(s)

specially see **especially**

specific gravity abbr: **sp gr**

specific heat abbr: **sp ht**

spectro- as a prefix, combines to form one word: *spectrometer, spectroscope;* if combining word starts with *o*, omit one *o*: *spectrology*

spectrum pl: *spectra* (pref) or *spectrums*

spelled; spelt *spelled* pref in Can. and US; *spelt* pref in Br

spilled; spilt *spilled* pref in Can. and US; *spilt* pref in Br

spiral(l)ed; spiral(l)ing *ll* pref in Br, rec in Can.; single *l* pref in US

split infinitive to split an infinitive is to insert an adverb between the word *to* and a verb: *to really insist* is a split infinitive; although some grammarians claim you should never split an infinitive, many now suggest you may do so if rewriting would result in awkward construction, ambiguity, or extensive rewriting

spoiled; spoilt *spoiled* pref in Can. and US; *spoilt* pref in Br

spotweld

square abbr: sq or ^{2}; other abbr:

square foot/feet	ft^2 (pref); sq ft
square inch(es)	$in.^2$ (pref); sq in.
square metre(s)	m^2
square centimetre(s)	cm^2
square millimetre(s)	mm^2
curies per square metre	Ci/m^2
milliwatts per square metre	mW/m^2

standard generalized markup language abbr: **SGML**

standby; standoff; standstill all combine into one word when used as noun or adjective

standing-wave ratio abbr: **swr** or **SWR**

startup one word as n or adj; two words as a v: **start up**

state-of-the-art

stationary; stationery *stationary* means not moving: *the vehicle was stationary when the accident occurred; stationery* refers to writing materials: *the main item in the October stationery requisition was an order for one thousand writing pads*

statute mile def: 1609 m (5280 ft); see **mile**

statutory

stencil(l)ed; stencil(l)ing *ll* pref in Br, rec in Can.; single *l* pref in US

stereo- as a prefix, combines to form one word: *stereometric, stereoscopic; stereo* can be used alone as a noun meaning multi-channel system

stimulus pl: *stimuli*

stocklist, stockpile

stop- as a prefix usually combines to form one word: *stopgap, stopnut, stopover* (when used as n or adj, but two words as v); but *stop payment, stop watch*

stoppage

straightened; straitened *straightened* means to make straight; *straitened* means restricted

strato- a prefix that combines to form one word: *stratocumulus, stratosphere*

stratum pl: *strata*

structural

stylus dictionaries list *styli* as the pref pl, but *styluses* is much more commonly used

sub- a prefix generally meaning below, beneath, under; combines to form one word: *subassembly, subcarrier, subcommittee, subnormal, subpoint*

subparagraph abbr: **subpara**; abbr for *subsubparagraph* is **subsubpara**

subpixel

subtle; subtlety; subtly

succinct; succinctly

sufficient in technical writing, *enough* is a better word than *sufficient*

sulphur; sulfur *sulphur* pref in Can. and Br; *sulfur* pref in US; the prefix **sulph-** (or **sulf-**) combines to form one word: *sulphanilamide* (or *sulfanilamide*)

summarize

super- a prefix meaning greater or over; combines to form one word: *superabundant, superconductivity, superregeneration*

superhigh frequency abbr: **shf**

superimpose; superpose *superimpose* means to place or impose one thing generally on top of another; *superpose* means to lay or place exactly on top of, so as to be coincident with

supersede see **-sede**

supra- a prefix meaning above; normally combines to form one word: *supramolecular;* if combining word starts with *a*, insert a hyphen: *supra-auditory*

surfeit def: to have more than enough

surveillance

surveyor

susceptible

switch- *switchboard, switchbox, switchgear*

swivel(l)ed; swivel(l)ing *ll* pref in Br, rec in Can.; single *l* pref in US

syllabus pl: *syllabuses* (pref) or *syllabi*

symmetry; symmetrical

symposium pl: *symposiums (pref)* or *symposia*

synchro as a prefix combines to form one word: *synchromesh, synchronize, synchronous, synchroscope; synchro* can also be used alone as a noun meaning synchronous motor

synonymous use *synonymous with*, not *synonymous to*

synopsis pl: *synopses*

synthesis pl: *syntheses*

synthetic

syphon *siphon* pref

syringe

syrup; syrupy

systemwide

T

tail- as a prefix normally combines to form one word: *tailboard, tailless, tailwind;* but *tail end, tail fin*

take- *takeoff; takeover; takeup;* as n or adj, these terms all combine into a single word; as a v, use two words

tangent abbr: **tan**

tangible

tape deck

target; targeted

taxable; tax-exempt; taxpayer

TCI/IP abbr for transmission control protocol/internet protocol; def: the basic communication language or protocol of the internet

teamwork

technician

Teflon

tele- a prefix meaning at a distance; combines to form one word: *teleammeter, telemetry, telephony, teletype(writer)*

telecom; telecon *telecom* is the abbr for *telecommunication(s); telecon* is the abbr for *telephone conversation*

television abbr: **TV**

Telnet

temperature abbr: **temp**; combinations are *temperature-compensating* and *temperature-controlled;* when recording temperatures, the abbr for *degree* (deg or °) may be omitted: *an operating temperature of 85C; the water boils at 100C or 212F;* the pref (SI) unit for temperature is the degree Celsius (C)

tempered

template; templet both spellings are correct; *template* pref in Can. and Br

temporary; temporarily

tenfold

tensile strength abbr: **ts**

tentative; tentatively

tenuous

tera def: 10^{12}; abbr: **T**; other abbr:

terabecquerel(s)	**TBq**
terahertz	**THz**
terajoule(s)	**TJ**
terawatt(s)	**TW**

terminus pl: *termini* (pref) or *terminuses*

tesla def: a unit of magnetic flux density, magnetic inductance (SI); abbr: **T**; other abbr: **mT, μT, nT**

that is abbr: **i.e.** (pref) or **ie**

their; there; they're the first two of these words are frequently used wrongly; *their* is a possessive, meaning belonging to them: *the staff took their holidays earlier than normal; there* means in that place: *there were 18 desks in the room,* or *put it there; they're* is a contraction of *they are* and should not appear in technical or business writing

there- as a prefix combines to form one word: *thereafter, thereby, therein, thereupon*

therefor(e) *therefore* pref

thermo- a prefix generally meaning heat; combines to form one word:

thermoammeter, thermocouple, thermoelectric, thermoplastic

thermodynamic temperature the SI unit is the kelvin (abbr: **K**), expressed in degrees Celsius (C)

thesis pl: *theses*

thousand abbr: **k**

thousand foot-pound(s)	**kip-ft**
thousand pound(s)	**kip**

three- when used as a prefix, a hyphen normally is inserted between the combining words: *three-dimensional, three-phase, three-ply, three-wire;* exceptions are *threefold* and *threesome*

threshold

through never use *thru*

tieing, tying *tying* pref

timber; timbre *timber* is wood; *timbre* means tonal quality

time always write time in numerals, if possible using the 24-hour clock: *08:17* or *8:17 a.m., 15:30* or *3:30 p.m.;* 24-hour times may be written as *20:45* (pref), *20:45 hr,* or *20:45 hours;* never use the term "o'clock" in technical writing: write *15:00* or *3 p.m.* rather than *3 o'clock*

time- typical combinations are *time base, time-card, time clock, time constant, time-consuming, time lag, timesaving, time-slot, timetable, time-wasting*

tinplate; tin-plate use *tinplate* as a noun, *tin-plate* as a verb or adjective

to; too; two frequently misspelled; *to* is a preposition that means in the direction of, against, before, or until; *too* means as well; *two* is the quantity 2

today; tonight; tomorrow never use *tonite*

tolerance abbr: **tol**

ton; tonne the US ton is 2000 lb and is known as a *short ton;* the Br ton is 2240 lb and is known as a *long ton;* the metric ton is 1000 kg (2204.6 lb) and is known as a *tonne* (abbr: **t**); other terms: *tonmile* and *tonnage*

toolbox; toolmaker; toolroom

top- top-heavy, top-loaded, top-up

torque; torqued; torquing

total(l)ed; total(l)ing *ll* pref in Br, rec in Can.; single *l* pref in US

touch-tone (dialing)

toward(s) *toward* pref

traceable

trade- as a prefix combines most often into a single word; *trademark, tradeoff*; but *trade-in, trade name,* and *trade show*

trans- a prefix meaning over, across, or through; it normally combines to form one word: *transadmittance, transcontinental, transship*; if combining word is a proper noun, insert a hyphen; *trans-Canada* (an exception is *transatlantic* and *transpacific*); *transonic* has only one *s*

transceiver def: a transmitter-receiver

transfer; transferred; transferring; transferable; transference

translator

transmission control protocol/internet protocol abbr: TCI/IP

transmit; transmitted, transmitting; transmittal, transmitter; transmission

transverse; traverse *transverse* means to lie across; *traverse* means to track horizontally

travel(l)ed; travel(l)er; travel(l)ing *ll* pref in Br, rec in Can.; single *l* pref in US

tri- a prefix meaning three or every third; combines to form one word: *triangulation, tricolour, trilateral, tristimulus, triweekly*

triple- all compounds are hyphenated: *triple-acting, triple-spaced*

trouble-free; troubleshoot(ing)

truncated

tumo(u)r *tumour* pref in Br, rec in Can.; *tumor* pref in US; but *tumorous* has only one *u*

tune; tunable; tuneup (n or adj); *tune up* as a v

tunnel(l)ed; tunnel(l)ing *ll* pref in Br, rec in Can.; single *l* pref in US; *tunnel* has only one *l*

turbo- a prefix meaning turbine-powered; combines to form one word: *turboelectric, turboprop*

turbulence; turbulent

turn- *turnaround* and *turnover* form one word when used as n or adj, but two words as a v; *turnstile* and *turntable* always form one word; *turns-ratio* is hyphenated

two- when used as a prefix to form a compound term, a hyphen normally is inserted: *two-address, two-phase,* *two-ply, two-position, two-wire*; an exception is *twofold*

type- as a prefix normally combines into one word: *typeface, typeset(ting)*

tyre Br spelling of *tire* (on a car wheel)

U

UCD user-centred drive

ultimatum pl: *ultimatums*

ultra- a prefix meaning exceedingly; normally combines to form one word: *ultrasonic, ultrasound, ultraviolet*; if combining word starts with *a*, insert a hyphen: *ultra-audible, ultra-audion*

ultrahigh frequency abbr: **uhf** or **UHF**

un- a prefix generally meaning not or negative; normally combines to form one word: *uncontrolled, undamped, unethical, unnecessary*; if combining word is a proper noun, or if term combines to form an existing word that has a different meaning, insert a hyphen: *un-Canadian, un-ionized* (meaning not ionized); if uncertain whether to use *un-, in-,* or *im-,* try using *not*

unadvisable; inadvisable both are correct; *inadvisable* pref

unbalance; imbalance for technical writing, *unbalance* pref; see **imbalance**

unbiased

under- a prefix meaning below or lower; combines to form one word: *underbunching, undercurrent, underexposed, underrated, undershoot, undersigned, underway*

underage means a shortage or deficit, or too young

unequal(l)ed *unequaled* pref; see **equal**

unessential; inessential *unessential* pref

unforeseen; unforeseeable

uni- a prefix meaning single or one only; combines to form one word: *uniaxial, unidirectional, unifilar, univalent*

uninterested def: not interested; avoid confusing with *disinterested*

unionized; un-ionized *unionized* refers to a group of people who belong to a union; *un-ionized* means not ionized

unique def: the one and only, without equal, incomparable; use with great care and never in any sense where a comparison is implied; you cannot

write *this is the most unique design*; rewrite as *this design is unique*, or (if a comparison must be made) *this is the most unusual design*

universal resource locator abbr: URL

universal serial bus abbr: USB

unmistakable

unnavigable

unparalleled

unpractical *impractical* pref

unsanitary

unserviceable abbr: u/s

unstable but *instability* is better than *unstability*

untraceable

unwieldy

up- as a prefix combines to form one word: *update, upend, upgrade, uprange, upswing*; but *up-to-date*

uppercase def: capital letters; abbr: **uc**

uppermost

URL abbr for universal resource locator

USB abbr for universal serial bus

use; usable; usage; using; useful

user-centred drive abbr: UCD

utilize; utilise *utilize* pref; avoid using *utilizes* when *uses* or *employs* would be a better word

V

vacuum

valance; valence *valance* means a cover over a drapery track; *valence* is an electronic or nucleonic term, as in *valence electron*

valve-grind(ing)

vari- as a prefix meaning varied, combines into one word: *varicoloured, variform*

variance write *at variance with*, never *at variance from*

varimeter; varmeter def for both: a meter for measuring reactive power; *varimeter* pref

V-chip

vdisk virtual disk

vehicle, vehicular

vender; vendor *vendor* pref

ventilator

verbatim def: written exactly as originally said

versed sine abbr: **vers**

versus def: against; abbr: **vs**

vertex def: top; pl: *vertices* (pref) or *vertexes*; avoid confusing with *vortex*

very high frequency abbr: **vhf** or **VHF**

VGA video graphics locator

vice; vise def: a clamping device; *vice* pref in Can. and Br; *vise* pref in US

vice versa def: in reverse order

video- as a prefix normally combines to form one word: *videocast, videocassette, videotape*; the abbr for videocassette recorder is **VCR** or **vcr**

video frequency abbr: **vf** or **VF**

video graphics array abbr: **VGA**

viewfinder; viewpoint

virtual disk abbr: **vdisk** (pref) or **VDISK**

vise see **vice**

visor; vizor *visor* pref

viz def: namely; this term is seldom used in technical writing

vocation; avocation *vocation* is a trade or calling; *avocation* means an interest or hobby

voice-over; voiceprint

volatile memory

volt def: electric potential or potential difference; abbr: **V**; other abbr: **MV, kV, mV, μV, nV**; also

volt-ampere(s)	**VA**
volt-ampere(s), reactive	**VAr**
volts, alternating current	**Vac**
volts, direct current	**Vdc**
volts, direct current, working	**Vdcw**
volts per metre	**V/m**

volt- combines into one word: *voltammeter, voltohmyst*

volume abbr: **vol**

vortex def: spiral; pl: *vortices* (pref) or *vortexes*; avoid confusing with *vertex*

VU-meter

W

WAIS wide area information server

waive; waiver; waver *waive* and *waiver* mean to forgo one's claim or give up one's right; *waver* means to hesitate, to be irresolute

walkie-talkie

war- as a prefix, combines to form one word: *warfare, wartime*

warranty

waste; wastage

water- combines irregularly: *water-cool(ed), water cooler, waterflow, water level, waterline, waterproof, water-soluble, watertight*

watt def: a unit of power, or radiant flux (SI); abbr: **W**; other abbr: **TW, GW, MW, kW, mW, μW, nW, pW, W/m^2**; the abbr for *watt-hour(s)* is **Wh** (pref) or **W-hr**; as a prefix, *watt-* forms *watthourmeter* and *wattmeter*

wave- normally combines to form one word: *waveband, waveform, wavefront, waveguide, wavemeter, waveshape*; exceptions are *wave angle* and *waveswept*

wavelength abbr: λ

waver see **waiver**

wear and tear *no* hyphens

weather use only as a noun; never write *weather conditions*; avoid confusing with *climate* and *whether*

weatherproof

web def: the world wide web (**the web**); also **website**

weber def: a unit of magnetic flux (SI); abbr: **Wb**; other abbr: **mWb**

Wednesday often misspelled

week(s) abbr: **wk**

weekend

weight abbr: **wt**

well- as a prefix normally combines with a hyphen: *well-adjusted, well-defined, well-timed*

west abbr: **W**; *westbound* and *westward* are written as one word; for rule on capitalization, see **east**

where- as a prefix combines to form one word: *whereas, wherein*; when combining word starts with *e*, omit one *e*: *wherever*

whether; weather *whether* means if; *weather* has to do with rain, snow, sunshine, wind, etc

while; whilst *while* pref

whoever

wholly not *wholely*

wide; width abbr: **wd**

wide area information server abbr: **WAIS**

wideband; widespread

wirecutter(s); wire-cutting; wirewound

withheld; withhold

word processor; word processing abbr: **WP**; as an adj, insert a hyphen: *the word-processing software*

words per minute abbr: **wpm**

work- as a prefix usually combines to form one word: *workbench, workflow, workforce, workload, workshop*; but *work station*

working volts, dc abbr: **Vdcw**

worldwide

world wide web abbr: **www** or **the web**; all the resources and users on the internet that use the Hypertext Transfer Protocol (http)

wrap; wrapped; wrapping; wraparound

writeoff; writeup both combine into one word when used as n or adj; use two words in v form

writer see **author**

writing only one *t*

www world wide web

wysiwyg def: What You See Is What You Get

X

x- *x-axis, X-band, x-particle, x-radiation, x-ray*

Xerox

X-Y recorder

Y

y- *Y-antenna, y-axis, Y-connected, Y-network, Y-signal*

Yahoo

yard(s) abbr: **yd**

yardstick

year(s) abbr: **yr**; typical combinations are *year-end* and *year-round*

yocta def: 10^{-24}; abbr: **y**

yotta def: 10^{24}; abbr: **Y**

your; you're *your* means belonging to or originating from you: *I have examined your prototype analyser*; *you're* is a contraction of *you are* and should not appear in technical or business writing

Z

z-axis

zepto def: 10^{-21}; abbr: **z**

zero pl: *zeros* (pref) or *zeroes*; typical combinations are *zero-access, zero-adjust, zero-beat, zero-hour, zero level, zero-set, zero reader*

zetta def: 10^{21}; abbr: **Z**

zip code

zoology; zoological; zoologist

Index

serif fonts, 276–277
SI units, 301–302
single curve in graphs, 198
speaking notes, 221–222
spelling
    Canadian spelling, 293–294
    spell-check programs, 15
student project proposals, 175, 176
style. *See* writing style; writing techniques
subject development
    for clarity, 30
    in formal reports, 110
subject lines
    in business letters, 37
    in email, 43
    in incident reports, 56
subjective comparative analysis, 89–91
subordinate clauses, 285, 287
summaries
    evaluation reports, 93
    executive summaries
        cover letters as, 92
        formal reports, 125
        proposals, 163–164
    formal reports, 106–107
    keywords, in resumes, 255
    summary statements
        pyramid technique, 4–5, 6, 18–20, 27–28
        in resumes, 241, 246, 249–250
        technical instructions, 187

table of contents, 116
tables
    guidelines, 212–213
    information design, 213–214, 279–280
    in investigation reports, 87
    "open" tables, 99
task analysis, 183
technical briefings
    assignments, 233–235
    circumstances
        audience, 217
        length of talk, 218
        location, 218
    planning
        audience-focused talk, 218–219
        capturing audience's attention, 219–221

organization of information, 219
"tell-tell-tell" method, 219–221
preparing
    handouts, 223–224
    practice, 223
    speaking notes, 221–222
    visual aids, 222–223
presenting
    controlling nervousness, 224
    distributing handouts, 225–226
    platform manner, 224–225
    speaker-audience relationship, 226
Technical Communication Quarterly, 2
technical instructions
    See also user's manual
    assignments, 192–195
    audience identification, 186
    avoiding ambiguity, 189–190
    components, 187–188
    description, 186
    imperative mood, 189
    instilling confidence in user, 188–189
    precautionary comments, 191
    purpose statement, 187
    short, one-paragraph steps, 191, 274
    step-by-step instructions, 187–188, 191, 274
    summary statements, 187
    tools and materials section, 187
    usability testing, 191–192
    writing plan, 187–188
technical proposals. *See* proposals
technical writing, history, 1–3
tenses (verb) in reports, 55–56
terminal summary, 93
third-person incident report, 57
Thompson, Karl Owen, 1–2
title pages
    formal reports, 115–116
    proposals, 163–164
titles of reports, 115
tone
    business letters
        antagonizing words, 35–36
        emails, 43, 44
        personal pronoun use, 35
        revision for, 13–15

sincerity, 34
    suitability for audience, 34
    email and memos, 34–36, 43, 44
    formal *vs.* informal, 272–274
    simple *vs.* pretentious words, 14
    wordiness, 31
    writing in reverse order, 129–130, 273–274
topic sentences, 32, 66, 280–281
topical summaries, 106–107
topics
    arranging topic groups, 10
    choosing headings, 7–8
    deciding on relevance, 9
    grouping related, 9
traditional resume, 241–244, 245
trip reports, 60–61, 62–63
troubleshooting techniques, 186
    See also user's manual

usability testing, 191–192
user's manual
    See also technical instructions
    assignments, 192–195
    audience identification, 181
    describing the product
        detailed description, 182–183
        overview, 182
        product description, 182
        summary, 182
    description, 181
    operating instructions
        grouping and labelling tasks, 183–184
        task analysis, 183
        writing the steps, 185–186
    troubleshooting techniques, 186
    writing plan, 181–182

van der Wyck, Phyllis, 88–90
variables, dependent and independent, 200, 201
verbs
    imperative mood, 189
    passive *vs.* active voice, 33, 288
    tenses in reports, 55–56
visual aids for presentations, 222–223
visual impression
    See also information design
    of business letters, 30
    formal reports, 105
voice, passive *vs.* active, 33, 288